Recreating Sustainable Retirement

Recreating Sustainable Retirement

Resilience, Solvency, and Tail Risk

EDITED BY

Olivia S. Mitchell,
Raimond Maurer, and
P. Brett Hammond

OXFORD
UNIVERSITY PRESS

OXFORD
UNIVERSITY PRESS

Great Clarendon Street, Oxford, OX2 6DP,
United Kingdom

Oxford University Press is a department of the University of Oxford.
It furthers the University's objective of excellence in research, scholarship,
and education by publishing worldwide. Oxford is a registered trade mark of
Oxford University Press in the UK and in certain other countries

First Edition published in 2014

Impression: 1

Published in the United States of America by Oxford University Press
198 Madison Avenue, New York, NY 10016, United States of America

British Library Cataloguing in Publication Data
Data available

Library of Congress Control Number: 2014940448

ISBN 978–0–19–871924–3

Printed and bound by
CPI Group (UK) Ltd, Croydon, CR0 4YY

Preface

The workforce of today and tomorrow must count on longer lives and deferred retirement, while at the same time it is taking on increased responsibility for managing retirement risk. This volume explores new ways to think about, manage, and finance longevity risk, capital market risk, model risk, and regulatory risk. We have gathered the provocative and insightful views of key academics, practitioners, and policymakers, to analyze ways to manage and finance these risks with a view to create more resilient retirement systems. Our volume is another valuable addition to the Pension Research Council/Oxford University Press series, and as such it will interest a wide range of readers, including consumers, researchers, and employers seeking to design better retirement plan offerings and policymakers charged with oversight and enhancement of the financial system.

In the process of preparing this book, many people and institutions played essential roles. Co-editors Raimond Maurer and Brett Hammond contributed many helpful suggestions as we designed and structured the analysis presented herein. We thank them, along with our Advisory Board, Senior Partners, and Institutional Members of the Pension Research Council, for intellectual and financial sustenance. Additional support was received from the Pension Research Council, the Boettner Center for Pensions and Retirement Research, and the Ralph H. Blanchard Memorial Endowment at the Wharton School of the University of Pennsylvania. We also offer deep appreciation to Oxford University Press, which publishes this series on global retirement security. The manuscript was expertly prepared and carefully edited by Donna St. Louis and Andrew Gallagher, with assistance from Irene Shaffer.

Our work at the Pension Research Council and the Boettner Center for Pensions and Retirement Security of the Wharton School of the University of Pennsylvania has focused on aspects of pensions and retirement wellbeing for over half a century. This volume contributes to the fulfillment of our mission, which is generating research and engaging debate on policy issues affecting pensions and retirement security.

Olivia S. Mitchell
Executive Director, Pension Research Council
Director, Boettner Center for Pensions and Retirement Research
The Wharton School, University of Pennsylvania

Contents

Part III. Regulatory and Political Risk

Part IV. Implications for Plan Sponsors

List of Figures

List of Tables

Notes on Contributors

Geoff Bauer is Associate in Mercer's Financial Strategy Group, where he focuses on the design and implementation of investment and risk management strategies for UK pension schemes and their corporate sponsors. Previously he worked for Alexander Forbes in South Africa on actuarial valuations and other projects for large government, union, and semi-government clients. He is Fellow of the Institute and Faculty of Actuaries and also holds a diploma in International Employee Benefits.

Enrico Biffis is Associate Professor of Actuarial Science at Imperial College Business School, London, and Associate Member of the Munich Risk and Insurance Center, LMU Munich. He is also Fellow of the Pensions Institute, and a member of the Institute of Actuaries Working Party on Centralized Clearing of OTC Derivatives. His research focuses on asset-liability management, valu-ation of insurance liabilities, and optimal design of risk transfers for long term risks. He has written on de-risking strategies for pensions/annuity businesses and longevity risk transfers. Previously he taught at Bocconi University and Cass Business School. He holds a Laurea degree in Statistics from Trieste, an M.Sc. in Actuarial Management from Cass Business School, and a Ph.D. in Mathematics of Economic Decisions from Trieste.

Patrick Brockett holds the Memorial Chair in Risk Management and Insurance in the Department of Information, Risk, and Operations Management at the McCombs School of Business of the University of Texas at Austin. His inter-ests include insurance, risk theory, risk management, statistics, actuarial science, data envelopment analysis, and quantitative models in business. He received his B.A. from California State University, Long Beach, and his M.A. and Ph.D. from the University of California, Irvine, all in Mathematics.

Andrew Cairns is Professor of Financial Mathematics at Heriot-Watt University, Edinburgh. His research focuses on financial risk management for pension plans and life insurers, and the modeling of longevity risk. He qualified as Fellow of the Faculty of Actuaries and has edited the leading international actuarial journal *ASTIN Bulletin*; he also is a corresponding member of the Swiss Association of Actuaries. He holds an M.A. in Mathematics from Cambridge University and a Ph.D. in Statistics from Heriot-Watt University.

Guy Coughlan works at Pacific Global Advisors and serves on the Society of Actuaries' Longevity Task Force. Previously he was Managing Director at J.P. Morgan and most recently held the positions of Global Head of Longevity

Solutions, Global Head of ALM Advisory, and Co-head of European Pension Advisory. He also founded the Global ALM Advisory group and set up J.P. Morgan's longevity business and helped establish the Life/Longevity Markets Association, a cross-industry body that promotes the market for longevity risk transfers. He earned a D.Phil. in Physics from Oxford University, where he was a Rhodes Scholar, and he also holds a B.Sc. degree from the University of Western Australia and an M.B.A. from Henley Business School in the UK.

E. Philip Davis is Senior Research Fellow, NIESR, and Pastor of the Penge Baptist Church. His research interests focus on the economics of pensions, aging, and financial stability. Previously he worked at the Bank of England and taught at Brunel University. He has consulted for the World Bank, ILO, Asian Development Bank, Financial Services Authority, European Investment Bank, OECD, and EBRD. His most recent work in the pension field was for the Dutch Central Bank (relating pension performance to sponsoring firm characteristics) and the Canadian OMERS fund (on asset returns and asset restrictions).

Gordon Fletcher is Principal and Actuary in Mercer's Financial Strategy Group, where he helps clients identify their pension risks and how best to manage them; he also chairs Mercer's U.S. LDI committee. He led Mercer's development of pension buyout online auctions and advised plan trustees in acquiring a longevity swap; he also works on LDI strategies, annuities, lump sums, derivative strategies, and longevity swaps. Previously he was a researcher at Cambridge University. He has received a Master's degree and Ph.D. in Mathematics and the Institute of Actuaries' Certificate in Derivatives.

Julien Halfon is Principal in London's Mercer Financial Strategy Group, where he advises UK and European clients on strategic risk management to manage exposures to interest and inflation rates, equity markets, and credit markets. Previously he has worked at P-Solve, Lazard, Hewitt, and Goldman Sachs. He earned his M.A. from the School of Advanced International Studies, John Hopkins University, and his M.B.A. from the Wharton School of the University of Pennsylvania. He also holds a Master's degree in International Economics and Finance from Dauphine University of Paris and a B.A. and Master's in Banking, Finance, and Insurance, also from Dauphine University of Paris.

P. Brett Hammond is Managing Director at MSCI and serves on the Pension Research Council Advisory Board. His research focuses on higher education and pensions, science and technology, finance, and health policy. Dr. Hammond previously was Manager of Corporate Projects at TIAA-CREF and worked at the National Academy of Science. He received a Ph.D. in Public Policy from MIT.

Tim Hodgson is a senior investment consultant with Towers Watson where he founded and now directs the Thinking Ahead Group. He is also a member of the firm's Global Investment Committee responsible for capital market and asset modeling assumptions. He earned his B.A. and M.A. in Economics from the University of Cambridge; he also completed the Investment Management Programme at London Business School. He is Associate of the CFA Society of the UK and is a qualified scuba divemaster, which is a hedge against his investment career not working out.

Amy Kessler is Senior Vice President and head of Longevity Reinsurance for Prudential Retirement's Pension Risk Transfer business. Previously she has worked at Bear Stearns and as Global Head of Pension ALM at Swiss Re in the United Kingdom. She earned her B.A. in Economics and M.A. in International Economics and Finance from Brandeis University, where she is a member of the Board of Overseers of the International Business School.

Robert Kosowski is Associate Professor of Finance at the Imperial College Business School, Imperial College London, and Director of the Risk Management Lab and Centre for Hedge Fund Research. He is also an associate member of the Oxford-Man Institute of Quantitative Finance at Oxford University and a member of AIMA's and PRMIA's research committees. Previously he worked for Goldman Sachs, the Boston Consulting Group, and Deutsche Bank. His research interests include asset pricing and financial econometrics with a focus on hedge funds, mutual funds, performance measurement, business cycles, and derivative trading strategies. He has taught at the Imperial College London and INSEAD. He holds a B.A. (First Class Honours) and M.A. in Economics from Trinity College, Cambridge University, and he earned an M.Sc. in Economics and a Ph.D. from the London School of Economics.

Ruben Laros works at All Pensions Group (APG) in the Netherlands, where he develops expertise on pension design, pension communication, and international pension provision. He received a Bachelor's degree in International Economics and Finance and a Master's degree in Economics and Finance of Aging from Tilburg University.

Marlena I. Lee is Vice President on Dimensional Fund Advisors' Research team, where she researches asset pricing and macroeconomics. Previously, Marlena has worked to explain complex financial concepts, and she was an economic consultant on antitrust litigation cases and a research assistant at the Manhattan Institute of Policy Research. She earned her Ph.D. in Finance from the University of Chicago's Booth School of Business; she also holds an M.B.A. from Booth, an M.S. in Agricultural and Resource Economics, and a B.S. in Managerial Economics from the University of California, Davis.

Yijia Lin is Assistant Professor of Finance at the University of Nebraska, Lincoln. Her research focuses on insurance securitization, enterprise risk management, and actuarial science. She received the Harold D. Skipper Best Paper Award, the Ernst Meyer Prize for University Research Work by the Geneva Association, and the North American Actuarial Journal Annual Prize for the Best Paper Published. She received both a B.A. in Insurance and an M.A. in Finance and

Insurance from Beijing Technology and Business University, and earned her Ph.D. in Risk Management and Insurance from Georgia State University. She is also a Chartered Financial Analyst Charterholder.

Stefan Lundbergh is Head of Innovation at Cardano Risk Management and a non-executive board member of the Fourth Swedish National Pension Fund; he also chairs the Research Committee of the Rotman International Centre for Pension Management. Previously he held positions at Algemene Pensioen Groep (APG) in the Netherlands and Skandia Life Insurance Company in Sweden. He holds a Ph.D. from Stockholm School of Economics.

Richard MacMinn is the first holder of the Edmondson-Miller Chair in Insurance and Financial Services at Illinois State University; previously he was the first holder of the Swiss Re Chair in the Management of Risk at the University of Nottingham. He has edited several top-field journals and has thrice won the prestigious Mehr Award, in addition to a number of other awards from the American Risk and Insurance Association, Casualty Actuarial Society, and General Insurance Research Organization in the United Kingdom and Asia-Pacific Risk and Insurance Association for his publications. He received his B.A. in Political Science from the University of California at Los Angeles, as well as an M.A. in Public Administration and a Ph.D. in Economics from the University of Illinois.

Raimond Maurer is the Chair of Investment, Portfolio Management, and Pension Finance at the Finance Department of the Goethe University Frankfurt, and recently held the Metzler Visiting Professorship at the Wharton School. His research focuses on asset management, lifetime portfolio choice, real estate, and pension finance. He has consulted for the World Bank, ECB, FED, and Ministry of Social Affairs Baden Württemberg; he also serves on the German Society of Actuaries, the Association of Certified International Investment Analysts (academic director and member of the International Examination Committee) and is a Member of the Supervisory Board of Union Real Estate Investment and the Advisory Board of the Wharton School's Pension Research Council. He received his habilitation, Ph.D., and diploma in Business Administration from Mannheim University, as well as an honorary doctorate from the University of St. Petersburg.

Olivia S. Mitchell is the International Foundation of Employee Benefit Plans Professor of Insurance/Risk Management and Business Economics/Public Policy at the Wharton School of the University of Pennsylvania. Her research focuses on private and public insurance, risk management, public finance, labor markets, compensation, and pensions, with both a U.S. and an international focus. She is also the Executive Director of the Pension Research Council and the Director of the Boettner Center on Pensions and Retirement Research at Wharton, Faculty Research Fellow at the National Bureau of Economic Research, and Associate Director of the Financial Literacy Center. She received her B.A. in Economics from Harvard University, and her M.S. and Ph.D. degrees in Economics from the University of Wisconsin-Madison.

James Moore is Managing Director in the Newport Beach PIMCO office where he leads the global liability-driven investments product management team and is co-head of the investment solutions group. He is also PIMCO's pension strategist. Previously he was in the corporate derivative and asset-liability strategy groups at Morgan Stanley, responsible for asset-liability, strategic risk management, and capital structure advisory work. He also taught investments and employee benefit plan design and finance while at the Wharton School of the University of Pennsylvania, where he earned his Ph.D. with concentrations in Finance, Insurance, and Risk Management. His undergraduate degrees are from Brown University.

Niels Pedersen is Senior Vice President in the client analytics group in the Newport Beach PIMCO office, where he specializes in asset allocation, quantitative risk management, and design of customized tail-risk hedging strategies. He earned his Ph.D. and Master's in Economics from Northwestern University, and he received an undergraduate degree in Economics from the University of Aarhus in Denmark.

Laura Rebel is as a risk manager at Cardano, servicing clients in the European pension industry. She obtained a Bachelor's degree in Economics and Business and an Honors Master's degree in Finance at VU University Amsterdam.

Stacy Scapino is Partner and the Global Leader for Mercer's Investments Multinational Consulting activities, where she focuses on pension, investment, and banking industries. Previously she was a senior financial analyst responsible for research and policy development for bank supervision at the Federal Reserve Bank of New York. She received the B.S. in Finance from the University of Illinois and an M.A. in International Economics and European History from the Johns Hopkins University Paul Nitze School for Advanced International Studies. She is also a CFA Charterholder.

Michael Sherris is Professor of Actuarial Studies at the Australian School of Business, UNSW, in Sydney, Australia; he is also Chief Investigator in the ARC Centre of Excellence in Population Ageing Research. His current research interests focus on longevity risk modeling and management, insurer risk management, and risk-based capital. He was awarded the IAA Bob Alting von Gesau AFIR Prize, the Casualty Actuarial Society (CAS) annual prize for the most valuable contribution to casualty actuarial science, the Geneva Association/IIS Research Program Shin Research Award for Excellence, the Redington Prize of the Society of Actuaries, and the H.M. Jackson Memorial Prize of The Institute of Actuaries of Australia. He is also past President of the Asia Pacific Risk and Insurance Association.

Ruilin Tian is Assistant Professor of Finance in the College of Business at North Dakota State University. Her research interests include pension fund management, longevity risk hedging, mathematical optimization, portfolio management, moment problem, and tail risk analysis via Value-at-Risk (VaR) or Conditional Value-at-Risk (CVaR). In addition, she is involved in research analyzing monetary policies and predict business cycles. She received her Ph.D. in Risk Management and Insurance from Georgia State University, and her M.S. in Applied Economics from Marquette University.

Jennifer Wang is Chair of the Risk Management and Insurance Department at National Chengchi University in Taiwan. Her research interests include risk management, social insurance, annuity, pension fund management, insurance accounting and finance, and asset liability management. She has held positions at the American Risk and Insurance Association, Asia-Pacific Risk and Insurance Association, and *Journal of Insurance*, among others. She received a Ph.D. in Risk Management, Insurance and Actuarial Science from Temple University.

Qiming Zhou is an Honours student in the School of Risk and Actuarial Studies at the University of New South Wales.

Chapter 1

Recreating Retirement Sustainability

Olivia S. Mitchell and Raimond Maurer

The financial crisis and the ensuing Great Recession alerted all those working to ensure old-age security about the extreme risks confronting the financial and political institutions comprising our retirement system. This volume offers an in-depth analysis of the recently glimpsed 'black swans' that threaten private and public pensions around the world. Capital market shocks, surprises to longevity, regulatory and political risk, and errors in modeling all have profound consequences for stakeholders ranging from pension plan participants and plan sponsors to policymakers and those who seek to make retirement more resistant. In this book we analyze such challenges to retirement sustainability, and explore ways to better manage and finance them, as well. This understanding is intended to help rebuild retirement systems capable of withstanding what the future will bring.

Modeling and Managing Capital Market Risk

One way that pension plans can better handle the capital market risks they inevitably confront is to undertake liability-driven investment (LDI). In their chapter, Enrico Biffis and Robert Kosowski outline the main principles behind this variant of asset liability management (ALM) and describe commonly used hedging tools. They also discuss emerging de-risking tools such as pension buyouts/ins, longevity swaps, and tail risk hedges that have gained popularity in light of the rise in cross-asset correlation associated with quantitative easing. The main challenges ahead they identify include changes in pension regulation, centralized clearing of derivatives, and risk-taking incentives in delegated asset management for pension plans. Recent innovations include risk on/off trading, stock-bond correlation longevity swaps, and Credit Support Annex (CSA) pricing. Non-cleared derivatives may also be part of the solution.

A different concern arises from the fact that projections 30 years out may be problematic when asset returns are not well-behaved. James Moore and Niels Pederson's chapter proposes that historical data suggest important deviations from normality in asset returns, so that fat tails and extreme events happen more often than we once anticipated. Their preferred approach to simulation therefore involves developing a macroeconomy-consistent structural model, which can be used to run simulations through real-world simulators. They devise and implement a regime-switching model with these features, and then they compare results to those obtained using more conventional approaches.

In her chapter, Marlena Lee brings her own measured perspective to the way in which many pension modelers use stochastic models to project the future. Monte Carlo simulation is commonly used in risk analysis and in financial planning, which generally assumes normal distributions of uncertainty. While such simulations will always be a useful financial planning tool, she also highlights their limitations. Specifically, she notes that returns of 40 percent would be anticipated to occur only once each 520 years if shocks were normally distributed, but these were seen in both 1931 and 2008. Moreover, returns in excess of 70 percent would be expected to occur only every 4002 years, but this happened in 1933.

In sum, experts agree that all statistical models can provide useful guides, but model risk remains a crucial problem that cannot be taken too lightly. Financial models played a key role in the global financial crisis, and new ways of modeling financial risk are greatly needed.

Measuring and Managing Longevity Risk

As the workforce ages and people live longer, analysts concerned with retirement security have focused increasingly on how financial markets can be constructed to help model and manage longevity risk. Andrew Cairns' chapter notes that many statistical models of the human life extension are not very robust, though good models are critical if we are to properly forecast future mortality patterns and protect retirement plans against this risk. Defined benefit (DB) plans in particular need ways to hedge against large increases in human survival rates, including longevity swaps. Nevertheless, pension plan sponsors must also evaluate their appetite for and tolerance to risk, in order to determine how much to pay for such protection. This is not always an easy task.

Taking the argument a step further, in his chapter Guy Coughlan proposes that DB pension plans should address longevity risk in the larger framework of corporate finance and financial economics. He points out that with the development of longevity swaps, this risk can now be hedged in a flexible and customized way. As a result, DB pension plans now have at their disposal a complete toolkit for ensuring they are managed in a sustainable fashion. In fact, because of the compounding effects between longevity and interest rate risks, he suggests that it is financially desirable to manage these two liability risks in concert. His proposed framework provides the basis for addressing key pension risk management decisions, including whether to consider a buyout/termination or pursue the hedging of longevity risk as part of the long-term management of the plan. He then shows how this approach helps understand the different ways in which Ford, General Motors, and Verizon handled risk management in their pensions.

The chapter by Michael Sherris and Qiming Zhou outlines several different actuarial approaches to modeling longevity risk. As they point out, systematic mortality risk models and Markov aging models that can handle heterogeneity have been developed, yet analysts often capture only one of these aspects of mortality risk. Their work, by contrast, includes both a mortality heterogeneity model and a frailty model, to show the impact of this risk on annuity fund values at older ages. In particular, when a mortality model includes systematic risk, this can increase the tail of the mortality distribution. They also allow for adverse selection to impact pension plan fund values.

Securitization of longevity risk is a topic that has generated much interest of late, as noted in the chapter by Richard MacMinn, Patrick Brockett, Jennifer Wang, Yijia Lin, and Ruilin Tian. These authors explore several ways to manage longevity risk in both DB and defined contribution (DC) plans, noting that longevity risk is a $2.2 trillion business in the U.S. and a $42 trillion business globally.

Preparing for Regulatory and Political Risk

No expert in the retirement security arena can ignore what many in the field call regulatory and political risk. This topic is the purview of Philip Davis, whose chapter focuses on how pension regulation has become more focused on risk, transparency, and governance. In fact, he points out that some regulatory developments have been counterproductive, inducing pension funds to become increasingly short-term focused in their investments. Whereas banks have been subjected to new regulation under the Basel III international agreements in the wake of the financial crisis, Davis contends that pension funds do not compete across borders, a pension failure does not usually produce significant externalities across borders, and pension policy remains national in scope. Nevertheless, he also recognizes that some global similarity in regulation of company funds would likely be beneficial to multinationals. Some countries have turned to a focus on risk-based supervision for DC pensions. Additionally, international accounting standards are a form of regulation, in particular the mark-to-market movement.

The chapter by Stefan Lundbergh, Ruben Laros, and Laura Rebel examines how regulation can replicate what traditional DB pension schemes offered: they completed the market by offering real deferred annuities to their members. Although the traditional DB design proved to be unsustainable due to the demographic developments, it still serves as a guide of what good pension solutions should provide, namely a lifelong stable inflation and linked cash flows at retirement. And in this context, they argue that risk should be defined as the probability of failing to provide stable retirement income. This approach to pension risk differs substantially from the wealth management portfolio approach. Against this backdrop, they see recent European Union (E.U.) regulatory changes as seeking to create a single market among member states for retirement provision and thus to remove an obstacle to labor mobility. In turn, this effort to bring coherence will increase transparency and create incentives for insurance companies and pension funds to manage the balance sheet risks in an economically meaningful way, while also providing regulators with an early warning system and tools for intervention. The authors also suggest that by applying the principles of market consistent valuation and pricing mechanisms to pension design, it will be possible to build a collective product that is fair to the members/customers and embodies an internally consistent risk-based framework.

In his chapter, Tim Hodgson points out that we cannot diversify our risk across time; hence he contends that analysts, regulators, and plan designers should give greater weight to the consequences of outcomes and less weight to their likelihoods. And in this context, extreme risks matter and deserve more attention than they have been given thus far. This is particularly worrisome since the global economic environment continues to be characterized by significant imbalances, and retirement for the masses is at serious risk, In fact he believes that retirement as currently configured was never affordable, but this reality was hidden by demographic and debt trends over many decades. He adds that a ranking system is a useful way to prioritize efforts to consider and manage potential risk exposures; as far as hedging is concerned, the major conclusion is that political, environmental, social, and technological risks are generally difficult to hedge. In view of this, a pragmatic solution is less about changing investment strategy and more about building a larger risk buffer.

Implications for Plan Sponsors

While population aging continues unabated, Amy Kessler notes in her chapter that the low growth/low interest rate environment is producing a deep funding gap for plan sponsors, who have been taking on more risk to bridge the gap. In fact, she questions whether there is any way to budget and moderate risk, provide for increasing longevity, manage the intergenerational risk in the pension plan, and create greater certainty that participant pension benefits can be met. One solution might be to increase retirement ages. Also, pension risk-transfer decisions made without taking longevity risk into account will consistently undervalue benefits of risk management. By contrast, she contends that a sustainability model will need to depart from the conventional approach, by building in a risk budget.

The study by Geoff Bauer, Gordon Fletcher, Julien Halfon, and Stacy Scapino argues that corporations have allocated a significant share of available cash originating from ongoing operations, as well as equity and debt, to finance pension obligations rather than to boost core productive activities or enhance shareholder value. And firms sponsoring under- or unfunded pension liabilities should assess whether they must provide additional voluntary funding, invest in alternative opportunities, or pursue other corporate activities. In their view, a holistic approach to pension risk and funding can prevent another decade of weak asset liability management strategies, conflicts with trustees, investment boards and unions, and lost pension contributions. Pension deficits ballooned after the 2008 crisis, and corporate finance decisions must be balanced in the face of pension risk and governance.

Conclusion

Many see the lengthening human life span as a welcome development. Nevertheless, longer time horizons also expose us to greater risk and reduce our ability to predict long-term returns. Moreover, managers of retirement systems grounded on social security and medical care benefit promises now fear that the latter face insolvency. For all these reasons, pensions will need to be reimagined if they are to survive in the face of demographic, capital market, model, and regulatory risk. In the United States and many other countries, an additional challenge arises from the fact that pensions had initially been designed to be an employer responsibility. But as the twenty-first century progresses, employer commitment to traditional benefit systems appears to be on the downturn. Inevitably, these trends highlight a profound need to reimagine pensions and other retirement benefits. This volume offers ideas and suggestions toward that end.

References

Bauer, G., G. Fletcher, J. Halfon, and S. Scapino (2014). 'The Funding Debate: Optimizing Pension Risk within a Corporate Risk Budget,' in P. B. Hammond, R. Maurer, and O. S. Mitchell, eds., *Recreating Sustainable Retirement: Resilience, Solvency, and Tail Risk*. Oxford, U.K.: Oxford University Press, pp. 273–292.

Biffis, E. and R. Kosowski (2014). 'Managing Capital Market Risk for Retirement,' in P. B. Hammond, R. Maurer, and O. S. Mitchell, eds., *Recreating Sustainable Retirement: Resilience, Solvency, and Tail Risk*. Oxford, U.K.: Oxford University Press, pp. 9–29.

Cairns, A. (2014). 'Modeling and Management of Longevity Risk,' in P. B. Hammond, R. Maurer, and O. S. Mitchell, eds., *Recreating Sustainable Retirement: Resilience, Solvency, and Tail Risk*. Oxford, U.K.: Oxford University Press, pp. 71–88.

Coughlan, G. (2014). 'Longevity Risk Management, Corporate Finance, and Sustainable Pensions,' in P. B. Hammond, R. Maurer, and O. S. Mitchell, eds., *Recreating Sustainable Retirement: Resilience, Solvency, and Tail Risk*. Oxford, U.K.: Oxford University Press, pp. 89–112.

Davis, E. P. (2014). 'Evolving Roles for Pension Regulations: Toward Better Risk Control?' in P. B. Hammond, R. Maurer, and O. S. Mitchell, eds., *Recreating Sustainable*

Retirement: Resilience, Solvency, and Tail Risk. Oxford, U.K.: Oxford University Press, pp. 163–185.

Hodgson, T. (2014). 'Extreme Risks and the Retirement Anomaly,' in P. B. Hammond, R. Maurer, and O. S. Mitchell, eds., *Recreating Sustainable Retirement: Resilience, Solvency, and Tail Risk.* Oxford, U.K.: Oxford University Press, pp. 215–243.

Kessler, A. R. (2014). 'Risk Budgeting and Longevity Insurance: Strategies for Sustainable Defined Benefit Pension Funds,' in P. B. Hammond, R. Maurer, and O. S. Mitchell, eds., *Recreating Sustainable Retirement: Resilience, Solvency, and Tail Risk.* Oxford, U.K.: Oxford University Press, pp. 247–272.

Lee, M. (2014). 'Stress Testing Monte Carlo Assumptions,' in P. B. Hammond, R. Maurer, and O. S. Mitchell, eds., *Recreating Sustainable Retirement: Resilience, Solvency, and Tail Risk.* Oxford, U.K.: Oxford University Press, pp. 60–67.

Lundbergh, S., R. Cardano, R. Laros, and L. Rebel (2014). 'Developments in European Pension Regulation: Risks and Challenges,' in P. B. Hammond, R. Maurer, and O. S. Mitchell, eds., *Recreating Sustainable Retirement: Resilience, Solvency, and Tail Risk.* Oxford, U.K.: Oxford University Press, pp. 186–214.

MacMinn, R., P. Brockett, J. Wang, Y. Lin, and R. Tian (2014). 'The Securitization of Longevity Risk and Its Implications for Retirement Security,' in P. B. Hammond, R. Maurer, and O. S. Mitchell, eds., *Recreating Sustainable Retirement: Resilience, Solvency, and Tail Risk.* Oxford, U.K.: Oxford University Press, pp. 134–160.

Moore, J., and N. K. Pederson (2014). 'Implications for Long-term Investors of the Shifting Distribution of Capital Market Returns,' in P. B. Hammond, R. Maurer, and O. S. Mitchell, eds., *Recreating Sustainable Retirement: Resilience, Solvency, and Tail Risk.* Oxford, U.K.: Oxford University Press, pp. 30–59.

Sherris, M. and Q. Zhou (2014). 'Model Risk, Mortality Heterogeneity, and Implications for Solvency and Tail Risk,' in P. B. Hammond, R. Maurer, and O. S. Mitchell, eds., *Recreating Sustainable Retirement: Resilience, Solvency, and Tail Risk.* Oxford, U.K.: Oxford University Press, pp. 113–133.

Part I
Capital Market and Model Risk

Chapter 2

Managing Capital Market Risk for Retirement

Enrico Biffis and Robert Kosowski

The Emergence of Liability-driven Investment

Liabilities of corporate and public defined benefit (DB) pension plans have reached unprecedented levels in the last decade, due to increases in life expectancy and underperformance of the assets backing the promises. Pension trustees have addressed the deterioration of funding levels in different ways, working both on the asset and liability sides. On the liability side, there have been closures of schemes to new members as well as to new accruals, in order to cap liabilities. On the asset side, there has been a stronger focus on asset liability management (ALM), which has translated into 'de-risking' strategies tilting asset allocations away from equities and toward liability-driven investment (LDI).

LDI differs from the simple approach to asset management which aims to maximize the return of a portfolio for a given level of portfolio risk (volatility) without taking liabilities explicitly into account. In fact, LDI is a strategy based on the cash flows needed to fund future liabilities. It can be applied to both DB and defined contribution (DC) pension plans. In the latter, investment decisions and risk rest with the employee; the plan's liability is employee-specific. In the former, pension plan sponsors, with the assistance of actuaries, forecast future anticipated cash payouts to pensioners over their expected lifetimes. From the perspective of a DB plan sponsor, risk entails two main components: investment risk and liability risk, the latter stemming from the stochastic value of pension liabilities. A pension plan's funded status can change due to a change in liabilities, even if investment risk is carefully managed. Although the notion of LDI is not new (there are references to it by U.K. actuaries going back to the 1930s), its adoption among pension plans has only recently become more widespread (Kessler 2014).

The ALM problem faced by a DB pension plan can be represented by a complex dynamic optimization problem. For simplicity, some academic studies abstract from the dynamic nature of the problem and use surplus optimization as a method to reflect the presence of liabilities and its effect on optimal portfolio choice (e.g. Sharpe and Tint 1990; Ezra 1991; Leibowitz et al. 1992; Nijman and Swinkels 2008). These works treat fund liabilities as a state variable and specify an objective function of assets relative to liabilities. The objective function takes into account the correlation between assets and liabilities in determining the optimal portfolio allocation. Surplus at each time t is defined as $S_t(k) = A_t \tilde{k} - L_t$, where A_t denotes the value of the assets at time t and L_t the value of the liabilities, whereas the parameter k measures the importance that the fund management attaches to the value of the liabilities. The return on the fund surplus can be then be defined as $R_t^s(k) = R_t^A - kR_t^L$, where $R_t^s(k)$, R_t^A, and R_t^L are the return on the surplus, the assets, and the liabilities, respectively, and $k = \tilde{k}L_{t-1/At-1}$ (e.g. Sharpe and Tint 1990).

If we assume that the pension fund manager has a mean-variance utility function with risk aversion coefficient γ in the return on surplus, we can derive a closed form solution for the optimal asset allocation. For example, Nijman and Swinkels (2008) use this framework to study whether the risk of investment portfolios of pension schemes investing in traditional asset classes can be reduced by non-traditional investment opportunities such as commodities. They find that the benefits for pension plans with inflation-indexed liabilities are substantial, but they are not large for those with nominal liabilities.

Dynamic ALM

One caveat to this simple static surplus return optimization framework is that it captures only time-varying asset allocation as a result of a repeated application of the static framework. In practice, however, pension asset allocation can be expected to change over time, as market conditions change and/or the plan matures. Over time, assets may be moved away from the return-seeking component of the portfolio and placed into the liability-hedging component. A pension plan sponsor may, for example, decide to take on more risk when a plan is underfunded, to generate a higher return in the hope that the funding status improves. But once a plan's ratio of assets to liabilities (that is, the funded status or funding ratio) reaches a comfortable enough level, sponsors often investigate the possibility of closing or terminating the plan in an effort to remove risk to the plan sponsor; see the discussion of pension buyouts below.

A more general approach to the pension manager's utility function was developed by Rudolf and Ziemba (2004).[1] They do so using a portfolio selection model for an investment company seeking to maximize the intertemporal expected utility of the surplus of assets net of liabilities. They show that the optimal portfolio consists of investors holding a combination of four portfolios: the market portfolio, a hedge portfolio for the relevant state variables, a hedge portfolio for the liabilities, and the riskless asset. In contrast to Merton's (1973) result in the asset-only case, the liability hedge is independent of preferences and depends only on the plan's funding ratio. Demand for the state variable hedge and the market portfolio depends on the investor's preferences. Detemple and Rindisbacher (2008) extend Rudolf and Ziemba (2004) by (a) allowing the factors in the model to follow a more general diffusion process, and (b) defining preferences over intermediate cash flows, instead of the surplus.[2]

The Spread of LDI

LDI has spread widely in recent years. The SEI Pension Management Research Panel (SEI 2012) has conducted an annual poll of corporate pension plans since 2007; in 2012, this poll was completed by 125 pension plans from the United States, Canada, the United Kingdom, and the Netherlands. Figure 2.1 shows that since the poll's inception, LDI more than tripled in use, from 20 percent in 2007 to 63 percent in 2011. The use of LDI dipped to 57 percent in 2012, probably as a result of low funding ratios and exceptional market conditions shaped by quantitative easing.

Of those organizations not utilizing an LDI strategy in 2012, 20 percent said they planned to implement one by the end of 2013. The portion of assets invested in LDI has also increased over time, as Figure 2.2 shows.

Of those plans using LDI in 2012, over half (52 percent) continued to invest more than 40 percent of their portfolio in an LDI strategy; only 11 percent of plans invested less than 20 percent. In other words, as a plan's funding status improves, a greater portion of its portfolio tends to be invested in LDI. It is instructive to see how pension sponsors and trustees define LDI. According to the SEI (2012) poll, most defined LDI in one of two ways: 'matching duration of assets to duration of liabilities' or 'a portfolio designed to be risk managed with respect to liabilities' (see Table 2.1).

Moreover, as shown in Table 2.2, most respondents to the SEI Global LDI Poll describe control of the year-to-year volatility of the funded status as the main goal of LDI.

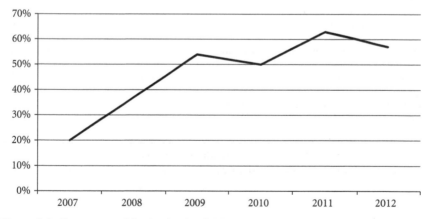

Figure 2.1. Percentage of funds adopting LDI strategies.

Source: SEI (2012).

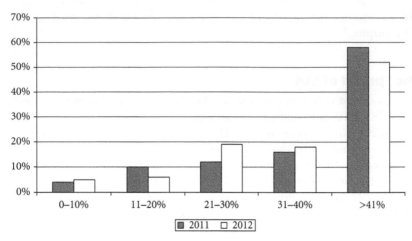

Figure 2.2. Percentage of funds that use LDI strategy.

Notes: This figure shows the portion of the portfolio invested in LDI among the funds that employ LDI. The percentages are shown for 2011 and 2012 as reported in the SEI 2012 poll.

Source: SEI (2012).

TABLE 2.1 Definition of LDI according to respondents (percent)

Definition of LDI	2007	2008	2009	2010	2011	2012
Matching duration of assets to duration of liabilities	41	30	40	30	46	39
A portfolio designed to be risk-managed with respect to liabilities	38	34	32	39	24	31
Consideration of liability poll and/or costs in setting asset allocations	12	14	7	12	5	11
Immunizing the plan's liabilities with fixed-income securities	2	6	5	7	12	8
Forcing asset performance to mimic liability performance	4	6	8	3	9	7
Use of derivative instruments such as interest-rate swaps	1	1	1	4	2	2
Use of asset classes with reduced volatility	1	9	7	5	2	2

Note: This shows how SEI poll respondents defined what LDI meant to them.
Source: SEI 6th Annual Global LDI Poll (SEI 2012).

TABLE 2.2 Goals of LDI (percent)

Goals of LDI	2007	2008	2009	2010	2011	2012
Control of year-to-year volatility of funded status	79	79	90	46	78	80
Control contribution and/or pension expense	46	45	51	43	46	53
Minimize/maximize impact on corporate liquidity/cash flow	31	30	35	23	41	30
Improve funding levels	19	14	24	28	26	30
Progress plan toward termination or buyout	8	8	13	20	15	26
Avoid the minimum funding liability	14	13	9	7	5	6

Note: This shows how SEI poll respondents described the goals of LDI.
Source: SEI 6th Annual Global LDI Poll (SEI 2012).

Pension De-risking

Next we provide an overview of some common tools used in LDI and recent innovations in pension de-risking solutions.

Interest-rate and Inflation-linked Derivatives

It is well known that the average duration of pension liabilities is very long and quite difficult to match with standard fixed-income instruments. According to J.P. Morgan (2006), for example, the average duration gap of European pension plans exceeded 13 years in 2006, with an average liability duration of 21 years, and an average duration of fixed-income portfolios falling short of eight years. These figures give an idea of the challenges faced by ALM strategies relying on standard duration gap analysis or interest-rate immunization. In countries where pension regulation has become more transparent and risk-based, notably the U.K. and the Netherlands, pension plans have made structural changes in asset allocation, gearing their portfolios toward liability matching by relying on interest-rate derivatives and hedging programs structured by investment banks and asset managers. The most common products include interest-rate swaps, forward-starting swaps, and 'swaptions' (i.e. options giving the right but not the obligation to enter a swap at a future date). These instruments represent a cheaper and more flexible alternative to bonds, as the latter are in limited supply at the long end of the yield curve, and in any case would typically fall short of the duration target that pension plans favor. Dynamic strategies in fixed-income derivatives also provide a natural way to take advantage of movements in the yield curve that may allow the hedger to lock in a higher funding ratio as a result of the valuation basis used in marking to market the liabilities. Moreover, the format of fixed-income derivatives provides a natural template to address the exposure to other sources of risk, such as inflation and other forms of indexation of pension payments. For example, in recent years, inflation swaps, inflation caps and floors, and related instruments have experienced a dramatic surge in popularity due to LDI programs. The market in these instruments is now quite liquid, provides an efficient alternative to inflation-linked treasuries, and can be used to gauge more precisely the market value of pension liabilities.

Pension Buyouts and Buy-ins

The most direct way for a sponsor to reduce its exposure to pension risk is to transfer part of its pension liabilities to a counterparty.[3] The transfer may take several forms:

- A *pension buyout*, in the case where the original employer's covenant is ended and the counterparty is another principal employer, meaning that all the liabilities of the pension plan, together with the responsibility to meet them, are transferred to another institution.
- A *pension buy-in*, in the case where the counterparty is a life insurer or reinsurer. The transaction essentially entails the purchase of bulk-annuities to insure some or all the liabilities while retaining responsibility for them.

An active pension buyout market developed in the U.K. beginning in 2006, enjoying significant growth and attracting the participation of major players in financial markets (LCP 2012). As a stylized example of pension buyout, consider the case of a DB plan with assets A and liabilities L, valued on an 'ongoing basis' by the plan actuary. When the plan's assets are insufficient to cover the liabilities (i.e. $A<L$), the company recognizes a deficit of $L-A$. If $A>L$ instead, the company's plan has a surplus of $A-L$. Life insurers are usually required to value liabilities under more prudent assumptions than pension plans (regarding future mortality improvements, inflation rates, and market yields), resulting in a larger valuation of the liabilities L'. This increases reported deficits or reduces reported surpluses when a company approaches an insurer for transfer of its pension assets and liabilities. In the case of a deficit, a company borrows the amount $max(L'-A,0)$ and pays it to an insurer to buy out its pension assets and liabilities. The transaction allows the employer to offload the pension liabilities from its balance sheet. This means that the volatility of assets and liabilities associated with the pension plan accounts, the payment of management fees on the plan's assets, and any levies charged for members' protection insurance can be avoided (Coughlan 2014; Kessler 2014). If buyout costs are financed by borrowing, a regular loan replaces pension assets and liabilities on the balance sheet. From the point of view of the plan members, the pensions are secured in full—subject, of course, to the solvency of the life insurer.

Other alternatives exist in addition to the full buyout transactions. *Partial buyouts/ins* may take different forms, and involve the transfer of liabilities originating from a subgroup of members (e.g. deferred pensions, pensions in payment, etc.) or payable over a limited time-horizon (e.g. liabilities above ten years' maturity). Another variation is represented by *synthetic buy-ins* (or do-it-yourself buy-ins), whereby the pension plan enters a series of swap contracts to hedge longevity, investment, and inflation risks, so that the overall effect is similar to a traditional buy-in (Biffis and Blake 2010*b*; LCP 2012). The fixed payments of the swaps are financed by using the income from the pension plan assets, which are retained by the hedger as collateral and hence reduce its exposure to counterparty risk.

Longevity Swaps

Longevity swaps represent a recent innovation relative to traditional buyouts and buy-ins. They are agreements between two parties to exchange fixed payments against variable payments linked to the number of survivors in a reference population. They are used by pension plans to hedge longevity risk: that is, the exposure to the systematic risk of mortality improvements, which cannot be mitigated by pooling together large numbers of lives. The non-financial nature of the exposure to longevity risk is only apparent: the number of active members or pensioners alive at each point in time acts as a multiplier for the financial exposure associated with (current and future) payments to the representative member of a cohort of active or retired individuals. In the language of derivatives, longevity risk introduces a 'quanto' component in pension liabilities,[4] which can dramatically undermine LDI programs based on average notional exposures, particularly if the latter are based on outdated mortality projections.

To date, longevity swaps transactions have mainly involved pension funds and annuity providers wanting to hedge their exposure to longevity risk without having to bear any basis risk (i.e. the risk of mismatch between the hedger's exposure and the reference population on which the hedging instrument is written). The variable payments in such longevity swaps are designed to match precisely the mortality experience of each individual hedger: hence the name *bespoke longevity swaps* (Biffis and Blake 2010*b*; LCP 2012). This is essentially a form of longevity risk insurance, similar to annuity reinsurance in reinsurance markets. A fundamental difference from other forms of reinsurance, however, is that longevity swaps are typically collateralized, whereas typical (re)insurance transactions are not (Biffis et al. 2012*a*). The main reason is that longevity swaps are often part of a wider de-risking strategy involving other collateralized instruments (interest-rate and inflation swaps, for example); additionally, pension plans have been increasingly concerned with counterparty risk in the wake of the subprime crisis (as discussed further on in the chapter).[5]

Financial Innovation in the Wake of the Global Financial Crisis

The subprime crisis has accelerated the deterioration of DB plans' funding levels. Pension sponsors and trustees have addressed the downturn by working on both the liability and the asset sides. To cap liabilities, there have been a number of closures of schemes to new members, as well as to new accruals. According to Hewitt Associates, 'more than half of all [private-sector] employers surveyed at the start of [2009] were considering closing their final salary pension schemes to existing members, effectively freezing retirement benefits at today's levels' (Cohen 2009). Even if liabilities are locked in once a DB plan is closed, there still remains the problem of meeting the pension payments as they fall due, which has led to keen interest in the U.K. pension buyout market experience on the part of pension sponsors the world over. On the asset side, there has been a stronger focus on LDI programs. The interest in de-risking strategies has extended beyond jurisdictions traditionally more active in LDI (such as the U.K., the Netherlands, and Scandinavian countries), and has materialized in large transactions taking place, for example, in North America.

In terms of innovation in de-risking solutions, some of the most important developments involve a stronger focus on tail-risk hedging, contagion, and cross-asset correlation, as well as counterparty risk management.

Tail-risk and Cross-asset Correlation

The secular increase in cross-asset correlation (due to the integration of global financial markets and the deployment of alpha-extraction strategies across asset classes) was taken to a new level by the macro uncertainty resulting from the subprime crisis. The risk-on/off trading style, whereby portfolio risk is adjusted up or down depending on macro-economic uncertainty, has exacerbated the co-movement of different markets and strengthened the view that tail risk can be effectively proxied by measures of correlation or contagion. This has boosted the structuring of tail hedges relying on cross-asset derivatives (also called hybrid products)—in other words, instruments whose payoff is contingent on the price of more than one asset class. As an example, we discuss the stock-bond correlation swaps used in some LDI programs.

Case Study: Stock–bond Correlation Swaps[6]

To illustrate tail-risk hedging based on hybrid products, consider the case of stock-bond correlation swaps. These are instruments paying the difference between a fixed rate agreed at inception (the swap rate) and the realized correlation between the changes in a stock market index and the changes in a bond yield or interest-rate swap rate.

Pension funds are natural candidates for entering a payer correlation swap (they pay fixed and receive the floating realized correlation), as they are net long stocks and net short bonds. Their position originates from their liabilities which are, to a first order, bond-like (although of course they also depend on inflation and mortality rates). The empirical evidence suggests that during financial crises the correlation between stock returns and bond yields increases dramatically, an effect known as 'flight-to-safety,' where investors sell stocks to buy treasuries (e.g. Fleming and

Remolona 1999; Gulko 2002; Connolly et al. 2005). This results in the liabilities of pension funds rising in value (due to an increase in discount rates) by more than the asset side, depending on the equity/bond mix, thus generating a significant asset-liability mismatch. The correlation between bond and equity markets is likely to again become very important in the future, as bond yields are at historical lows and bond prices appear to be in bubble territory. Going forward, the risk is that short-term interest rates will eventually rise, leading to a significant sell-off in long-term bonds, as last happened in 1994. If central banks raise rates in an environment of improved economic growth and rising stock prices, the correlation between bond yields and stock returns can again suddenly increase.

To illustrate how a pension fund might benefit from a position in a payer stock-bond correlation swap, consider the following stylized example. Liabilities are proxied by 20-year duration bonds, whereas assets are invested in a 60/40 split across stocks and ten-year duration bonds. The split is consistent with the findings of Rauh (2009) and the duration mismatch with J.P. Morgan (2011). For a fully funded plan, we apply a shock of 10 percent to the stock price and the yield curve, which for simplicity is assumed to be flat. Figure 2.3 reports the percentage decrease in the funding ratio resulting from the individual shocks and a joint shock to stocks and bonds. The impact of the interest-rate shock is higher than for stocks due to (a) the mismatch between the asset and liability stock/bond split, and (b) the duration mismatch. The effects are greatly amplified by a simultaneous shock, which can be regarded as a proxy for high stock-bond correlation.

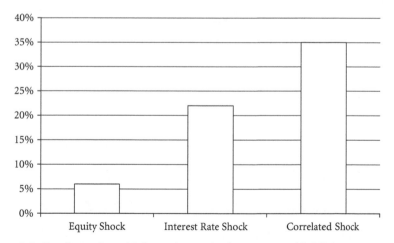

Figure 2.3. Funding ratio at risk from adverse shocks to assets and liabilities.

Note: The figure reports the percentage decrease in the funding ratio from the initial level of 100 percent (i.e. $A = L$), as a result of the 10 percent adverse shock to the stock price level and the (flat) yield curve separately, as well as jointly (correlated shock bar in the plot).

Source: Biffis et al. (2012*b*).

If the correlation between stocks and bonds were completely predictable, a pension fund manager with an ALM mandate would be able to adjust his portfolio today to take account of changes in correlation tomorrow. Although some studies find common factors that display some predictability of the second moments of stocks and bonds (e.g. Viceira 2012), the predictability of correlation is far from perfect out-of-sample. Hence, correlation swaps offer an effective way to hedge against unexpected changes in correlation. Figure 2.4 shows the price (in correlation points) of an OTC swap contract written on the correlation between changes in S&P 500 returns and in the ten-year constant maturity swap (CMS) rate. The swap rate at the end of April 2011 for the swap expiring in April 2012 (2013, 2014, 2015, 2016) was 25 percent (31 percent, 32 percent, 34 percent, 35 percent). An investor could have thus entered a payer correlation swap allowing him to enter a long position in the realized correlation at the price of a fixed correlation level equal to 32 percent over two years.

By taking a position in this product, the pension fund is exposed to the net payments from the instrument at each payment date, as well as to changes in the market's expectation of future stock-bond correlation via the marking-to-market/model procedure. Both the cashflow and mark-to-market channel can provide

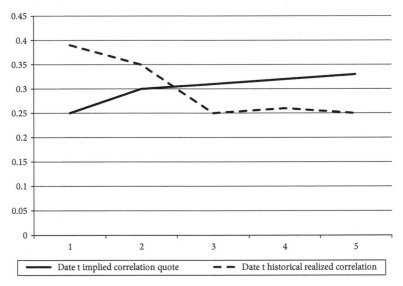

Figure 2.4. Correlation swap rates for different maturities as of April 8, 2011.

Notes: We plot the historical realized correlation (over one to five years to date) for comparison, demonstrating how the swap rate embeds a positive premium for short maturities and a negative premium for longer maturities. Gauging the correlation swap premium heavily depends on the methodology used to estimate the realized correlation.

Source: Biffis et al. (2012b); the investment bank which provided these quotes wishes to remain anonymous.

significant benefits *ex post* (in case of market distress) and *ex ante* (for regulatory valuations and stress testing exercises). These benefits typically come at a lower price than for standard tail-risk hedging strategies relying on put options or VIX derivatives. The reason is that the hybrid product provides insurance on a joint event (low stock prices and low yields) that may not occur in a downturn affecting both asset classes simultaneously, or in a stagflation environment characterized by rising yields and falling markets. The product can be priced even more cheaply as a result of the inventories and rebalancing needs of structuring desks operating across the LDI and other spaces.

To provide an example of how a pension fund might go about choosing the allocation to a correlation swap, Biffis et al. (2012*b*) first compute the implied volatilities of stocks and bonds.[7] Using the model-free methodology of Britten-Jones and Neuberger (2000), they back out the one-year implied volatility from options on the S&P 500 index and on ten-year Treasury bonds, and find evidence of time-varying linkages between the implied volatilities of stock and bond options which are not spanned by the available securities (see Biffis et al. 2012*b*). The presence of unspanned correlation risk means that one cannot rely on replication arguments to price the correlation swap. The authors therefore take a stance on preferences and use a utility indifference argument. Specifically, they consider a representative DB pension plan manager with mean-variance preferences on surplus returns; they then determine the correlation swap rate as the fixed leg that zeros the price of the swap at inception and makes the pension fund indifferent between entering the position or not. The dynamics of stock prices and bond yields are modeled (under the realistic measure) with a Wishart process allowing for stochastic volatilities and correlation (see Fonseca et al. 2007, for example).

Calibration of the model to historical data gives model-implied quotes falling within the range of quotes obtained from market participants such as those provided in Figure 2.4. The results on the optimal allocation to the correlation swap are presented in Table 2.3. Biffis et al. (2012*b*) define the surplus as above, where we recall that k captures the importance of the plan's liabilities, the limiting case $k = 0$ representing the asset-only case. From Table 2.3 we see that the optimal allocation to bonds increases as the liabilities become more important (higher k). The optimal allocation to the correlation swap is financed by reducing the position in both equities and bonds, and is decreasing in k. The intuition is that mean-variance optimization increases the allocation to bonds as the importance of the liabilities increases (because bonds have a risk profile closer to that of the liabilities), thus reducing the exposure to stock-bond correlation risk. The higher the pension plan's aversion to the volatility of the surplus, the stronger the effect.

Collateralization of Hedging Instruments

The global financial crisis has highlighted the importance of bilateral counterparty risk and collateralization for over-the-counter instruments, spurring a number of responses from market participants and regulators (e.g. ISDA 2009, 2010*a*).

TABLE 2.3 Portfolio weights for a pension plan with mean-variance preferences over surplus returns

k	$\gamma = 5$			$\gamma = 30$		
	0	0.5	1	0	0.5	1
Panel A. Without stock-bond correlation swap						
Stocks	0.415	0.371	0.336	0.415	0.262	0.190
Bonds	0.585	0.629	0.664	0.585	0.738	0.810
Panel B. With stock-bond correlation swap						
Stocks	0.401	0.360	0.327	0.401	0.256	0.187
Bonds	0.568	0.612	0.647	0.568	0.723	0.796
Correlation swap	0.031	0.028	0.026	0.031	0.021	0.017

Notes: This table reports the asset portfolio weights for differing values of k, the importance of liabilities, and γ, the risk aversion of the pension plan. Panel A reports the weights for when investable assets include only stocks and bonds. Panel B reports the weights for the case when correlation swaps are available for trade.

Source: Biffis et al. (2012*b*).

Although there is no commonly accepted framework yet for marking to market/model such exotic instruments as longevity swaps, hedgers and hedge suppliers look to other markets to provide a reference model for counterparty risk assessment and mitigation. In interest-rate swap markets, for example, the most common form of credit enhancement is the posting of collateral. According to the International Swap and Derivatives Association (ISDA), almost every swap at major financial institutions is 'bilaterally' collateralized (ISDA 2010*b*), meaning that either party is required to post collateral depending on whether the market value of the swap is positive or negative. Collateralization addresses the concerns aired by pension trustees regarding the safety of hedging instruments, but introduces an additional dimension in the cost/benefit assessment of de-risking solutions. The 'risk premium' embedded in a transaction then reflects not only the compensation for the risk being transferred and the cost of regulatory capital involved in the transaction, but also the expected costs to be incurred from posting collateral during the life of the trade. In an environment where good quality collateral is scarce, counterparty risk mitigation may therefore lead to higher prices and reduce the appeal of OTC instruments commonly used by pension plans in LDI programs.

To give an example, let us consider the case of a longevity swap and first take the perspective of a reinsurer (the hedge supplier) dealing with a pension plan (the hedger). Whenever the swap is sufficiently out-of-the-money to the hedge supplier, the hedge supplier is required to post collateral, which can be used by the hedger to mitigate losses in the event of default. Although interest on collateral is typically rebated, there is both a funding cost and an opportunity cost, as the posting of collateral depletes the resources the hedge supplier can use to meet her capital requirements at aggregate level as well as to write additional business. Conversely, whenever the swap is sufficiently in-the-money to the hedge supplier, the hedge supplier will receive collateral from the counterparty, thus benefiting from capital relief in regulatory valuations and freeing up capital that can be used to sell additional longevity protection. The benefits can be far larger if collateral can be re-hypothecated—that is, if collateral is not segregated and can be re-pledged for other purposes. The same considerations can be made from the viewpoint of the hedger, but the funding needs and opportunity costs of the two parties are unlikely to offset each other exactly. Hence they will ultimately affect the pricing of the hedging instrument. This is particularly relevant for transactions involving parties subject to different regulatory frameworks. In the U.K. and several other countries, for example, pension liabilities are more capital intensive for hedge suppliers, such as insurers, than for pension plans.[8]

Challenges Ahead

Pension plans face a number of challenges threatening the sustainable and orderly provision of retirement income to plan members. Well-known issues affecting the liability side, such as low interest rates and rising life expectancy (e.g. IMF 2012), are exacerbated by dangerous incentives on the asset side ('hunt for yield' in markets distorted by quantitative easing), as well as by a changing regulatory landscape that may force pension plans to recognize funding levels that are much lower than lenient accounting standards might suggest. There is an opportunity for regulation to create the right incentives for sponsors and trustees to consider the value of de-risking strategies, and engage with financial institutions and the insurance community to ensure that the risks of retirement provisions can be shared more widely and more efficiently. We give some examples of current challenges facing the demand and supply of de-risking solutions: collateralization of OTC derivatives; differential regulatory standards in the pension buyout market; and risk-taking incentives in delegated asset management.

A Changing Regulatory Landscape

Both the Dodd–Frank Wall Street Reform and Consumer Protection Act (signed into law by President Barack Obama on July 21, 2010) and the European Market Infrastructure Regulation (EMIR) in Europe are likely to have a major impact on the way financial institutions will manage counterparty risk in the coming years. It is unclear whether centralized clearing will lead to lower utilization of derivative instruments due to scarcity of collateral and funding costs associated with initial margins and possibly variation margins (Singh and Aitken 2009; Heller and Vause 2012; Sidanius and Zikes 2012; Bauer et al. 2013). What seems likely is that, for derivatives exempted from centralized clearing (such as inflation and longevity swaps), pension plans will be treated as 'covered entities' by regulators—in other words, in the same way as financial firms and systemically important non-financial firms. EMIR, for example, captures pension funds as financial counterparties, so one might expect pension plans to be considered as covered entities when E.U. regulators finalize the rules. This could possibly result in pension funds being required to exchange variation margins from the beginning of 2015, after which they would be subject to two-way posting of initial margins that will be segregated (see BIS-IOSCO 2013). These requirements will be phased in over 2015–2019 and will mainly affect large plans. For example, only covered entities with more than a notional €3 trillion of non-cleared swaps will be subject to these initial margin requirements, whereas entities with less than €8 billion of non-cleared swaps will be required to meet the requirements from 2019 onwards. The proposals currently being discussed suggest that initial margins will rely on standard risk measures (value-at-risk at 99 percent confidence interval over a 10-day horizon) computed with a model or standard tables. Eligible collateral will range from cash and bonds to corporate bonds and major equity indices (with haircuts).

The costs associated with these regulatory changes could be significant. For smaller and larger plans, in particular, the collateral management process will have to become an integral part of ALM and LDI. This could make pension buyouts and buy-ins more appealing because of their 'hedge and forget' nature, although the regulatory changes described above will also affect the LDI programs of buyout firms, making buyouts more expensive.

At the same time, recent innovation in the European marketplace is making it easier for smaller plans to cope with counterparty risk mitigation protocols. For example, the Credit Support Annex (CSA—the legal document that supports the collateral of derivatives transactions; see ISDA 1996) may now take the form of an umbrella CSA covering a consortium of pension plans engaging in LDI with a common asset manager. It is also increasingly common to see multi-currency cash/bond CSAs, as well as investment-grade credit CSAs, offering pension plans the option to deliver collateral in different forms and currency. Similarly, there are instruments being designed around the collateral management process, such as margin lending facilities and collateral swaps.[9] This suggests that the tools to respond to regulatory changes are already available and are being currently tested in the LDI programs of several pension plans.

Pension Buyouts and Regulation

Biffis and Blake (2013) explain the mechanics of pension buyouts by looking at the role of informational asymmetries and differences in regulatory standards between hedgers and hedge suppliers. They show that the adverse selection problem faced by unsophisticated pension plans (a seller's curse) transferring their liabilities to more informed insurers subject to stricter regulatory rules can have an adverse impact on prices, and has prevented a number of pension plans from accessing the buyout market. This suggests that greater transparency on the liability side could provide a more level playing field for pension plans and buyout firms. On the other hand, naive information disclosure may exacerbate the adverse selection problem by making informed buyers even more informed.

There is an opportunity here for regulators to align the broad actuarial assumptions used in DB pension accounting with a more realistic assessment of market risk and longevity risk, while leaving the choice of detailed information disclosure to pension funds and their advisors. This could favor the aggregation of liabilities and bulk buyouts (as a tool to reduce the information advantage of buyout firms), while narrowing the gap between buy-side and sell-side valuations due to differences in regulatory environments. Transparency can further have a beneficial effect in the secondary market for pension liabilities (e.g. the market for insurance-linked securities), as it mitigates the adverse selection problem faced by investors acquiring longevity-linked securities issued by buyout firms. Here, specialized insurers can use their information advantage to suitably pool longevity exposures and issue securities minimizing the impact of information asymmetries (e.g. Biffis and Blake 2010*a*). Regulators can therefore play an important role, for example by requiring rating agencies to use sufficiently granular data to assess the risk profile of securitized products, or by providing incentives to disclose and use detailed information from the very same internal models used to demonstrate the capital resilience of buyout firms in the primary market.

Risk-taking Incentives in Delegated Asset Management

Anchoring asset management to long-term liabilities via surplus-based performance measures leads to complex risk-taking and risk mitigation incentives. The value of assets and liabilities depends on regulation and accounting rules. On the asset side, financial instruments may be valued by using average historical yields to smooth out fluctuations in prices, or using historical cost rather than market value (e.g. under the accounting standard IAS 39, historical cost can be used for instruments classified as held-to-maturity as opposed to available for trading). On the liability side, accounting rules often rely on simplified and unrealistic assumptions that result in a distorted representation of the risk profile of pension liabilities (e.g. the use of outdated mortality tables in discounting future liabilities). The recent push toward market-consistent valuation methods (e.g. IAS 19, IAS 39, and IFRS4) has mitigated the distortions induced by accounting measures, at the price of introducing substantial short-term volatility in funding ratios and liability portfolios and giving rise to considerable modeling uncertainty when non-tradable risks (such as longevity risk) are considered (e.g. Biffis et al. 2010). The first effect is due to the use of market-implied information that may diverge from long-term fundamental values; the second is due to model risk (a reference model is used to compute market-consistent values) and parameter risk (mark-to-model exercises are affected by uncertainty in parameter estimates). On the one hand, discounting by current yields guarantees an accurate description of the fund's financial situation. On the other, using a constant yield smooths out temporary fluctuations in the present value of the liabilities and gives a longer-term description of a fund's financial condition.

Risk-taking incentives can be classified as arising in the presence of *ex ante* prevention measures (e.g. short-sale and other constraints in asset allocation, Value-at-Risk constraints) and *ex post* punishment (such as curb in compensation, reputational losses, or the costs associated with additional funding from the sponsors). Despite their relevance, these issues are still largely unexplored. We now review some recent contributions offering some interesting insights on the trade-offs at play in this space.

Van Binsbergen and Brandt (2009) study the impact of regulations on the investment decisions of a DB pension plan. In their model, the optimal asset allocation decisions of the investment manager are a function of the plan's funding ratio (defined as the ratio of its assets to liabilities), interest rates, and the equity risk premium. They compare the optimal investment decisions under several policy alternatives to understand better the real effects of financial reporting and risk management rules. They evaluate the influence of *ex ante* (preventive) and *ex post* (punitive) risk constraints on the gains to dynamic, as opposed to myopic, decision-making. They show that, in their model, preventive measures, such as Value-at-Risk constraints, tend to decrease the gains to dynamic investment. In contrast, punitive constraints, such as mandatory additional contributions from the sponsor when the plan becomes underfunded, lead to very large utility gains. They also show that financial reporting rules have real effects on investment behavior. For example, they argue that the current U.S. requirement to discount liabilities at a rolling average of yields, as opposed to at current yields, induces grossly suboptimal investment decisions. The way liabilities are computed can drive an important wedge between the fund manager's long-term objective of maximizing the funding ratio and his short-term objective (and/or requirement) of satisfying risk constraints and avoiding additional financial contributions from the plan sponsor.

Buraschi et al. (2012) study the implications of non-linear managerial incentives and funding contracts for risk-taking and traditional reduced-form tests of performance attribution for hedge funds. The authors solve the structural optimal portfolio choice problem of a hedge fund investor who is subject to (a) performance fee-based incentives, (b) funding options by the prime broker, and (c) equity investors' redemption options, which together create a non-linear payoff structure that affects endogenous hedge funds' risk-taking. The resulting optimal portfolio choice is state-dependent due to the time-varying endogenous incentives perceived by the manager, depending on the distance of the assets under management from the high-water mark. This implies that optimal leverage and reduced-form alphas fluctuate over time. This is important since it implies that traditional performance regressions with constant coefficients are potentially mis-specified. The call option-like performance fee incentive motivates the manager to use more leverage, while put option-like features (together with the concern about the future value of the incentive options) induce the manager to reduce leverage when his fund underperforms below a given threshold. Although this study uses hedge funds in the empirical application, its results have a much broader economic motivation. Separating the effect of risk-taking and skill, based on observed investment performance, is a fundamental problem that affects not only investors in alternative investment funds, but also investors in (and regulators of) levered financial institutions such as investment banks or pension funds which employ incentive contracts.

Ang et al. (2012) note there are significant penalties associated with the failure to meet liabilities which are not captured by the variance of the surplus return in the static surplus return maximization. They also point out that the 2006 Pension Protection Act (PPA) in the U.S. required that plan funding equal 100 percent of the plan's liabilities, so underfunded plans were required to fund their plans according to rules that result in higher employer contributions.[10] The authors list additional downside risks associated with underfunding such as higher insurance premia, holding higher reserves, and the opportunity costs associated with transferring money to the pension plan, as well as the cost to beneficiaries who face higher default risk of their plan. To incorporate these real-world effects into their model, the authors propose a new model that incorporates downside risk penalties for not meeting liabilities. In their model, the shortfall between the asset and liabilities can be valued as an option which swaps the value of the endogenously determined optimal portfolio for the value of the liabilities. The optimal portfolio selection exhibits endogenous risk aversion and as the funding ratio deviates from the fully funded case in the direction of underfunding or overfunding, effective risk aversion decreases. When funding is low, it is optimal for the manager in the model to take on risk, betting on the chance that liabilities can be covered. When the plan is overfunded the manager also takes on more risk, as liabilities are already well matched, and so the manager decides to invest aggressively in risky securities. In contrast to Detemple and Rindisbacher (2008), where shortfall costs have a utility cost for a risk-averse fund sponsor, the shortfall cost is reflected in an actual real-world value through an option calculation in Ang et al. (2012).[11] Amenc et al. (2010) also present an LDI model that incorporates an option, but it is exogenous rather than endogenous in their framework.

Conclusion

This chapter reviewed the key drivers behind the emergence of LDI, illustrating the main principles behind this variant of ALM, as well as some of the most commonly used hedging tools. We also described several emerging de-risking tools such as pension buyouts/ins, longevity swaps, and tail-risk hedges that have gained popularity in light of the rise in cross-asset correlation associated with quantitative easing. Some of the main challenges ahead include changes in pension regulation, centralized clearing of OTC derivatives, and risk-taking incentives in delegated asset management for pension ALM.

Notes

1. Other examples include Boulier et al. (1995), Sundaresan and Zapatero (1997), Cairns (2000), and Van Binsbergen and Brandt (2009).
2. The authors examine a dynamic asset allocation problem of a fund manager with von Neumann–Morgenstern preferences with (a) terminal utility function defined over the excess of liquid wealth over minimum liability coverage tolerated, and (b) intermediate utility function defined over dividends.
3. See, for example, Biffis and Blake (2010b, 2013).
4. A quanto option is a cash-settled option whose payoff is converted into a third currency at maturity at a pre-specied rate, called the quanto factor. In our case, the pension payments toward a homogenous cohort of pensioners are obtained by multiplying the payments due to a representative pensioner by the number of survivors in that cohort. A similar feature exacerbated the problems faced by Equitable Life when dealing with guaranteed annuity options (see Biffis and Millossovich 2006).
5. For details on the collateralization of these instruments and its impact on their valuation, see Biffis et al. (2012a).
6. This section draws on Biffis et al. (2012b).
7. Such an approach is justified by the work of Fleming et al. (1999), Chordia et al. (2005), and Connolly et al. (2005), who find evidence of volatility linkages between stock and bond markets which also drive the correlation between these markets.
8. See Biffis et al. (2012a), and Biffis and Blake (2013), Davis (2014), and Lundbergh et al. (2014) for additional discussion.
9. 'In these arrangements a [pension plan] lends a bank liquid securities such as government bonds—for which the bank pays a small fee—and in return the bank pledges highly rated but less liquid collateral such as mortgage-backed securities—bonds backed by pools of loans—where the markets are still tainted by the "toxic" tag from the financial crisis' (Hughes 2011).
10. Ang et al. (2012) illustrate the penalties associated with underfunding by pointing to the case of AT&T, whose funding status changed from $17 billion surplus in 2007 to a nearly $4 billion deficit in 2008, contributing to the decline of AT&T's stock from 2007 to 2008.
11. They specify the objective function of the fund as mean-variance over the asset returns plus a downside risk penalty on the liability shortfall:

$$\max_{W} E(r_A) - \frac{\gamma}{2}\text{var}(r_A) - \frac{c}{A_0}P(W,L_0,A_0)$$

where c is a penalty cost associated with the downside and $P(w, L_0, A_0)$ is the endogenous value of the option as the fund manager can reduce the value of this option by increasing the correlation of the optimal portfolio with the pension liabilities.

References

Ang, A., B. Chen, and S. Sundaresan (2012). 'Liability-Driven Investment with Downside Risk,' Netspar Discussion Paper DP10/2012-051. Tilburg, The Netherlands: Netspar.

Amenc, N. L., L. Martellini, F. Goltz, and V. Milhau (2010). 'New Frontiers in Benchmarking and Liability-Driven Investing,' EDHEC Business School Risk Institute Research Paper. Paris, France: EDHEC.

Bauer, D., E. Biffis, and L. R. Sotomayor (2013). 'Optimal Collateralization with Bilateral Default Risk,' Imperial College Business School Working Paper. London, U.K.: Imperial College.

Biffis, E. and D. Blake (2010a). 'Securitizing and Tranching Longevity Exposures,' *Insurance: Mathematics and Economics*, 46(1): 186–197.

Biffis, E. and D. Blake (2010b). 'Mortality-linked Securities and Derivatives,' in M. Bertocchi, S. Schwartz, and W. Ziemba, eds., *Optimizing the Aging, Retirement and Pensions Dilemma*. Hoboken, NJ: John Wiley & Sons, pp. 275–298.

Biffis, E. and D. Blake (2013). 'Informed Intermediation of Longevity Exposures,' *The Journal of Risk and Insurance*, 80(3): 559–584.

Biffis, E., D. Blake, L. Pitotti, and A. Sun (2012a). 'The Cost of Counterparty Risk and Collateralization in Longevity Swaps,' Pensions Institute Working Paper PI-1107. London, U.K.: Pensions Institute.

Biffis, E., M. Denuit, and P. Devolder (2010). 'Stochastic Mortality Under Measure Changes,' *Scandinavian Actuarial Journal*, 2010(4): 284–311.

Biffis, E., F. Jivraj, and R. Kosowski (2012b). 'Pension Funds and Stock-bond Correlation Risk: The Case for a Correlation Swap,' Imperial College Business School Working Paper. London, U.K.: Imperial College.

Biffis, E. and P. Millossovich (2006). 'The Fair Value of Guaranteed Annuity Options,' *Scandinavian Actuarial Journal*, 2006(1): 23–41.

BIS-IOSCO (2013). *Second Consultative Document on Margin Requirements for Non-centrally Cleared Derivatives*. Bank for International Settlements and International Organization of Securities Commissions. Basel, Switzerland: BIS-IOSCO.

Boulier, J.-F., E. Trussant, and D. Florens (1995). 'A Dynamic Model for Pension Funds Management,' in *Proceedings of the 5th AFIR International Colloquium*, 1: 361–384.

Britten-Jones, M. and A. Neuberger (2000). 'Option Prices, Implied Price Processes, and Stochastic Volatility,' *The Journal of Finance*, 55(2): 839–866.

Buraschi, A., R. Kosowski, and W. Sritrakul (2012). 'Incentives and Endogenous Risk Taking: A Structural View on Hedge Fund Alphas,' Working Paper presented at the Chicago AFA Meetings 2012.

Cairns, A. (2000). 'Some Notes on the Dynamics and Optimal Control of Stochastic Pension Fund Models in Continuous Time,' *ASTIN Bulletin*, 30(1): 19–55.

Chordia, T., A. Sarkar, and A. Subrahmanyam (2005). 'An Empirical Analysis of Stock and Bond Market Liquidity,' *The Review of Financial Studies*, 18(1): 85–129.

Cohen, N. (2009). 'Final Salary Pension Threat,' *Financial Times,* June 5.

Connolly, R., C. Stivers, and L. Sun (2005). 'Stock Market Uncertainty and the Stock-bond Return Relation,' *Journal of Financial and Quantitative Analysis*, 40(1): 161–194.

Coughlan, G. (2014). 'Longevity Risk Management, Corporate Finance, and Sustainable Pensions,' in P. B. Hammond, R. Maurer, and O. S. Mitchell, eds., *Recreating Sustainable Retirement: Resilience, Solvency, and Tail Risk*. Oxford, U.K.: Oxford University Press, pp. 89–112.

Davis, E. P. (2014). 'Evolving Roles for Pension Regulations: Toward Better Risk Control?' in P. B. Hammond, R. Maurer, and O. S. Mitchell, eds., *Recreating Sustainable Retirement: Resilience, Solvency, and Tail Risk*. Oxford, U.K.: Oxford University Press, pp. 163–185.

Detemple, J. and M. Rindisbacher (2008). 'Dynamic Asset Liability Management with Tolerance for Limited Shortfalls,' *Insurance: Mathematics and Economics*, 43(3): 281–294.

Ezra, D. (1991). 'Asset Allocation by Surplus Optimization,' *Financial Analysts Journal*, 47(1): 51–57.

Fleming, M. J. and E. M. Remolona (1999). 'Price Formation and Liquidity in the U.S. Treasury Market: The Response to Public Information,' *Journal of Finance*, 54(5): 1901–1915.

Fonseca, J. D., M. Grasselli, and C. Tebaldi (2007). 'Option Pricing when Correlations are Stochastic: An Analytical Framework,' *Review of Derivatives Research*, 10(2): 151–180.

Gulko, L. (2002). 'Decoupling,' *The Journal of Portfolio Management*, 28(3): 59–66.

Heller, D. and N. Vause (2012). 'Collateral Requirements for Mandatory Central Clearing of Over-the-counter Derivatives,' Bank for International Settlements (BIS) Working Paper No. 373. Basel, Switzerland: BIS.

Hughes, J. (2011). 'Concern Mounts over Rise of Collateral Swaps,' *Financial Times,* June 30.

International Monetary Fund (IMF) (2012). 'The Financial Impact of Longevity Risk,' in *Global Financial Stability Report 2012*. Washington, DC: IMF, pp. 123–153.

International Swaps and Derivatives Association (ISDA) (1996). *Guidelines for Collateral Practitioners*. New York, NY: ISDA.

International Swaps and Derivatives Association (ISDA) (2009). *Big Bang Protocol*. New York, NY: ISDA.

International Swaps and Derivatives Association (2010a). *Market Review of OTC Derivative Bilateral Collateralization Practices*. New York, NY: ISDA.

International Swaps and Derivatives Association (2010b). *2010 Margin Survey*. New York, NY: ISDA.

J.P. Morgan (2006). *J.P. Morgan Liability-Driven Investment (LDI) Survey*. London: J.P. Morgan Asset Management.

J.P. Morgan (2011). 'Rise of Cross-asset Correlations,' *Global Equity Derivatives & Delta One Strategy*, May 16. New York, NY: J.P. Morgan.

Kessler, A. R. (2014). 'Risk Budgeting and Longevity Insurance: Strategies for Sustainable Defined Benefit Pension Funds,' in P. B. Hammond, R. Maurer, and O. S. Mitchell, eds., *Recreating Sustainable Retirement: Resilience, Solvency, and Tail Risk*. Oxford, U.K.: Oxford University Press, pp. 247–272.

Leibowitz, M. L., S. Kogelman, and L. N. Bader (1992). 'Asset Performance and Surplus Control: A Dual-shortfall Approach,' *Journal of Portfolio Management*, 18(2): 28–37.

Lane, Clark & Peacock LLP (LCP) (2012). 'Pension Buy-ins, Buy-outs and Longevity Swaps 2012,' LCP Publication, 5 April.

Lundbergh, S., R. Cardano, R. Laros, and L. Rebel (2014). 'Developments in European Pension Regulation: Risks and Challenges,' in P. B. Hammond, R. Maurer, and O. S. Mitchell, eds., *Recreating Sustainable Retirement: Resilience, Solvency, and Tail Risk*. Oxford, U.K.: Oxford University Press, pp. 186–214.

Merton, R. C. (1973). 'Theory of Rational Option Pricing,' *Bell Journal of Economics and Management Science*, 4(1): 141–183.

Nijman, T., and L. A. P. Swinkels (2008). 'Strategic and Tactical Allocation to Commodities for Retirement Savings Schemes,' in F. J. Fabozzi, R. Fuss, and D. G. Kaiser, eds., *The Handbook of Commodity Investing*. Hoboken, NJ: John Wiley & Sons, Inc., pp. 522–546.

Rauh, J. D. (2009). 'Risk Shifting versus Risk Management: Investment Policy in Corporate Pension Plans,' *Review of Financial Studies*, 22(7): 2687–2733.

Rudolf, M., and W. T. Ziemba (2004). 'Intertemporal Asset-Liability Management,' *Journal of Economic Dynamics and Control*, 28(4): 975–990.

SEI (2012). *6th Annual Global Liability-Driven Investment Poll*. Oaks, PA: SEI.

Sharpe, W. F., and L. G. Tint (1990). 'Liabilities: A New Approach,' *Journal of Portfolio Management*, 16(2): 5–10.

Sidanius, C., and F. Zikes (2012). 'OTC Derivatives Reform and Collateral Demand Impact,' Financial Stability Paper No. 18. London, U.K.: Bank of England.

Singh, M., and J. Aitken (2009). 'Counterparty Risk, Impact on Collateral Flows, and Role for Central Counterparties,' International Monetary Fund (IMF) Working Paper 09/173. Washington, DC: IMF.

Sundaresan, S., and F. Zapatero (1997). 'Valuation, Optimal Asset Allocation and Retirement Incentives of Pension Plans,' *Review of Financial Studies*, 10(3): 631–660.

van Binsbergen, J. H., and M. W. Brandt (2009). 'Optimal Asset Allocation in Asset Liability Management,' National Bureau of Economic Research (NBER) Working Paper No. 12970. Cambridge, MA: NBER.

Viceira, L. (2012). 'Bond Risk, Bond Return Volatility, and the Term Structure of Interest Rates,' *International Journal of Forecasting*, 28(1): 97–117.

Chapter 3

Implications for Long-term Investors of the Shifting Distribution of Capital Market Returns

James Moore and Niels Pedersen

> *It's tough to make predictions, especially about the future.*
>
> (attributed to Yogi Berra)

Despite the caution from Hall of Fame baseball player *cum* philosopher Mr. Berra, few people have stopped trying to predict the future. And nowhere is prediction more common than in the financial markets. One cannot watch financial television for more than an hour without a guest being asked where he believes the level of the S&P 500, an individual stock, the price of gold, or the ten-year Treasury yield will be at year-end. Given the vagaries of the market, short-term forecasting, particularly for high volatility assets, is little more than a toss of the dice. The media soon forget the many whose predictions are off the mark. The few whose prognostications end up close to the mark are ascribed sage-like properties and develop cults of followers. While short-run forecasting has value for financial entertainment and speculation, in the United States and much of the developed world, there is perhaps no field where long-run forecasting has wider implications for personal welfare than that of forecasting asset returns.

The expected returns of stocks, bonds, and other investments play a critical role in retirement planning, budgeting, and determining future savings adequacy. Of course, practitioners in the space—plan sponsors, investment advisors, consultants, asset managers, and others versed in statistics—know that future returns are random variables. Actual returns through time are drawn from a distribution of possibilities. Given this fact, outcomes that are functions of the realized returns are themselves distributions of random variables. The specific form of the ultimate distribution in question relies on (a) the stochastic processes governing the returns themselves, (b) the functional form that these returns are 'filtered' through, and possibly (c) convolutions of multiple functional forms. Even when the underlying stochastic processes are known with certainty and the generating distributions are well behaved, the transforming nature of the real-world functions overlaid can lead to significant alterations of the resultant distributions. In some cases this may compress distributions; in others it may lead to tails that are exaggerated.

Yet it is important to remember that *we do not know the true statistical generating process of asset returns*. The vast majority of work done by practitioners relies on the lessons learned in undergraduate statistics courses. The insights absorbed there rely heavily on the Law of Large Numbers and asymptotic convergence to normality. These in turn rely on the stronger assumptions of stationarity and ergodicity. What if these do not hold?

To explore this question, this chapter looks at the implications of long horizon asset returns that flow from three different generating processes for stock and bond returns.[1] The first, a multivariate normal distribution, is widely used due to its familiarity and analytic tractability and has been used for Monte Carlo statistical analyses since the Second World War. The second, a block bootstrap approach, has become more common in the past few decades with increases in computing power and questions as to the appropriateness of normality given limited historical data. The third approach uses a nested structural model that links asset returns to macroeconomic fluctuations in the real economy. The core of this model relies on a non-stationary, Markov-switching evolution of real GDP as first modeled by Hamilton (1994).

Each of these approaches has different pros and cons. The first approach is easy to implement. The second makes heavy use of actual historical precedence and can capture short-intermediate-horizon autocorrelation and cross-correlation structures. The third allows for the strongest linkage between economic theory and simulation results, dynamic correlation behavior, and differential, conditional sub-period dynamics. But this comes with additional complexity in model design and calibration difficulty. In what follows we explore the differences in model outcomes focusing on the behavior of distribution tails and the implications for potentially differing intra-path dynamics. This may have great importance for pensions. For defined benefit (DB) plans, this can meaningfully impact the magnitude and timing of required contributions. For defined contribution (DC) plans, it can have meaningful welfare implications—especially if there are behavioral responses to participant asset allocations around extreme performance periods.

Preliminaries

Before we elaborate on model differences, it is worth spending some time looking at the nature of uncertainty about the first moments of our return distributions. In Figure 3.1, we see three different averages of historic real equity returns—rolling ten- and 30-year geometric average returns, as well as the full sample geometric average.[2] Both rolling averages display quite a bit of variation. The ten-year numbers range from a low of −4.3 percent to a high of 17.9 percent. The 30-year numbers range from 3.1 percent to 9.9 percent and have deviated above or below the full sample average of 6.5 percent for periods as long as 19 years.[3]

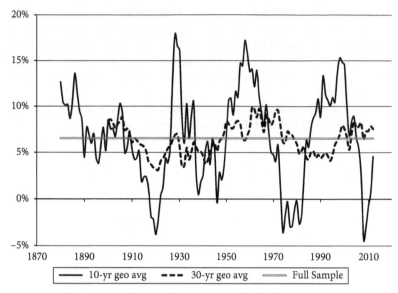

Figure 3.1. Averages of S&P Composite real returns, 1871–2012.

Note: 1871–2010 data from Shiller (2013); 2010+ from Bloomberg (2013).

Source: Authors' illustration.

Standard theory would instruct us to 'use all the data.' Yet while this may work for a return series as long-lived and as widely followed as the S&P 500, note that even here, the standard error of the estimate is 1.55 percent. If the meandering of the rolling averages gives us reason to question stationarity, the standard error could be still wider than that. For other return series—foreign markets or new asset classes—30 years of reliable data may be difficult to obtain. Dimson et al. (2002) contains a nice discussion of additional problems due to censoring, survivorship bias, market discontinuities, and other factors that plague offshore equity markets, even for developed economies.

The economic impact of such volatility on savers can be tremendous. Taking the extremes of our 30-year rolling averages for illustration, imagine a 35-year-old putting a dollar of her 401(k) in the S&P for a planned age-65 retirement. If she assumes her dollar saved will grow at a conservative 3.1 percent *per annum*, it will be worth 2.5 times as much in real dollars. At a more robust 9.9 percent, that dollar would grow to $17.

It should be noted that a 30-year horizon is frequently cited in corporate and public sector DB plans to justify future expected return assumptions that would imply implausibly large forward-looking equity return spreads over available risk-free debt of long maturities.[4] Despite the market crashes of 2000–2002 and 2008–2009, the most recent 30-year real equity returns exceeded the very long-term average by 2.0 percent *per annum*. This is due to the power of the bull run of the 1980s and 1990s. The 30-year horizon also conveniently leaves out the poor returns in the 1970s. A similar story holds for bonds.

The focus on equity alone raises to some degree the question about expected bond returns and the interplay between expected equity returns and bond returns. A serious analysis of returns should not explore the return dynamics of stocks in isolation. It should also analyze other investment choices and account for relevant conditioning variables. Bonds play a role in both cases. The body of literature on expected returns is large and growing (see Ilmanen 2011). A key implication of the literature is that expected returns vary over time. Factors such as interest rates, the spread between high yield and investment-grade debt, aggregate dividend yields and earnings yields, and book-to-market ratios, for instance, all have some predictive power in forecasting stock returns. More recently, longer-term factors such as demographic variables have been shown by Arnott and Chavez (2012), among others, to have some explanatory value.

In addition to uncertainty as to the *ex ante* mean, there is some uncertainty regarding the long-run generating process and how uncertainty compounds over time. There appears to be different behavior in the short run and the long run. Lo and MacKinlay (1988) used variance ratios to demonstrate that returns show positive serial correlation (momentum) over short horizons. Moreover, Poterba and Summers (1988), Campbell and Viciera (2005), and others have demonstrated that in long horizons there appears to be some evidence of mean reversion.

But even with conditioning variables, the specification of the *ex ante* mean expected return is an imprecise exercise. If that is the case, how much faith can we have in characterization of higher moments or distribution tails? In what follows, we first discuss the slow nature of convergence of financial variables to a true mean, even if one assumes stationarity. Next we lay out our three different simulation approaches. A macroeconomic regime-switching model is introduced as a mechanism to be able to capture both shorter-term and longer-term behavior of financial markets. We then describe the two real-world filtrations of interest: (a) a long-term glide path for a defined contribution plan, and (b) the funding and contribution impact over a more moderately long horizon for a corporate DB plan. After a summary of the results, we compare the dynamics for the three model approaches.

Slow Convergence to a True Mean

Uncertainty about the true mean or expected return is quantitatively large, even if we assume that the annual stock return can be viewed as a realization from a stationary distribution. The solid dark lines in Figure 3.2 show the 95 percent confidence interval for the expected excess stock return based on a 16 percent annual volatility and a sample average of 7 percent. The figure reminds us of the

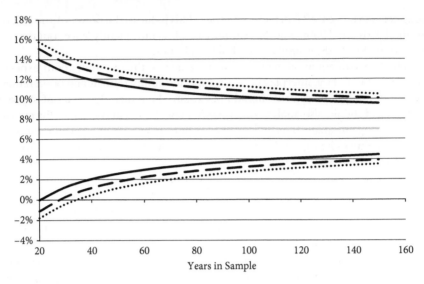

Figure 3.2. Slow convergence to true mean.

Note: 1871–2010 data from Shiller (2013); 2010+ from Bloomberg (2013).

Source: Authors' illustration.

unnerving statistical uncertainties associated with some of the key parameters that most simulation techniques take as given.

Of course, if the true process is not stationary, convergence can be even slower still. Figure 3.2 also shows the convergence in estimation for another process with true mean of 7 percent and volatility of 16 percent. In this case, the generating process is a Markov-switching mixture of normal distributions where the two sub-sample means are set at a level ±3.5 percent around our true mean (i.e. 3.5 percent and 10.5 percent). The parameters are chosen to correspond approximately to the widest deviations of the 30-year rolling averages from the full sample mean in the Shiller dataset (2013) shown previously.

A total of 10,000 150-year paths were run with starting draws equally split between the high and low conditional mean return states. State transitions occurred according to a two-state Markov chain set with $p = q$ so that each state is equally probable over the course of the simulation and the distribution of returns is symmetric.[5] Values of p and q are set at 0.90 (dashed line) and 0.95 (dotted line) corresponding to average durations of the conditional states of ten and 20 years. Bootstrap standard errors are calculated from the 10,000 simulation trails to construct confidence intervals.

We see that this generates consistently wider confidence intervals. At the 30-year sample point, the ten-year average regime duration process would yield a confidence interval with a 1.93 percent wider spread (3.32 percent for the 20-year average duration process). Convergence is also slower: comparing the ratio of the confidence intervals as the sample increases, at 30 years, the 20-year, slow switch process is 29 percent wider than our baseline case; at 150 years it is 36 percent wider.

Three Different Return-generating Models and Their Results

We compare three different return-generating models—a multivariate normal distribution model, a block bootstrap model which resamples from past historical data, and a third structural model that is designed and calibrated to capture a number of economic features. The more involved macroeconomic long horizon simulation model is described in some detail below, with a more detailed technical appendix at the end of the chapter. The other two models, multivariate normal and block bootstrap, are commonly used by both academics and practitioners and are presented later as counterparts for comparison and evaluation of the more expansive macroeconomic approach. Limitations of both of these models provided the impetus for the development of this modeling approach.

Macroeconomic Long Horizon Simulation (LHS) Model

The premise of the macro-driven long horizon simulation model is that the dynamic processes for macroeconomic growth, inflation, and risk aversion jointly determine both the short-term dynamics as well as the variations in discount factors applied to these cash flows in financial markets to form asset prices and valuations for both risk-free and risky investments. When we impose restrictions and assumptions on the dynamics of these fundamental variables that are based on theory and academic research, we indirectly imply a set of 'structural' restrictions for the long-term valuations of asset prices, such as bond prices and equity prices, which restrict the plausible range of average investment returns and volatility over a given investment horizon. Cochrane (2011) contains a discussion of some these issues.

The secular dynamics of productivity growth or 'potential' GDP growth, inflation rates, and equilibrium risk premiums shape the distributions of real interest rates and nominal interest rates and equity yields (dividends and earnings yields) over a long-term investment horizon. Similarly, the business cycle dynamics of unemployment, output gap, and central bank policy, as well as the accompanying temporary bouts of extreme uncertainty and risk aversion in financial markets, shape the distribution of asset returns and yield curves in the short term.

A structural macroeconomic regime-switching (LHS) model combines these guiding principles and ideas within a unified structural framework designed to

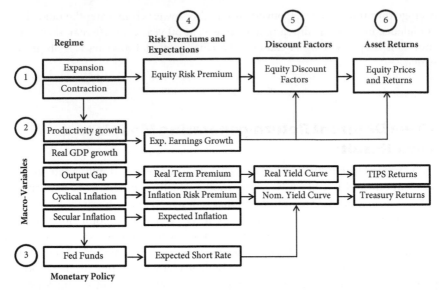

Figure 3.3. Schematic of structural LHS process.

Source: Authors' illustration.

remain highly empirically and quantitatively relevant. Figure 3.3 summarizes the structure of the model at a high level.

This LHS model explicitly incorporates the main dynamic linkages between economic growth and inflation, monetary policy, risk aversion, and realized asset returns. In this way it provides a suitable framework for assessment of both long-term and short-term distributions of asset returns and yields curves. The framework allows us to quantify both the short-term and long-term tail risks that strategic long-term investors face based on inputs for the main drivers of returns (long-term growth, long-term inflation, and equity risk premium) and allows us to explore the impact of parameter uncertainty.

A key feature of the model is the regime-switching component, which generates realistic business cycle dynamics in the model (see Hamilton 1989). The regime-switching dynamics directly translate into realistic cyclical fluctuations in inflation, GDP growth, and risk premiums. They also enable the model to more closely match the higher frequency moments of asset returns distributions, as well as the general correlations with macro variables over the business cycle. More specifically, such regime-switching models can produce the type of rapid changes in risk premiums required to generate the 'boom–bust' characteristics of asset returns experienced historically. The regime-switching behavior ultimately also generates a strong tendency for mean reversion in average returns, and it reduces volatility of those returns over long-term investment horizons. A more detailed description of each component of the model is provided next.

Macro Regimes

The business cycle dynamics are determined by a regime-switching model that places the macro economy in either a 'contraction' or an 'expansion,' similar to the specification first introduced by Hamilton (1989). One extension is that the transitions between these two regimes are governed by time-varying probabilities modeled with duration-dependent hazard functions. The duration dependence is such that the hazard rate increases exponentially with the time the economy has been in a specific regime. The probability that a specific recession or expansion comes to an end consequently increases with the duration of the current stage of the business cycle. The parameters of the hazard function for contractions and expansion are calibrated to match the characteristics of National Bureau of Economic Research (NBER) business cycle durations, both in terms of their average length and their standard deviation. Since contractions tend to be shorter-lived than expansions, the transition probabilities are inherently asymmetric.

Real Activity, Growth, and Output Gaps

The business cycle dynamics of real GDP growth are derived from the specification of a dynamic process for the output gap. In a recession, the output gap converges to a negative level, whereas it converges to a positive level in an expansion. The specification that is used within regimes ensures that real GDP growth rate is generally most negative at the beginning of a recession and most positive at the beginning of an expansion. Overall the parameters are calibrated to match the distribution of real GDP growth and the distribution of output gap realizations within both expansions and contractions. The long-term potential GDP growth is set to an exogenous rate in the model, which can reflect forward-looking views on productivity growth or simply the historical growth rate of about 2 percent per year. In principle the long-run growth rate can have its own dynamics.

Inflation

Inflation in the model has both a cyclical business cycle-driven component and a persistent, long-term component. The business cycle component of inflation is assumed to be driven by cyclical fluctuations in aggregate demand and, as such, it is based on the simulated level of the output gap. A positive output gap is associated with high cyclical levels of inflation, whereas a large negative output gap will reduce the inflation rate to a level below the long-term 'structural' inflation rate that is prevailing at a given point in time. This feature of the model resembles the well-known 'Phillips' curve from theoretical economic models. The long-run level of realized inflation, and hence also the long-run level of inflation expectations, is determined by shocks to a stationary but highly persistent process for non-business cycle-related inflation fluctuations. Shocks to this process have a very significant impact on the expected inflation rates many years into the future, which are important in shaping the long-term distribution of nominal yields.

Monetary Policy

The central bank is assumed to respond to the cyclical components of inflation and real activity. The response function is calibrated with a Taylor rule that implies positive real rate responses to both the cyclical component of inflation and the output gap. Both effects will tend to push the Federal Reserve to reduce short-term real rates in recessions (absent any short-term supply shocks to inflation) and increase the short-term real rate in expansions. The current unusual monetary policy stance, however, warrants an explicit adjustment to this general description of monetary policy. The impact of quantitative easing (QE) is therefore explicitly modeled. Specifically, for the two years until the end of 2014, our model assigns only a small probability that the Fed exits its current stance (with a fixed fed funds rate at 25 basis points) and raises the fed funds rate toward the level implied by the Taylor rule. After that, it is assumed that the probability of exiting the regime increases over time.

Yield Curve and Bond Returns

The nominal yield curve is derived as the expected future short rate plus an inflation risk term premium and a real rate risk term premium. The 'expectations component' of the yield curve is implicitly derived from the expected dynamics of the output gap and inflation because they 'pass through' the Taylor rule to the expected future fed funds rate. As a consequence, the expectations component of the yield curve responds to the current state of the business cycle and becomes logically consistent with the specified dynamics for monetary policy, inflation, and real activity. The business cycle dynamics of short maturity yields are dominated by business cycle-driven fluctuations in expectations about monetary policy, which creates interesting and very realistic endogenous dynamics in the yield curve simulations. For instance, at the beginning of an expansion the market will price additional rate increases resulting in a steepening yield curve, whereas at the beginning of a recession the market will anticipate further easing of monetary policy over the course of the recession and yield curves will potentially be inverted for some time as the economy enters a contraction. Overall, the yield curve will be 'steepest' in the middle of or at the end of a recession, whereas the curve will be 'flattest' in the middle of an expansion. The current shape of the yield curve is consistent with our modeling of QE.

The cyclical dynamics of long maturity yields in the model are, on the other hand, mostly driven by fluctuations in inflation and real rate risk premiums, since long-term expectations for real rates and inflation (and hence expectations for

distant future policy rates) are fairly stable across the business cycle. This is consistent with empirical evidence suggesting that survey-based measures of long-term
expectations and real activity are quite constant over time and simply do not fluctuate enough to generate the observed volatility in long-term real and nominal yields
at annual frequencies.

While risk premiums fluctuate in the short run and drive dynamics in the short
run for long maturity yields, they remain fairly constant and are 'bounded' in the
long run. The main driver of any significant dispersion in the simulated long-run
dispersion of nominal yields is therefore gradual accumulation of small but persistent shocks to inflation. Generally speaking, significant changes in long-term
interest rate changes must be accompanied by persistent changes in the level of
inflation.

Finally, we note that, on average, long maturity bonds have higher expected
returns due to the maturity-dependent term premium that is specified in the model.
As a result of this risk premium, the average yield curve tends to be upward sloping at maturities out to about 20–25 years. After that convexity, effects in the yield
curve flattens the curve and cause even longer-term yields to decline gradually with
maturity.

Equity Returns

Equity prices are based on expected dividends discounted with the term structure of risk-free yields as well as the equity risk premium. The equity return
is composed of dividend yields plus capital appreciation (re-pricing of equities). Earnings growth is based on future GDP growth and mean reversion in
corporate profit margins. We assume a constant payout ratio for dividends.
Consequently, short-term earnings growth expectations will rationally fall when
the probability of entering a recession increases in the model, but long-term
earnings growth and dividend growth expectations do not fluctuate a lot over
time. The dominant component of equity returns and return volatility is the
're-pricing' component of returns and the associated changes in the price to
'stabilized' earnings ratio. The dynamics of the P/E ratio are inherently linked
to the behavior of both long-term real rates and, especially, the dynamics of the
equity risk premium. The re-pricing return in a given period is approximately
equal to the change in the equity discount factor times the equity price duration with respect to yield and equity risk premium changes. The equity price
duration can be inferred from the discounted cash flow model but will be about
20–30 years depending on current valuations. In the recessionary regime, equity
risk premiums will tend to widen (capital loss) with higher volatility, but will
narrow (capital gain) in an expansion. Similarly, the volatility of risk aversion
levels and hence equity premiums are assumed to be higher in recessions than
expansions.

To summarize, most of the annual volatility in equity returns is due to the fluctuations in the discount rate and hence fluctuations of the equity risk premium and long-term interest rates. The volatility is not due to shocks to expected future cash flows. These features are consistent with the extensive body of academic research associated with Robert Shiller.

Comparison to Alternative Simulation Approaches

To highlight some of the major advantages of the macro-based approach to long-run simulations we compare our simulation results with two simpler and more commonly used approaches to simulation of both the yield curve and the equity market returns. These approaches do not incorporate the same inter-temporal structural relationships between equity returns and bond returns and macro variables that the macro model 'enforces.'

One model which we can compare results with is a normal approximation to the LHS model dynamics, where we match the average annual return, volatility, and correlations of two-, five-, ten-, and 30-year maturity points on the yield curves, as well as equity returns. A second model is a 'bootstrap' model, similar in that we match the average return and volatility to the structural model, but this instead samples historical quarterly data to also match the higher moments of the empirical distribution that a normal approximation may be missing. The bootstrap generally produces fatter tails in equity returns, since they are non-normal on an annual basis. But for long-term investment horizons, the difference between the bootstrap and normal approximation is small.

The structure of the LHS model serves to limit the plausible range of outcomes over longer periods of time. It induces mean reversion in excess bond and equity returns over time, which means that the long-run volatility of real returns decreases with the investment horizon. For instance, following an increase in the equity risk premium, investors are 'hit' by an immediate capital loss, but they face higher returning investment opportunities afterwards. Similarly, a shock to interest rates causes negative bond returns in the short run, but investors then face an environment with higher yields subsequently. Figure 3.4 shows how the term structure of volatility is downward-sloping in our model, whereas it is flat in both the normal model and the bootstrap model.

The downward-sloping term structure of volatility that the macro-based model generates means that there are very large differences between the long-term predictions of the macro-based structural model and the two 'naïve' memoryless simulations of returns. Over time the cumulative volatility of returns explodes in both of the non-structural, reduced-form approaches. This gives rise to exaggerated tail behaviors in these two simulation approaches. This can be seen in Figure 3.5,

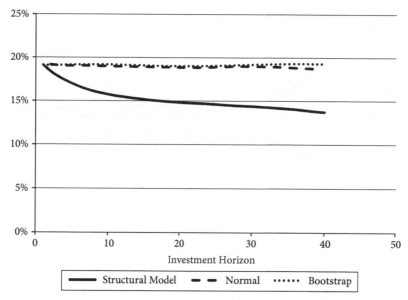

Figure 3.4. Volatility term structure: equity returns.

Source: Authors' illustration.

which shows the distribution of equity and bond returns from the three different models.

For example, both the normal and bootstrap processes give roughly 5 percent likelihoods of negative annualized equity returns over a 20-year horizon. It is difficult to imagine such persistence in an economy without a fundamental structural shift in markets, given the implied long-term real capital decimation. Similarly, the 95th percentile of 20-year annualized compounded equity returns is nearly 14 percent for both simple models. Here either growth or inflation would have to be materially higher for a sustained economic period than we have witnessed, or price–earnings ratios would eclipse historic levels. Similarly implausible relationships would have to hold to generate bond return behavior as seen at the outer percentiles.

Importantly, the specific paths that generate the tail events in pure 'engineering' models, such as the independent and identically distributed (i.i.d.) normal distribution model, of asset price returns cannot be linked to a specific economic environment or assumption. It is not possible to assess whether the 'tail' outcomes are reasonable from an economic standpoint as the fundamental economic parameters that shape the distribution of returns are hidden from the visible eye. In the macro model, it is much easier to pinpoint the economic assumptions that have to be made to generate a given tail scenario, and hence to assess whether it is 'plausible' or not.

Panel A. Annualized horizon equity returns.

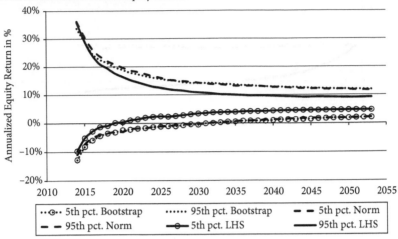

Panel B. Annualized horizon bond returns.

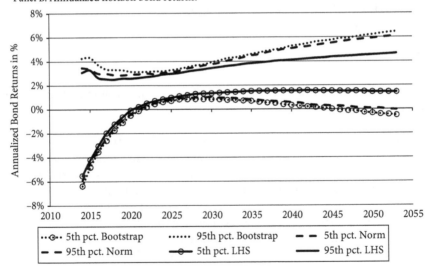

Figure 3.5. Models' distributions of equity and bond returns.

Note: Panel A: Annualized horizon equity returns; Panel B: Annualized horizon bond returns; Panel C: Horizon annualized 60/40 returns.

Source: Authors' illustration.

Panel C. Horizon annualized 60/40 returns.

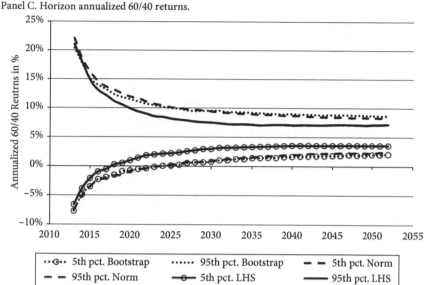

Figure 3.5. (*Continued*)

Implications for Projections of DC and DB Plans

To get a sense of the impact of the three different return-generating processes in real-world settings, we construct two examples: one for a DC plan and another for a DB plan. The returns and yield curves generated by our models can then be used to assess the impact on key decision variables used by plan sponsors. While the annualized distributions of return dynamics are informative, without the overlay of the pension-specific models, key inferences may be missed. In addition, the long-term nature of the pension saving/funding dynamic introduces a series of other effects due to the changing dynamics of contributions. In the case of the DC plan, the representative saver is increasing contributions though time as she ages and presumably has a higher income from which to save. For the DB plan, there is an endogenous, path-dependent relationship between contributions, asset returns, and changes in the discount rate that can be highly non-linear through time.

For our DC case, we look at the cumulative savings dynamics of our return process over a 40-year glide path.[6] With the passage of the Pension Protection Act (PPA) in 2006 and its codification of target date funds as Qualified Default Investment Alternatives (QDIAs), there has been explosive growth in these target date funds. According to Morningstar (Furman 2013),[7] total target date fund assets reached $475 billion by November 2012—a four-fold increase since the passage of the PPA. In practice each fund family has its own glide path, and most have individual nuances. Yet as a rule, the glide paths are invariably designed so that financial market risk in portfolios is decreasing in time-to-retirement. This is akin to the financial planning heuristic that one saving for retirement should hold (100 − age) in equities or other similarly risky assets. The essential motivation here is that as the DC plan participant is moving through his career toward retirement, he is replacing the present value of future human capital with financial assets. In the early years, with many years to retirement, the reservoir of this store of human capital is large relative to financial assets and provides a buffer against market shocks. As the individual approaches retirement, the relative size of the combined portfolio = PV(Human Capital) + Financial Savings, tilts toward an increasing fraction on the financial assets side. To maintain a relatively balanced risk position, the mix in the financial portfolio (here the target date fund) decreases in risk as one moves closer to retirement.

In practice, target date portfolios may have many different asset classes and gradations within each asset class. MarketGlide calculates indices of weighted-average glide paths from 37 fund families (see Abidi and Quayle 2010). For our purposes we use a simplified version of the glide path that maps assets into cash, fixed income, and equities. This provides a relatively accurate representation of key risks as the indices are dominated by U.S. aggregate fixed income and U.S. large cap equities. As a general rule, asset classes with distinct dynamics, principally commodities and real estate, comprise less than 2 percent each at any point along the industry average glide path. The glide path used is shown in Figure 3.6.

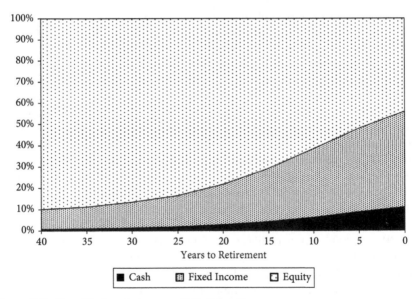

Figure 3.6. Simplified market average DC glidepath.

Source: Authors' illustration.

Our hypothetical participant starts his participation in our DC plan with a salary of $30,000 per year, which grows at a rate of 1 percent per year in excess of inflation.[8] He contributes 6 percent of pay and has a match of 4 percent from his employer. Moreover, he is assumed to invest solely in the target date fund corresponding to the 40-year glide path.

The variables of interest are the plan account balances at various points along his progression to retirement. Note that for each individual simulation, there will be some path-dependency as the values grow by the contributions as well as asset returns and the asset allocation is changing through time, so timing and order of specific return draws can be very important. Table 3.1 shows the characteristics of two hypothetical DB plans that we examine.

We assume both plans are currently 80 percent funded, approximately equal to the funding level (81.7 percent) estimated for the Milliman Pension Funding Index as of January 31, 2013 (Milliman 2013). The funding rules for contributions are those as set out in the PPA.[9] Unfunded amounts are subject to a seven-year amortization basis. Each year the amount of underfunding is compared to the rolled-forward amortization bases. If the new underfunding exceeds the value of the unamortized prior-year bases, a new basis is created with a seven-year amortization. Once a plan is fully funded, all existing bases are erased. The required contributions are the sum of the amortization charges from these bases and the plan's normal (service) cost.[10] For simplicity, we handled the plan's current underfunding by assuming that equal amortization charges were established in the current and each of the three prior years. Funding levels are a function of both the plan's assets and liabilities. In reality, plan sponsors have some latitude in the yield curve used to determine liabilities—this is currently even more the case given the rules promulgated by MAP-21 in 2012. For our purposes we use an approach closer to the mark-to-market liability valuation as set forth by the FASB for accounting purposes and use a point-in-time yield curve rather than one that is a moving average through time.

Assets are rolled forward assuming asset returns per a 60/40 mix of stocks and bonds rebalanced quarterly, less current year benefit payments. Liabilities are revalued each year given changes in the discounting yield curve. We examine two

TABLE 3.1 Characteristics of DB plans

	Frozen plan	Accruing plan
PV (liabilities)	$1.25 billion	$1.25 billion
0–10 years	42%	32%
10–20 years	35%	36%
20–30 years	16%	20%
30+ years	7%	12%
Duration of liabilities	13.8 years	16.5 years
Normal cost (%) of liabilities	–	5%

Source: Authors' tabulations.

cases: a frozen plan and an open accruing plan. For the frozen plan, benefits are paid and the $t+1$ set of cash flows becomes the current year's benefit payments (we assume that the actuaries have perfect foresight into plan demographics). For the accruing plan, we make the simplifying assumption that normal cost is applied *pro rata* in future years. This yields a stationary distribution of liabilities which, as a first order approximation, only shifts duration in response to changes in the yield curve.

The principal variable of interest is the value of required plan contributions. For the DB case, we expect scenario results to be highly path-dependent. Unlike the DC case where we had a time-varying asset allocation, here the path-dependency is a result of the interplay between assets and liabilities (stocks and the yield curve) and the contribution rules. Strong equity markets and/or large increases in the discount rate can abruptly halt required contributions, and they may stay at zero for some time. Poor equity markets/flat-to-declining rates, combined with benefit outflows, can cause required contributions to increase and stay persistently high.

Results for DC Simulations

Results for our 40-year DC glide path are presented in Figure 3.7 and Table 3.2. Over time, we see a pattern emerging. The spread of the block bootstrap

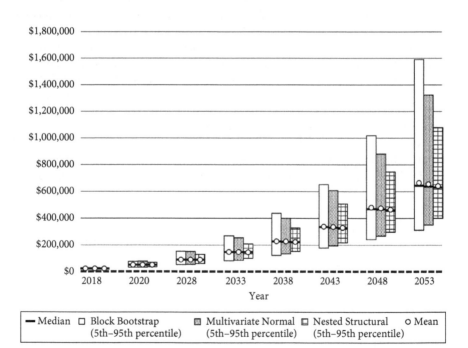

Figure 3.7. Total savings in DC plan.

Source: Authors' illustrations.

TABLE 3.2 Total savings in DC plan

Structural ($)	2018	2023	2028	2033	2038	2043	2048	2053
1st percentile	15,122	30,537	51,002	83,016	128,019	188,575	260,682	335,884
5th percentile	17,341	36,168	60,584	100,360	151,868	216,685	295,950	397,964
10th percentile	18,513	39,179	66,852	108,428	164,470	237,206	325,632	432,843
25th percentile	20,363	44,014	77,175	124,257	188,668	273,212	382,817	514,899
Median	22,490	50,207	88,966	144,981	220,990	324,748	458,374	629,008
75 percentile	24,564	56,930	103,199	168,051	259,750	385,915	549,521	778,129
90th percentile	27,003	64,669	117,039	192,388	298,291	458,437	664,364	952,725
95th percentile	28,518	68,642	128,872	206,481	326,813	504,899	744,054	1,076,167
99th percentile	31,366	77,712	147,174	245,714	382,644	590,109	904,104	1,431,140
Mean	22,364	50,103	88,809	144,339	221,569	326,856	462,825	638,618

Bootstrap ($)	2018	2023	2028	2033	2038	2043	2048	2053
1st percentile	14,079	25,777	41,732	65,719	96,981	141,697	184,930	231,906
5th percentile	16,619	32,288	52,603	81,677	121,999	176,682	240,333	310,006
10th percentile	17,911	35,756	58,710	93,381	140,008	201,478	278,002	361,897
25th percentile	20,103	42,704	72,530	115,284	173,771	255,539	350,723	467,323
Median	22,639	50,872	90,233	145,922	225,470	332,590	467,660	641,948
75 percentile	25,180	60,403	112,530	186,935	293,122	440,524	637,955	918,742
90th percentile	27,688	69,510	134,961	235,436	366,077	562,444	850,329	1,258,562
95th percentile	29,366	75,592	151,949	267,700	434,956	649,153	1,016,471	1,588,341
99th percentile	32,485	89,988	187,266	335,609	532,169	854,683	1,349,915	2,263,013
Mean	22,399	50,388	89,801	146,925	226,834	336,252	477,879	661,902

Normal ($)	2018	2023	2028	2033	2038	2043	2048	2053
1st percentile	14,820	27,836	45,457	70,568	106,233	153,494	218,312	276,610
5th percentile	16,603	32,775	54,421	86,520	133,322	194,091	267,094	348,871
10th percentile	17,725	36,096	60,757	96,957	146,713	213,807	297,960	395,908
25th percentile	19,907	42,079	71,883	116,552	177,523	263,153	367,440	487,140
Median	22,464	50,538	89,817	145,566	222,230	327,427	464,200	634,796
75 percentile	25,252	60,067	110,930	182,323	282,972	418,014	599,582	856,484
90th percentile	27,955	70,093	134,154	227,201	354,872	531,657	761,865	1,105,678
95th percentile	29,672	77,677	149,767	252,908	397,478	604,754	878,447	1,320,910
99th percentile	33,480	94,584	188,617	333,923	552,279	814,311	1,248,614	1,945,710
Mean	22,402	50,408	89,822	146,573	225,607	333,430	472,565	652,603

Source: Authors' tabulations.

distributions of account balances is wider than the spread of the multivariate normal distributions, which in turn is wider than those seen for the structural LHS model. A similar pattern is seen when we examine the means and medians of the distribution as we go out to the far years of the distribution. We might expect differences in the width of the distributions given the different generating processes, but one must recall that the models were calibrated to have the same mean and volatility of returns for any single year. Hence, *ex ante*, most readers would probably expect the means and the medians of the distributions to stay quite close for our entire horizon. But note that we are showing the means and medians of the distributions at each point in time, not the values corresponding to compounding the mean or median single-year returns.

The same forces that give rise to longer-run mean reversion in returns in the structural model affect the means and medians of the distributions as well. For shorter horizons, these effects are small—even out to 20 years, values of medians stay within 1 percent or less (means within 2 percent), but this drift compounds out to 40 years where there is as much as a 4 percent discrepancy in mean account balances in the difference between the bootstrap simulations and the structural model results.

Both tails of the account balances are also quite different. After 20 years, the saver has combined employee and employer contributions of just over $92,000. In both the bootstrap and normal models, he would expect that, almost 10 percent of the time, his account balance would be less than cumulative contributions. Under the LHS model, this would happen less than 3 percent of the time. The LHS model produces downside accumulation results that are 26 percent better in the lowest percentile of the distribution, and 23 percent better at the 5th percentile. On the flip side, the LHS approach also produces smaller account balances in the good scenarios. Balances are approximately 18–23 percent (26–27 percent) lower at the 95th (99th) percentiles than in the bootstrap and normal distributions.

It is also instructive to look at the implied geometric average returns in the upper tails. For the normal and bootstrap cases, these are approximately 11 percent and 13.3 percent. These do not seem too extreme when one considers that the average glide path weight in equity in the first 20 years is roughly 85 percent. Yet they may appear wider when viewed against the backdrop of current bond yields of less than 2 percent on ten-year Treasuries, and also given that higher equity returns have tended to coincide with periods of persistently moderate or declining inflation. A back-of-the-envelope calculation assuming he gets 2.5 percent from bonds over the period would imply either 10.0 percent or 12.7 percent excess returns for equities. This seems inordinately high for such a long period.

At the 40-year horizon, the bootstrap-driven model has the widest distribution, with both more negative and more positive outcomes. It should also be noted here that the asset allocation changes the most dramatically in the last 20 years of the glide path. Equities drop from 78 percent with 20 years to go, to 44 percent at retirement. The bond allocation rises from 19 percent to 45 percent.

The lack of mean reversion in the bootstrap and normal models may be most distortionary here, since there is natural reason to expect negative serial correlation of returns over the medium to longer term in fixed income markets. If a riskless bond, which is held to maturity, returns less than its yield to maturity it *must* be followed by returns greater than the initial yield to maturity. This mathematical fact is lessened somewhat if we think about rolling portfolios and portfolios containing spread product, but for the investment-grade fixed income assumed here, these factors would be insufficient to overcome the rationale for longer-term mean reversion in returns.

After 40 years, the account balances in the bootstrap simulations are on average 1.5 percent higher than those for the normal simulations, and 3.5 percent higher than for the structural model. At the upper extremes of the distributions (99th percentile) the bootstrap gives account balances nearly 40 percent greater than those in the normal model, and nearly 60 percent greater than those seen in the structural model. The implied annualized return is approximately 10.3 percent. Again this number seems inordinately large over a 40-year horizon, given the mix of assets and our current starting point. In the bottom percentile, the bootstrap model lags the normal model by 16 percent and the structural model by 31 percent. The persistent negative returns required to get approximately 1.8 percent *per annum* seem implausibly low for a 40-year implied compounded average.

The spread for the normal model seems more reasonable by comparison, yet it also spans a range where the 99th percentile outcome is almost seven times that seen in the 1st percentile results. Its median and mean results are 1–2 percent higher than those seen in the structural simulation model. For the extreme percentiles, the normal model is about 20–25 percent wider than the structural model. In the worst percentile case, we again see negative nominal returns over a 40-year horizon. Upside effective annual asset appreciations are 8.0 percent annualized at the 95th percentile (9.7 percent annualized for the 99th percentile). This does not seem terribly unreasonable given our horizon length and the fact that these are for the extremes of the distribution.

The LHS model produces an annualized return of 0.8 percent in the worst percentile. This would be depressing, but much less so than for the other two models. Results to the upside are more muted as well producing effective annualized returns of 7.1 percent at the 95th percentile (and 8.4 percent for the 99th). It should be noted, however, that annualized returns can be a bit deceiving in this context when one thinks about the asset-weighted averages. Time-weighted, the averages have substantially more exposure to equities, but when viewed against the construct of the glide path and increasing reliance on bonds in the future, the average effective weight is likely more closely balanced.

Results for DB Plans

Turning our attention to the DB plans, we first analyze the behavior of contributions across the three models for the frozen plan over a ten-year horizon. Recall that asset allocation is kept at 60 percent equity and 40 percent fixed income with quarterly rebalancing. Under the contribution rules, median minimum required contributions drop to zero by 2017 (see Figure 3.8, Panel A). This is largely driven by the upward drift in the discount curve, assumed to increase by 100 basis points on average at the ten-year point of the yield curve and somewhat more for short–intermediate maturities with the two-year rate rising by some 240 basis points. Average required contributions stay positive in all years given the funding rules. For the first three years, there is little difference across the models given the nature of the amortization bases. Average contribution results differ a bit as we move forward in time, but even at their widest they amount to approximately $6 million in ten years' time, or less than 1 percent of current liabilities. At the 99th percentile, the potential contributions display greater and widening variance. For 2014, the spread between the bootstrap and LHS models is a little over $9 million. In ten years' time, this grows to $61 million.

Panel B in Figure 3.8 shows a distribution of the present value of contributions for the three models. Interestingly, all three models have average required contributions less than current shortfalls, given the central tendency for rates to rise. The present value of average contributions ranges from a low of $170 million in the LHS model to a high of $210 million in the bootstrap model. The bootstrap and normal models display significantly higher distribution in the possible future contributions. This difference is again largely attributable to the lack of mean reversion of returns in the bootstrap and normal distribution models and to the propensity for a greater left skew in the historic return distribution for equities.

Contribution requirements for the plan still accruing benefits are more interesting (see Figure 3.9, Panel A). There is a similar pattern of mean and median required contributions for the first few years, but then there is some divergence. Means and medians stay positive, as additional benefits are earned while the combined increase in the yield curve and current asset levels are not sufficient to award 'free' additional benefit accruals. Interestingly, the medians and means diverge most for the bootstrap simulations, with the bootstrap ultimately having the lowest median contribution requirements, but the highest mean requirements. After the first few years, the bootstrap consistently produces the largest mean and 99th percentile contributions.

Over the next ten years, the average present value of contributions for the open plan ranges from $789 million in the structural model to $866 million in the bootstrap model. The normal model is in between, at $841 million. The bootstrap model also displays the widest variation in contributions and a substantial tail (Panel B, Figure 3.9).

Conclusion

This chapter examines three alternative methods to simulate long horizon yield curves and asset returns: a 'block bootstrap' simulation, a normal 'Monte Carlo'

Panel A. Minimum required contribution ($ millions): frozen plan.

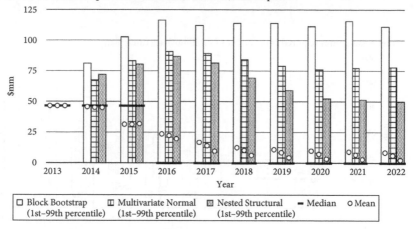

Panel B. Distribution of ten year cumulative contributions.

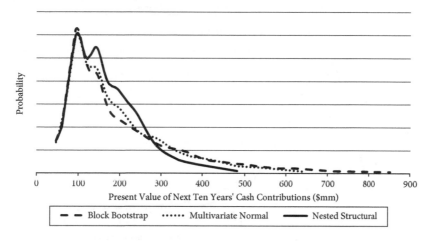

Panel C. Distribution of five year cumulative contributions.

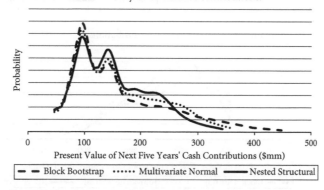

Figure 3.8. Contribution patterns under alternative scenarios: frozen plan.

Notes: Panel A: Minimum required contribution ($mm): frozen plan. Panel B: Distribution of ten-year cumulative contributions. Panel C: Distribution of five-year cumulative contributions.

Source: Authors' illustration.

Panel A. Minimum required contributions ($ millions): accruing plan.

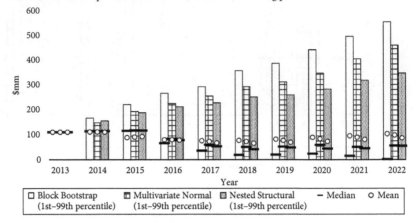

Panel B. Distribution of ten-year cumulative contributions.

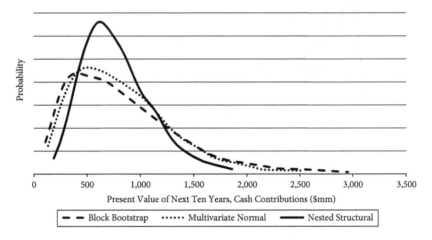

Panel C. Distribution of five-year cumulative contributions.

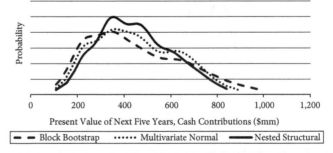

Figure 3.9. Contribution patterns under alternative scenarios: accruing plan.

Notes: Panel A. Minimum required contribution ($mm): accruing plan. Panel B. Distribution of ten-year cumulative contributions. Panel C. Distribution of five-year cumulative contributions.

Source: Authors' illustration.

simulation, and a structural economic regime-switching model. We explore how the choice of modeling approach affects the simulated distribution of future returns and outcomes (such as plan contributions and retirement wealth) for both DC and DB plans.

The bootstrap model has desirable properties for shorter simulations of a few years or less, but it produces very questionable results for long horizons. Examination on a path-by-path basis yields individual scenarios that strain credibility, both in individual variables and between variables. The normal model with independently, identically distributed returns also fails along several dimensions. Over a longer horizon, fundamental tenants of economic rationality dictate bounds on valuations that would almost certainly rule out a true memoryless process, which the normal and bootstrap models assume. The weak linkages between variables that correlation provides are not sufficient to ensure reasonable long-term relationships. A simple correlation matrix cannot capture the complex dynamic relationship between stock returns, bond returns, and macro variables. These relationships are better characterized by a model that generates correlations which vary with the macroeconomic regime, such as our proposed macro-driven regime-switching model (LHS). This model captures many desirable properties at both the secular and cyclical frequencies and overcomes many of the flaws of simpler models. The model also makes it possible to directly link investment returns with simulated macroeconomic time series for inflation and GDP growth. For this reason we would argue that the structural model should be preferred for longer horizon simulations. The model can be used to evaluate different asset allocations, market or macro-contingent dynamic asset allocations, and hedging strategies.

A key implication of the LHS model is mean reversion of returns at longer investment horizons, which implies a downward sloping term structure of volatility. This feature or idea is supported by the work of Campbell and Viceira (2005) and by Siegel's well-known work (1994) on long-run stock returns. We initially described the statistical uncertainty surrounding estimates of risk premiums and expected returns that may even vary over time. So, what is the equity risk premium we are supposed to be converging to in the simulation? The task ahead of us is to incorporate some essence of the uncertainty about the mean processes (risk premiums) into our long-term simulation models (see Pastor and Stambaugh 2012).

Our results and discussion should provide some cautionary lessons. Characterizing distributions of outcomes ten or 40 years hence is an exercise that should be taken with more than a single grain of salt. One should look at such models (no matter how sophisticated) only as one among a number of guides to answers, rather than the sole guide—or, worse yet, the answer in and of itself.

Appendix: The Regime-Switching Long Horizon Simulation Model

Regime Dynamics

The transition probabilities between regimes are a function of the time spent in the regime. Formally, it is assumed that the transitions are governed by a Weibull distribution. The survival function (the probability of staying in a given regime past time t is given by $S(t) = e^{((t)/(a))^b}$, with associated probability density function $f(t) = ba^{-b}t^{b-1}$ $e^{((t)/(a))^b}$, and hazard rate function $h(t) = (f(t))/(S(t)) = ba^{-b}t^{b-1}$. As discussed above, we calibrate the parameters to match the empirical mean and standard deviation of the durations of economic expansions and contractions.

Output Gap Dynamics

The output gap is assumed to follow an Ornstein-Uhlenbeck process within regimes. In a regime-switching setting the key feature of this specification is that changes in GDP growth are going to be more pronounced at the business cycle turning points.

$$dy = -\kappa_{y,s}[y - \theta_{y,s}]dt + \sigma_{y,s}\sqrt{dt} \cdot \varepsilon_r$$

Mechanically, the reason why the most dramatic changes occur around turning points is that it is typically at the business cycle turning points in the simulation (where the regime changes from one to the other) that the difference between the current output gap and the new 'target level' for the regime is the greatest. As a result, extreme levels of GDP growth are going to be realized at the beginning of a recession (from positive to highly negative) and the beginning of an expansion (from negative/zero to highly positive).

Inflation Dynamics

Inflation is assumed to have two components.

$$\pi = \pi_{cyclical} + \pi_{persistent}$$

$$d\pi_{cyclical} = -\kappa_{cyclical,s}\,ydt + \sigma_{cyclical,s}\sqrt{\delta\tau} \cdot \varepsilon_{\pi}$$

The first component is meant to capture excess 'demand'-driven inflation. Its behavior is strongly linked to the output gap. It is in other words a short-term Phillips-type inflation vs. aggregate demand relationship.

$$d\pi_{persistent} = -\kappa_{\pi,s}(\pi_{persistent} - \theta_\pi)dt + \sigma_{\pi,s}\sqrt{dt} \cdot \varepsilon_\pi$$

The second component is a very low frequency/almost permanent component of inflation. This component captures secular changes in inflation levels in the economy.

The Taylor Rule for Monetary Policy

Monetary policy is assumed to follow a modified Taylor rule, such that the targeted short-term real rate responds to deviations of inflation from its long-run level and the output gap.

$$r = (r* + \pi) + \beta_\pi(\pi - \pi_{long}) - \beta_{y,s}[y - y_{long}]$$

Monetary policy is neutral when the current inflation equals the current value for the time-varying long-term component of inflation. This captures the notion that a substantial increase in long-run inflation expectations and average future realized inflation has to be a monetary phenomenon. On a path toward higher inflation, which would correspond to a shock in the permanent component of inflation, we would expect to see 'unsustainable' or overly accommodating levels of (low) short-term real rates of interest. It is implausible for real policy rates to remain very high during inflationary periods. The general cyclical dynamics of monetary policy in the model are however determined by the business cycle. In recessions the central bank cuts real rates, and in expansions the central bank tightens, increasing real short-term rates.

The Yield Curve Model

The nominal yield at maturity T is given by the average expected future short rate plus a nominal risk premium minus a nominal rate volatility convexity adjustment. The real yield for maturity T is given by the average expected future short real rates plus a real risk premium (which may be negative) plus a liquidity risk premium–real rate volatility convexity adjustment. Mathematically, the nominal yield at time T can be written as

$$y_T = E\left[\frac{1}{T}\sum_{j=1}^{T} r_j\right] + \delta_T + \theta_T - \gamma_T$$

where r is the short rate (three-month T-Bill), δ is the real rate risk premium for maturity T, θ_T is the duration/inflation risk premium, and γ_T is the convexity adjustment at maturity T. The real rate risk premium is driven by the business cycle in that we relate it to the output gap and is given by:

$$\delta_T = \alpha_{\delta,T} + \beta_{\delta,T}\, y_{\text{gap}} + \epsilon$$

$\beta_{\delta,T}$ is assumed to be positive, which captures the positive correlation between the real risk premium and the output gap. This captures the 'flight-to-safety' characteristics of U.S. securities in general and U.S. Treasuries in particular. The nominal duration (inflation) risk premium is given by:

$$\theta_T = \alpha_{\theta,T} + \beta_{\theta,T}\, \pi_{\text{inf}} + \epsilon$$

Since $\beta_{\theta,T}$ is assumed to be positive, we generally expect a positive correlation between the inflation risk premium and the level of inflation. The convexity adjustments to the nominal and real yield curves are simply given by the conventional expression of:

$$\gamma_T = \frac{1}{2}T^2\sigma^2$$

The convexity adjustment plays a significant role in shaping the longer-term maturities of the yield curve, but does not in itself affect the expected term premium.

Overall the dynamics of the shorter end of the curve (maturities inside five years) are heavily influenced by the business cycle and the expected federal funds rate.

The Equity Model

Equities are priced according to discounted dividend model with a terminal condition:

$$P = E\left[\sum_{t=1}^{30} \frac{D_t}{(1+r_t+\lambda)^t}\right] + E\left[\frac{1}{(1+r_{30}+\lambda)^{30}} P_T\right]$$

The equity risk premium is assumed to follow a regime-switching process (Ornstein–Uhlenbeck process). Each regime is characterized by a mean, volatility, and mean reversion parameter.

Equity Risk Premium

The dynamics of the equity risk premium are specified as an Ornstein–Uhlenbeck process that depends on the regime (contraction or expansion) that the economy is currently in. Formally,

$$d\lambda_{erp} = -\kappa_{s,erp}\left[\lambda_{erp} - \theta_{j,erp}\right]dt + \sigma_{s,erp}\sqrt{dt}\cdot\varepsilon_{erp}$$

The parameters of the model are calibrated to generate higher volatility in recessions and more violent changes in equity risk premiums around business cycle turning points.

This means that the parameters satisfy the following conditions: $\theta_{contraction,erp} > \theta_{expansion,erp}$, $\kappa_{contraction,erp} > \kappa_{expansion,erp}$, $\sigma_{contraction,erp} > \sigma_{expansion,erp}$. The first condition ensures that the P/E ratio will tend to decline when the economy goes into a recession. The second condition means that changes in P/E ratios are asymmetric in that they decline faster in recessions than they improve in expansions. The final condition gives more idiosyncratic volatility in the recession phase of the business cycle. This is consistent with the skewness of empirical equity returns where the left tail of equity returns is 'fatter' than the right tail and consistent with higher market volatility and uncertainty in recessions.

The Terminal Condition on Equity Valuations

In steady state the expected return on equity should equal the required rate of return on equity. We impose this condition to pin down the expected terminal valuation of equities, beyond the 30-year forecasting horizon at each 'node' in the simulation.

$$P_T = E_T / (r + \lambda)$$

The steady state condition can be derived as follows. The terminal expected price level is $P_T = d_T / (r + \lambda - g_D)$, where d is dividends, r is long-term interest rate, and *roe* is the return on equity. Now use the fact that $d_T = po_T e_T$, $g_D = (1 - po_T)roe$, and impose $roe = r + \lambda$ in equilibrium.

A Note on Expectations in the Model

The complicated regime-switching dynamics of the model do not admit a closed-form solution for expected future fed funds rate, real GDP growth and inflation at any given 'simulation node' in the simulation. To deal with this issue, the expected future values of a specific variable are set to model consistent linear functions (projections) onto the most relevant current state variables in the model. The expected future fed funds rate at a given point in time in a given regime is for instance based on the linear projection of future simulated realizations of the fed funds rate, the current fed funds rate, the current level of cyclical and persistent inflation, and the current output gap for a given set of model parameters. To get a term structure of expectations at a given point in time, the parameters for a given variable vary at different forecast horizons, which are one, two, three, four, five, seven, ten, 20, and 30 years. The expectations are in this way by construction 'unbiased,' conditional on the current state of the economy.

Notes

1. In practice, most modern implementations would extend to a broader array of asset classes (e.g. real estate, commodities, private equity, hedge funds, etc.). The reduced set of asset classes is chosen to reduce complexity of computation and to focus development of intuition.
2. Data are taken from Robert Shiller's (2013) website for 1871–2010 and from Bloomberg (2013) thereafter.
3. In nominal terms, the corresponding average ranges are ten-year rolling: (1.7 percent)–20.4 percent; 30-year rolling: 5.2 percent–13.6 percent; Full Sample Average: 8.7 percent. On a cumulative basis using Shiller's CPI series, nearly 60 percent of the cumulative inflation has occurred in the past 30 years.
4. Discussed in Moore (2011).
5. p is the probability if in the high state to stay in that state, $1-p$ is the probability of transition to the low state. Symmetric results hold for q with respect to the low and high states.
6. Schaus (2010) provides a thorough treatment of the design and motivations behind DC glide paths.
7. Furman (2013) cites sources at Morningstar in her January 13, 2013, *New York Daily News* article.
8. For the Multivariate Normal and Bootstrap models inflation is assumed to be 3 percent over the period. For the Nested Structural model, inflation is a stochastic process which drives yield curve dynamics and feeds into equity valuations. Here the process is calibrated to a long-run mean of 3 percent.
9. This analysis assumes zero funding balances (Prefunding Balance and Funding Standard Carryover Balance), which impacts the funding ratio and minimum required contribution.
10. Provided the plan is underfunded or 100 percent funded. If the plan is overfunded, the required contribution is Max (Normal Cost – Overfunding,0).

References

Abidi, N., and D. Quayle (2010). 'Fixing the Flaws with Target Date Funds,' *Journal of Indexes*, 13(2): 46–51.

Arnott, R. D., and D. B. Chavez (2012). 'Demographic Changes, Financial Markets, and the Economy,' *Financial Analysts Journal*, 68: 1–24.

Bloomberg (2013). *S&P 500 Index* [website]. <http://www.bloomberg.com/quote/SPX:IND>.

Campbell, J. Y., and L. M. Viceira (2005). 'The Term Structure of the Risk-return Tradeoff,' *Financial Analysts Journal*, 61(1): 34–44.

Cochrane, J. H. (2011). 'Discount Rates,' *Journal of Finance*, 66(4): 1047–1108.

Dimson, E., P. Marsh, and M. Staunton (2002). *Triumph of the Optimists*. Princeton, NJ: Princeton University Press.

Furman, P. (2013). 'Target-date Funds as a Retirement Investment Option are Growing in Popularity, But Do Your Homework,' *New York Daily News*, January 13.

Hamilton, J. D. (1989). 'A New Approach to the Economic Analysis of Non-stationary Time Series and the Business Cycle,' *Econometrica*, 57(2): 357–384.

Hamilton, J. D. (1994). *Time Series Analysis*. Princeton, NJ: Princeton University Press.

Ilmanen, A. (2011). *Expected Returns: An Investor's Guide to Harvesting Market Rewards*. Hoboken, NJ: Wiley Finance.

Lo, A., and A. C. MacKinlay (1988). 'Stock Market Prices Do Not Follow Random Walks: Evidence from a Simple Specification Test,' *Review of Financial Studies*, 1(1): 41–66.

Milliman (2013). 'Milliman Analysis: Pension Plans Off to a Roaring Start in 2013 as Funded Status Improves by $106 Billion,' Milliman 100 Pension Funding Index [website]. <http://www.milliman.com/expertise/employee-benefits/products-tools/pension-funding-index/pdfs/pfi-february-2013.pdf>.

Moore, J. (2011). *PIMCO Viewpoints: Prediction? Pain* [website]. <http://www.pimco.com/en/insights/pages/prediction-pain.aspx>.

Pastor, L. and R. Stambaugh (2012). 'Are Stocks Really Less Volatile in the Long Run?' *Journal of Finance*, 67(2): 431–478.

Poterba, J. M., and L. H. Summers (1988). 'Mean Reversion in Stock Returns: Evidence and Implications,' *Journal of Financial Economics*, 22(1): 27–60.

Schaus, S. L. (2010). *Designing Successful Target-Date Strategies for Defined Contribution Plans*. Hoboken, NJ: John Wiley & Sons.

Shiller, R. J. (2013). 'Shiller, R., U.S. Stock Price Data, Annual, with Consumption, both Short and Long Rates, and Present Value Calculations.' *Online Data Robert Shiller* [website]. New Haven, CT: Yale University Department of Economics. <http://www.econ.yale.edu/~shiller/data.htm>.

Siegel, J. J. (1994). *Stocks for the Long Run: The Definitive Guide to Financial Market Returns & Long Term Investment Strategies*. New York, NY: McGraw-Hill.

Chapter 4
Stress Testing Monte Carlo Assumptions

Marlena I. Lee

Monte Carlo simulations are a useful financial planning tool serving several purposes. They are often used to forecast wealth outcomes into the future for the purposes of financial planning.[1] One can input assumptions about returns, saving, and spending needs, and the simulation reports how likely these goals are to be achieved, given the assumptions of the model. This framework is immensely valuable for helping investors understand the key factors that can influence their long-term investment goals. But Monte Carlo simulations also require some key assumptions to simplify a very complex problem.

This chapter examines the importance of three assumptions central to most Monte Carlo simulations: that stock returns are normally distributed, expected returns are constant over time, and return parameters are known to the user. None of these assumptions is completely consistent with reality. Returns are known to have fat tails, meaning extreme events have occurred more often than expected under a normal distribution. Expected returns also likely vary through time and, most importantly, they are unobservable, let alone precisely measured. Although underlying Monte Carlo assumptions are not an exact description of the world, the usefulness of the simulations depends on whether they can still provide useful insights to guide financial planning. Given that we know the assumptions are only approximations, this chapter assesses how users might interpret Monte Carlo results that attempt to forecast wealth outcomes into the future.

The Behavior of Black Swans

Stock returns tend to have more extreme observations than would be expected under a normal distribution. For example, global market declines in excess of 40 percent should occur once every 540 years according to a normal distribution.[2] Yet since 1900, global markets have seen two such declines, once in 1931 during the Great Depression, and again in 2008 during the global financial crisis. Researchers have studied these tail returns since the early 1960s, although popular interest in these 'black swans' has risen with the recent bestselling book of the same name.[3]

Figure 4.1 shows a histogram of global equity returns relative to the normal distribution. This is generated using annual returns on global equities from 1900

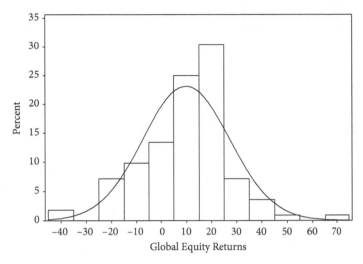

Figure 4.1. Histogram of annual equity returns: 1900–2011.

Source: Dimson et al. (2011).

to 2011 from the Dimson, Marsh, and Stauton Global Returns Database (Dimson et al. 2011). Much attention is often devoted to the negative tail events, although Figure 4.1 shows that extreme positive events also occur, such as the 71 percent return in 1933. Returns also tend to cluster around the mean much more than expected under a normal distribution. These patterns tend to offset, so that the assumption of normality does not greatly impact the results of Monte Carlo simulations.

To illustrate this point, 100,000 outcomes of a 100 percent global equity portfolio are simulated for 30 years. In the baseline Monte Carlo simulation, returns are assumed to be normally distributed with mean and standard deviation equal to that observed in historical data. A second simulation 'bootstraps' returns from actual historical data. This bootstrap simulation preserves many of the characteristics of the actual distribution including the mean, standard deviation, fat tails, and skewness of returns. This means that market drops of 40 percent will occur 1.79 percent of the time, instead of 0.19 percent of the time. We repeat each simulation 100,000 times.

Results are shown in Table 4.1. Historical returns appear in Row A, and the simulated returns in Rows B1–B2. As expected, both simulations produce averages and standard deviations t which are very similar to those observed in the historical data. Annualized average returns are within a few basis points, an acceptable range for sampling error. The bootstrap methodology better captures specific percentiles of the historical distribution. Tail percentiles and the median match up

TABLE 4.1 Summary statistics of global equity returns, 1900–2011

	Avg.	Std. dev.	Percentiles					N
			5th	10th	50th	90th	95th	
A. Historical returns	9.91	17.26	−18.09	−13.11	11.45	28.23	36.38	112
B. Simulated returns								
B1. Baseline Monte Carlo	9.93	17.27	−18.50	−12.21	9.92	32.05	38.31	3,000,000
B2. Bootstrap	9.97	17.20	−18.09	−13.11	11.73	28.23	36.38	3,000,000
B3. Bootstrap 10yr	9.92	17.19	−18.09	−13.11	11.73	28.23	36.38	3,000,000
B4. Random mean	9.90	17.34	−18.64	−12.34	9.91	32.12	38.41	3,000,000
C. Difference in annualized return from historical								
C1. Baseline Monte Carlo	0.02		−0.41	0.90	−1.53	3.82	1.93	
C2. Bootstrap	0.07		0.00	0.00	0.28	0.00	0.00	
C3. Bootstrap 10yr	0.01		0.00	0.00	0.28	0.00	0.00	
C4. Random mean	−0.01		−0.55	0.77	−1.54	3.89	2.03	

Source: Author's calculations derived from Dimson et al. (2011).

almost perfectly in the bootstrap, while small discrepancies appear when returns are simulated from a normal distribution.

Table 4.2 shows growth of wealth statistics after 30 years.[4] The baseline Monte Carlo simulation, in Row A1, produces very similar results to the bootstrap simulation in Row A2, although with slightly narrower tails. In other words, fat tails in the return distribution also result in fat tails in the wealth distribution over time. Annualized returns at the fifth percentile differ by 22 basis points per year. Accordingly, the assumption that returns are normally distributed does not greatly impact the results of Monte Carlo simulations.[5]

Time-varying Expected Returns

Both theoretical and empirical research indicates that the expected equity risk premium varies over time. Investors demand a higher expected return to hold risky assets such as stocks, and this expected return should be higher during times of greater uncertainty, such as at the onset of a recession. Some argue that this results

TABLE 4.2. Simulated growth of $1

	Average	Std dev	Percentiles				
			5th	10th	50th	90th	95th
A. Growth of $1 over 30 years							
A1. Baseline Monte Carlo	15.55	15.74	2.51	3.47	10.89	32.63	44.02
A2. Bootstrap	15.79	15.97	2.35	3.36	11.03	33.29	45.10
A3. Bootstrap 10yr	14.59	14.13	3.15	3.97	10.21	29.85	40.88
A4. Random mean	15.44	15.78	2.44	3.41	10.74	32.50	43.73
B. Difference in annualized returns from baseline Monte Carlo (basis points)							
B1. Baseline Monte Carlo	–	–	–	–	–	–	–
B2. Bootstrap		6	–22	–11	4	8	9
B3. Bootstrap 10yr	–23		79	48	–23	–33	–28
B4. Random mean	–3		–9	–6	–5	–2	–3

Source: Author's calculations derived from Dimson et al. (2011).

in mean reversion in returns: following periods of poor market returns, expected returns should be higher than average.[6]

All time series patterns in stock returns such as autocorrelation or variation around business cycles are assumed away in a typical Monte Carlo simulation. Each year, expected returns are assumed to be the same, regardless of economic conditions or recent returns. It turns out that this is not a bad assumption. Using the framework from the previous section, next we show that incorporating time series patterns in returns has only a mild impact on simulation results.

We simulate a 100 percent global equity portfolio using a bootstrap simulation very similar to that in the previous section, but with one important difference. Instead of randomly selecting annual returns, we now randomly select ten-year returns by picking a random year t between 1900 and 2011. The return of a simulated portfolio for its first ten years equals the return in years t to $t + 9$.[7] We repeat the process two more times, until we have returns for a 30-year investment horizon. Row B3 in Table 4.1 shows that the simulated returns are very similar to the actual distribution of returns. The benefit of this method is that it captures any variation in expected returns that might occur over the course of ten-year return cycles.

This simulation generates portfolio outcomes with lower averages and less wealth dispersion than the baseline Monte Carlo simulation, as shown in Row A3 of Table 4.2. Tighter wealth outcomes are the result of very slight mean reversion in the global equity data. Average returns are slightly higher following periods of poor returns. This makes long-run returns, such as the ten-year returns in the simulations, less risky than ten independently drawn annual observations.[8] The effect is that very bad and very good outcomes are less likely. In the lower tail at the fifth percentile, this reduction in long-term risk works out to a positive difference in annualized returns of 79 basis points. This benefit comes at the cost of lower annualized returns in the upper part of the wealth distribution.

Although mean reversion is good news for long-run investors, investors should be cautious about whether mean reversion will also occur in the future. Most of the mean reversion in the global portfolio comes from the U.S., and results using World ex-U.S. do not display evidence of mean reversion. Mean reversion is difficult to assess since even with more than a century of returns, the sample contains only 11 completely independent ten-year return observations. Given uncertainty about whether these patterns will hold in the future, one sensible approach would be to assume that expected returns are constant through time. If mean reversion did appear in the future, this assumption will prove to be slightly conservative.

Uncertain Inputs

All of the simulations thus far make a critical assumption, namely that the true return distribution is known. Of course it is not. Nominal global equity returns have averaged about 10 percent over the period from 1900 to 2011, but there is substantial uncertainty about future expected returns.[9] Even if the distribution has not changed over time, there is a good chance that the expected nominal equity return ranges anywhere from 7 to 13 percent.[10]

To examine the impact of uncertainty around expected returns, next we run a two-step simulation. We first randomly draw an expected return, $\tilde{\mu}$, from a normal distribution with mean equal to the historical average and standard deviation equal to the standard error.[11] Next, we randomly draw a return from a normal distribution with random mean $\tilde{\mu}$ and standard deviation equal to the sample standard deviation. This simulation accounts for uncertainty around the expected return, but still assumes the standard deviation is known without error.

Return summary statistics in Row B4 of Table 4.1 show that this simulation produces a very similar return profile to the other simulations. The extreme tails of the distribution are slightly wider than the baseline Monte Carlo simulation, and because it assumes returns are normally distributed, it does not perfectly match all points of the historical distribution.

Wealth outcomes in Row A4 of Table 4.2 show essentially identical results to the baseline Monte Carlo simulation. As long as the historical average is an unbiased estimate of the true mean, which is true if the distribution of returns does not change over time, then uncertainty about the mean has no impact on the simulation. But it is unclear whether historical averages can be considered an unbiased estimate of future expected returns.

TABLE 4.3. Monte Carlo simulations with varying expected returns

		Avg.	Std dev	Percentiles				
				5th	10th	50th	90th	95th
C =	−2%	9.13	9.48	1.41	1.96	6.31	19.31	26.18
	−1%	11.93	12.23	1.88	2.61	8.30	25.14	33.99
	0%	15.55	15.74	2.51	3.47	10.89	32.63	44.02
	1%	20.22	20.21	3.33	4.59	14.26	42.27	56.89
	2%	26.24	25.90	4.41	6.06	18.61	54.64	73.33

Note: Growth of $1 over 30 years; expected return = historical average + C.
Source: Author's calculations derived from Dimson et al. (2011).

The average historical excess return of U.S. stocks over one-month Treasury bills has been about 8 percent from 1926 to 2011. Some Monte Carlo users may also use this figure as their assumption for the expected equity premium going forward. But there are reasons to believe this estimate might be high. Extending the sample back to 1900 yields a U.S. equity premium of about 7 percent, and expanding globally lowers the equity premium to about 6 percent. Using long-term dividend and earnings growth, Fama and French (2002) estimate an equity premium in the range of 2.6 to 4.3 percent. If future expected returns are lower than historical averages, the impact on Monte Carlo simulations can be large.

Table 4.3 shows wealth outcomes for standard Monte Carlo simulations but with different levels of expected return. The simulation with mean equal to the historical average embeds an equity premium of about 6 percent. If the equity premium is actually 8 percent, the simulations in the first row (C = −2 percent) would apply. Similarly, the last row corresponds to simulations with expected return of about 8 percent over T-bills. The results are dramatically different, with each percentage difference in expected return cumulating to a 30 percent difference in wealth over 30 years. These results dwarf the minor deviations that result from fat tails and mean reversion, and they highlight a critical flaw in Monte Carlo simulations when users use an upward-biased expected return assumption.

Conclusion

Monte Carlo simulations incorporate many assumptions that simplify reality. These assumptions are not perfect descriptions of the world, but they appear to be decent approximations for some purposes. Moreover, simulation methods that better reflect historical returns do not dramatically impact results in our setting. Bootstrapping returns to account for extreme tail returns has little impact on the simulations relative to a simple assumption that returns are normal. And although expected returns on equities do vary through time, it seems reasonable to simply assume that expected returns are constant through time.

One important assumption that does have a critical impact when using Monte Carlo simulations to project absolute future wealth is the long-run expected rate of return on equities. Changing expected return assumptions dwarfs differences that arise from all other assumptions examined in this study. When using Monte Carlo to project future wealth, no tool, no matter how many bells and whistles, can escape this fundamental problem. Expected future returns are unobservable and are incredibly difficult to estimate precisely.

In our view, Monte Carlo simulations are a very useful financial planning tool. But understanding the tool's limitations will help prevent its misuse. Monte Carlo output cannot be interpreted as a guarantee, since the model does not account for a myriad of factors that can impact investment outcomes. Instead, Monte Carlo simulations should be viewed as a directional guide to let investors know if they are roughly on track. Combined with frequent evaluation and investor discipline, Monte Carlo simulations are a useful component of a sound financial plan to help increase the probability of investor success.

Disclaimer

The projections or other information generated by Monte Carlo analysis tools regarding the likelihood of various investment outcomes are hypothetical in nature, do not reflect actual investment results, and are not guarantees of future results. Results may vary with each use and over time. These hypothetical returns are used for discussion purposes only and are not intended to represent, and should not be construed to represent, predictions of future rates of return. Actual returns may vary significantly.

Notes

1. This chapter studies the use of Monte Carlo simulations for predicting future wealth outcomes. Other uses, such as to assess liability hedging, are not analyzed in this chapter.
2. Computed using a mean of 9.9 percent and standard deviation of 17.26 percent, the sample estimates from annual global returns from 1900 to 2011.
3. See Mandelbrot (1963), Fama (1963), and Taleb (2010).
4. Investment horizons of ten and 20 years yield similar conclusions.
5. A greater impact would be observed as one moves more into the tails. I have only examined the fifth percentile here, although the differences in results may be more pronounced in the first percentile.
6. Jorion (2003) shows that the empirical evidence on mean reversion in historical stock returns is weak, particularly in global returns.
7. For $t \geq 2003$, I use returns from t to 2011, then from 1900 on until I have a ten-year period. This is to ensure that returns in the first and last ten years are not under-sampled.

8. This is not to say that long-term returns are less risky than short-term returns. The distribution of wealth outcomes grows with the investment horizon.
9. It is more common to assume an expected equity premium over a risk-free rate. Since my goal is to illustrate the impact of uncertainty around expected returns, I examine total equity returns for the sake of simplicity.
10. If returns are normally distributed, a 95 percent confidence interval for the mean would range from 6.7 percent to 13.1 percent.
11. The standard error equals the standard deviation divided by $\sqrt{N}$.

References

Dimson, E., P. Marsh, and M. Staunton (2011). *The Dimson-Marsh-Staunton Global Investment Returns Database*. New York: Morningstar, Inc.

Fama, E. F. (1963). 'Mandelbrot and the Stable Paretian Hypothesis,' *Journal of Business*, 36: 420–249.

Fama, E. F., and K. R. French (2002). 'The Equity Premium,' *Journal of Finance*, 57: 637–659.

Jorion, P. (2003). 'The Long-Term Risks of Global Stock Markets,' *Financial Management*, 32: 5–26.

Mandelbrot, B. (1963). 'The Variation of Certain Speculative Prices,' *Journal of Business*, 36(4): 394–419.

Taleb, N. N. (2010). *The Black Swan: The Impact of the Highly Improbable*. New York, NY: Random House.

Part II
Longevity Risk

Chapter 5

Modeling and Management of Longevity Risk

Andrew Cairns

This chapter considers recent developments in the modeling and management of longevity risk: the risk that, in aggregate, people live longer than anticipated. There are a number of aspects to this problem. First, we need to develop good models that will help us to measure and understand the risks that will arise in the future, with longevity risk being one of a number of risks, such as interest-rate risk and other market risks. Pension plan trustees and sponsors then need to consider the results of this exercise in relation to the plan's stated risk appetite and risk tolerances. Finally, they need to make active risk management decisions on how best to manage the plan's exposure to longevity risk as part of a bigger package of good risk management.

We start with a review of developments in the modeling of longevity risk. We consider how three distinctively different approaches to modeling have 'interbred' in recent years and we discuss some difficulties with the most recent and also more complex models. Alongside this, we discuss uncertainties in the underlying population data that, to date, have not received much attention from the modeling community but are beginning to cause practitioners some anxiety.

We then move on to discuss the question of robustness. There are many outputs from a modeling exercise, but here, our ultimate goal is to ensure that a particular model produces recommendations for risk management actions that are robust, and which the end users can understand and trust. Without this endpoint, the efforts of those researchers who do the modeling will be fruitless.

Modeling Challenges

Recent years have seen the development of new stochastic models for future improvements in mortality rates. One element of this chapter is to challenge the usefulness of all of these models. Our hypothesis is that developing new models is relatively easy. That is, additional features can easily be added to existing models such as the Lee–Carter model (Lee and Carter 1992) or the CBD model (Cairns et al. 2006b), and it is normally straightforward to fit these models to the usual datasets and to get a better fit. However, a question remains as to whether this added complexity actually improves our ability to forecast future developments in mortality. Answering this question is much more difficult, if it can be answered at all.

Alongside the modeling and consequent measurement of longevity risk, we must also think about the management of that risk. The transfer of longevity risk from pension plans to reinsurers, insurers, and the capital markets (for example, hedge funds specializing in insurance-linked securities) is a relatively new phenomenon, as plan sponsors have begun to get a better grip on the risks inherent in the running of these plans. This market has been slowly gaining momentum, with most activity in the U.K., but with large and notable transactions in the Netherlands (e.g. Aegon 2013) and the U.S. more recently. Again we consider which transactions are easy and which ones are difficult. For an actuarial consultancy, it is easy to recommend a customized longevity swap. This would be part of a package of over-the-counter transactions that hedge out the interest-rate, inflation, and longevity risks that are embedded in a portfolio of pensions in payment. Recommending a longevity swap is 'easy' from the consultant's perspective because the end result of zero risk is guaranteed (notwithstanding counterparty risk). All that remains is to negotiate a good price for the swap or, perhaps, to conclude that the price is too high and that the plan should wait until market conditions and the plan funding position improve.

But is a customized longevity swap actually the best solution? Alternatives do exist in the form of q-forwards and S-forwards (see <www.LLMA.org>). These are derivative securities whose payoffs are linked to an index of mortality rather than the pension plan's own mortality. As a consequence, therefore, their use gives rise to basis risk. But for many pension plans (the hedgers), some residual risk might be acceptable if the hedge is relatively cheap compared to the customized longevity swap. But many consultants will completely avoid consideration of such contracts, for a variety of reasons:

- Assessment of basis risk is difficult and, perhaps, beyond the capabilities of the consultant;
- Assessment of the risk appetites of the plan trustees and sponsor is difficult;
- Communication of the nature of the underlying derivatives (e.g., q-forwards) is difficult (what does a q-forward have to do with long-term survivorship?); and
- Perceived reputational risk from the consultant's perspective if he/she recommends an index-linked solution that subsequently requires topping up (a customized swap might be suboptimal but the reputational risk is minimal).

A significant issue concerns establishment of the risk appetites of a plan sponsor and trustees. The use of a customized longevity swap seems to be consistent with zero appetite for risk. But the paradox here is that pension plans seem to be left with two parts: the part of the plan that deals with pensions in payment and is completely intolerant of risk; and the pre-retirement liabilities and associated assets. Typically, for the latter portion of the plan, trustees and sponsors are apparently happy to continue with a risky, equity-driven investment strategy. This apparent paradox is discussed further below.

   With the above discussion in mind, the objective of this paper is to focus minds on the development of a longevity risk management strategy for pension plans and annuity providers that we can have confidence in; that we believe is (close to) optimal; and that we know is robust.

Model Development: A Genealogy

We next review briefly some of the key developments in modeling over the past 20+ years, before discussing in a later section where efforts might be focused in the future on the development of new models (especially in a multifactor setting). We choose to refer here to the modeling 'genealogy,' because the majority of new models can be thought of as being modifications (that is, the descendants) of earlier models. This is illustrated in Figure 5.1.

   Models for mortality are typically expressed in terms of the death rate, $m(t, x)$, for age x in year t or the corresponding mortality rate (probability of death), $q(t, x)$. A commonly used approximation that links the two is that $1 - q(t, x) \approx \exp[-m(t, x)]$. Stochastic mortality modeling in demography and actuarial work can mainly be traced back to the model of Lee and Carter (1992) (model M1 in Table 5.1). The medical statistics literature does contain the Age–Period–Cohort model (APC), which pre-dates the Lee–Carter model (see, for example, Osmond 1985). It is only since 2000 that a variety of models has been proposed as alternatives to the

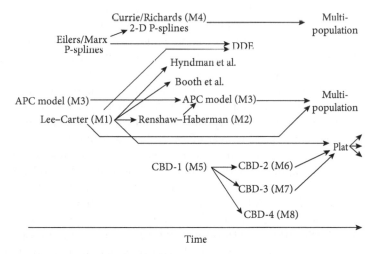

Figure 5.1. Timeline for the development of stochastic mortality models.

Note: Arrows indicate the influence that individual models have had on the development of later generations.

Source: Cairns et al. (2008).

TABLE 5.1 Formulae for the mortality models

Model	Formula
M1	$\log m(t,x) = \beta_x^{(1)} + \beta_x^{(2)}\kappa_t^{(2)}$
M2	$\log m(t,x) = \beta_x^{(1)} + \beta_x^{(2)}\kappa_t^{(2)} + \beta_x^{(3)}\gamma_{t-x}^{(3)}$
M3	$\log m(t,x) = \beta_x^{(1)} + \kappa_t^{(2)} + \gamma_{t-x}^{(3)}$
M4	$\log m(t,x) = \sum_{i,j} \theta_{ij} B_{ij}^{ay}(x,t)$
M5	$\operatorname{logit} q(t,x) = \kappa_t^{(1)} + \kappa_t^{(2)}(x-\bar{x})$
M6	$\operatorname{logit} q(t,x) = \kappa_t^{(1)} + \kappa_t^{(2)}(x-\bar{x}) + \gamma_{t-x}^{(3)}$
M7	$\operatorname{logit} q(t,x) = \kappa_t^{(1)} + \kappa_t^{(2)}(x-\tilde{x}) + \kappa_t^{(3)}((x-\tilde{x})^2 - \hat{\sigma}_x^2) + \gamma_{t-x}^{(4)}$
M8	$\operatorname{logit} q(t,x) = \kappa_t^{(1)} + \kappa_t^{(2)}(x-\bar{x}) + \gamma_{t-x}^{(3)}(x_c - x)$

Notes: The functions $\beta_x^{(i)}$, $\kappa_t^{(i)}$, and $\gamma_t^{(i)}$ are age, period, and cohort effects, respectively. The $B_{ij}^{ay}(x,t)$ are B-spline basis functions and the θ_{ij} are weights attached to each basis function. $\bar{x}$ is the mean age over the range of ages being used in the analysis. $\hat{\sigma}_x^2$ is the mean value of $(x-\bar{x})^2$. See text.
Source: Cairns et al. (2009).

Lee–Carter model to address its deficiencies (although, because of its simplicity, the Lee–Carter model does still have its supporters). Some of these new models can be thought of as direct descendants of the Lee–Carter model (such as Booth et al. 2002 and Hyndman and Ullah 2007), by adding additional age-period effects. Other models had distinctly different roots. Currie et al. (2004), building on Eilers and Marx (1996), proposed the use of two-dimensional P-splines (M4 in Table 5.1). Cairns et al. (2006b) (CBD) proposed a two-factor model with parametric age effects in contrast to the fully non-parametric Lee–Carter model (M5 in Table 5.1).

Analysis of underlying mortality data in the early 2000s (Willets 2004) revealed patterns in the data related to year of birth that could not be easily explained through the use of age-period models. This gave rise to a number of new models based on three approaches that built cohort effects into the model: Renshaw and Haberman (2006), building on Lee–Carter (M2); Cairns et al. (2009), building upon CBD (M6, M7, and M8); and Richards et al. (2006), building on Currie et al. (2004) (M4). The growing number of models led to the comprehensive studies of Cairns et al. (2009, 2011a) and Dowd et al. (2011a, b), who used a wide range of criteria to compare different models, as well as providing a framework for developing and analyzing other new models in the future. Of the models considered in these comparative studies, several fit historical data well but M2 and M8 were found to have significant (and apparently insurmountable) problems with robustness (see also Continuous Mortality Investigation, CMI 2007), leading to a recommendation that these models not be used in practical work except with extreme caution, and then only in expert hands.

Other strands of work have sought to take the best features of the different approaches to create new models. Delwarde et al. (2007) introduced the use of P-splines into the Lee–Carter model. Plat (2009) and Currie (2011) added a non-parametric age effect into the CBD family of models (M5, M6, and M7), with the key benefit that these models could be extended to a wider range of ages than was previously recommended by Cairns et al. (2006b, 2009). Plat's work has since been developed further by Börger et al. (2011).

Most recently, new models have begun to emerge that attempt to model mortality in multiple populations, by adapting standard single population models. So far, these have focused on the simpler single population models. These include the work of Li and Lee (2005), Cairns et al. (2011b), Li and Hardy (2011), Jarner and Kryger (2011), and Dowd et al. (2011a). Much work remains to be done in this direction, but a better understanding of multipopulation dynamics is central to the development of a vibrant market in longevity transactions.

In addition to the models discussed above, a variety of other approaches has been proposed. Cairns et al. (2006a) reviewed how arbitrage-free frameworks for modeling interest-rate risk and credit risk can be adapted to form different frameworks for modeling mortality risk. The models covered in Figure 5.1 and Table 5.1 can best be described as 'short-rate' models in the interest-rate context. Of the alternatives proposed, most progress has been made on so-called 'forward-rate' models (Olivier and Jeffery 2004; Miltersen and Persson 2005; Smith 2005; Bauer 2006; Bauer and Russ 2006; Cairns 2007). In a similar spirit, Cairns et al. (2008) describe in more detail the Survivor Credit Offered Rate (SCOR) market model. Compared to the extended family models illustrated in Figure 5.1, these forward-rate models bring with them greater challenges in terms of complexity and calibration, but they also offer good prospects for efficient market-consistent valuation from one time period to the next. Finally, other avenues that concern the use of additional covariates, such as smoking prevalence (Kleinow and Cairns 2013) or income (Kallestrup-Lamb et al. 2013), are also under consideration, but such approaches are constantly hindered by the lack of good quality data on relevant covariates.

So why do we need all of the extra complexity that these models bring? The answer lies with the quality of the fit of the model to historical data. Cairns et al. (2009) compared eight models, and then found that, using the Bayes Information Criterion, the more complex models (e.g. M7) fitted the historical data much better. Additionally, an analysis of standardized residuals reveals that simple models such as Lee–Carter and CBD violated key assumptions such as conditional independence of the death count in individual (t, x) cells. Figure 5.2, for example, shows strong diagonal clusters of gray and black cells (left-hand plot) when, in fact, these should be distributed randomly throughout the plot. This contrasts with the more complex CBD model with a cohort effect (M7) (which includes a cohort effect), where the plot of residuals is much more random (Figure 5.2, right).

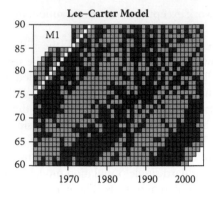
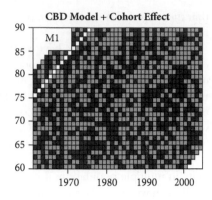

Figure 5.2. Standardized errors for actual versus expected deaths.

Notes: $\in (t,x)=(D(t,x)-\hat{m}(t,x)E(t,x))/\sqrt{\hat{m}(t,x)E(t,x)}$ where the $E(t,x)$ are the exposures, the $D(t,x)$ are the actual deaths, and the $\hat{m}(t,x)$ are the estimated death rates under the Lee–Carter model (M1; left) and the CBD model, M7, with three period effects and a cohort effect. Black (t,x) cells correspond to $\epsilon(t,x) < 0$, gray cells correspond to $\epsilon(t,x) \geq 0$, and white cells correspond to missing or excluded data. If the model is true then the $\epsilon(t,x)$ should be independent and approximately standard normal.

Source: Author's computations from England and Wales data on males aged 60 to 89 from 1961 to 2005.

But this raises a potential problem. Models such as Lee–Carter and the basic CBD approach (Cairns et al. 2006*b*) are known to be simple and robust, but then violate the underlying assumptions when they are fitted to the data (specifically that deaths are conditionally independent and have a Poisson distribution). The more complex models such as the CBD-M7 or Plat (2009) fit much better and satisfy the underlying assumptions. But, as a general rule of thumb, greater complexity brings with it an increased possibility that forecasts will be less robust. Backing this up, Dowd et al. (2010*a*, *b*) compared six models and found that complex models that fit historical data much better did not obviously outperform simple models in out-of-sample forecasting (nor did they underperform).

A final problem with more complex models is that the more random processes we have in a single population model, the more complex it becomes to extend the model to multiple populations.

Data Reliability

Model fitting generally makes the assumption that the exposures data, $E(t, x)$, are accurate. However, for many national datasets and, potentially, smaller specialized sub-populations, it is acknowledged that exposures are estimates and sometimes quite poor estimates of true values. This issue was mentioned in passing in the discussion of U.S. mortality data in Cairns et al. (2009). More recently, the Office

for National Statistics in the U.K. (ONS 2012) made significant revisions to estimated exposures from 2001 to 2011 for higher ages in the U.K. (including England
and Wales). The U.K. carries out population censuses every ten years (the most
recent being in 2011). Even in the census years, population estimates are subject
to error, and between censuses the ONS needs to estimate population sizes at each
age through estimates of deaths and net migration. In their analysis, Cairns et al.
(2009) noted that even for the best fitting models, standardized errors were bigger
in magnitude than they ought to be under the conditional Poisson model. One
explanation for this is the fact that exposures are approximations. Indeed, for at
least some smaller countries with much better systems in place for estimating population sizes at each age, it seems that the standard mortality models fit better: a fact
that might be the result of greater accuracy of the exposures.

Applications of Models

The models themselves have a number of applications. As a starting point, the
outputs of models need to be communicated to end users in a clear way. Various
graphical methods, in particular, have been proposed by Renshaw and Haberman
(2006), Cairns et al. (2009, 2011a), and Dowd et al. (2010c).

A larger body of papers has sought to consider the pricing of longevity-linked
financial contracts. Solvency II and related issues have been discussed by Olivieri
and Pitacco (2009) and, with a one-year time horizon, Plat (2010); annuity pricing
by Richards and Currie (2009); and pricing in a more general context by Zhou and
Li (2013) and Zhou et al. (2011). This includes a requirement to calculate prices or
values at future points in time, which creates a challenge in its own right: namely,
that most stochastic mortality models do not give rise to simple analytical formulae
for even annuity prices. Some papers, therefore, propose methods for calculating
approximate values for key quantities (see, for example, Denuit et al. 2010; Cairns
2011; Dowd et al. 2011b).

More recent work has focused on the use of models to develop and assess hedging strategies (see Dahl et al. 2008; Coughlan et al. 2011; Dowd et al. 2011c; and Li
and Luo 2012; Cairns 2013; Cairns et al. 2014). Much more needs to be done in
this direction, in particular, to persuade end users to consider a wider range of risk
management options, a topic discussed later in this chapter.

Robustness

A key theme in this chapter is the need for robustness in the models, forecasts, and
decisions that we might take in the measurement and management of longevity
risk. If any elements lack robustness, then end users will not have sufficient trust in

what is being recommended, and potentially a significantly suboptimal decision might be taken. The assessment of robustness takes many forms.

Model Fit

Models M1 to M8 in Table 5.1 consist of combinations of age, period, and cohort effects. We wish to know how robust the estimated age, period, and cohort effects are relative to changes in: the range of ages used to calibrate the model; the range of years (especially adding one new year's data); and the method of calibration. Additionally, it is important to ask whether estimated age, period, and cohort effects are robust relative to uncertainties in the estimated exposures. Where results are found to be sensitive to these choices, it could be that the sensitivity is just a manifestation of identifiability constraints (as discussed, for example, by Cairns et al. 2009) or a genuine lack of robustness.

The method of calibration relates to the underlying statistical assumptions (for example, the conditional independent Poisson assumption—see Brouhns et al. 2002; see also Li et al. 2009). A Bayesian or frequentist approach might be taken, smoothing might be imposed, and the objective being optimized might differ (for example, maximum likelihood or a more simple form of linear regression).

Model Forecasts

In a similar vein, how robust are stochastic forecasts (both central trajectories and the level of uncertainty around that trend) to changes in: the range of ages used to calibrate the model; the range of years (especially adding one new year's data); the method of calibration; and the choice of stochastic model for simulating future period and cohort effects? Moreover, analysts must explore the robustness of forecasts relative to the more general treatment of model and parameter risk and uncertainty in exposures data.

Business Decisions

Related to the forecasts of future mortality rates, one must ask how robust, relative to the factors discussed above, financial variables such as the market-consistent value of liabilities, and the prices of, for example, q-forwards; risk management metrics (such as hedge effectiveness); and risk management decisions (such as the choice of hedging instrument and the number of units of that instrument) are.

Future Developments

The preceding sections have revealed a tension between the need for robustness on the one hand, and the temptation to add complexity to models to better explain smaller and smaller details of single population data on the other. We focus next on the development of models to meet the needs of industry and for a better understanding of the objectives that longevity risk hedgers seek to optimize.

Modeling

The key challenge on the modeling front is to develop robust multipopulation models. There are several reasons for this.

First, pension plans seek to measure accurately trends in mortality rates for their own membership: both central trends and uncertainty around that. In the majority of cases pension plans either have relatively small populations or limited amounts of historical mortality data for their own population, and this makes it difficult to develop a reliable single population stochastic mortality model. The use of a two-population model means that limited data for the pension plan itself can be augmented by, for example, a much larger national dataset. The use of Bayesian methods, as in Cairns et al. (2011), means that missing data can be easily dealt with, including earlier years for which pension plan mortality data has been discarded.

Pension plans seeking to manage their longevity risks need robust multi-population models that will allow them to compare the various customized and index-linked derivative solutions. Such models are necessary for both price establishment and comparison, as well as the assessment of residual risk (such as basis risk in index-linked hedges).

Life insurers seeking to measure accurately trends in mortality rates and the uncertainty around them need good multipopulation models because they have exposure, potentially, to many populations: males and females; different contract types (e.g. assurances and annuities); smokers and non-smokers; or multinational portfolios.

Life insurers might bid to take over pension liabilities from pension plans. The underlying risks being transferred need to be measured accurately (i.e. the central trend and uncertainty around that) in order to price the deal accurately. This needs a multipopulation model.

Last, life insurers themselves might seek to transfer longevity risk to third parties, and so the same issues as for pension plans apply but, perhaps, on a different scale.

As remarked earlier, if a stochastic mortality model has, as its stochastic drivers, additional numbers of processes, then this makes extension to two or more populations much more challenging because of the need to consider correlations between all of the driving processes in both populations. Therefore, there is a need to develop a new approach that goes back to basics and focuses on models with fewer period effects in particular. For example, an approach being developed by Cairns et al. (2013) moves away from the usual assumption that deaths in different (t, x) cells have a conditionally independent Poisson distribution. Their approach is to model the difference between actual and expected as a mixture of traditional Poisson errors and a new residuals process $R(t, x)$ that allows for correlation between individual cells.[1] With this type of approach, multipopulation modeling will focus only on correlation between the processes driving the long-term $\bar{m}(t, x)$ processes: that is, assuming that the $R(t, x)$ processes for each population are independent (an assumption that obviously needs verification!).

A different and, perhaps, less radical approach is to start with more complex single population models but reduce the number of correlated processes between populations. An example would be the model M7 in Cairns et al. (2009), which has three period effects and one cohort effect in each population. If we have two populations, then a full time-series model needs to consider correlations between six period effects (that is, 15 correlation parameters) and two cohort effects. With three populations, the number of correlation parameters starts to become unmanageable. Instead, we can seek to minimize the number of non-zero correlations: for example, correlations between the principal period effects, $\kappa1(t)$ (affecting the level of mortality) might be found to be significant, while correlations between the slope and curvature period effects between the two populations might be negligible. Alternatively, we might seek to establish a correlation between some linear combinations of the period effects with zero correlation otherwise. A second modeling challenge concerns the treatment of exposures. As remarked earlier, modelers have, in the past, always treated exposures as accurate point estimates or (as in Cairns et al. 2009) treated specific cohorts as missing data. There is an urgent need to develop a new statistical methodology that considers exposures themselves as being subject to uncertainty. A key question then is to consider whether or not *ex ante* forecasts that assume that exposures are accurate are themselves robust. We also must consider how, in individual populations, exposures might from time to time be revised up or down. These revisions could potentially result in significant changes in base mortality tables and also in central trajectories.

Risk Appetite

Derisking Glide Paths

We will now discuss how a pension plan might choose between the various hedging options.[2] Anecdotal evidence based on recent deals and professional magazines (e.g. Khiroya and Penderis 2012) points to one situation as being typical for what consultants recommend to U.K. pension plans. Consultants typically refer to a derisking glide path, especially for defined benefit plans that are closed to new members and potentially have no further accrual for existing members.

This glide path is characterized by a number of features. For pensions in payment, the plan should seek to hedge the liabilities in a way that minimizes or even eliminates the risk of deficit for that subset of the pension plan membership. For a fully derisked position this means one of a collection of individual buyouts, a bulk buyout (both of which transfer legal responsibility for payment of the pension to the insurer), a bulk buy-in, or a customized longevity swap. For active members where pensions are linked to future salary increases, the plan continues to invest in a mixed portfolio of risky assets (e.g. 60 percent equities, 40 percent bonds). Where the plan is in deficit, then derisking activities are deferred until the funding level has improved. In this situation, a generally more risky asset strategy is adopted to increase the chances of achieving a fully funded position. Intermediate options might be considered for deferred pensioners and also active members if the defined benefit does not include future salary increases. In this case customized buyouts and longevity swaps are potentially very expensive due to significantly elevated levels of longevity risk inherent in such transactions relative to pensions that are already in payment to older plan members.

Against this background we ask: what type of risk appetite or objective do the pension plan trustees have in mind that results in the derisking glide paths described above? A candidate for this lies in the realm of utility theory. Specifically, we consider a semi-quadratic utility function of the form $u(x) = -(1-x)^2$ if the funding level $x < 1$, and $u(x) = 0$ if $x \geq 1$ (see Figure 5.3). In some sense, this utility is consistent with the strategies recommended above to follow a derisking glide path. For pensions in payment, in particular, once the plan is fully funded, then derisking means that there is no chance to fall below the bliss point, B, in Figure 5.3. If the funding level is below 100 percent, then the plan should adopt a more risky investment strategy until it can get back up to 100 percent funding, at which point it should derisk as a one-off, irreversible transaction. But, this logic only follows if the plan has no unhedgeable liabilities such as salary risk for active members. In that case, it is less clear that 100 percent removal of risk for one sub-population is actually optimal.

Now consider the setting where there is a mixture of member classes (e.g. actives, deferred pensioners, and pensioners). An open question is the following: is there a

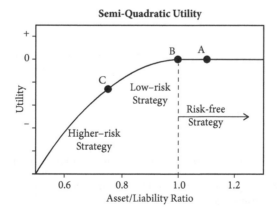

Figure 5.3. Semi-quadratic utility function for a pension plan.

Source: Cairns et al. (2008).

realistic formulation of risk appetite (e.g. a utility function) under which it is locally optimal to totally derisk in relation to one population, and to maintain a substantially risky strategy for a different sub-population? Intuition suggests that it will be difficult, if not impossible, to find such a formulation. Total derisking of one population suggests that the plan sponsor and trustees are totally intolerant of risk. In this case, for active members, the plan should also hedge all hedgeable risks (e.g. price inflation risk and longevity risk), leaving only the residual non-hedgeable risks (e.g. the difference between salary inflation and price inflation). Countering this criticism, one might argue that typical hedging strategies are illiquid and cannot be reversed easily without incurring substantial cost. But, taking this into account, it might still be preferable to gradually derisk the actives' liabilities in a planned series of 'irreversible' hedging transactions.

Size Matters

We will now consider other reasons why a pension plan might consider alternatives to bulk buyouts and customized longevity swaps.[3]

In Figure 5.4 we present a stylized view of the relative costs of four options for a pension that contains only pensions in payment. The four options (relative to inaction) are as follows.

Individual Buyout

The plan buys individual annuities one by one for its pensioners. In this case the cost does not depend on the size of the plan (that is, the number of members).

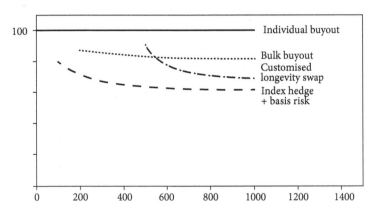

Figure 5.4. Potential prices per unit for different longevity hedging instruments as a function of the size of a transaction.

Note: Quantities and relationships are illustrative only and have no scientific basis.

Source: Cairns et al. (2008).

A Bulk Buyout of the Full Set of Pensioners

This type of transaction enjoys economies of scale, so that the price per unit falls as the size of the plan increases. Additionally, the price will fall with size because sampling risk in the runoff of the liabilities will, relatively, be smaller. There is a minimum size to this type of transaction, below which the receiver (for example, a monoline insurer) would not be interested in taking over the liabilities.

A Customized Longevity Swap

This is part of a buy-in strategy involving additional hedges, for example, against inflation risk in pensions in payment. Customized longevity swaps have a much higher threshold for engagement with the receiver of the longevity risk than bulk buyouts. The price of a longevity swap would also reward scale and reductions in sampling risk and there might be a crossover of the price per unit of risk relative to bulk buyout.

Use of Index-Linked Longevity Hedging Instruments

This type of transaction has a much lower threshold for engagement (in theory, a single q-forward or S-forward contract). In theory, the price should not reflect the size of the transaction, but in practice, the expenses related to the contract would push up the price per unit of smaller deals.

This list of options is not exhaustive: for further longevity risk-management options, see Blake et al. (2006), Coughlan et al. (2007), Cairns et al. (2008), and <www.llma.org>.

Figure 5.4 and the remarks above point to lower prices for larger plans, but potentially, as we move further up the scale, transactions might become so large that the receivers' appetite for taking on longevity risk diminishes. So the price per unit might actually have to rise in order to balance supply and demand.

Now consider the impact of each of these types of transaction on a pension plan's expected utility. Figure 5.5 presents a stylized view of this in a way that is consistent with Figure 5.4, and plots the difference in expected utility of a given strategy relative to the individual buyout strategy. Figure 5.5 assumes a strictly concave and strictly increasing utility implying that the plan always has some appetite for risk, rather than (as in Figure 5.3) zero appetite for risk above some threshold.

We include no hedging as one option. The normalized utility increases with scale relative to individual buyout because the plan benefits from lower levels of sampling risk. The two curves cross over because individual buyout includes expenses and a risk premium.

Bulk buyout and customized longevity swaps achieve essentially the same endpoint as individual buyouts using different vehicles, and so the differences between

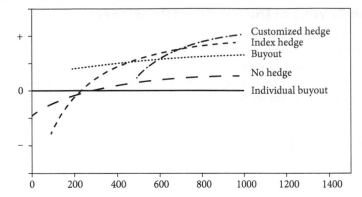

Figure 5.5. Potential expected utilities for different longevity hedging strategies relative to the individual annuitization strategy (normalized to have zero utility).

Note: Quantities and relationships are illustrative only and have no scientific basis.

Source: Cairns et al. (2008).

the three simply reflect the different prices per unit of risk and the scale thresholds for bulk buyouts and longevity swaps.

The curve for an index hedge falls from right to left because of two factors. First, the increasing cost of a smaller transaction size as in Figure 5.4. Second, the relative level of basis risk that arises with an index-linked transaction rises as the size of the plan gets smaller, and this pushes down further the normalized utility.

We have constructed our stylized plot so that the optimal hedge will depend on the size of the pension plan. For small transactions up to 'liability sizes' of 200 (Figures 5.4 and 5.5), individual buyouts are optimal even though index-linked hedges are available over some of that range. Bulk buyouts take over between liability sizes in the range 200 to 440, index hedges between 440 and 680, and finally, customized longevity swaps are optimal above 680. However, we stress that, in practice, the bands over which each strategy might be optimal will vary substantially from situation to situation without any guarantee that the order is the same as that presented here or that individual strategies will be optimal at any level of scale (for example, higher levels of risk aversion will push down the utility of the index hedge relative to the customized transactions).

The point of this example, though, is to show that, particularly if the pension plan has some appetite for risk at all funding levels, then all options should be considered, and that there is no default option that will always come out top. Instead a variety of factors comes into play: price per unit of risk as a function of scale; sampling risk; basis risk; and risk aversion.

Conclusion

In this chapter we contrast aspects of longevity risk measurement and management that are easy versus those that are difficult. Building new and ever more complex models and the recommendation of customized longevity hedges are tasks that are (relatively) easy. In contrast, the development of models that are robust and fit for purpose in a multipopulation setting is much tougher. Robustness, in particular, is a criterion that cannot be ignored or glossed over: without a proper analysis of robustness, practitioners will not engage with a model or, therefore, use it in the development of risk management strategies.

A rigorous assessment of all of the risk management options, including index-linked hedges, is also a much tougher call, and this includes a proper prior assessment of the pension plan's risk appetite and risk tolerances.

Acknowledgments

Part of this research was conducted while the author was in receipt of a research grant from Netspar, the Netherlands.

Notes

1. As an example, let $\log m \cdot (t,x) = \beta_1(x) + \kappa_2(t) + \kappa_3(t)(x = \bar{x})$ be an adaptation of the CBD (Cairns et al. 2006b) and Plat (2009) models. This is used to model the long-term developments in mortality. *Local* mortality adds the residuals process, $R(t,x)$, thus $\log m(t / x) = \dot{m}(t,x) + R(t,x)$. Lastly, deaths follow the usual Poisson model $D(t,x) \sim Poisson\big(m(t / x)E(t,x)\big)$.
2. The use of the expression 'glide path' is an interesting one. Relative to a 'flight' path it suggests no further contributions from the sponsor (which is what they would like), but also only limited controls relative to powered flight.
3. An example of this is the Pall Pension Plan longevity hedge for active members transacted with J.P. Morgan LifeMetrics early in 2011.

References

Aegon (2013). 'Aegon Grows Earnings and Sales in Q4; Proposes Increased Final Dividend.' The Hague, Netherlands: Aegon, February 15. <http://www.aegon.com/Documents/aegon-com/Sitewide/Quarterly-results/2012-Q4/EN/2012-Q4-Full-version-English.pdf>.

Bauer, D. (2006) 'An Arbitrage-Free Family of Longevity Bonds,' University of Ulm Working Paper. Ulm, Germany: University of Ulm. <http://www.mortalityrisk.org>.

Bauer, D., and J. Russ (2006). 'Pricing Longevity Bonds Using Implied Survival Probabilities,' University of Ulm Working Paper. Ulm, Germany: University of Ulm. <http://www.mortalityrisk.org>.

Blake, D., A. J. G. Cairns, and K. Dowd (2006). 'Living With Mortality: Longevity Bonds and Other Mortality-Linked Securities,' *British Actuarial Journal*, 12: 153–197.

Börger, M. D. Fleischer, and N. Kuksin (2011). 'Modeling Mortality Trend Under Modern Solvency Regimes,' *ASTIN Bulletin*, 41: 1–38.

Booth, H., J. Maindonald, and L. Smith (2002). 'Applying Lee–Carter Under Conditions of Variable Mortality Decline,' *Population Studies*, 56: 325–336.

Brouhns, N., M. Denuit, and J. K. Vermunt (2002). 'A Poisson Log-Bilinear Regression Approach to the Construction of Projected Life Tables,' *Insurance: Mathematics and Economics*, 31: 373–393.

Cairns, A. J. G. (2007). 'A Multifactor Generalization of the Olivier–Smith Model for Stochastic Mortality,' in *Proceedings of the 1st IAA Life Colloquium*. Stockholm, 2007.

Cairns, A. J. G. (2011). 'Modeling and Management of Longevity Risk: Approximations to Survival Functions and Dynamic Hedging,' *Insurance: Mathematics and Economics*, 49: 438–453.

Cairns, A. J. G. (2013). 'Robust Hedging of Longevity Risk,' *Journal of Risk and Insurance*, 80(3): 621–648.

Cairns, A. J. G., D. Blake, and K. Dowd (2006a). 'Pricing Death: Frameworks for the Valuation and Securitization of Mortality Risk,' *ASTIN Bulletin*, 36: 79–120.

Cairns, A. J. G., D. Blake, and K. Dowd (2006b). 'A Two-Factor Model for Stochastic Mortality with Parameter Uncertainty: Theory and Calibration,' *Journal of Risk and Insurance*, 73: 687–718.

Cairns, A. J. G., D. Blake, and K. Dowd (2008). 'Modelling and Management of Mortality Risk: A Review,' *Scandinavian Actuarial Journal*, 2008: 79–113.

Cairns, A. J. G., D. Blake, K. Dowd, G. D. Coughlan, D. Epstein, A. Ong, and I. Balevich (2009). 'A Quantitative Comparison of Stochastic Mortality Models Using Data from England & Wales and the United States,' *North American Actuarial Journal*, 13: 1–35.

Cairns, A. J. G., D. Blake, K. Dowd, G. D. Coughlan, D. Epstein, and M. Khalaf-Allah, (2011a). 'Mortality Density Forecasts: An Analysis of Six Stochastic Mortality Models,' *Insurance: Mathematics and Economics*, 48: 355–367.

Cairns, A. J. G., D. Blake, K. Dowd, G. D. Coughlan, and M. Khalaf-Allah (2011b). 'Bayesian Stochastic Mortality Modelling for Two Populations,' *ASTIN Bulletin*, 41: 29–59.

Cairns, A. J. G., K. Dowd, D. Blake, and G. D. Coughlan (2014). 'Longevity Hedge Effectiveness: A Decomposition,' *Quantitative Finance*, 14(2): 217–235.

Cairns, A. J. G., G. Mavros, G. Streftaris, and T. Kleinow (2013). 'New Directions in the Modeling of Longevity Risk,' Presented at the International AFIRERM/Life/ASTIN Colloquium, Mexico City, October 2012.

Continuous Mortality Investigation (CMI) (2007). 'Stochastic Projection Methodologies: Lee-Carter Model Features, Example Results and Implications,' CMI Working Paper No. 25. London, U.K.: Institute and Faculty of Actuaries.

Coughlan, G., D. Epstein, A. Sinha, and P. Honig (2007). 'q-Forwards: Derivatives for Transferring Longevity and Mortality Risk' [website]. <http://www.lifemetrics.com>.

Coughlan, G. D., M. Khalaf-Allah, Y Ye, S. Kumar, A. J. G. Cairns, D. Blake, and K. Dowd (2011). 'Longevity Hedging 101: A Framework for Longevity Basis Risk Analysis and Hedge Effectiveness,' *North American Actuarial Journal*, 15: 150–176.

Currie, I. D., M. Durban, and P. H. C. Eilers (2004). 'Smoothing and Forecasting Mortality Rates,' *Statistical Modeling*, 4: 279–298.

Currie, I. D. (2011). 'Modeling and Forecasting the Mortality of the Very Old,' *ASTIN Bulletin*, 41: 419–427.

Dahl, M., M. Melchior, and T. Møller (2008). 'On Systematic Mortality Risk and Risk Minimization with Survivor Swaps,' *Scandinavian Actuarial Journal*, 2–3: 114–146.

Delwarde, A., M. Denuit, and P. Eilers (2007). 'Smoothing the Lee–Carter and Poisson Log-Bilinear Models for Mortality Forecasting: A Penalized Log-Likelihood Approach,' *Statistical Modeling*, 7: 29–48.

Denuit, M., S. Haberman, and A. E. Renshaw (2010). 'Comonotonic Approximations to Quantiles of Life Annuity Conditional Expected Present Values: Extensions to General ARIMA Models and Comparison with the Bootstrap,' *ASTIN Bulletin*, 40: 331–349.

Dowd, K., A. J. G. Cairns, D. Blake, G. D. Coughlan, D. Epstein, and M. Khalaf-Allah (2010*a*). 'Evaluating the Goodness of Fit of Stochastic Mortality Models,' *Insurance: Mathematics and Economics*, 47: 255–265.

Dowd, K., A. J. G. Cairns, D. Blake, G. D. Coughlan, D. Epstein, and M. Khalaf-Allah (2010*b*). 'Backtesting Stochastic Mortality Models: An Ex-Post Evaluation of Multi-Period-Ahead Density Forecasts,' *North American Actuarial Journal*, 14: 281–298.

Dowd, K., D. Blake, and A. J. G. Cairns (2010*c*). 'Facing up to Uncertain Life Expectancy: The Longevity Fan Charts,' *Demography*, 47: 67–78.

Dowd, K., A. J. G. Cairns, D. Blake, G. D. Coughlan, and M. Khalaf-Allah (2011*a*). 'A Gravity Model of Mortality Rates for Two Related Populations,' *North American Actuarial Journal*, 15: 334–356.

Dowd, K., D. Blake, and A. J. G. Cairns (2011*b*). 'A Computationally Efficient Algorithm for Estimating the Distribution of Future Annuity Values under Interest-Rate and Longevity Risks,' *North American Actuarial Journal*, 15: 237–247.

Dowd, K., D. Blake, A. J. G. Cairns, G. D. Coughlan (2011*c*). 'Hedging Pension Risks with the Age-Period-Cohort Two-Population Gravity Model,' Presented at the Seventh International Longevity Risk and Capital Markets Solutions Conference, Frankfurt, September.

Eilers, P. H. C., and B. D. Marx (1996). 'Flexible Smoothing with B-Splines and Penalties,' *Statistical Science*, 11: 89–121.

Hyndman, R. J., and S. M. Ullah (2007). 'Robust Forecasting of Mortality and Fertility Rates: A Functional Data Approach,' *Computational Statistics and Data Analysis*, 51: 4942–4956.

Jarner, S. F., and E. M. Kryger (2011). 'Modeling Adult Mortality in Small Populations: The SAINT Model,' *ASTIN Bulletin*, 41: 377–418.

Kallestrup-Lamb, M., A. B. Kock, and J. T. Kristensen (2013). 'Lassoing the Determinants of Retirement,' CREATES Research Paper 2013-21. Aarhus, Denmark: Aarhus University Department of Economics and Business.

Khiroya, N., and M. Penderis (2012). 'Using LDI as Part of a Glide Path De-Risking Program,' in Professional Pensions, ed., *The Guide to Risk Reduction*. London, U.K.: Professional Pensions, pp. 8–9.

Kleinow, T., and A. J. G. Cairns (2013). 'Mortality and Smoking Prevalence: An Empirical Investigation in Ten Developed Countries,' *British Actuarial Journal*, 18(2): 452–466.

Lee, R. D., and L. R. Carter (1992). 'Modeling and Forecasting U.S. Mortality,' *Journal of the American Statistical Association*, 87: 659–675.

Li, J. S.-H., M. R. Hardy, and K. S. Tan (2009). 'Uncertainty in Model Forecasting: An Extension to the Classic Lee-Carter Approach,' *ASTIN Bulletin*, 39: 137–164.

Li, J. S.-H., and A. Luo (2012). 'Key q-Duration: A Framework for Hedging Longevity Risk,' *ASTIN Bulletin*, 42: 413–452.

Li, J. S.-H., and M. R. Hardy (2011). 'Measuring Basis Risk in Longevity Hedges,' *North American Actuarial Journal*, 15: 177–200.

Li, N., and R. Lee (2005). 'Coherent Mortality Forecasts for a Group of Populations: An Extension of the Lee–Carter Method,' *Demography*, 42(3): 575–594.

Miltersen, K. R., and S.-A. Persson (2005). 'Is Mortality Dead? Stochastic Forward Force of Mortality Determined by No Arbitrage,' University of Bergen Working Paper. Bergen, Norway: University of Bergen.

Olivier P., and T. Jeffery (2004) 'Stochastic Mortality Models,' Presentation to the Society of Actuaries of Ireland.

Olivieri, A., and E. Pitacco (2009). 'Stochastic Mortality: The Impact on Target Capital,' *ASTIN Bulletin*, 39: 541–563.

Office for National Statistics (ONS) (2012). *Population Estimates for England and Wales, Mid-2002 to Mid-2010 Revised (National)*. Newport, South Wales: Office for National Statistics.

Osmond, C. (1985). 'Using Age, Period and Cohort Models to Estimate Future Mortality Rates,' *International Journal of Epidemiology*, 14: 124–129.

Plat, R. (2009). 'Stochastic Portfolio Specific Mortality and the Quantification of Mortality Basis Risk,' *Insurance: Mathematics and Economics*, 45: 123–132.

Plat, R. (2010). 'One-Year Value-at-Risk for Longevity and Mortality,' Pensions Institute Working Paper PI-1015. London, U.K.: Pensions Institute.

Renshaw, A. E., and S. Haberman (2006). 'A Cohort-Based Extension to the Lee-Carter Model for Mortality Reduction Factors,' *Insurance: Mathematics and Economics*, 38: 556–570.

Richards, S. J., and I. D. Currie (2009). 'Longevity Risk and Annuity Pricing with the Lee-Carter Model,' *British Actuarial Journal*, 15: 317–343.

Richards, S. J., J. G. Kirkby, and I. D. Currie (2006). 'The Importance of Year of Birth in Two-Dimensional Mortality Data,' *British Actuarial Journal*, 12: 5–61.

Smith, A. D. (2005). 'Stochastic Mortality Modelling,' Workshop on the Interface between Quantitative Finance and Insurance, International Centre for the Mathematical Sciences, Edinburgh.

Willets, R. C. (2004). 'The Cohort Effect: Insights and Explanations,' *British Actuarial Journal*, 10: 833–877.

Zhou, R., and J. S.-H. Li (2013). 'A Cautionary Note on Pricing Longevity Index Swaps,' *Scandinavian Actuarial Journal*, 2013: 1–23.

Zhou, R., J. S.-H. Li, and K. S. Tan (2011). 'Economic Pricing of Mortality-Linked Securities in the Presence of Population Basis Risk,' *Geneva Papers on Risk and Insurance: Issues and Practice*, 36: 544–566.

Chapter 6

Longevity Risk Management, Corporate Finance, and Sustainable Pensions

Guy Coughlan

Longevity risk poses a significant threat to the provision of retirement income. With life expectancy having steadily risen in most of the world's countries, so too has the cost of providing adequate income in retirement. Moreover, the fact that actuaries and demographers have consistently underestimated these increases in life expectancy is a cause for concern and calls into question the sustainability of defined benefit (DB) pension plans and the adequacy of individual retirement savings.[1]

Until recently, longevity risk was an unacknowledged risk in DB pension plans, despite being an obvious risk for individuals who financed their retirement directly from savings. Just how big longevity risk actually is depends on the details of each pension plan: in particular, the precise nature of its benefits and the demographic profile of its members (or beneficiaries). For most DB pension plans, longevity risk has generally been smaller than both the investment risk associated with the pension assets and the interest rate risk associated with the pension liability. Yet for pension plans that have substantially de-risked and/or have a low funded status, longevity risk can emerge as much more significant.

The development of new tools to measure and manage longevity risk means that DB pension plans now have at their disposal a complete toolkit for ensuring the plan is managed in a sustainable fashion. But simply having the tools available is not enough. To make sustainability a real possibility requires not only appropriate implementation, but also, for many plan sponsors, a change in mindset. In particular, it means taking a perspective which has a greater focus on the financial economics of the plan and a reduced focus on the accounting. For corporate pension plans, this means also taking account of the principles of corporate finance and the inter-relationships between the pension plan and the sponsor.

This chapter emphasizes the importance of addressing longevity risk in DB pension plans and presents a framework for the sustainable management of these plans based on these observations. Our framework provides a basis for long-term management of the plan, in a way that minimizes the likelihood that the sponsor will be required to make an excessively large unplanned contribution at some future date, and also maximizes the likelihood that plan members will receive their full pension benefits.

In what follows, we address the notion of sustainability for DB pension plans and what it means for pension management. We then discuss the size of longevity risk and its significance for DB plans. Subsequently we review the development of the longevity market and the new instruments for managing longevity risk that make sustainability a realistic goal. The corporate finance context of pensions is then presented as the appropriate stage for addressing longevity risk management decisions. Our discussion emphasizes the importance of understanding the differing, but interrelated, perspectives of the sponsor and the plan. Finally, we present a framework for sustainable management of DB pension plans, which incorporates decisions related to management of longevity risk.

Long-term Alternatives for DB Plans

Over the long term, there are only two possible strategic alternatives for the sponsor of a DB pension plan: transfer it or keep it. The decision to transfer it, now or at some time in the future, means executing a pension buyout, or termination, with an insurance company. This is the traditional approach to managing longevity risk and it involves selling the longevity risk along with all other risks and transferring pension obligations to the insurer, thereby removing the pension from the sponsor's balance sheet. In contrast, a decision to keep the pension plan entails a commitment to maintain it for the long term. This involves managing the longevity risk (along with all other risks) over the life of the plan.

In both cases, the management of the pension assets against the pension liability requires a focus on the underlying economics of the plan, rather than the accounting. When the objective is a buyout/termination, the insurer will certainly take this long-term economic perspective. So moving from an accounting focus to an economic focus soon becomes prudent. When the objective is to keep the plan over the long term, this necessitates a long-term perspective on performance and risk, along with a long-term commitment to manage the plan sustainably. Since it is the economics that matters over the long term, an economic perspective is also vital in this case.

Managing DB Pension Plans Sustainably

Insurance companies in the business of providing life annuities and pension buyouts are practical examples of the kind of sustainable management relevant to DB pension plans. These insurers, in fact, make a profitable business out of managing what are effectively (at least in economic terms) DB pension plans. They do so by fully (or indeed over-) funding the liability, hedging unrewarded and unwanted risks, and managing a carefully designed, diversified investment strategy. Moreover, they do so within the tightly controlled regime of insurance regulation, which effectively places limits on the minimal level of funding, the risk profile, and the investment strategy. It is partly because of these restrictions that the annuity business has remained profitable and sustainable.

Clearly DB pension plans are different from annuity portfolios and cannot be managed in exactly the same way. In particular, unlike annuity portfolios, they may be underfunded and are associated with a sponsor for whom managing pensions is not the main business line. Nevertheless, the insurance example provides practical pointers as to what pension plans and their sponsors can do to make them more sustainable.

Sustainability for DB pension plans means being able to manage the plans for the long term, without (a) exposing the sponsors to the potential requirement of making excessively large contributions at some future date and (b) exposing plan members to increased risk that the sponsors are unable to pay pension benefits in full. In practice, sustainability can only be achieved by ensuring two things. The first is that a credible and sustainable strategy is in place for funding the pension plan through contributions. The second is that the risks facing the plan are appropriately sized and diversified, relative to the plan's funded status and relative to the size, risk profile, and financial strength of the sponsor. These require a thorough understanding of both the perspective of the pension plan and the perspective of the sponsor, which reflects the interdependencies between them in the context of corporate finance. This is a point on which we elaborate further on in the chapter.

How Significant is Longevity Risk for DB Pension Plans?

As mentioned, the significance of longevity risk for a DB pension plan depends on the details of the plan:: specifically, the nature of its benefits and the demographic profile of its members. Some key factors determining the size of this risk are listed

TABLE 6.1 Factors that impact the longevity risk in a DB pension plan

Category	Factor
Demographic	Number of members
	Age profile
	Gender profile
	Socioeconomic profile
	Aggregate health profile
	Profile of spouses and dependents
	Willingness of members to take lump sums (if available)
	Utilization of other optional benefits
Benefit structure	Fixed benefits vs. inflation- or COLA-linked benefits
	Nature of lump sum options
	Nature of spouse and dependent benefits
	Nature of other optional benefits and payment adjustments

Source: Author's tabulation.

in Table 6.1. The principal demographic factors relate to the age and socioeconomic profiles of the members, whereas the factors relating to benefit structure include whether the benefit payments are fixed or rise in line with inflation, or some other cost of living adjustment (COLA). If a plan has an inflation- or COLA-linked benefit structure, the longevity risk is significantly magnified. Another benefit structure-related factor is the nature of lump sum options. If a plan permits members to take a lump sum payment in lieu of a pension at an attractive conversion price, then longevity risk will be diminished by an amount that depends on the take-up rate.

Relative to the financial risks faced by most DB pension plans, longevity risk is usually smaller. For most U.S. and U.K. plans, their traditional high allocation to growth assets (principally equities) has meant that longevity risk has generally been smaller than investment risk. Additionally, longevity risk has been typically smaller than the interest rate risk associated with the pension liability. Despite this, longevity risk can emerge as much more significant in relative terms if the plan has low funded status, has substantially de-risked by reducing its equity allocation, and/or has hedged a significant amount of its liability interest rate risk.

Unfortunately, the significance of longevity risk must be measured in detail for each pension plan. This involves a two-stage process, where the first stage involves evaluating the likelihood and size of potential increases in life expectancy for the plan members/beneficiaries. The second stage involves evaluating how these potential future increases in life expectancy impact the pension liability. The resulting longevity risk depends on the factors related to the demographics and benefit structure, as listed in Table 6.1.

Stage 1: Projecting Future Mortality

Life expectancy is estimated by measuring current mortality rates and forecasting future rates, taking account of how the observed historical trend of falling mortality rates—referred to as mortality 'improvements'—is likely to evolve in the future. So the first stage in evaluating longevity risk requires quantifying the potential range of outcomes for the trend of future mortality improvements, relative to the initial (or base) mortality table.

Typically, actuaries develop longevity forecasts based on extrapolative methods that project future mortality from historical trends (Lee and Carter 1992; Currie et al. 2004; Cairns et al. 2006).[2] These are complex models that are widely used for valuation and risk assessment of pension plans and insurers' annuity portfolios.

So historical mortality improvements provide a useful input into how mortality rates might evolve in the future. Figure 6.1 shows average annualized mortality improvements for U.S. males in five-year age groups over the 41-year period 1968–2008.[3] These average improvements range from 0.96 percent *per annum* (p.a.) for ages 25–29 to 1.92 percent p.a. for ages 60–64. Note that a mortality improvement of 0.96 percent p.a. means that next year's mortality rate will be 99.04 percent of

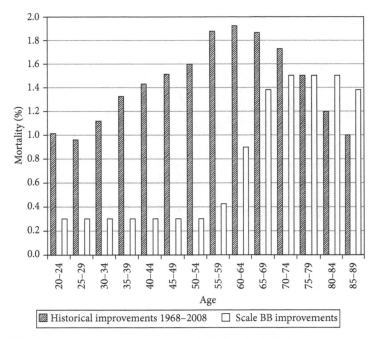

Figure 6.1. Average mortality improvements for U.S. males in different age groups over the period 1968–2008 compared with Scale BB.

Source: LifeMetrics data for the U.S. national population and Society of Actuaries (2012).

this year's mortality rate, then the following year's mortality rate will be 99.04 percent of the next year's rate, etc.

It is important to note that the average improvements in Figure 6.1 obscure considerable variation over time. This is illustrated in Figure 6.2, which shows annualized five-year mortality improvements for ages 70–74.[4] The average mortality improvement for this age group is 1.74 percent p.a., but over the period it shows an upward trend rising from 0.70 percent p.a. to 2.44 percent p.a. with significant volatility.

For comparison, Figure 6.1 also shows the Scale BB forecast improvements published by the Society of Actuaries (2012) for use in pension valuations. The Scale BB improvements are generally below the historical averages, except for ages 75 and over, but even for these higher ages the Scale BB improvements are significantly below the most recent five-year improvements.

If we take an aggregate view of five-year mortality improvements across all age groups and all years collectively, then the average improvement comes to 1.43 percent p.a. with a standard deviation of 1.51 percent and a 95 percent confidence 'worst case' improvement of 3.38 percent p.a. Figure 6.3 shows a histogram of all these mortality improvements, which illustrates the degree of volatility in the

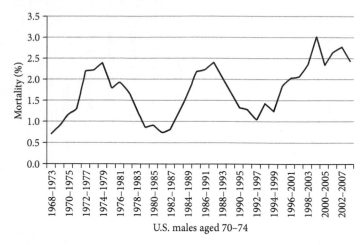

Figure 6.2. Annualized five-year mortality improvements for U.S. males aged 70–74 over 1968–2008.

Source: LifeMetrics data for the U.S. national population and author's calculations.

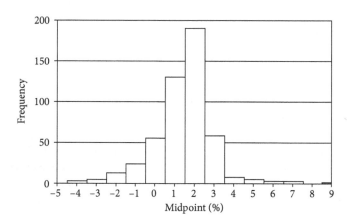

Figure 6.3. Histogram of mortality improvements 1968–2008. Annualized five-year mortality improvements for U.S. males in five-year age groups from 20–24 to 85–89.

Source: LifeMetrics data for the U.S. national population and author's calculations.

historical observations. Note the absolute worst case is an improvement of 8.55 percent p.a., which occurred for ages 30–34 over the period 1995–2000.

Stage 2: Impact on the Pension Liability

The second stage in the evaluation of longevity risk involves measuring the impact of projected mortality improvements on the pension liability. This can be evaluated

TABLE 6.2 Mortality *q*-duration and interest rate duration for generic U.S. pension benefits without a lump-sum option

	45-year-old pre-retirement	65-year-old retiree (pensioner)
Initial life expectancy	37.1 years	19.2 years
Impact on life expectancy of an unexpected mortality improvement of 1% p.a.	+3.9 years	+1.4 years
q-duration for a fixed pension*	16	5
q-duration for an inflation- or COLA-linked pension*	22	8
Interest rate duration for a fixed pension**	36	11
Interest rate duration for an inflation- or COLA-linked pension**	39	13

Notes:

* % increase in pension value due to a 1% p.a. unexpected improvement in mortality rates

** % increase in pension value due to a 1% fall in interest rates

Source: Author's calculations.

either in terms of a stochastic value-at-risk (VaR) metric or in terms of a sensitivity metric similar to interest rate duration called mortality duration, or '*q*-duration' (Coughlan et al. 2007a).

Mortality *q*-duration is defined as the percentage increase in the value of a pension liability if mortality improvements are higher (and mortality rates correspondingly lower) than expected by 1 percent per year compounded (Coughlan et al. 2008a). Table 6.2 compares the mortality *q*-duration and interest rate duration for generic U.S. pension benefits without lump sums for 45-year-old and 65-year-old U.S. males. Note that *q*-duration, although much smaller than interest rate duration, is still significant. This is partly due to the mortality improvement expectations for these individuals and partly due to the current interest rate environment, in which nominal interest rates are very low and real rates are negative at all but the longest maturities.[5] Table 6.2 shows that if mortality improvements are underestimated by 1 percent p.a. then a fixed pension liability (with no inflation or COLA linkage) increases by 15 percent for 45-year-olds and by 5 percent for 65-year-olds. For an inflation- or COLA-linked liability the increases are 22 percent and 8 percent respectively. Note that the longevity risk and interest rate risk are both higher for younger plan members than for older members, reflecting the longer duration (*q*-duration and interest rate duration) of pensions for the former.

Longevity, Interest Rate, and Inflation Risks

Longevity risk, interest rate risk, and inflation risk are the key risks to which DB pension liabilities are subject,[6] but the relationship between them is often overlooked. For example, despite the fact that mortality rates and interest rates appear to be uncorrelated, longevity risk and interest rate risk are actually interdependent. When interest rates fall, longevity risk increases, and when life expectancy increases, interest rate risk increases. Moreover, the impact of a combined change

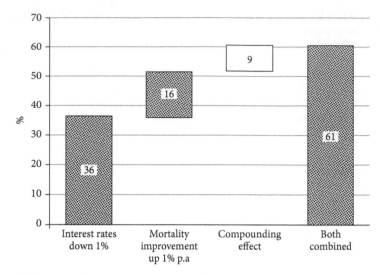

Figure 6.4 Impact of an interest rate stress and mortality improvement stress on the value of the pension liability (fixed benefit payments) for 45-year-olds.

Source: Author's calculations.

in interest rates and longevity is greater than the sum of the parts. In other words, the impact of a combined fall in interest rates and an increase in mortality improvements is actually greater than the sum of the impacts of these changes separately. This compounding effect can be seen clearly in Figure 6.4. The same is true of the combination of longevity risk and inflation risk.

The obvious implication of this interrelationship is that longevity risk and interest rate risk (and inflation risk where appropriate) should be measured and managed together in a coordinated fashion. Moreover, the advent of longevity swaps now makes it practical to coordinate the hedging of longevity risk and interest rate risk of pension liabilities. This brings a new dimension to so-called liability-driven investing (LDI) strategies and to other strategies that are liability 'aware.'

The Significance of Longevity Risk

Such analysis shows that longevity risk can be very significant for many DB pension plans, depending on their benefit structure and demographics. It can lead to higher benefit payments than expected over a longer period of time than expected, thereby increasing the value of the pension liability. This can have a devastating impact on the funded status of the plan over the medium term—even if the investment and risk management strategies are best in class.

Ignoring longevity risk means that pension plans cannot be credibly managed for the long term. It also means that pension buyouts/terminations will appear relatively more expensive. For these reasons, longevity risk needs to be incorporated into both the process of measuring risk and the strategy for managing risk.

Evolution of Longevity Risk Management

The development of new tools such as longevity swaps has made longevity risk management viable for DB pension plans. Before the development of such tools, the management of longevity risk was rigidly tied to both funding and the management of other pension-related risks. In particular, instruments for removing longevity risk also removed other risks and, moreover, required that the pension be funded at least to the level of the risk mitigation. In this section, we briefly review the evolution of longevity risk management from traditional annuities to the flexible, new capital markets solutions. The different types of longevity risk management solutions are summarized in Table 6.3.

Longevity risk management essentially began as an insurance activity. This involves individuals and DB pension plans buying annuities from insurers, in order to provide certainty of retirement income regardless of how long people live. The annuity insurers then invest the proceeds from selling annuities and manage the

TABLE 6.3 Summary of longevity risk management solutions that have been transacted

Solution	Type of contract	Risks transferred or hedged	Comments
Buyout or termination	Insurance	Longevity risk and all other financial and demographic risks	Removes pension plan from the sponsor's balance sheet
Buy-in	Insurance	Longevity risk and all other financial and demographic risks	Annuities become pension plan assets and the plan remains on the sponsor's balance sheet
Lump sum offer	Agreement between sponsor and beneficiaries	Longevity risk and all other risks	Removes pension plan from the sponsor's balance sheet
Longevity swap	Capital markets or insurance	Longevity risk only	Exchanges actual pension benefit payments (based on realized longevity) for a fixed set of payments
q-forward	Capital markets	Longevity risk only	Exchanges a payment based on a realized mortality rate for a fixed payment
Synthetic buy-in	Capital markets or insurance	Longevity risk and selected other financial risks	Combines longevity swaps with hedges of financial risks (e.g. interest rate swaps) in a flexible way. May also include asset swaps
Out-of-the-money longevity swap	Capital markets or insurance	A portion of the longevity risk. Specifically just that associated with large increases in life expectancy	Does not hedge increases in life expectancy that are below a certain level

Source: Author's tabulation.

assets (i.e. investments) against these liabilities (i.e. annuities). Since annuities are of very long duration, insurers manage these portfolios using a carefully constructed long-term investment and risk management program.

Pension Buyouts, Buy-ins, and Terminations

The traditional solution for managing the longevity risk in a DB pension plan is to transfer the liability, along with all its risks, to an insurer via a contract of insurance. This type of transaction is called a pension buyout, or pension termination. A buyout is one endgame for a DB pension plan, in that it removes the pension liability from the plan sponsor's balance sheet. This process involves transferring the pension assets and liabilities to an insurer, together with a top-up payment. This payment is required to bring the assets up to the level of the so-called 'buy-out liability,' which is typically larger than the size of the liability recorded in the accounts. This liability is larger because it generally reflects more realistic longevity assumptions, market-based risk-free discount rates, expenses, and a risk premium.

A related type of solution is a pension buy-in, which, in contrast to a buyout, does not remove the pension liability from the sponsor's balance sheet. It involves the bulk purchase of annuities by the pension plan to match the obligations and risks associated with a subset of the plan's liabilities, typically associated with retired members. In a buy-in, the annuities become assets of the plan and reflect the exact mortality and demographic characteristics of the plan's beneficiaries. Buy-ins are often used as stepping stones to a buyout. They effectively reduce the size of the pension plan in economic terms, but not necessarily in accounting or regulatory terms. Their utility lies in their ability to enable the plan to move towards a buyout gradually over time, allowing the sponsor to avoid the large upfront payment that is required in a buyout (at least for plans that are underfunded on this basis) and also allowing the sponsor to take advantage of periods in which annuity pricing is favorable.

Note that as a result of innovation, actual transactions have recently become more complex and in many cases cannot be accurately characterized as a simple buyout or buy-in.

The modern longevity market, of which buyouts and buy-ins are a part, effectively began in 2006 in the U.K. with the launch of several new monoline insurers set up specifically to acquire DB pension plans.[7] Prior to this time, the buyout market in the U.K., like that in the U.S. and elsewhere, comprised pension plans that were being wound up, often due to the insolvency of the sponsor. This proto-market was characterized by a large number of small buyout transactions typically totaling £1.5–2 billion a year in the U.K., and similar levels in the U.S. and Canada.

Crucially for the development of the market, the new specialist insurers were backed by investment banks and private equity, which brought a new mindset and helped crystallize innovation within the market. This has led to the creation of new capital market-based solutions, as well as new insurance-based solutions.

New Solutions for Longevity Risk

Shortly after the birth of the longevity market, capital markets-based solutions for managing longevity risk began to emerge. These solutions were motivated by a perceived need for additional capacity for bearing longevity risk; greater diversity of counterparties; liquidity and flexibility; fungibility; and better management of counterparty credit risk.

Longevity Bonds

One of the earliest proposals for a capital markets-based longevity hedging instrument was the so-called longevity bond (Blake and Burrows 2001; Blake et al. 2006), which predated the birth of the longevity market. A longevity bond (or survivor bond) is essentially a life annuity bond with no return of principal, whose payments decline in line with the survivorship profile of a population of individuals. If the individuals in the population live longer than expected, then the bond makes correspondingly larger payments than expected.

The first attempt to issue a longevity bond to manage the longevity risk of DB pension plans took place in 2004, when the European Investment Bank (EIB) sought to launch a 25-year, £540 million longevity bond with an initial coupon of £50 million (Azzopardi 2005). The reference population for calculating survivorship was all 65-year-old males from the national population of England and Wales as reflected in mortality statistics produced by the U.K. Government Actuary's Department. The structurer and lead manager for the bond was the French bank BNP Paribas, which intended to assume the longevity risk and then reinsure it through PartnerRe. Unfortunately, the bond was unsuccessful for several reasons connected with its structure and the lack of education of its target market (Blake et al. 2006).

Then in 2006, the World Bank, with the help of the Chilean insurance regulator, the Superintendencia de Valores y Seguros (SVS), made another attempt to issue a longevity bond, but this time in Chile (Zelenko 2011). The bond was targeted at insurers who provide retirement annuities and the SVS agreed to provide explicit regulatory capital relief to insurers who hedged the risk. A feasibility project was conducted with BNP Paribas, but the effort foundered due to the high cost of what was envisaged to be a World Bank-issued longevity bond. Following this, the World Bank turned to J.P. Morgan to develop a more cost-effective 25-year maturity bond structure that was designed to provide an effective hedge, with minimal basis risk. The longevity bond was to be issued out of a collateralized special purpose entity, with Munich Re taking the longevity risk and J.P. Morgan managing the cash flow mismatch between the various payment streams (Coughlan 2009; Life & Pension Risk 2010). This bond, like others before it, was not successful for reasons related to its novelty and what was perceived to be little need to hedge.

The First Successful Capital Markets Solutions

In 2007, a very different capital markets instrument for transferring longevity risk, called a 'q-forward,' was proposed (Coughlan et al. 2007b). This instrument was a mortality forward-rate contract, a financial derivative that locks in a fixed mortality rate at a future time. Its name comes from the actuarial symbol for a mortality rate, 'q.'

A q-forward is an agreement in which two parties agree to exchange an amount proportional to the actual, realized mortality rate of a given population, in return for an amount proportional to a fixed mortality rate at a future date (the maturity of the contract). The importance of q-forwards derives from the fact that they are building-blocks from which other, more complex, instruments can be constructed. When appropriately designed, a portfolio of q-forwards can be used to hedge the longevity exposure of an annuity or a pension liability with a high degree of effectiveness.

The first successful capital markets transaction to hedge longevity risk was in fact a q-forward contract. It was executed by Lucida PLC, a pension buyout insurer, in January 2008 (Lucida 2008; Symmons 2008). The instrument was a q-forward linked to a longevity index based on England and Wales national male mortality for a range of different ages.[8] The hedge was provided by J.P. Morgan, and was novel not just because it involved a longevity index and a new kind of product, but also because it was designed as a hedge of liability value rather than a hedge of liability cash flow. In other words, it hedged the value of the annuity, not the actual annuity payments.

Soon afterwards, in July 2008, J.P. Morgan completed another capital market-based longevity hedge, this time with Canada Life in the U.K. (Trading Risk 2008; Life and Pension Risk 2008). But in this case, the hedging instrument was different from that used by Lucida. It was a 40-year maturity £500 million longevity swap linked not to an index, but to the actual mortality experience of the 125,000-plus annuitants in Canada Life's annuity portfolio. It also differed in being a cash flow hedge of longevity risk by hedging the variability in pension benefit cash flows rather than just the variability in the value of the liability. And most significantly, this transaction brought capital markets investors into the longevity market for the very first time, as the longevity risk was passed from Canada Life to J.P. Morgan and then directly on to investors. The Canada Life–J.P. Morgan longevity swap has become a standard instrument for transferring longevity risk. Such a longevity swap involves the exchange on a regular basis of the actual realized annuity, or pension benefit, payments for a fixed set of payments based on fixed life expectancy.

The third capital markets longevity swap to be completed was a hybrid of the first two, involving a hedge of both cash flow and value provided by RBS to U.K. insurer Aviva in March 2009. It was a £475 million hedge based on the actual mortality experience of Aviva's annuitants. The longevity risk in this transaction was also placed with a group of capital markets investors (Towers Perrin 2009; Trading Risk 2010).

June 2009 saw the execution of the first longevity swap implemented by a pension plan. Babcock International implemented a series of customized longevity swaps totaling £1.2 billion to hedge the longevity risk in its three U.K. pension plans. These were capital markets swaps transacted with Credit Suisse. Although the structure of the swap was not new, being essentially the same as that of the Canada Life–J.P. Morgan swap, it was significant in that it demonstrated the practical relevance of longevity swaps for managing longevity risk in DB pension plans.

New Insurance Solutions

At the same time, product innovation was also occurring in insurance-based solutions. An example of this was the 'synthetic pension buy-in,' the first of which was transacted in July 2009 by the pension plan of RSA Insurance Group. This was essentially an asset-swap-funded longevity swap executed in insurance format with Rothesay Life, which also incorporated hedges of inflation risk and interest rate risk. An important component in this £1.9 billion transaction was a total return swap— of U.K. government securities (gilts) for higher-yielding government-backed bonds—whose cash flows were used to fund the longevity swap. The key to this synthetic buy-in was the effective combination of insurance and capital markets capabilities across Rothesay Life and its parent, Goldman Sachs (Tsentas 2011). Also in 2009, the first public sector pension plan transacted a longevity swap in the U.K. The Royal County of Berkshire Pension Fund entered a £750 million insurance-based longevity swap with Swiss Re to hedge a portion of its longevity risk.

Initiatives to Facilitate Market Development

In addition to the developments described which were designed to facilitate individual transactions, there were also a number of initiatives broadly aimed at facilitating the development of the longevity market as a whole. Here we mention the most significant.

The first of these was LifeMetrics (Coughlan et al. 2007a, 2007c, 2008b), launched by J.P. Morgan in association with the Pensions Institute and Towers Watson in 2007, with the aim of promoting standardization and education. LifeMetrics was from its launch a publicly available set of resources for measuring and managing longevity risk that included a risk management framework, longevity indices (for the U.S., England and Wales, Germany, and the Netherlands), analytics, and software. The framework blended actuarial and financial perspectives on longevity, in order to educate and establish a common basis for longevity risk management across the insurance, pension, banking, and investment management industries.

Then in November 2008, Hymans Robertson, a pension consultant, launched an organization to enable U.K. pension plans to pool mortality data in return for regular analysis and reporting on longevity (Hymans Robertson 2008). Called Club Vita, it aimed to provide pension plans with better and timelier information on longevity trends. By 2011, Club Vita had amassed a huge longevity database with more than 130 large pension plans contributing data, including the U.K.'s Pension Protection Fund (PPF).[9]

Another facilitating initiative was the formation in 2010 of a not-for-profit, cross-industry trade association called the Life & Longevity Markets Association (LLMA). The LLMA aims to 'promote a liquid, traded market in longevity and mortality-related risk' by supporting the development of 'consistent standards, methodologies and benchmarks.'[10] In April 2011, the LLMA acquired the LifeMetrics Longevity Index from J.P. Morgan.

Developments in the U.S. Market

The U.K. initiated the development of the longevity market, but progress has also been made recently in other countries, notably the U.S., Canada, and the Netherlands. The U.S., in particular, has seen several important transactions since 2011. For example, in May 2011, U.S. insurer Prudential announced a high-profile $75 million buy-in for the pension plan of Hickory Springs Manufacturing Company. Then 2012 saw several significant transactions, including very large deals by General Motors and Verizon. We return to these in the next section.

Pension Risk Management and Corporate Finance

Next we describe the corporate finance context of DB pension plans, which provides the backdrop for the management of longevity risk and also has important implications for the sustainable management of these plans.

In 2012, four major U.S. corporations announced significant initiatives to address the challenges associated with their U.S. pension plans. Each of these was very different from the other. The first took place in April, when Ford announced it was offering lump sum payments to some 90,000 retirees (pensioners) and terminated vested (i.e. deferred) plan members as part of a long-term de-risking strategy. This offering effectively transferred the longevity risk, investment risk, and all other pension-related risks to the individual members. This was followed by General Motors' (GM) announcement in June of its intention to remove $29 billion of pension liability from its balance sheet, with a combination of (a) retiree lump sums, (b) a spin-off of active and terminated vested members into a new GM pension plan, and (c) the termination of the residual retiree plan. This combination transferred the longevity risk to external parties, including retirees and an insurance company (Prudential). Then in October, Verizon announced the buyout (with accounting settlement) of $7.5 billion of pension liabilities. The same month, AT&T announced a plan to contribute $9.5 billion of preferred stock in its wireless business into its pension plans. This last transaction was a pension funding transaction without an annuity purchase or a lump sum offering.

The diversity of these transactions is striking, reflecting as it does the varied circumstances and objectives of the sponsors and their associated pension plans. This diversity also emphasizes the importance of understanding the situations and perspectives of both the sponsor and the pension plan when evaluating risk management and funding. It is particularly important to note the interrelationships between them. For corporate pension plans, these interrelationships need to be understood in the context of corporate finance.

The literature addressing DB pensions in the context of corporate finance goes back several decades (e.g. Tepper and Afflect 1974; Sharpe 1976; Treynor 1977; Black 1980; Tepper 1981). However, those papers involved simple models used to illustrate the principles. It was not until the 2000s that these ideas began to be widely promoted, and researchers and investment banks began to develop practical methods to incorporate them into decision-making (Coughlan and Ong 2003; Bodie 2004; Jurin and Margrabe 2005; Frieman et al. 2005; Jin et al. 2006).

Impact of the Pension Plan on the Sponsor

The relevant corporate finance implications of DB pension plans relate to their impact on the firm's (a) capital structure, (b) risk profile, and (c) enterprise value. In particular, we note the following.

A DB pension liability is a form of debt, which is held by the plan members and collateralized by pension assets (Feldstein and Morck 1983; Bodie 2004). In fact, investors view pension deficits, or underfunding, as being like debt, but riskier (Long et al. 2010). As a result, an underfunded pension has an impact on the credit rating of the firm as it is effectively a claim against the future operating cash flows of the business, which reduces the security of other debtholders. Carroll and Niehaus (1998) established empirically that debt market valuations actually do reflect the funded status of the plan.

The funded status of a DB pension plan is also reflected in equity market valuations of the sponsor, as established by a number of empirical studies (Feldstein and Seligman 1981; Feldstein and Morck 1983; Bodie et al. 1987; Bulow et al. 1987; Bodie and Papke 1992; Long et al. 2010).

Pension risk adds volatility to the sponsor's stock price, increases the equity beta of the firm, and raises the weighted average cost of capital or WACC. Moreover, a pension plan typically decreases the firm's optimal leverage ratio and reduces debt capacity (Frieman et al. 2005; Jin et al. 2006; Gold 2008; Long et al. 2010).

Pension risk adds to the overall risk profile of the corporation, consuming risk budget and displacing business opportunities that might have otherwise been pursued. If the risk of the pension is too great, then it can impact liquidity and/or financial strength, leading to reduced access to the capital markets and threatening the execution of business plans (Coughlan and Ong 2003; Frieman et al. 2005; Gold 2008).

These points demonstrate that a DB pension plan can have a significant impact on the value of a firm's debt and equity through both the plan's funding level and its risk profile. In particular, Long et al. (2010) present an empirical analysis that suggests that the sponsor's stock price is inversely related to the size of the pension liability and directly related to its funded status. Moreover, it appears that the impact of funded status on debt and equity prices is asymmetric. Jurin and Margrabe (2005) developed a theoretical model for this based on the option-like profile created by the U.S. excise tax on the reversion of pension surpluses. See also Coronado et al. (2008).

Impact of the Sponsor on the Pension Plan

Conversely, a firm's capital structure decisions, corporate risk profile, and financial strength have an impact on the fair value of the claims of pension plan members. The members of an underfunded plan rely on the sponsor to make contributions to eliminate the deficit and ensure all pensions are paid in full at some future time. The sponsor's ability to do so depends on these factors and is summarized in its credit rating. Note that even if plan members' claims are collateralized by a fully funded asset portfolio, this may only be temporary because of a risky asset allocation or a liability that is growing faster than asset returns. In other words, the plan members hold a contingent call on the firm's future cash flows even if the plan is currently fully funded. As a result, the capital structure, corporate risk profile, and financial strength of the sponsor should be of great interest to plan members and fiduciaries.

Both Perspectives Matter: Sponsor and Plan

While a DB pension plan must always be managed in the best interest of its members, the previous discussion suggests that the management of any such plan should take into account the perspectives of both the sponsor and the plan itself. Furthermore, despite the existence of some conflicts, we argue that the relationship between the two is in many ways symbiotic: what is good for the plan is often good for the sponsor, and vice versa. In considering these two perspectives, the interrelationships between sponsor and plan necessitate a holistic approach to evaluating pension decisions. This has a long history, and it involves consolidating the pension plan and the sponsor into each other's economic balance sheet (see Treynor et al. 1978). It was originally referred to as the 'augmented balance sheet,' but we shall use the term 'holistic balance sheet.'

From the sponsor's perspective, the pension plan should be consolidated into the corporate balance sheet and evaluated using the principles of corporate finance, with the aim of maximizing shareholder, or firm, value. We call this consolidation the *holistic corporate balance sheet*. Pensions need to be economically consolidated along with the rest of the corporation despite the fact that the company is not the legal owner of the assets in the pension fund, because it does effectively own the risks and rewards associated with those assets. In particular, if the assets outperform, the company's contributions into the pension fund will fall. On the other hand, if the assets underperform, then contributions will need to rise. For this reason, pensions must be economically consolidated for the purposes of risk management and the management of capital structure.

Conversely, from the plan's perspective, the sponsor should be consolidated into the pension balance sheet using the principles of financial economics, with the aim of maximizing the probability that pension plan members (beneficiaries) receive the full benefits they have been promised. We call this consolidation the *holistic pension balance sheet*. An important component on the asset side of this holistic balance sheet is the so-called 'sponsor covenant,' which reflects the ability and willingness of the sponsor to fund the plan and ensure that pensions are paid in full. All underfunded plans rely on the sponsor covenant, the value of which reflects the credit rating of the sponsor, the level and timing of planned contributions, and the associated risks. Also included on the asset side are other contingent assets such as benefit guarantees from bodies such as the Pension Benefit Guaranty Corporation (PBGC) in the U.S. and the PPF in the U.K. These organizations make payments in the event that the assets fall short of what is needed for a specified guaranteed benefit level. Recently, the European Insurance and Occupational Pension Authority (EIOPA) has been discussing the notion of a holistic balance sheet for pension plans as the basis of future European pension regulation. This version of the holistic balance sheet also includes contingent assets, such as benefit guarantees and the sponsor covenant (European Commission 2012).

The holistic balance sheet concept, as applied to both the sponsor and the pension plan, neatly summarizes the interdependencies between these two entities and provides an objective basis for evaluating strategies for sustainable management of the plan. This concept is fundamentally based on a purely economic view of pensions, rather than the more traditional accounting view.

Managing Longevity Risk in Pension Plans

With the advent of longevity swaps and the other new solutions for longevity risk management described earlier in the chapter, pension longevity risk can now be managed in a flexible and customized way, similar to the way in which other pension risks are managed. This is an important element of ensuring the sustainability of a DB pension plan over the long term. Prior to the development of these new instruments, longevity risk could only be fully hedged with annuities in the form of a buyout or a buy-in, which required all risks to be hedged at the same time and was not possible unless the plan was adequately funded.

As we have argued, corporate finance provides the appropriate context for managing longevity risk and developing sustainable DB pension strategies. As such, it provides important insights into the economics of pension decisions from the perspectives of the key stakeholders: the plan beneficiaries and the corporate sponsor.

Framework for Sustainability

Now that all the tools are available to manage pension plans sustainably, what is required is a framework for evaluating the key decisions such as whether to transfer or keep the pension plan; how much longevity risk to hedge (this is relevant if the plan is being kept, or if a buyout is planned at a distant time in the future); and the degree to which funding and the management of other risks should be pursued in conjunction with longevity risk management.

The framework we propose acknowledges the interrelationships between the pension plan and the sponsor, and the connections with corporate finance discussed earlier. In particular, from the sponsor's perspective, the relevant decision metrics are linked to valuation in terms of shareholder value and/or enterprise value. This will be driven by the impact of the pension plan on the corporate cost of capital, corporate risk profile, and competing uses of cash flow. On the other hand, from the pension plan's perspective the relevant decision metrics are linked to the valuation of the sponsor covenant. This will be driven by the impact of the pension plan on corporate credit quality, corporate risk profile, and cash flow.

Several tools are important in implementing this framework. Foremost among these are the holistic balance sheets of both the sponsor and the pension plan, as illustrated in Figure 6.5. These capture the economic impact of contingent assets and liabilities, a realistic measurement of the pension liability, and the interdependencies between the sponsor and the plan. Note the contingent liability on the sponsor's balance sheet, which incorporates additional claims on the sponsor, including the additional liability that would result if the funded status falls below its current level, as well as the excise tax that would accrue should the plan become significantly overfunded.

Also important are the risk profiles, or risk decompositions, of both the sponsor and the pension plan. Table 6.4 summarizes the main financial and demographic risks in the risk profile of a typical DB pension plan.

The framework can be summarized as follows. First, evaluate the pension liability in economic terms. This includes the use of market interest rates for discounting liability cash flows, up-to-date mortality base tables, and realistic projections for future mortality improvements. Second, model the interdependencies between the pension plan and the sponsor, and their differing perspectives. This includes taking account of the optionality in the holistic balance sheet of each. Important metrics include materiality of the plan as measured by the ratio of economic pension liability to equity market capitalization (or enterprise value) and the ratio of economic pension deficit to the market value of corporate debt. Third, evaluate

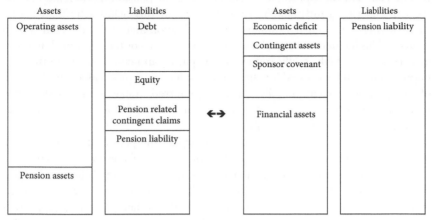

Figure 6.5. The holistic balance sheets for the sponsor and the pension plan reflect the economic interdependencies between them.

Note: Illustrative only, not to scale.

Source: Pacific Global Advisors.

TABLE 6.4 Major financial and demographic risks impacting DB pension plans

Risk origin	Risk type
Asset-related risk	Equity risk
	Interest rate risk
	Nominal interest rate risk
	Real interest rate risk
	Includes inflation risk
	Credit risk
	Alternatives risk
Contingent asset-related risk	Sponsor covenant risk
	Benefit guarantee risk
	Credit risk
	Regulatory risk
Liability-related risk	Interest rate risk
	Nominal interest rate risk
	Real interest rate risk
	Includes inflation risk
	Demographic risk
	Longevity risk
	Other

Source: Author's tabulation.

the risk profile for the plan and the sponsor. This refers to the size and composition of risks. For the sponsor, it includes the scale of pension risk in relation to the sponsor's operating and financing risks. For the plan, this includes the impact of the sponsor covenant. Fourth, evaluate the key valuation metrics for the plan and the sponsor. This includes the actual and contingent impact of the pension plan on cost of capital, risk profile, credit rating, debt capacity, and cash flow. From these the implications can be assessed for shareholder value, enterprise value, and the value of the sponsor covenant. Finally, select the preferred strategy on the basis of how it impacts the pension plan and the sponsor in terms of higher valuation metrics, sustainable risk levels, and diversification.

This framework provides a basis for managing the pension plan for the long term, which minimizes the likelihood that the sponsor will be required to make an excessively large unplanned contribution and maximizes the likelihood that plan members receive their full pension benefits. In particular, it facilitates a consistent approach to evaluating decisions connected with the hedging and management of longevity risk, along with liability-related interest rate risk and investment risks.

Conclusion

Longevity risk can be a significant risk for many DB pension plans and should, at the very least, be measured along with the other risks facing these plans. With the development of longevity swaps and other solutions, this risk can now be hedged in a flexible and customized way. As a result, DB pension plans now have at their disposal a complete toolkit for ensuring they are managed in a sustainable fashion. In fact, because of the compounding effects between longevity and interest rate risks, it is highly desirable to manage these two liability risks in concert.

We have argued that longevity risk management should be addressed in a framework for managing DB plans based on corporate finance and financial economics. Our proposed framework acknowledges the different, but interrelated, perspectives of the sponsor and the plan, and it argues that both must be taken into account for optimal decision-making. Even fiduciaries acting in the interest of the plan members/beneficiaries must take account of the sponsor's perspective in order to maximize the probability that pensions will be paid in full. This framework provides the basis for addressing key pension risk management decisions, including whether to consider a buyout/termination or pursue the hedging of longevity risk as part of the long-term management of the plan.

Disclaimer

Information herein is obtained from sources believed to be reliable but Pacific Global Advisors does not warrant its completeness or accuracy. Opinions and estimates constitute the judgment of the authors and are subject to change without notice. Past performance is not indicative of future results. This material is provided for informational purposes only and is not intended as a recommendation or an offer or solicitation for the purchase or sale of any security or financial instrument and should not serve as a primary basis for investment decisions.

Notes

1. See IMF (2012). The authors point out that mortality tables used by U.S. pension actuaries in particular have been consistently out of date.
2. Recently new models have emerged based on modelling the causes of mortality improvement that provide greater insight into forecasting future mortality rates (Coburn and Nakada 2012).
3. These mortality improvements are derived from LifeMetrics data for U.S. males, which are available at www.lifemetrics.com.
4. The data in Figures 6.2 and 6.3 reflect rolling five-year mortality improvements that are annualized.
5. The mortality assumptions for this example include expected mortality improvements averaging 1 percent per year. At the time of writing, nominal swap rates are close to 2 percent at the ten-year point and 3 percent at the 30-year point, and with inflation expectations of 2.5 percent, real rates are negative to slightly positive across the yield curve.
6. Inflation risk can be considered an interest rate risk.
7. These specialist pension insurers included Paternoster, Synesis, Lucida, Pension Insurance Corporation and Rothesay Life.
8. The mortality rates used in this first q-forward transaction were based on the LifeMetrics Index for the mortality of the population of males in England and Wales (Coughlan et al. 2007a).
9. The PPF plays a similar role to the PBGC in the U.S. It was established by the U.K. Pensions Act 2004 to provide compensation to DB plan members, when the employer suffers an insolvency event and there are insufficient assets in the plan to cover the PPF level of benefits.
10. Taken from the LLMA website, <www.llma.org>.

References

Azzopardi, M. (2005). 'The Longevity Bond,' presentation at Longevity One: The First International Conference on Longevity Risk and Capital Markets Solutions, Cass Business School, London (February 18).

Black, F. (1980). 'The Tax Consequences of Long-Run Pension Policy,' *Financial Analysts Journal*, 36(4), Jul.–Aug.: 21–28.

Blake, D., and W. Burrows (2001). 'Survivor Bonds: Helping to Hedge Mortality Risk,' *Journal of Risk and Insurance*, 68: 336–348.

Blake, D., A. J. G. Cairns, and K. Dowd (2006). 'Living with Mortality: Longevity Bonds and Other Mortality-linked Securities,' *British Actuarial Journal*, 12: 153–197.

Bodie, Z., J. Light, R. Morck, and R. Taggart (1987). 'Funding and Asset Allocation in Corporate Pension Plans: An Empirical Investigation,' in Z. Bodie, J. Shoven, and D. Wise, eds., *Issues in Pension Economics*. National Bureau of Economic Research Project Report Series, Chicago and London: University of Chicago Press, pp. 15–48.

Bodie, Z., and L. Papke (1992). 'Pension Fund Finance,' in Z. Bodie and A. Munnell, eds., *Pensions and the Economy*. Philadelphia: University of Pennsylvania Press.

Bodie, Z. (2004) 'Pensions: A Corporate Finance Perspective.' Presentation at the Seminar on Pension Finance and Economics, June 11, Staple Inn, London.

Bulow, J., R. Morck, and L. Summers (1987). 'How Does the Market Value Unfunded Pension Liabilities?' in Z. Bodie, J. Shoven, and D. Wise, eds., *Issues in Pension Economics*. National Bureau of Economic Research Project Report Series, Chicago and London: University of Chicago Press, pp. 81–110.

Cairns, A. J. G., D. Blake, and K. Dowd (2006). 'A Two-Factor Model for Stochastic Mortality with Parameter Uncertainty: Theory and Calibration,' *Journal of Risk and Insurance*, 73: 687–718.

Carroll, T. J., and G. Niehaus (1998). 'Pension Plan Funding and Corporate Debt Ratings,' *The Journal of Risk and Insurance*, 65(3): 427–441.

Coburn, A., and P. Nakada (2012). 'Insights from Structural Cause-of-improvement Models.' *Longevity Risk Management for Institutional Investors*, Fall: 92–99.

Coronado, J., S. Sharpe, O. S. Mitchell, and S. Blake Nesbitt (2008). 'Footnotes aren't Enough: The Impact of Pension Accounting on Stock Values,' *Journal of Pension Economics and Finance*, 7(3): 257–276.

Coughlan, G. D., and A. Ong (2003). 'CALM: Holistic Corporate Risk Management Including Pensions,' London: J.P. Morgan.

Coughlan, G. D., D. Epstein, A. Ong, A. Sinha, I. Balevich, J. Hevia-Portocarrero, E. Gingrich, M. Khalaf Allah, and P. Joseph (2007*a*). *LifeMetrics, A Toolkit for Measuring and Managing Longevity and Mortality Risks: Technical Document*, London: J.P. Morgan.

Coughlan, G. D., D. Epstein, A. Sinha, and P. Honig (2007*b*). '*q*-Forwards: Derivatives for Transferring Longevity and Mortality Risk,' London: J.P. Morgan.

Coughlan, G. D., D. Epstein, J. Hevia-Portocarrera, M. Khalaf-Allah, C. S. Watts, and P. Joseph (2007*c*). *LifeMetrics: Netherlands Longevity Index: Technical Document Supplement*, London: J.P. Morgan.

Coughlan, G. D., D. Epstein, M. Khalaf-Allah, and C. Watts (2008*a*). 'Hedging Pension Longevity Risk: Practical Capital Markets Solutions,' *Asia-Pacific Journal of Risk and Insurance*, 3(1): 65–88.

Coughlan, G. D., D. Epstein, C. S. Watts, M. Khalaf-Allah, P. Joseph, and Y. Ye (2008*b*). *LifeMetrics: Germany Longevity Index: Technical Document Supplement*, London: J.P. Morgan.

Coughlan, G. D. (2009). 'Hedging Longevity Risk.' Presentation at the SVS Longevity Conference, Santiago, Chile (March 19) [electronic file]. <http://www.svs.cl/sitio/pub licaciones/doc/seminario_rentas_vitalicias/present_gcoughlan_19_03_2009.ppt>.

Currie, I. D., M. Durban, and P. H. C. Eilers (2004). 'Smoothing and Forecasting Mortality Rates,' *Statistical Modelling*, 4: 279–298.

European Commission (2012). 'Quantitative Impact Study (QIS) on Institutions for Occupational Retirement Provision (IORPs)—Technical Specifications,' Brussels: Directorate General Internal Market and Services, Financial Institutions, Insurance and Pensions.

Feldstein, M., and R. Morck (1983). 'Pension Funding Decisions, Interest Rate Assumptions and Share Prices,' in Z. Bodie and J. Shoven, eds., *Financial Aspects of the United States Pension System*. Chicago: University of Chicago Press.

Feldstein, M., and S. Seligman (1981). 'Pension Funding, Share Prices, and National Savings,' *Journal of Finance*, 36(4): 801–824.

Frieman, A., J. Pettit, A. Badakhsh, and K. Barket (2005). 'Optimal Capital Structure and the Corporate Pension,' New York: UBS (April).

Gold, J. (2008). 'The Intersection of Pensions and Enterprise Risk Management,' in D. Broeders, S. Eiffinger, and A. Houben, eds., *Frontiers in Pension Finance*. Cheltenham, UK: Edward Elgar Publishing, Ltd., pp. 23–47.

Hymans Robertson (2008). 'Longevity Comparison Club Launches: Club Vita,' Press Release (November 13).

International Monetary Fund (2012). 'The Financial Impact of Longevity Risk,' in *Global Financial Stability Report: The Quest for Lasting Stability*. Washington, DC: International Monetary Fund, pp. 123–151.

Jin, L., R. C. Merton, and Z. Bodie (2006). 'Do a Firm's Equity Returns Reflect the Risk of its Pension Plan?' *Journal of Financial Economics*, 81(1): 1–26.

Jurin, B., and W. Margrabe (2005). 'The JPMorgan Framework for Measuring—and Managing the Risk of—Overfunding and Underfunding in a Defined Benefit Pension Plan.' New York: J.P. Morgan.

Lee, R. D., and L. R. Carter (1992). 'Modeling and Forecasting U.S. Mortality,' *Journal of the American Statistical Association*, 87: 659–675.

Life and Pension Risk (2008). 'Canada Life Hedges Equitable Longevity with JPMorgan Swap,' *Life and Pension Risk*, October: 6.

Long, C., E. Bronsnick, H. Zwiebel, S. Haas, C. Crevier, R. Vetter, and M. Jordon (2010). 'Pensions in Practice: How Corporate Pension Plans Impact Stock Prices,' New York, NY: Morgan Stanley.

Lucida PLC. (2008). 'Press Release: Lucida and JPMorgan First to Trade Longevity Derivative,' London, February 15.

Sharpe, W. (1976). 'Corporate Pension Funding Policy,' *Journal of Financial Economics*, 3(2): 183–193.

Society of Actuaries (2012). 'Mortality Improvement Scale BB Report,' Schaumburg, IL: Society of Actuaries.

Symmons, J. (2008). 'Lucida Guards Against Longevity,' *Financial News* [website]. February 19. <http://www.efinancialnews.com>.

Tepper, I., and A. Affleck (1974). 'Pension Plan Liabilities and Corporate Financial Strategies,' *Journal of Finance*, 29(5): 1549–1564.

Tepper, I. (1981). 'Taxation and Corporate Pension Policy,' *Journal of Finance*, 36(1): 1–13.

Towers Perrin (2009). 'Aviva Transfers Longevity Risk to the Capital Markets,' Stamford, CT: Towers Perrin.

Trading Risk (2008). 'JPMorgan Longevity Swap Unlocks U.K. Annuity Market,' *Trading Risk*, September/October: 3.

Trading Risk (2010). 'Longevity Swap Case Study,' *Trading Risk*, January: 15.

Treynor, J. L. (1977). 'The Principles of Corporate Pension Finance,' *The Journal of Finance*, 32: 627–638.

Treynor, J. L., P. J. Regan, and W. W. Priest (1978). 'Pension Claims and Corporate Assets,' *Financial Analysts Journal*, 34(3): 84–88.

Tsentas, T. (2011). 'RSA: Anatomy of a Longevity Swap,' *Life & Pensions Risk*, February.

Woolner, A. (2010). 'Bond Ambition,' *Life and Pension Risk*, May: 10–12.

Zelenko, I. (2011). 'Longevity Risk Hedging and the Stability of Retirement Systems: The Chilean Longevity Bond Case.' Paper presented at Longevity 7: Seventh International Longevity Risk and Capital Markets Solutions Conference, Frankfurt (September 8).

Chapter 7

Model Risk, Mortality Heterogeneity, and Implications for Solvency and Tail Risk

Michael Sherris and Qiming Zhou

Mortality improvements have been systematic in that they have impacted individuals of all ages, although to varying extents by age and across time for many countries. Mortality improvement rates have also shown varying trends (Njenga and Sherris 2011). Pension funds and insurance companies issuing life annuities have been exposed to this systematic risk, and this has the potential to impact solvency, especially in the tail of the distribution of survivors. Although some of this risk has been transferred to reinsurers using reinsurance and longevity swaps, much of this risk is accumulating with insurers, pension funds, and reinsurers, and it has not been diversified into the broader financial markets (Blake et al. 2011).

Systematic longevity risk is usually modeled with a doubly stochastic survival model, where the mortality rate follows a stochastic process and all individuals of the same age and gender are assumed to experience the same realized mortality rate. Given the mortality rate, individual survival is subject only to idiosyncratic risk, which can be diversified in large pools of lives. Even if there is only idiosyncratic risk, at older ages in the tails of the survival distribution, the number of lives surviving becomes small and the variability in benefit payments and liability values increases. This is exacerbated by systematic risk from uncertain but common rates of improvement across individuals.

Many models of systematic mortality risk have been proposed. These vary from models such as the Lee–Carter model (Lee and Carter 1992) and variations, to models that model random changes in a parametric survival curve (Cairns et al. 2006), to those that model the dynamics of mortality rates in a financial framework similar to that used for interest rate models (Biffis 2005). These models do not include allowance for heterogeneity. Individuals of the same age are assumed to experience the same aggregate mortality rate.

Increasingly, attention is being devoted to the impact of mortality heterogeneity and its effect on insurers and pension funds (Lin and Liu 2007; Liu and Lin 2012 ; Su and Sherris 2012). Along with systematic mortality risk, this mortality heterogeneity has implications for the solvency and tail risk of annuity and pension providers. Even if there were no systematic, or aggregate, mortality risk, heterogeneity generates variability in future experience and volatility in financial results. Heterogeneity requires underwriting of risks to avoid adverse selection. Without full information about the risks that insurers underwrite, the financial consequences of adverse selection has its greatest impact for annuities in the tail of the survival distributions long after the annuities have been issued.

Solvency and tail risk for life annuities and pensions have two dimensions. First, there is an effect on insurer profitability from adverse experience as well as an impact on variability at the older ages. Trends in mortality that arise from uncertain mortality improvements and from the deaths of less healthy lives in a heterogeneous pool have their greatest influence at the older ages. Second, the volatility of financial results arises from both systematic mortality changes, with higher volatility experienced at older ages, and from heterogeneity, also producing higher volatility at older ages (Su and Sherris 2012; Meyricke and Sherris 2013).

There are many different approaches to modeling mortality heterogeneity. Recent advances have seen the calibration and application of more advanced models in the form of Markov aging models (Lin and Liu 2007; Liu and Lin 2012; Su and Sherris 2012) that are extensions of the Le Bras model (1976). The other, more commonly used, approach is to apply frailty models to capture unobserved heterogeneity (Vaupel et al. 1979).

In this chapter, we develop and apply a stochastic Markov aging model of heterogeneity that also includes systematic mortality risk, calibrated to population aggregate mortality and health data. We compare results with a well-known frailty model and the Le Bras–Markov multiple state model to assess model risk, neither of which includes systematic mortality risk. These models are used to quantify solvency and tail risk for a portfolio of life annuities using risk measures standard deviation and value-at-risk for fund values at the older ages. Results illustrate the effects of heterogeneity and model risk on the assessment of longevity risk for these portfolios, as well as the impact of selection and pool size.

Mortality Heterogeneity Models

The main approaches to modeling mortality heterogeneity that we consider are frailty models and Markov multiple state models. Frailty models treat heterogeneity as unobservable. An often-used frailty model is that of Vaupel et al. (1979), where an individual is assumed to have frailty Z at age x with force of mortality: $\mu(x, Z) = Zae^{bx} + c$. The frailty factor Z is Gamma distributed $Z \sim Gamma(1, \sigma^2)$ so that the average frailty at age x is

$$\bar{Z}(x) = \left(1 + \sigma^2 \frac{a}{b}\left(e^{bx} - 1\right)\right)^{-1}$$

and the average force of mortality is given by $\bar{\mu}(x) = \bar{Z}(x)ae^{bx} + c$.

The Markov multiple state mortality model was developed by Le Bras (1976), who used a continuous time Markov chain with an infinite number of states and a discrete state space to model senescence. The model starts at state 1 and progresses to state 2, 3, etc. In any state, the rate of jump to the next higher state and the rate of death are assumed proportional to the state number. All individuals start in state 0 at time 0. In state i, the transition rate to state $i + 1$ is $\lambda_0 + i\lambda$, and the transition to death (an absorbing state) is $\mu_0 + i\mu$. For the Le Bras model, the probability of being in state i at time t is (Yashin et al. 2000):

$$P_i(t) = \frac{e^{-(\lambda_0 + \mu_0)t}}{i!}\left(\frac{\lambda - \lambda e^{-(\lambda + \mu)t}}{\lambda + \mu}\right)^i \prod_{k=1}^{i}\left(\frac{\lambda_0}{\lambda} + (k - 1)\right)$$

The probability of survival to time t, given the individual was in state n at time 0, is given by

$$S_n(t) = e^{-(\lambda_0 + \mu_0 + n(\lambda + \mu))t}\left(\frac{\lambda + \mu}{\mu + \lambda e^{-(\lambda + \mu)t}}\right)^{\frac{\lambda_0 + n\lambda}{\lambda}}$$

Yashin et al. (1994) show the representation of the average force of mortality in the fixed frailty model to be equivalent to the Le Bras model.[1] Markov aging models allow for heterogeneity because of the differing mortality rates in the different states.

There have been several applications of Markov chains to failure time distributions in mortality, also known as phase-type distributions. Lin and Liu (2007) devised a deterministic survival rate model based on a Markov aging process. Each state in the model represents a 'physiological age,' as opposed to calendar age. The model assumes that there is a maximum physiological age, n, and that $n = 200$ is appropriate as an approximation to the potentially infinite aging process in the Le Bras model. Subsequently, Su and Sherris (2012) developed the Lin and Liu model (2007) to assess population heterogeneity for life annuity portfolios and relate states and mortality rates to aggregate population mortality.

These two Markov aging models have parameters that capture the changes in observed period life tables. Liu and Lin (2012) make the model stochastic by adding a time change component. The small number of states and the transition matrix facilitate the incorporation of health information. The time change allows a probabilistic statement of mortality uncertainty. The initial distribution is estimated from health condition data, and closed forms for the expected value and variance of the survival probability exist if the stochastic time change process has a closed form moment generating function.

These Markov aging models are the basis of the model used in what follows. We extend the Su and Sherris (2012) approach to include health states calibrated to health conditions data as well as aggregate population mortality data. We also subordinate this underlying model to a Gamma time change, so that survival distributions are stochastic. The underlying model allows an assessment of model risk by comparison of results for solvency and tail risk with the other models of heterogeneity. The subordinated model shows the significance of heterogeneity if mortality is stochastic.

The Markov aging model used has a time-inhomogeneous five-state transition matrix fitted to ages 30–110. Transition occurs as a Markov process from one transient state to its next state, or to the absorbing state, and the model takes into account both health status and mortality data. Aggregate survival rates are determined by a deterministic underlying multiple states survival model $S_0(\cdot)$ and a time change process γ_t. The underlying model assumes the individual mortality process moves through a series of deteriorating health statuses. Health and mortality is made stochastic by a random time change. The aggregate survival rate at time t is $S_t = S_0(\gamma_t)$. Time until death in this system has a phase-type representation (π, T), where π is the initial distribution on the transient states, and T is the states' transition rates matrix. The probability of survival up to time x is $S_0 = \pi \exp(Tx) e$ where e is a column of ones. Under the assumption that deterioration in health is more likely than improvement, transition is assumed to be acyclic. Since all acyclic phase-type distributions have a Coxian representation, T can be written as:

$$\begin{pmatrix} -(\lambda_{1,t}+q_{1,t}) & \lambda_{1,t} & 0 & 0 & 0 \\ 0 & -(\lambda_{2,t}+q_{2,t}) & \lambda_{2,t} & 0 & 0 \\ 0 & 0 & -(\lambda_{3,t}+q_{3,t}) & \lambda_{3,t} & 0 \\ 0 & 0 & 0 & -(\lambda_{4,t}+q_{4,t}) & \lambda_{4,t} \\ 0 & 0 & 0 & 0 & -q_5 \end{pmatrix}$$

where

$$q_{1,t} = q_{2,t} = q_{3,t} = q_{4,t} = a \times e^{bt}.$$

$$q_{5,t} = a \times e^{bt} + c$$

$$\lambda_{i,t} = m_i \times (t-1) + n_i \quad for\ i = 1...4$$

$$a,b,c,m,n \geq 0$$

Here, $\lambda_{i,t}$ is the rate of transition from state i to state $i+1$ at time t, and $q_{i,t}$ is the rate of transition from state i to the absorbing (death) state at time t. The time change is modeled as a Gamma process which is non-decreasing, additive, and has a closed form moment generating function. It is defined as starting at $\gamma_0 = 0$ with independent increments $(\gamma_{t+s} - \gamma_t)$, which are Gamma distributed with mean s and variance vs.

The Markov aging model is used in two ways. Its deterministic component (i.e. the underlying Markov process) is used for comparisons with other deterministic heterogeneity models. The subordinated model is used to assess the impact of systematic mortality risk.

Data

Modeling mortality heterogeneity requires a basis to divide the population into groups of individuals anticipated to experience similar rates of mortality, distinct from other groups. Calibration of these models requires information about the health status distribution and survival probability. This can be done using socioeconomic status, health conditions, or health risk factors. Socioeconomic status and income level are related to mortality, yet the correlation is not definitive and mortality is driven by more specific factors than socioeconomic status. Health risk factors based on individual panel data can be used to relate failure time to health characteristics of individuals. Characteristics include various factors such as diastolic and systolic blood pressure, body mass index, cholesterol, blood sugar, vital capacity, and cigarettes per day. This approach has significant data availability imitations at a population level.

Health risk factors such as obesity or smoking habits are less effective in capturing heterogeneity than existing health conditions such as heart disease or lung cancer. In addition, health condition data is more readily available than health risk factor information, which requires both the risk factor and its duration. The ideal form of data is that which records a cohort's experience through time. However, health data are generally only available for the population alive in a particular year, so period mortality data must be used to match period health data.

For calibration of the Markov aging model, the data used for estimating severity of the health conditions and health status distribution were derived from a variety of sources. The National Health Survey (NHS) data (ABS 2009) are used to capture prevalence of long-term conditions, at ten-year intervals from age 15 to 75, from years 2007–2008. We also use estimated average dementia prevalence by Ritchie et al. (1992) in five-year age intervals from 60 to 85. The Australian Cancer Incidence and Mortality Books (ACIMB) (AIHW 2012) are used for cancer incidence and mortality for five-year age intervals up to 85, to the year 2008. Mortality by cause data (other than cancer) was taken from the following sources: the WHO mortality database (WHO 2010) for Australia gives the number of deaths from a health condition, for five-year age intervals until 95, to the year 2006; the Australian Bureau of Statistics Causes of Death database (ABSCD) (ABS 2013) gives number of deaths from each condition, aggregate of all ages, to the year 2010. Infectious diseases or accidents were not taken into account, which means that the calibrated model assumes all individuals to have the same exposure to these baseline risks.

In order to determine population health status distributions, health conditions are ranked according to their severity and divided into five groups (or health states); the distribution of the population for these five health states was estimated from the prevalence of health conditions. Health conditions are ranked by the probability of death from cause-of-death data given the prevalence of a condition. Since deaths by cause from WHO are only available up to 2006, and prevalence is only available for 2007–2008, the 2006 WHO data are scaled by the ratio of 2008 to 2006 numbers of deaths in ABSCD.

Some assumptions are made in estimating the proportion of the population in each health state. It is assumed that the prevalence of a condition for individuals for a ten-year age range could be used to represent the expected prevalence at the midpoint age, since health data are available at ten-year intervals, but the model requires distributions across ages. It is also assumed that long-term conditions are independent and that for a person affected by more than one condition, the highest death rate among all of the conditions is assumed to be the death rate. The proportion of individuals with a specific condition as their most severe condition is assumed equal to the proportion of individuals not affected by any worse condition multiplied by the proportion of the total population affected by the specific condition.

Aggregate mortality data are taken from the Human Mortality Database (HMD 2013). The 2008 Australian period life table (male and female combined) is used for coherence with health data.

Calibration of Mortality Heterogeneity Models

Figure 7.1 shows the survival curve for the fitted Le Bras model and the Australian 2008 life table used for calibration. The model provides a better fit to the survival curve when fitted for ages above 20. The parameter values estimated for the Le Bras model 20+ are given in Table 7.1. The model is equivalent to the frailty model.

The Markov aging model is fitted using observed health and survival distributions as expected values. The sum of squared differences with the model's estimation of $E(S(t))$ is minimized. A lower limit of 0.001 is imposed for v to prevent a near zero denominator in the numerical estimation procedure. Other parameters are assumed to have a lower limit of 0. Parameter estimates for the Markov aging model are given in Table 7.2.

Figure 7.2 shows the fitted survival curve. Figure 7.3 shows the fitted versus observed data by the health states for the model. The model provides a good fit to the survival distribution and health states data used for calibration.

Solvency and Tail Risk

In order to assess solvency and tail risk arising from heterogeneity, a portfolio of life annuities is projected using simulation. Annuity contracts are assumed to be written at age 65 under differing assumptions about the health status of the lives purchasing the annuity. The annuities pay an annual payment of $1 for as long as the individual lives. Expenses and other costs are not included. The distribution of health status is generated from each model. For comparison purposes health status ranges are aggregated into comparable groups for the purpose of calculating premiums and simulating annual balances.

Panel A. Le Bras fitted to ages 0 to 105.

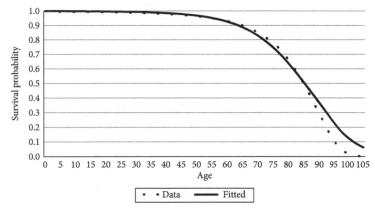

Panel B. Le Bras fitted to ages 20 to 105.

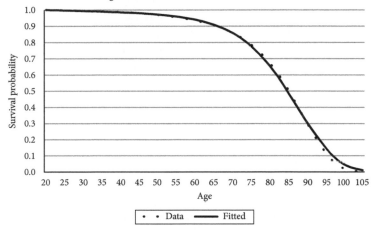

Figure 7.1. Survival curve fit of the Le Bras model.

Notes: Figures show the fit of the Le Bras model to the 2008 Australian life table survival curve (male and female combined). The model provides a better fit to survival data starting from age 20 than that starting from birth.

Panel A. Le Bras fitted to ages 0–105.
Panel B. Le Bras fitted to ages 20–105.

Source: Authors' calculations.

Premiums are calculated to be equal to the actuarial expected present value of all payments. Survival rates conditional on health states are used to allow for selection. Population average survival rates are used for the cases where no anti-selection is assumed for mixed health status groups. A fixed interest rate of 3 percent *per annum* is assumed along with an assumption of random investment returns.

TABLE 7.1 Parameter estimates for Le Bras
Model fitted to ages above 20

λ_0	0.489972
μ_0	0.000608
λ	0.117869
μ	0.00001

Notes: The table shows the parameters estimates
for the Le Bras model based on the Yashin et al.
parameterization (1994). Parameter definitions
are given in the text.
Source: Authors' calculations.

TABLE 7.2 Parameter estimates for subordinated
Markov model fitted to ages 30–110.

a	0.000022
b	0.143882
c	0.907697
m_1	0.001753
n_1	0.004911
m_2	0.000919
n_2	0.020675
m_3	0.00038
n_3	0.046633
m_4	0
n_4	0.032396
v	0.146892

Notes: The table shows the parameters estimates for
the subordinated Markov aging model. Parameter
definitions are given in the text.
Source: Authors' calculations.

Random returns are simulated using a model (including calibration) adopted
directly from Nirmalendran et al. (2012). Assets were assumed allocated according to the Australian Prudential Regulation Authority statistics (APRA 2010) of
5.5 percent in cash, 86.8 percent in bonds, and 7.7 percent in stocks (rebalanced
every year). Cash rates and stock prices are modeled with geometric Brownian
motion. Short rates generated by the Vasicek model are used for single-period bond
returns. For the random returns case, premiums are calculated with discount factor based on bonds yields. However, unlike Nirmalendran et al. (2012), the market
price of investment risk is not included.

The distributions of healthy states for the Markov aging model are given in Table
7.3. These percentages are calibrated to the health data. The table shows the shift

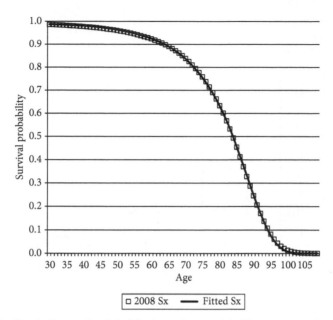

Figure 7.2. Survival curve fit of the Markov aging model of heterogeneity based on both health and survival data.

Note: Figure shows the fit of the Markov aging model used in the chapter compared to the 2008 Australian life table survival curve. The model fit is shown for ages 40 and above.

Source: Authors' calculations.

from the healthier states to the less healthy states and eventually to the death states with increase in age. The percentage in the healthiest state diminishes rapidly from age 50 to 70, with a reduction from 47.5 percent to 14.5 percent. By age 70 the distribution across health states has shifted to the less healthy states with higher mortality.

Figure 7.4 shows the distribution of heterogeneity at age 65 given by the three models by showing the distribution of expected future lifetimes for the different models. The Vaupel frailty model and the Le Bras Markov model forecast a higher proportion with higher life expectancies than the Markov aging model. The Markov aging model reflects a calibration to health status data as well as population mortality. By not reflecting health status, the expected future lifetime is overstated in the other models.

Impact of Heterogeneity and Adverse Self-selection

The impact of heterogeneity is illustrated for the three models in Figure 7.5 with a comparison of a 'best health' case and a 'mixed' case using the standard deviation of the fund values in the older ages for a pool size of 1,000 individuals. The best

Panel A. Age 40.

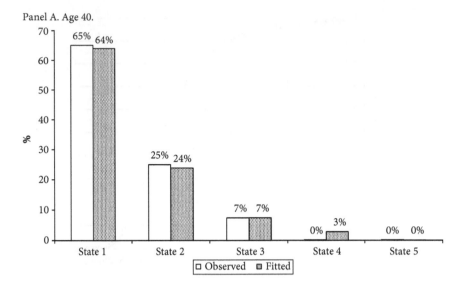

Panel B. Age 60.

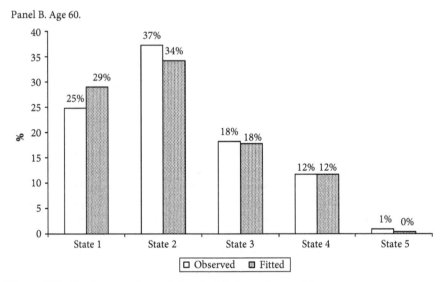

Figure 7.3. Fitted versus observed data for Markov aging model.

Note: Figure shows distribution of health states for the Markov aging model used in the paper compared to the actual data use dot fit the model. The model fit is shown for ages 40 and 60.

Panel A. Age 40.
Panel B. Age 60.

Source: Authors' calculations.

TABLE 7.3 Markov aging model: Percentage distribution of health states for ages 40–70

	State: 1(%)	2(%)	3(%)	4(%)	5(%)	Deceased (%)
Age:						
30	72.7	20.5	5.0	0.4	0.0	1.3
40	65.1	25.0	7.4	0.2	0.2	2.1
50	47.5	31.3	12.5	4.7	0.3	3.7
60	24.8	37.3	18.2	11.7	0.9	7.1
70	14.5	29.6	20.4	18.3	2.2	14.9

Notes: The table shows the distribution of health states for varying ages based on the Markov aging model. Health state 1 is the best health state with the lowest mortality rate, and 5 is the worst health state with the highest mortality rate.

Source: Authors' calculations.

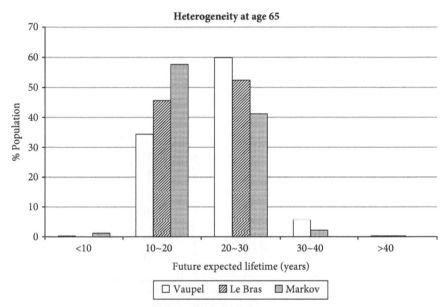

Figure 7.4. Heterogeneity based on expected future lifetimes at age 65.

Note: The figure shows the distribution of future expected lifetime according to the three modes used in the text to quantify heterogeneity of mortality. The Markov model has a noticeably different distribution from the other models, reflecting its calibration to both health and survival data.

Source: Authors' calculations.

health case assumes that only individuals in the best health class of the Markov aging model purchase annuities. The mixed cases assume a portfolio of annuitants with similar health proportions to that of the population purchases annuities with an average premium for the group, and there is no selection based on health.

The standard deviation of the annuity pool amount increases with older ages for all models. Even though frailty models imply reduced relative heterogeneity in

Panel A. Markov model standard deviation.

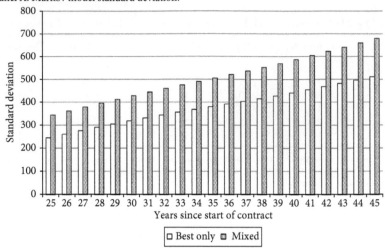

Panel B. Le Bras model standard deviation.

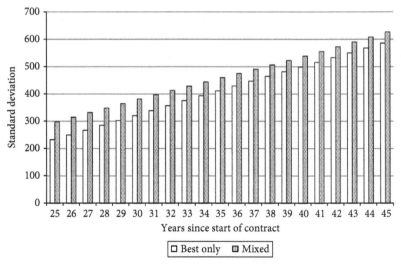

Figure 7.5. Standard deviation risk measure for the annuity pool amount at older ages for the different models of heterogeneity for a pool size of 1,000.

Note: The figures show standard deviation of the annuity fund for annuities commencing at age 65 at the older ages for a pool size of 1,000 individuals. The standard deviations are shown for the three different models and for the assumption that only the best health individuals purchase annuities (best only), and also assuming a mixture of health states representative of the population purchase annuities (mixed).

Panel A. Markov model standard deviation.
Panel B. Le Bras model standard deviation.
Panel C. Vaupel model standard deviation.

Source: Authors' calculations.

Panel C. Vaupel model standard deviation.

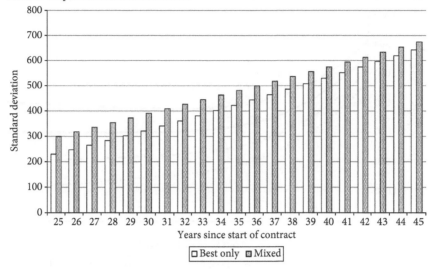

Figure 7.5. (*Continued*)

mortality at older ages, there is an increase in variability of pool fund amounts. The Le Bras and Vaupel models produce similar results, with the Vaupel model producing higher standard deviations.

The most interesting aspect shown here is the Markov aging model, whose measure of heterogeneity is specifically calibrated to population health data. The heterogeneity for cases when only people in the best health states purchase annuities is significantly lower than for the mixed-population pool. These differences do not arise in the other two models, where heterogeneity in health is derived from aggregate survival rates only.

Figure 7.6 shows the Markov aging model results for the best health state compared with the mixed health case in order to illustrate the differences in the expected value of the fund as well as the variability. The best health case expected value starts higher but both fund values converge to zero, since the premiums are fair. In the mixed population case the distribution of fund sizes is much wider, with significantly higher probabilities of adverse fund sizes.[2] This illustrates how the strategy of writing annuities for a select group of individuals reduces the volatility arising from heterogeneity and is a lower risk strategy for an annuity provider.

In practice individuals can self-select against the annuity provider. This is referred to as adverse selection. To consider this we assume that the premium charged is based on the mixed population distribution of health states but individuals purchase annuities based on their health state. Thus lives in better health than the mixed group find the annuity rate attractive and purchased annuities. As shown in Figure 7.7, the effect of this anti-selection is that the average fund size

Panel A. Best health state only annuity fund balance.

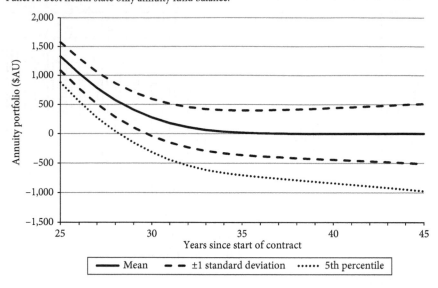

Panel B. Mixed population annuity fund balance.

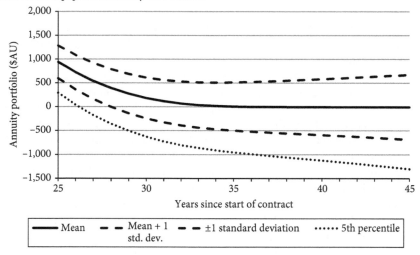

Figure 7.6. Balance of annuity fund for the best health state and the population mix showing uncertainty and downside risk.

Note: The figures show the annuity fund for annuities commencing at age 65 at the older ages for a pool size of 50 individuals. Panel A shows an annuity portfolio with only the best health state and Panel B shows annuities assuming a mixture of health states representative of the population purchase annuities (mixed).

Panel A. Best health state only annuity fund balance.
Panel B. Mixed population annuity fund balance.

Source: Authors' calculations.

Panel A. Mean balance.

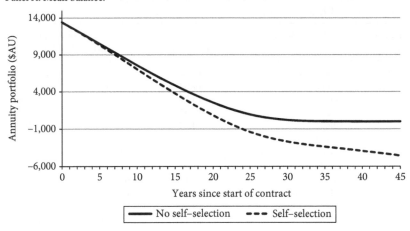

Panel B. Standard deviation.

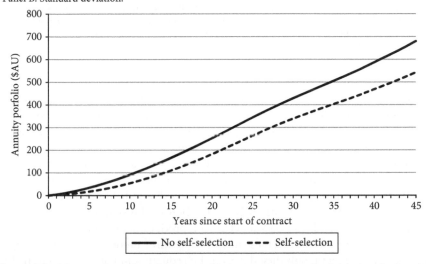

Figure 7.7. Mean and standard deviation of balance of annuity fund showing the impact of adverse selection.

Note: The figures show the annuity fund for annuities commencing at age 65 for a pool size of 50 individuals assuming that a population annuity rate is charged. The top figure shows the mean balance and the bottom figure the standard deviation. Two cases are shown: one where there is no self (adverse) selection and the other where only the healthy lives purchase annuities.

Panel A. Mean balance.
Panel B. Standard deviation.

Source: Authors' calculations.

TABLE 7.4 Annuity premiums and tail risk measures assuming a fixed investment return for different models of heterogeneity

Mortality model	Heterogeneity	Annuity premium	Risk measures at age 110 Stdev	95% VaR
Markov	best health only	15.22	511.76	821.67
	state 2	14.94	519.94	855.21
	state 3	13.97	566.82	922.96
	state 4	11.45	687.93	1112.05
	state 5	0.64	118.03	199.83
	mixed	13.42	682.91	1122.83
	mixed w/self-selection	13.42	540.05	5452.06
Le Bras	best health only	17.49	588.21	947.61
	mixed	14.15	634.72	1052.37
	mixed w/self-selection	14.15	608.96	6816.63
Vaupel	best health only	18.39	639.50	1029.39
	mixed	14.72	676.94	1130.14
	mixed w/self-selection	14.72	656.93	7369.68

Notes: The table shows the premium for a life annuity of 1 *per annum* and tail risk measures for a pool of 1,000 individuals aged 65 assuming different pool compositions for health statuses for a fixed investment return of 3% *per annum*. Results are shown for the different deterministic models of heterogeneity. See text.

Source: Authors' calculations.

drops significantly, as expected, and the chance of major losses increases. Adverse selection does produce lower standard deviations of pool fund balances, but this is primarily because the mean level of the fund falls more rapidly and the self-selected group is less heterogeneous than the mixed group.

Table 7.4 shows the premiums and risk measures at the ultimate age of 110 for the cases of best health, mixed health, and adverse selection for a pool size of 1,000. Annuity premiums vary significantly according to health state in the Markov aging model. They vary from 15.22 for the best health state to 0.64 in the worst health state. The Le Bras and Vaupel models produce higher premiums, reflecting the higher life expectancy in these models. The three models agree on the impact of self-selection, although they differ on the reduction in volatility when the best health group is priced separately. These results illustrate the extent of model risk in allowing for heterogeneity when assessing a pricing strategy and solvency of an annuity pool. Large variations in premiums occur as well as in tail measures of risk.

Impact of Random Investment Returns

Table 7.5 shows the annuity premiums and risk measures for pool sizes of 1,000 assuming random investment returns. Premiums are lower since the average interest rate in the stochastic model is higher than the deterministic 3 percent used in Table 7.4. The best health annuity premium for the Markov aging model is now 12.68,

TABLE 7.5 Annuity premiums and tail risk measures assuming random investment returns for different models of heterogeneity

Mortality model	Heterogeneity	Annuity premium	Risk measures at age 110 Stdev 95% VaR	
Markov	best health only	12.68	4,570.53	7,372.69
	state 2	12.49	4,454.89	7,150.40
	state 3	11.80	4,250.96	6,755.93
	state 4	9.85	3,494.09	5,688.37
	state 5	0.63	386.70	638.02
	mixed	11.34	4,096.90	6,528.22
	mixed w/self-selection	11.34	3,912.58	17,878.91
Le Bras	best health only	13.93	5,480.72	9,047.16
	mixed	11.84	4,328.60	6,910.74
	mixed w/self-selection	11.84	4,218.89	19,635.98
Vaupel	best health only	14.35	5,725.39	9,188.87
	mixed	12.14	4,500.81	7,286.31
	mixed w/self-selection	12.14	4,428.48	20,553.27

Notes: The table shows the premium for a life annuity of 1 *per annum* and tail risk measures for a pool of 1,000 individuals aged 65 assuming different pool compositions of health statuses for a random investment return. Results are shown for the different deterministic models of heterogeneity. See text.
Source: Authors' calculations.

compared to 13.93 for the Le Bras model and 14.35 for the Vaupel model. Risk is substantially increased with the addition of investment return risk. The Le Bras and Vaupel models show similar risk measures for the different cases of selection and these are higher than the Markov aging model. For the Markov aging model the better health states contribute significantly to the overall fund risk measures.

Impact of Stochastic (Systematic) Mortality

The subordinated Markov aging model incorporates stochastic mortality through a Gamma time change. This changes the survival probabilities for all individuals in a random manner. The result is a distribution of survival probabilities for each health state. The degree of uncertainty in future survival probabilities is determined by the variance v of the Gamma time change.

Table 7.6 shows the impact of the Gamma time change parameter on the fund standard deviation at age 110. The annuity fund tail risk is not very sensitive to this assumption. Higher values of the parameter result in reduced standard deviations for a mixed health state fund as compared with the best health only case.

Impact of Pool Size

Table 7.7 compares the standard deviation at age 110 for pool sizes 100 to 100,000 given by the Markov aging model with and without the stochastic time change.

TABLE 7.6 Standard deviation of annuity fund for different assumptions of stochastic mortality risk

	Stdev at age 110	
v	Best health	Mixed
0.01	956.16	1,027.44
0.05	1,859.89	1,817.99
0.1	2,603.98	2,509.03
0.5	5,660.73	5,474.22

Notes: The table shows the standard deviation for a life annuity fund of a pool of 1,000 individuals age 65 assuming different pool compositions for health statuses for annual payments of $1 and a fixed investment return of 3% *per annum*. See text.

Source: Authors' calculations.

TABLE 7.7 Standard deviation at age 110 for different pool sizes using Markov model without and with stochastic mortality risk

Pool size	Deterministic Markov	Subordinated Markov
100	215.54	354.96
1,000	684.12	2,954.66
10,000	2,147.19	28,913.66
100,000	6,832.39	287,749.89

Notes: The table shows the standard deviation of the fund at age 110 for life annuity of 1 *per annum* for best health individuals age 65, assuming a fixed investment return of 3% *per annum*. The stochastic model assumes variance of Gamma time change $v = 0.095$. See text.

Source: Authors' calculations.

With deterministic mortality rates, standard deviation increases approximately in proportion to the square root of pool size, showing a diversification of idiosyncratic mortality risk. Thus as the pool size grows by 10 times from 1,000 to 10,000, the tail risk, as given by the fund standard deviation at age 110, increases by approximately 3.16 times (square root of 10). In contrast, with the inclusion of systematic risk, the effect of diversification of mortality risk increases by 9.8 times (almost 10). Systematic mortality risk dominates as the pool size increases.

Figure 7.8 shows how the impact of systematic mortality risk increases through the older ages. The standard deviation of the pool amount for ages above 90 for the deterministic and subordinated Markov aging models, for pool sizes 500 and 1,000, increases significantly. The effect of larger pool sizes at the older ages is clearly seen.

Panel A. Without systematic risk.

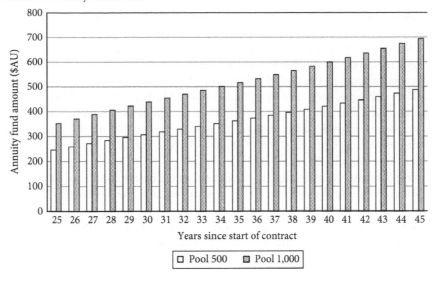

Panel B. With systematic risk.

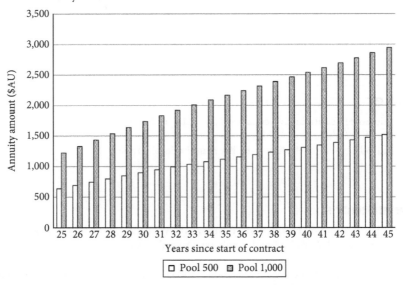

Figure 7.8. Standard deviation of annuity pool amount at older ages for the Markov aging model.

Note: The figures show the standard deviation of the annuity fund for annuities of $1 *per annum* for best health individuals aged 65, assuming a fixed investment return of 3 percent *per annum*.

Panel A. Without systematic risk.
Panel B. With systematic risk.

Source: Authors' calculations.

Conclusion

This chapter has deployed a recently developed Markov aging model for mortality heterogeneity, along with more commonly used frailty models, to show the impact of heterogeneity and systematic mortality risk on annuity fund values at the older ages, the tail of the mortality distribution. Model risk for longevity arises from a misspecification of the underlying process being modeled. Systematic mortality risk models have been developed and applied. Markov aging models for heterogeneity have also been developed. Standard models of heterogeneity do not capture observed health differentials or the effect of systematic mortality risk. Using a model that captures only one of these aspects of mortality risk has limitations because of model risk.

We illustrate the impact of this model risk in the determination of annuity premiums and fund risk measures. Heterogeneity results in a wide variation in annuity premiums depending on health status. Selection of lives in better health states by insurers when writing life annuities is a less risky strategy than writing annuities on all health states in the population, even if premium rates vary by health state and there is no adverse selection. Adverse selection negatively impacts both profitability and fund risk.

Increasing pool sizes increase tail risk almost linearly with the size of the pool for the cases where the Markov aging mortality model includes systematic risk. This effect is not captured by standard models of heterogeneity where mortality pooling results in only a square root of pool size increase in fund risk.

Notes

1. The two are equivalent when: $a = [(\lambda_0) / (\lambda)] \times \mu$, $b = \lambda + \mu$, $c = \mu_0 - [(\lambda_0) / (\lambda)] \times \mu$, $\sigma^2 = [(\lambda) / (\lambda_0)]$.
2. The other two models show a smaller magnitude; see Table 7.3.

References

Australian Institute of Health and Welfare (AIHW) (2012). *Australian Cancer Incidence and Mortality (ACIM) Books* [website]. Canberra, Australia: Australian Government. <http://www.aihw.gov.au/acim-books/>.

Australian Bureau of Statistics (ABS) (2009). '4364.0—National Health Survey: Summary of Results, 2007–2008 (Reissue),' *Statistics* [website]. Canberra, Australia: ABS, 25 August. <http://www.abs.gov.au/AUSSTATS/abs@.nsf/productsbyCatalogue/1A1B89187E1D2B13CA2575B0001399C8?OpenDocument>.

Australian Bureau of Statistics (ABS) (2013). '3303.0—Causes of Death, Australia, 2010,' *Statistics* [website]. Canberra, Australia: ABS. <http://www.abs.gov.au/AUSSTATS/abs@.nsf/DetailsPage/3303.02010>.

Australian Prudential Regulatory Authority (APRA) (2010). *Half Yearly Life Insurance Bulletin, June 2010*. Sydney, Australia: APRA.

Blake, D., C. Courbage, R. MacMinn, and M. Sherris (2011). 'Longevity Risk and Capital Markets: The 2010–2011 Update,' *The Geneva Papers*, 36: 489–500.

Biffis, E. (2005). 'Affine Processes for Dynamic Mortality and Actuarial Valuations,' *Insurance: Mathematics and Economics*, 37(3): 443–468.

Cairns, A. J. G., D. Blake, and K. Dowd (2006). 'A Two-factor Model for Stochastic Mortality with Parameter Uncertainty: Theory and Calibration,' *Journal of Risk and Insurance*, 73(4): 687–718.

Human Mortality Database (HMD) (2013). 'Australia,' *The Human Mortality Database* [website]. Berkeley, CA: University of California, Berkeley, Department of Demography, and Rostock, Germany: Max Planck Institute for Demographic Research. <http://www.mortality.org/cgi-bin/hmd/country.php?cntr=AUS&level=1>.

Le Bras, H. (1976). 'Lois de Mortalité et Âge Limite,' *Population*, 33(3): 655–691.

Lee, R. D. and L. Carter (1992). 'Modeling and Forecasting U.S. Mortality,' *Journal of the American Statistical Association*, 87(419): 659–671.

Lin, X. S. and X. Liu (2007). 'Markov Aging process and Phase-type Law of Mortality,' *North American Actuarial Journal*, 11(4): 92–109.

Liu, X. and X. S. Lin (2012). 'A Subordinated Markov Model for Stochastic Mortality,' *European Actuarial Journal*, 2(1): 105–127.

Meyricke, R. and M. Sherris (2013). 'The Determinants of Mortality Heterogeneity and Implications for Pricing Underwritten Annuities,' ARC Center of Excellence in Population Ageing Research (CEPAR) Working Paper 2013/05. Sydney, Australia: CEPAR. Forthcoming in *Insurance: Mathematics and Economics*.

Nirmalendran, M., M. Sherris, and K. Hanewald (2012). 'Solvency Capital, Pricing and Capitalization Strategies of Life Annuity Providers,' ARC Center of Excellence in Population Ageing Research (CEPAR) Working Paper 2012/14. Sydney, Australia: CEPAR.

Njenga, C. N. and M. Sherris (2011). 'Longevity Risk and the Econometric Analysis of Mortality Trends and Volatility,' *Asia-Pacific Journal of Risk and Insurance*, 5(2): 22–73.

Ritchie, K., D. Kildea, and J. M. Robine (1992). 'The Relationship Between Age and Prevalence of Senile Dementia: A Meta-analysis of Recent Data,' *International Journal of Epidemiology*, 21(4): 763–769.

Su, S. and M. Sherris (2012). 'Heterogeneity of Australian Population Mortality and Implications for a Viable Life Annuity Market,' *Insurance: Mathematics and Economics*, 51(2): 322–332.

Vaupel, J. W., K. G. Manton, and E. Stallard (1979). 'The Impact of Heterogeneity in Individual Frailty on the Dynamics of Mortality,' *Demography*, 16(3): 439–454.

World Health Organization (WHO) (2010). *International Statistical Classification of Diseases and Related Health Problems, 10th Revision* [website]. Geneva, Switzerland: WHO. <http://apps.who.int/classifications/icd10/browse/2010/en>.

Yashin, A. I., I. A. Iachine, and A. S. Begun (2000). 'Mortality Modeling: A Review,' *Mathematical Population Studies: An International Journal of Mathematical Demography*, 8(4): 305–332.

Yashin, A. I., J. W. Vaupel, and I. A. Iachine (1994). 'A Duality of Aging: The Equivalence of Mortality Models Based on Radically Different Concepts,' *Mechanisms of Aging and Development*, 74(1–2): 1–14.

Chapter 8

The Securitization of Longevity Risk and Its Implications for Retirement Security

Richard MacMinn, Patrick Brockett, Jennifer Wang, Yijia Lin, and Ruilin Tian

The simplest notion of individual longevity risk is that it is the possibility that one will outlive one's accumulated wealth. The risk of outliving one's accumulated wealth has many unpleasant consequences for individuals and societies, and because the risk is increasing it must be addressed. If an individual is covered by a defined contribution (DC) plan, the employee contributes to the plan until retirement. The employer may or may not match the employee's contribution. Accumulated wealth generated during the individual's working life yields the wealth that the individual will use to generate a retirement income stream. If the individual is covered by a defined benefit (DB) plan, the employer guarantees to provide the employee a designated amount of money upon retirement up until the employee's death. The employee may or may not contribute to the plan. The designated amount is based on the employee's earnings, length of employment, and age. With a DC plan, the employee is responsible for ensuring that enough money has been contributed to the account to avoid longevity risk. With a DB plan, the employer is liable for ensuring that the plan does not run out of money before the employee dies. In the first case the individual faces the longevity risk, while in the second case the pension provider faces the longevity risk.

Both plans have distinctive risks and in this chapter we examine the risks from the perspective of the individual and the institution. Longevity risk is important in part because of its size; international pension liabilities have been estimated at approximately $21 trillion. Longevity risk is also important because as life expectancy increases, individuals must increase contributions to their DC plans to mitigate longevity risk and the size of the necessary additional contribution is uncertain, as it depends in part on how life expectancies change over time. Hence the questions of interest here include: What happens to the financial well-being of a retired cohort in the event of an unexpected change in life expectancy or financial stability? What happens if it does not manage these risks? What happens if it does manage these risks using currently available instruments? How might it manage the longevity risk with longevity instruments?

In what follows, we first explore the meaning of longevity risk and consider its magnitude. Next we consider how mortality and longevity risks have been transformed from pure risks to speculative risks. Subsequently we examine longevity risk and financial market risks from the perspective of those who bear them; we show a need for more longevity instruments in the retail market and some of the benefits of the existing longevity instruments in the wholesale market for longevity risk. A final section concludes.

Longevity Risk

Risk can be defined as the negative consequences of uncertainty. Both uncertainty (multiple possible outcomes) and negative consequences are necessary prerequisites for risk to exist (Baranoff et al. 2009). Since most people find longer life desirable, the term 'longevity risk' needs further explication to provide the context in which longevity presents a 'risk' rather than a 'benefit' to individuals and/or institutions. Longevity risk is the risk that an individual life span or the average population life span will exceed expectations. The negative consequences of an extended life span can include outliving one's friends, diminished mobility and cognitive flexibility/focus, and outliving one's financial resources after retirement without the remedial possibility of rejoining the workforce to produce necessary income at the later date wherein the probability (or the eventuality) that financial assets will soon be depleted becomes recognized. Longevity risk has an unsystematic or idiosyncratic component, as well as a systematic component. The idiosyncratic component is sometimes described as the risk of an individual outliving one's accumulated wealth; Milevsky (2006) describes this as 'retirement ruin.' The systematic component corresponds to the more general hazard that people in the aggregate will live longer than expected (Oppers et al. 2012), thus causing strain on pensions, employers, and society in general. The systematic component is often referred to as aggregate longevity risk in the literature (MacMinn et al. 2006; Blake et al. 2013). The aggregate longevity risk discussed here is the risk of living longer than one expects; it is also a systematic risk because life expectations are themselves random variables.

From a financial perspective, the unsystematic component of longevity risk may be handled by holding a sufficiently diversified and adequately funded asset portfolio to decumulate during retirement. If life expectancy were certain, the individual could purchase an annuity certain designed to provide the desired cash flow for the certain life expectancy. Alternatively, the individual could purchase a bond with the desired flow of coupon payments and leave the principal repayment as a bequest to beneficiaries but because life expectancy is uncertain, the individual must design a portfolio of assets to provide a desired cash flow for an undetermined period of time. This portfolio may consist of equity, bonds, and possibly a life annuity. The life annuity is an asset that provides a specified cash flow for the remaining years of an individual's life. If the unsystematic component of life expectancy were the only risk faced by an individual then a life annuity may be shown to dominate other assets (Yaari 1965). However, the risk of outliving one's accumulated wealth is not the only unsystematic risk. Increased life expectancy includes morbidity (and other) risks as well, implying that just a life annuity would not cover a long-term illness, dementia, etc., and therefore a diversified asset portfolio is still needed (Sinclair and Smetters 2004; Horneff et al. 2009; MacMinn and Weber 2010; Chai et al. 2011).

From a financial perspective, at the firm or society level, aggregate longevity risk (the systematic component) must be managed. The management choices include bearing the risk or transferring or trading the risk to some other entity willing to bear it. In deciding among these alternatives, a determination must be made on how to price this risk transfer appropriately. This aspect of longevity risk might be thought of as a trend risk or the risk of underestimating life expectancy (Blake et al. 2013). Alternatively, as noted, we may think of life expectancy itself as a random variable. Oeppen and Vaupel (2002) show the record life expectancy for females as projected by a number of authors and organizations and report the rather surprising result that the record female life expectancy has increased by three months per year for more than 150 years. Hence, Oeppen and Vaupel also show that each historical life expectancy prediction has been wrong. With reference to 2005 mortality rates, they note that U.K. mortality rates had declined over the previous 10–15 years by over 2 percent *per annum* for the age groups over 60. Referring to the 2 percent decline and using government actuarial department (GAD) figures, Turner made the following comment about mortality rates (2006: 562):

> If they continue at that rate, male life expectancy at sixty-five, currently estimated at nineteen, will reach about thirty by 2050. If the rate accelerates to 3 percent, life expectancy would soar to 37 years. Only if it decelerates to 1 percent would the GAD's 2002-based principal projection of 22 years in 2050 be correct. So the GAD 2002 projection—a major increase from previous projections—nevertheless still assumed a major deceleration of mortality rate improvement.

The errors in life expectancy estimates noted here highlight the systematic risk of longevity risk and the magnitude of the risk.

It is important to understand the vast financial size of the longevity risk problem. Turner (2006) estimated £2.5 ($4.3) trillion in liabilities subject to longevity risk in the U.K. Swiss Re has since estimated $20.7 trillion in pension liabilities subject to longevity risk internationally (Burne 2011). Oppers et al. (2012: 8) provide a different perspective by calculating the cost of maintaining the retirement living standard due to aging and longevity shocks as a percentage of gross domestic product (GDP) for advanced and emerging countries. Using the demographic trends predicted by the United Nations, they note:

> In the baseline population forecast and with a 60 percent replacement rate, the annual cost rises from 5.3 percent to 11.1 percent of GDP in advanced

economies and from 2.3 percent to 5.9 percent of GDP in emerging economies ... Taken over the full period, the cumulative cost of this increase because
of aging in this scenario is about 100 percent of 2010 GDP for the advanced
economies and about half that amount in emerging economies.

The authors also observe that a longevity shock of three years would add almost
an additional 50 percent to these cumulative costs of aging by 2050. There is
uncertainty surrounding all of these predictions, but the magnitudes are hard
to ignore.

Ignoring longevity risk is indeed a significant problem. Oppers et al. (2012) use
data from the U.S. Department of Labor (DOL) to estimate the longevity risk faced
by DB plans. They report many plans used outdated mortality tables; the majority
of the plans used the 1983 Group Annuity Mortality (GAM) until recently. Using
out-of-date mortality tables exposes pension plans to longevity risk and risk of ruin.
Dushi et al. (2010) compare pension liability values based on the plans' longevity
assumptions versus the pension liability values forecast by the Lee–Carter mortality model and find that the outdated mortality tables could understate the pension
liability for a typical male participant by approximately 12 percent.

Longevity risk can be borne or transferred, in whole or in part. The retail market
for longevity risk allows consumers to transfer all or part of the risk with life annuities. In the U.K., this market amounts to £135 billion, but this is because consumers
are required by law to at least annuitize before they turn 75 (Loeys et al. 2007).[1] The
retail or life annuity market remains very small in the U.S. since there is no similar
requirement that individuals annuitize when they retire. In fact, this general lack of
a sizable life annuity market has been described as the annuity puzzle, since Yaari
(1965) and Davidoff et al. (2005), among others, have shown that in the absence
of a bequest motive, the life annuity instrument for retirement funding dominates
other asset choices.

A wholesale market for longevity risk would allow pension funds and insurers the
ability to transfer some of the longevity risk rather than bearing it. The U.K. wholesale market has been active and many of the transactions take the form of buyouts
and buy-ins.[2] In a buyout, there is a transfer of pension assets and liabilities for a
particular cohort; the cost of the buyout is the difference between the values of the
assets and the liabilities transferred. The difference between the asset and liability
values may be covered by a loan with a known cash flow that is well understood
by investors. In the buy-in, there is a bulk purchase of annuities from an insurer to
hedge the risk of the liabilities associated with one or more cohorts. This immu-
nizes the pension fund from the liability risk for the cohorts covered.

The retail and wholesale markets noted here do provide a transfer mechanism
for the market participants but the mechanisms are crude instruments. More than
one risk is transferred and the risks are aggregated rather than disaggregated; this
generates more concentration of risk and hence amplifies the eventual probability
of insolvency for those concentrations. Given the size of the longevity risks, this

becomes a new problem that is inconsistent with the history of financial markets. 'Indeed, the history of the development of risk instruments is a tale of the progressive separation of risks, enabling each to be borne in the least expensive way' (Kohn 1999: 2).

Securitization

Longevity risk has put corporations, governments, and individuals under a significant financial burden. One common way to manage this risk is securitization (i.e. isolating the cash flows that are linked to longevity risk and repackaging them into cash flows that are traded in capital markets). The earliest securitizations were 'block of business' securitizations used to capitalize expected future profits from a block of life business, such as to recover embedded values[3] or to exit from a geographical line of business. Cowley and Cummins (2005) introduced the early development of the securitization in life insurance. More recently, Blake et al. (2013) provided a more comprehensive and global overview of the emergence of the market in traded assets and liabilities linked to longevity and mortality and referred to this market as the New Life Market. They noted that the New Life Market would act as a catalyst to help facilitate the development of annuity markets both in the developed and the developing world and protect the long-term global viability of retirement income provision.

The idea of mortality securitization was initially proposed by Cox et al. (2000). The first mortality bond, known as Vita I, was issued by Swiss Re in 2003; it was designed to hedge mortality risk rather than to hedge longevity risk. Nevertheless, it provides an important successful example of a Life Market instrument. Vita I was a success, and led to additional bonds being issued to investors on less favorable terms.[4] Blake and Burrows (2001) were the first to advocate the use of mortality-linked securities to transfer longevity risk to capital markets. They suggested that the governments should help pension funds and insurance companies hedge their mortality risks by issuing survivor bonds. In 2004, the European Investment Bank (EIB) and BNP Paribas launched a longevity bond that was the first securitization instrument designed to transfer longevity risk; ultimately it was not issued due to insufficient demand. Design issues, such as the introduction of basis risk, pricing issues, institutional issues, and educational issues, were among the reasons why the EIB/BNP bond did not launch (Lin and Cox 2008).

The lack of success in issuing long-dated longevity bonds has led to a derivatives design effort. Various new securitization instruments and derivatives for longevity risk, such as mortality forwards, survivor swaps, survivor futures, and survivor options have received attention among academics and practitioners.[5] In 2007, J.P. Morgan introduced the first capital market derivative for a longevity hedge; it has become known as a 'q-forward.' A q-forward can be used to hedge the value of the pension liability or the associated cash flows. More complex, life-related derivatives can be constructed by using the q-forward as a basic building block. A portfolio of q-forwards can be used to replicate and to hedge the longevity exposure of an annuity or a pension liability or to hedge the mortality exposure for a book of life business. Following the introduction of a q-forward transaction, a longevity swap was used to exchange actual pension payments for a series of pre-agreed fixed payments. This particular swap was legally constituted as an insurance contract and was not a capital market instrument. There have been 16 publicly announced transactions of longevity swaps executed between 2007 and 2012 in the U.K. (Blake et al. 2013).

A Financial Market Model

Suppose the financial market consists of the S&P 500 index, the Merrill Lynch corporate bond index, and a three-month T-bill. Following Cox et al. (2013), we describe the return dynamics of the S&P 500 index as $A_{1,t}$ and the Merrill Lynch corporate bond index as $A_{2,t}$ at time t as a combination of Brownian motion and a compound Poisson process. The stochastic process of the three-month T-bill return $A_{3,t}$ is simply described as Brownian motion. The three returns are as follows:

$$A_{1,t+\Delta} \mid F_t = A_{1,t} \exp\left[(\alpha_1 - \frac{1}{2}\sigma_1^2 - \lambda_1 k_1)\Delta + \sigma_1 \Delta W_{1t}\right] \prod_{j>N_t^1}^{N_{t+\Delta}^1} Y_{1j} \qquad (8.1)$$

$$A_{2,t+\Delta} \mid F_t = A_{2,t} \exp\left[(\alpha_2 - \frac{1}{2}\sigma_2^2 - \lambda_2 k_2)\Delta + \sigma_2 \Delta W_{2t}\right] \prod_{j>N_t^2}^{N_{t+\Delta}^2} Y_{2j} \qquad (8.2)$$

$$A_{3,t+\Delta} \mid F_t = A_{3,t} \exp\left[(\alpha_3 - \frac{1}{2}\sigma_3^2)\Delta + \sigma_3 \Delta W_{3t}\right] \qquad (8.3)$$

where the constants $\alpha_1, \alpha_2, \alpha_3$ and $\sigma_1, \sigma_2, \sigma_3$ are the drift and volatility measures of the S&P 500 return, the Merrill Lynch corporate bond return, and the three-month T-bill rate given no jumps. The parameter $k_1 \equiv E(Y_1 - 1)$ is the expected percentage change in the S&P 500 return and k_2 is similarly defined for the Merrill Lynch corporate bond return if a Poisson event occurs. The parameters λ_1 and λ_2 are the mean numbers of arrivals per unit time of the Poisson processes N_t^1 and N_t^2 respectively. The jump size Y_{1j} or Y_{2j} is independent and identically distributed as a lognormal random variable with the size parameter m_1 and the volatility parameter S_1 or m_2 and S_2. Y_{1j} and Y_{2j} are independent for all i and j. The correlation between the standard Brownian motions of the S&P 500 index and the Merrill Lynch corporate bond index, W_{1t} and W_{2t}, is captured by the correlation coefficient ρ_{12} (i.e. $Cov(W_{1t}, W_{2t}) = \rho_{12}\sigma_1\sigma_2 t$).

We further assume the three-month T-bill is uncorrelated with either the S&P 500 index or the Merrill Lynch corporate bond index. Based on the annual data of the S&P 500 and the Merrill Lynch corporate bond provided by the DataStream

TABLE 8.1 Maximum likelihood parameter estimates of three pension assets using annual data

Parameter	Estimate	Parameter	Estimate	Parameter	Estimate
α_1	0.0866	α_2	0.0691	α_3	0.0515
σ_1	0.0864	σ_2	0.0547	σ_3	0.0329
λ_1	0.2742	λ_2	0.0505	ρ_{12}	0.6016
m_1	−0.3048	m_2	−0.1468		
s_1	0.0000	s_2	0.0000		

Notes: α_1, α_2, α_3 and σ_1, σ_2, σ_3 are the drift and volatility measures of the returns of the S&P 500 index, Merrill Lynch corporate bond index, and three-month T-bill. λ_1 and λ_2 are the mean numbers of arrivals per unit time of the Poisson processes for the returns of the S&P 500 and Merrill Lynch corporate bond indices. m_1 (m_2) and s_1 (s_2) are the size parameter and volatility parameter of the lognormal jump size for the return of S&P 500 (Merrill Lynch corporate bond) index. ρ_{12} is the correlation coefficient between the geometric Brownian motions of the returns of S&P 500 and Merrill Lynch corporate bond indices.

Source: Authors' calculations; see text.

and the three-month T-bill rates from FRED at Federal Reserve Bank of St. Louis from 1989 to 2010, we estimate models (8-1), (8-2), and (8-3) to obtain the model parameters. The estimated parameters are based on annual data and are reported in Table 8.1.

In what follows we will use these estimates to forecast returns for investor portfolios and for DB plans.

DC Plans

Given the financial market model developed in the previous section, suppose the individual investor or, equivalently, the retiree selects a portfolio $(\omega_1, \omega_2, \omega_3)$ in the S&P 500 index, the Merrill Lynch corporate bond index, and the three-month T-bill, respectively. Given our interest in longevity risk we investigate the length of a sustainable retirement period under the following two assumptions: (1) The individual invests in a TIAA-CREF-type lifecycle fund;[6] (2) The individual invests in a portfolio based on his own preferences.

Assumption (1): Investment in a TIAA-CREF-type Lifecycle Fund

The TIAA-CREF Lifecycle Funds consist of a series of target retirement date funds in five-year increments (2010, 2015, 2020, etc.), where an investor selects the fund that most closely matches his or her retirement year (e.g. a Lifecycle 2040

TABLE 8.2 Asset allocation at different ages (percentage)

Age	65	66	67	68	69	70	71	72	73	74	75 and older
Equity	50	49	48	47	46	45	44	43	42	41	40
Bonds	38	38	38	38	39	39	39	39	39	40	40
Risk Free	12	13	14	15	15	16	17	18	19	19	20

Note: All the numbers for equity, bonds, and risk-free assets are in percentages.
Source: TIAA-CREF (2013).

Fund is for an investor planning to retire in or around 2040). The funds are professionally managed and automatically adjust over time. For a retiree who invests in a TIAA-CREF-type Retirement Fund, the portfolio allocation at different ages is illustrated in Table 8.2.[7]

Assumption (2): Investment in a Self-selected Portfolio.

To consider all possible combinations of ω_1 and ω_2, we note that short selling is not allowed. In this case the investment in equity and bond indices satisfies $0 \leq \omega_1 + \omega_2 \leq 1$.

Investor Portfolio Analysis

We investigate the sustainable length of a retiree's retirement savings when the financial market experiences the following two scenarios:

Base Case

Suppose the financial market maintains the same trend and volatility that it has demonstrated over the past 20 years.[8] As such, we use the parameters in Table 8.1 calibrated with historical data to forecast the returns of the three pension assets. Under the Base case, the stock market will experience about $10/(1/0.2742) = 2.74$ crashes every ten years. The crashes in the bond market take place less frequently. Every ten years, an investment in corporate bonds is expected to face $10/(1/0.505) = 0.51$ crashes.[9]

BaseX2 Case

Suppose financial crashes happen twice as frequently as what the market experienced in the past 20 years. As such, we double the parameters λ_1, m_1, and s_1 for the stock index and λ_2, m_2, and s_2 for the bond index. Under the BaseX2 case, the stock and bond markets will experience 5.48 and 1.01 crashes every ten years.

We simulate the returns of three pension assets from $t = 0$ when the individual retires. Based on the United States male population mortality data from 1901 to 2007,[10] we assume the maximal age he can live is 103. For each yield path, we simulate 58 years after $t = 0$. Suppose the initial retirement fund at time 0 is $M_0 = M$ and the retiree withdraws W_d per period starting from $t = 1$. The value of the retirement fund M_t at time t depends on the amount invested in asset i at time $t-1$, $A_{i,t-1}$ and its return in period t and $r_{i,t}$. Hence,

$$M_t = \sum_{i=1}^{3} A_{i,t-1}(1 + r_{i,t}), \quad t = 1,2,3,... \tag{8.4}$$

and the following equation holds for the retiree:

$$\sum_{i=1}^{3} A_{i,t} = M_t - W_d, \quad t = 1,2,3,... \tag{8.5}$$

The sustainable length of the retirement fund, $\tilde{S}$, is calculated as:

$$\tilde{S} = \max\left\{t \in \mathcal{N}^+ \mid M_t \geq W_d\right\} \tag{8.6}$$

We run 1,000 simulations with the market parameters to generate 1,000 yield paths for each pension asset. For each yield path, we calculate sustainable length S_i based on equations (8.4), (8.5), and (8.6). For the random variable $\tilde{S}$, we investigate three measures (the mean, $VaR_{1\%}$, and $CVaR_{1\%}$) as shown in models (8.7), (8.8), and (8.9) respectively.

$$E(\tilde{S}) = E\left(\sum_{i=1}^{1000} S_i\right) \tag{8.7}$$

$$VaR_{1\%}(\tilde{S}) = s = \min\left\{s \in R \mid P\left\{\tilde{S} \geq s\right\} \leq 99\%\right\} \tag{8.8}$$

$$CVaR_{1\%}(\tilde{S}) = E\left\{\tilde{S} \mid \tilde{S} \leq s\right\} \tag{8.9}$$

where $\tilde{S}$ stands for the sustainable length of the retiree's retirement fund, $VaR_{1\%}(\tilde{S})$ gives the smallest sustainable period such that the probability of observing a sustainable period greater than it is 99 percent, and $CVaR_{1\%}(\tilde{S})$ gives the expected sustainable period conditional on the sustainable period being shorter than $VaR_{1\%}(\tilde{S})$. The impact of portfolio allocation on the mean, $VaR_{1\%}$, and $CVaR_{1\%}$ of the sustainable length is sensitive to the initial retirement savings M and the annual withdrawal W_d, which can be explained following two lines of thought that lead to opposite conclusions. First, due to the risk and return tradeoff, we should be able to observe a negative relationship between the mean and $CVaR_{1\%}$ (or $VaR_{1\%}$) because the latter is a measure of risk. Second, the mean and the tail expectation of a random variable could move in the same direction, since both come from the same distribution.

Results for the TIAA-CREF-type Lifecycle Fund

Given an initial retirement fund $M = \$1,000,000$, we assume the retiree invests in a TIAA-CREF-type retirement fund. That is, the portfolio allocation changes over time as specified in Table 8.2. The sustainable length of the fund for the Base case and the BaseX2 case under different annual withdrawal strategies is illustrated in Table 8.3.

We further investigate how the individual's funding status would be affected if the financial market deteriorates due to more frequent crashes (BaseX2 case). Setting the Base case as the benchmark, the influence of market deterioration on the individual retirement fund is expressed as the difference of the sustainable length between the Base and BaseX2 cases. The differences in mean, $VaR_{1\%}$, and $CVaR_{1\%}$ are illustrated in Figure 8.1. Figure 8.1 shows that if the financial markets

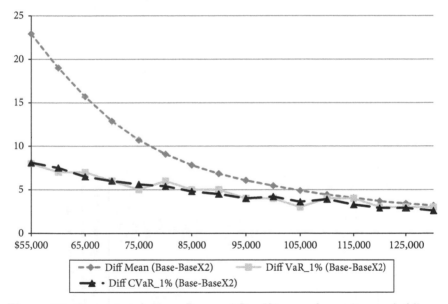

Figure 8.1. Comparison between Base and BaseX2 cases for an investor holding a TIAA-CREF-type retirement fund.

Note: The Base case assumes the financial market maintains the same trend and volatility that it has demonstrated throughout the past 20 years. The BaseX2 case supposes financial crashes happen twice as frequently as the market has experienced in the past 20 years. The vertical axis shows the sustainable periods in years and the horizontal axis is the annual withdrawal.

Source: Authors' calculations; see text.

TABLE 8.3 Sustainable lengths when investing in a TIAA-CREF-type retirement fund

Base Case				BaseX2 Case			
Withdraw ($)	Mean ($)	$VaR_{1\%}$ ($)	$CVaR_{1\%}$ ($)	Withdraw ($)	Mean ($)	$VaR_{1\%}$ ($)	$CVaR_{1\%}$ ($)
55,000	35.305	14	13.4971	55,000	12.382	6	5.3951
60,000	30.558	13	12.5974	60,000	11.541	5.99	5.09
65,000	26.501	12	11.4963	65,000	10.795	5	4.9999
70,000	23.054	11	10.5974	70,000	10.163	5	4.5975
75,000	20.281	10	9.8996	75,000	9.574	5	4.2936
80,000	18.154	10	9.395	80,000	9.068	4	4
85,000	16.411	9	8.799	85,000	8.588	4	4
90,000	15.016	9	8.4963	90,000	8.19	4	4
95,000	13.862	8	7.8996	95,000	7.801	4	3.8996
100,000	12.877	8	7.5974	100,000	7.433	4	3.3951
105,000	12.024	7	6.8996	105,000	7.131	4	3.2936
110,000	11.267	7	6.8996	110,000	6.846	3	3
115,000	10.612	7	6.2935	115,000	6.542	3	3
120,000	10.008	6	5.8996	120,000	6.323	3	3
125,000	9.483	6	5.8996	125,000	6.07	3	3
130,000	9.023	6	5.5975	130,000	5.837	3	3

Notes: The Base case assumes the financial market maintains the same trend and volatility that it has demonstrated throughout the past 20 years. The BaseX2 case supposes financial crashes happen twice as frequently as what the market experienced in the past 20 years.

Source: Authors' calculations; see text.

become more volatile, in the sense that crashes become more frequent, then the individual can expect to lose more than 20 periods from the sustainable retirement fund. Figure 8.1 and Table 8.3 also show that, under the same circumstances, a retiree can lose eight sustainable periods from the $VaR_{1\%}$ at the lowest annual withdrawal ($55,000). Finally, the difference in CVaR represents the loss in sustainable periods in the tail of the distribution sustainable periods and Figure 8.1 shows that for the lowest withdrawal rate the investor can expect to lose 8.1 of the sustainable retirement periods; the expected tail loss eventually diminishes with the withdrawal rate since the number of sustainable retirement periods also diminishes.

When both the initial fund M and annual withdrawal W_d are allowed to change, we demonstrate the impact of M and W_d on the sustainable number of periods in Figure 8.2. This figure shows that the BaseX2 case deteriorates from the Base case. As one expects, the figure shows that the sustainable number of retirement years increases with M and decreases with W_d. Given $M = \$1,000,000$ and $W_d = \$55,000$, the expected number of sustainable retirement periods is 35 in the Base case, while it is about 13 periods if W_d is increased to $100,000.

If the investor realizes returns in the tail of the portfolio distribution, then the $CVaR_{1\%}1$ yields 13 and 8 periods for these two withdrawal rates respectively in the Base case. Again given $M = \$1,000,000$, the expected number of sustainable retirement periods is greater than the life expectancy of a 65-year-old U.S. male (i.e. 19.4 years) if he withdraws no more than $75,000 per year; even here, however, a withdrawal rate of $55,000 will not sustain that 65-year-old to his life expectancy. Since there is a 30 percent chance that the 65-year-old will live to 90, the $M = \$1,000,000$ and $W_d = \$55,000$ may be adequate unless he experiences returns in the tail of the portfolio distribution; then the sustainable retirement period is clearly inadequate. In the event that crashes are more frequent, Table 8.3 shows that given $M = \$1,000,000$ and $W_d = \$55,000$, the expected and conditional tail-expected values for sustainable periods become 12.38 and 5.4 respectively. Hence, the expectations fall far short of the life expectancy if the financial market deteriorates, as in the BaseX2 case. One of the additional difficulties for the investor facing financial risk and longevity risk is that his perceived life expectancy may fall short of his actual life expectancy (i.e. the individual may get the trend wrong).

Results for Other Portfolios

Next we suppose the investor selects a portfolio for retirement based on his own preferences.[11] Given an initial retirement asset M at $t = 0$ of $1,000,000, we show how the sustainable periods are affected by the annual withdrawal W_d and portfolio allocation under the Base and BaseX2 scenarios. Figures 8.3 and 8.4 show the mean and $CVaR_{1\%}$ of the sustainable lengths respectively. The three surfaces from top to bottom stand for sustainable periods with withdrawal rates of $75,000, $100,000, and $125,000 respectively. As Figure 8.3 shows, in the Base case, the initial investment of $M = \$1,000,000$ and $W_d = \$75,000$ allows the investor to

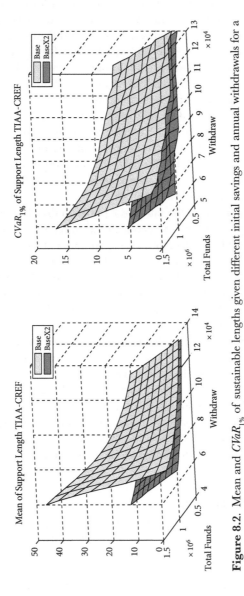

Figure 8.2. Mean and $CVaR_{1\%}$ of sustainable lengths given different initial savings and annual withdrawals for a TIAA-CREF-type lifecycle portfolio.

Note: The Base case assumes the financial market maintains the same trend and volatility that it has demonstrated throughout the past 20 years. The BaseX2 case supposed financial crashes happen twice as frequently as the market has experienced in the past 20 years.

Source: Authors' calculations; see text.

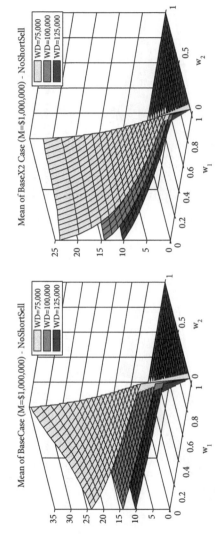

Figure 8.3. Mean of sustainable length when investing in customized portfolios.

Note: The Base case assumes the financial market maintains the same trend and volatility that it has demonstrated throughout the past 20 years. The Base X2 case supposed financial crashes happen twice as frequently as the market has experienced in the past 20 years. w_1 and w_2 stand for the proportions of the retiree's fund invested in equity and long-term fixed-income securities, respectively.

Source: Authors' calculations; see text.

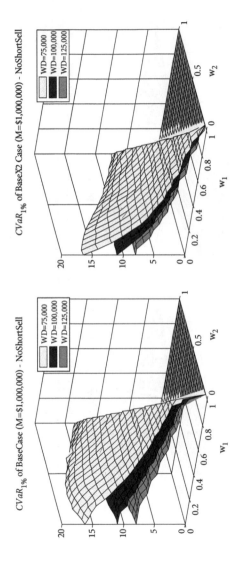

Figure 8.4. *CVaR*~1%~ of sustainable length when investing in customized portfolios.

Note: The Base case assumes the financial market maintains the same trend and volatility that it has demonstrated throughout the past 20 years. The Base X2 case supposed financial crashes happen twice as frequently as the market has experienced in the past 20 years. w_1 *and* w_2 stand for the proportions of the retiree's fund invested in equity and long-term fixed-income securities, respectively.

Source: Authors' calculations; see text.

generate an expected sustainable retirement of almost 35 periods given the portfolio $(\omega_1, \omega_2, \omega_3) = (0, 1, 0)$ (i.e. the investor plunges in the bond index fund). Figure 8.3 also shows that in the BaseX2 case, the investor can generate an expected sustainable retirement of almost 24 years by investing in the portfolio $(\omega_1, \omega_2, \omega_3) = (0, 0, 1)$ (i.e. the investor plunges in T-bills). Again in the case of an initial investment of $M = \$1,000,000$ and $W_d = \$75,000$, Figure 8.4 shows that to maximize the number of sustainable retirement years in the tail measured by $CVaR_{1\%}$, the investor should invest 30 percent of his fund in the bond index and the remaining 70 percent in T-bills (i.e., $(\omega_1, \omega_2, \omega_3) = (0, 0.3, 0.7)$) in the Base case; this portfolio yields almost 18 sustainable retirement periods. Figure 8.4 also shows that in the BaseX2 case, the investor should choose the portfolio with 10 percent invested in the bond index and 90 percent invested in T-bills (i.e. $(\omega_1, \omega_2, \omega_3) = (0, 0.1, 0.9)$)[12] to maximize the number of sustainable retirement periods in the tail; this portfolio yields 11 sustainable retirement periods. In other words, to reduce tail risk, the investor should choose a more conservative portfolio and invest more in risk-free assets such as T-bills.

DB Plans

DB plans put longevity risk on the pension provider, not the individual. The DB provider is a trustee who should act in the interests of the retirement cohort; we consider one retirement cohort. Since the DB plan is exposed to financial and longevity risks, one objective is to minimize the total unfunded liability (TUL) of the plan subject to any appropriate constraints. The TUL up to the terminal age of the retirees is defined as the present value of the sequence of unfunded liabilities. Hence TUL is

$$TUL = \sum_{t=1}^{\infty} \frac{UL_t}{(1+\rho)^t}$$

where the random variable UL_t is the underfunding at time t. We suppose that T is the retirement date of the cohort. Then for $t \le T$, the plan's unfunded liability UL_t equals

$$UL_t = PBO_t - (PA_t + C), \quad t = 1, 2, \ldots, T. \tag{8.10}$$

In (8.10) PBO_t is the pension benefit obligation and PA_t is the date t pension asset value. When $t > T$, UL_t equals

$$UL_t = PBO_t - PA_t + B \cdot {}_{t-T}\hat{p}_{x,T} \quad t = T+1, T+2, \ldots \tag{8.11}$$

where B is the survival benefit and $_{t-T}\hat{p}_{x,T}$ is the conditional expected probability that a plan member age x at time T survives $t - T$ years when $t > T$.

Following Cox et al. (2013), who investigate capital market and longevity risks, we solve the following constrained minimization problem, or equivalently the pension optimization problem:

$$\text{Minimize Var}\left[\sum_{t=1}^{\infty}\frac{UL_t}{(1+\rho)^t}\right]$$

$$\text{subject to } E\{TUL\} = 0$$

$$CVaR_\alpha(TUL) = \tau \qquad\qquad (8.12)$$

$$0 \leq \omega_i \leq 1, \ i = 1,2,\ldots,n$$

$$\sum_{i=1}^{n}\omega_i = 1$$

$$C \geq 0$$

In (8.12), we require the expected TUL to equal zero. To control the underfunding risk, we impose an α-level conditional value-at-risk (CVaR) constraint on the total unfunded liability (i.e. $E(TUL | TUL \geq VaR_{95\%}) = \tau$).[13] Short selling is not allowed for the plan, so $\omega_i \geq 0$.

DB Base Case

To obtain the optimal solutions for the Base case for a DB plan given the pension optimization problem in (8.12) with the Lee and Carter (1992) mortality model and the pension asset models (8.1), (8.2), and (8.3), suppose the DB plan has members who all join the plan at age $x_0 = 45$ ($t = 0$) and retire at age $x = 65$ ($T = 20$). The annual survival benefit payment after retirement is $B = \$10$ million and the pension fund at $t = 0$ is \$5 million. Following Cox et al. (2013), we set the pension valuation rate at $\rho = 0.08$ and the life annuity discount rate at $r = 0.05$. In addition, the plan will amortize the unfunded liability over $m = 7$ years as in Panteli (2010) and following Maurer et al. (2009), we set the penalty factors on the supplementary contributions and withdrawals at $\psi_1 = \psi_2 = 0.2$. Our objective is to find the optimal pension asset allocation and contribution strategies for the plan throughout the life of the cohort.

We set year 2007 as our base year $t = 0$ and run a Monte Carlo simulation with 1,000 iterations to generate forecasts for the three financial asset returns and pension liabilities PBO_t for $t = 1,2,\ldots$. The downside risk parameter is set at 60 and given $\tau = 60$, the optimal solution for (8.12) is shown in Table 8.4.

To achieve the lowest underfunding variance J and the target $CVaR_{95\%}(TUL)$ of 60, the plan should invest 27 percent of its funds in the S&P 500 index, 43 percent in the Merrill Lynch corporate bond index, and the remaining 30 percent of its funds in three-month T-bills. In addition, given $E(TUL) = 0$, the optimal annual

TABLE 8.4 Optimal solution for the Base case with model (5.13)

C	ω_1	ω_2	ω_3	$\mathcal{J}$
3.34	0.27	0.43	0.30	624.41

Notes: C stands for the normal contribution. $\mathcal{J}$ is the value of the objective function in Model (5-13), which measures the variance of total unfunded liability. (ω_1 , ω_2 , ω_3) represents the investment strategy where ω_1 , ω_2 , and ω_3 are the proportions invested in the S&P 500 index, Merrill Lynch corporate bond index, and 3-month T-bill, respectively. The Base case assumes the financial market maintains the same trend and volatility that it has demonstrated throughout the past 20 years.

Source: Authors' calculations; see text.

contribution is $C = 3.34$. The total pension cost represents the present value of all normal contributions, C, supplementary contributions, SC_t and withdrawals, W_t. A higher TPC lowers the plan's underfunding risk but imposes a higher cost on the plan sponsor. To achieve the level of $CVaR_{95\%}(TUL) = 60$, the expected total pension cost is $ETPC = 36.08$.

Longevity Risk Effect

To examine the adverse effect of an unexpected mortality improvement on the plan, we change the value of the Base case g in the model to other possible values; in the Lee–Carter model, mortality is a function of a common risk factor and the risk factor is described as a random walk with drift g. This drift g may be thought of as the systematic risk component of mortality. A more negative value of g implies a more substantial mortality improvement. Given $CVaR_{95\%}(TUL) = 60$, the adverse effect of the longevity risk is captured by the higher E(TPC), since the plan must adjust E(TPC) upward to reflect higher longevity risk.

Table 8.5 shows the optimization results given different assumptions on g after solving the optimization problem (8.12). As g decreases from the Base case -0.20 to -0.40, E(TPC) increases notably from 36.08 to 39.06 (i.e. an 8.3 percent rise); this is due to the higher normal contribution $C = 3.62$ with $g = -0.40$, compared to $C = 3.34$ with $g = -0.20$. The increased longevity risk increases the normal contribution and puts more weight in the tails of the underfunding distribution. Hence an increase in longevity risk increases the variance $\mathcal{J}$ of the underfunding distribution. That variance increases from 624.41 to 709.96 as g decreases from -0.2 to -0.4. In addition, as g decreases, the plan invests more in the safe asset. Equivalently, the plan manager must elect a higher portfolio weight for the safe asset, so as to satisfy his downside risk constraint (that is, the $CVaR_{95\%}(TUL) = 60$).

TABLE 8.5 Optimal normal contribution and asset allocation for the Base case given $CVaR_{95\%}(TUL) = 60$ and $E(TUL) = 0$ and different mortality improvement parameters g in the Lee and Carter Model (1992)

g	C	ω_1	ω_2	ω_3	$E(TPC)$	$\mathcal{J}$
−0.20	3.34	0.27	0.43	0.30	36.08	624.41
−0.30	3.50	0.28	0.39	0.33	37.77	670.84
−0.40	3.62	0.28	0.36	0.36	39.06	709.96

Notes: C stands for the normal contribution. $\mathcal{J}$ is the value of the objective function in Model (13), which measures the variance of total unfunded liability. (ω_1, ω_2, ω_3) represents the investment strategy where ω_1, ω_2, and ω_3 are the proportions invested in the S&P 500 index, Merrill Lynch corporate bond index, and 3-month T-bill, respectively. g is the mortality improvement parameter in the Lee and Carter Model (1992). $E(TPC)$ represents the expected total pension cost of the plan. The Base case assumes the financial market maintains the same trend and volatility that it has demonstrated throughout the past 20 years.

Source: Authors' calculations; see text.

Capital Market Risk Effects

To examine the capital market risk effect on the pension plan, we double the values of the volatility, jump size, and jump arrival rate parameters for the S&P 500 index and the Merrill Lynch corporate bond index in Table 8.1, simulate, and resolve the optimization model (8.12). The results with the doubled parameter values of the S&P 500 index and the Merrill Lynch corporate bond index are shown in Table 8.6; they provide important insights for the pension plan with respect to possible market crashes. Given g equal to the Base case level of −0.20 and a more volatile capital market, the $E(TPC)$ increases by 16.6 percent from 36.08 in Table 8.5 to 42.08 in Table 8.6. In addition, to meet the downside risk constraint, the annual normal contribution C increases by 17.8 percent to 3.93 and the proportion invested in the low-risk three-month T-bill rises by 54 percent to $\omega_3 = 0.47$, compared with the Base case levels of $C = 3.34$ and $\omega_3 = 0.30$ in Table 8.5.

It is worth noting that if the adverse longevity and capital market events both occur, it will push up the expected total pension cost $E(TPC)$ dramatically by 24.9 percent, from 36.08 in Table 8.5 to 45.05 in Table 8.6. These changes could cause significant financial consequences to the pension sponsor. Both longevity risk and capital market risk affect the financial stability of a pension sponsor.

Next we investigate how pension hedging strategies can mitigate the adverse effects arising from these two sources of risk.

Pension Hedging Strategies

Here we investigate two pension longevity risk-hedging strategies: a ground-up hedging strategy, and an excess-risk hedging strategy. The ground-up hedging strategy not only reduces longevity risk but also manages capital market risk, as it

TABLE 8.6 Optimal normal contribution and asset allocation for the BaseX2 case given $CVaR_{95\%}(TUL) = 60$ and $E(TUL) = 0$ and different mortality improvement parameters g in the Lee–Carter Model (1992)

g	C	ω_1	ω_2	ω_3	$E(TPC)$	$\mathcal{J}$
−0.20	3.93	0.08	0.45	0.47	42.08	619.92
−0.30	4.12	0.08	0.43	0.48	43.97	660.39
−0.40	4.22	0.08	0.42	0.49	45.05	697.99

Note: C stands for the normal contribution. $\mathcal{J}$ is the value of the objective function in Model (5-13), which measures the variance of total unfunded liability. (ω_1, ω_2, ω_3) represents the investment strategy where ω_1, ω_2, and ω_3 are the proportions invested in the S&P 500 index, Merrill Lynch corporate bond index, and 3-month T-bill, respectively. *g* is the mortality improvement parameter in the Lee and Carter Model (1992). E(*TPC*) represents the expected total pension cost of the plan. The Base case assumes the financial market maintains the same trend and volatility that it has demonstrated throughout the past 20 years.

Source: Authors' calculations; see text.

transfers both pension asset and liability risks to pension risk takers. The ground-up hedging strategy, given a full hedge, is equivalent to a pension buyout, and the excess-risk hedging, also given a full hedge, is equivalent to a mortality option; see Cox et al. (2013) for a discussion of both.

The Ground-up or Buyout Hedging Strategy

Suppose the plan implements a ground-up hedging strategy and transfers a proportion h^G of pension assets and liabilities to a hedge provider by paying a price equal to

$$HP^G = \frac{h^G \left(1 + \delta^G\right) \overline{Ba}\left(x(T)\right)}{\left(1 + \rho\right)^T}$$

where $\overline{Ba}\left(x(T)\right)$ is the expected present value of pension payments at retirement T and δ^G is the unit hedge cost. Given that the plan pays a hedge price HP^G, the available fund for pension asset investment at $t = 0$ is $PA_0^G = M^G = M - HP^G$, which is lower than that of the no-hedge case with $PA_0 = M$. In our example, $M = 5$. With the hedge ratio h^G, the pension liability retained by the plan becomes

$$PBO_t^G = \begin{cases} \dfrac{\left(1 - h^G\right) Ba\left(x(T)\right)}{\left(1 + \rho\right)^{T-t}} & t = 1, 2, \ldots, T \\[2ex] \left(1 - h^G\right) Ba\left(y(t)\right) & t = T + 1, T + 2, \ldots \end{cases}$$

In this expression, $a(x(T))$ is the life annuity factor for age x at retirement T and $a(y(t))$ is the life annuity factor for age y after retirement T with $t = T+1, T+2, \ldots$.

Suppose the plan adopts the optimal asset allocation and normal contribution strategies shown in Table 8.5. Table 8.7 shows how the ground-up hedging strategy mitigates the funding downside risk caused by the capital market risk and longevity risk for the Base case with different hedge ratios.

With the ground-up hedging strategy, when $h^G > 0$, all $CVaR_{95\%}(TUL)$s in Table 8.7 are lower than $CVaR_{95\%}(TUL) = 60$ without hedging. Table 8.7 also shows that as h^G increases, $CVaR_{95\%}(TUL)$ and E(TPC) decrease, indicating a lower pension risk to the plan. For example, when $\delta^G = 0$, as h^G increases from 0.1 to 0.15, $CVaR_{95\%}(TUL)$ decreases from 46.91 to 40.38 and E(TPC) decreases from 34.81 to 34.18. The hedge cost δ^G, however, reduces the risk reduction effect of the ground-up hedging. For example, when $\delta^G = 0$ and $h^G = 0.15$, $CVaR_{95\%}(TUL)$ is only 40.38 but it increases to 42.16 when $\delta^G = 0.1$ and $h^G = 0.15$. As a robustness check, we also examine the ground-up hedging strategy with different combinations of g and the pension asset parameters. All of them echo the pattern we observe in Table 8.7. We conclude that the ground-up hedging strategy can effectively reduce the capital market and longevity risks imbedded in a pension plan.

TABLE 8.7 Ground-up edging strategy for Base case with $g = -0.2$

	$\delta^G = 0$		$\delta^G = 0.05$		$\delta^G = 0.1$	
	$h^G = 0.1$	$h^G = 0.15$	$h^G = 0.1$	$h^G = 0.15$	$h^G = 0.1$	$h^G = 0.15$
C	3.34	3.34	3.34	3.34	3.34	3.34
ω_1	0.27	0.27	0.27	0.27	0.27	0.27
ω_2	0.43	0.43	0.43	0.43	0.43	0.43
ω_3	0.31	0.31	0.31	0.31	0.31	0.31
E(TUL)	−7.93	−11.90	−7.31	−10.96	−6.68	−10.02
E(TPC)	34.81	34.18	35.03	34.52	35.26	34.86
$CVaR_{95\%}(TUL)$	46.91	40.38	47.50	41.27	48.09	42.16
J	625.75	628.73	631.62	637.40	637.58	646.26
HP^G	2.36	3.54	2.48	3.72	2.60	3.90

Note: C stands for the normal contribution. (ω_1, ω_2, ω_3) represents the investment strategy where ω_2, ω_2, and ω_3 are the proportions invested in the S&P 500 index, Merrill Lynch corporate bond index, and 3-month T-bill, respectively. g is the mortality improvement parameter in the Lee and Carter Model (1992). TUL and TPC represent the total unfunded liability and total pension cost of the plan. J is the value of the objective function in Model (5-13), which measures the variance of total unfunded liability. HP^G, h^G, and δ^G are the hedge price, hedge ratio, and unit hedge cost under the ground-up hedging strategy. The Base case assumes the financial market maintains the same trend and volatility that it has demonstrated throughout the past 20 years.

Source: Authors' calculations; see text.

The Excess-risk Hedging or Insurance Option Strategy

The second pension hedging strategy, the excess-risk hedging strategy, focuses on transferring the high-end longevity risk. With the excess-risk hedging strategy, the plan needs to determine a strike level on the s-year survival probability $_s\tilde{p}_{x,T}$ for age x at retirement T in each year t, $t = T+1, T+2,\ldots$ above which to transfer a proportion h^E of the longevity risk. The conditional expected s-year survival rate, $_s\hat{p}_{x,T}$, is defined as $_s\hat{p}_{x,T} = E[_s\tilde{p}_{x,T} | \tilde{p}_{x,T}, \tilde{p}_{x+1,T+1}, \ldots, \tilde{p}_{x+s-1,T+s-1}]$, where $\tilde{p}_{x+s-1,T+s-1}$ is the one-year survival rate for age $x+s-1$ in year $T+s-1$.

Suppose at $t=0$, the plan purchases a series of European call options with strike levels set at the expected survival rates, $_s\bar{p}_{x,T} = E[_s\hat{p}_{x,T}]$, $s = 1,2,\ldots$. The option payoffs in years $T+1, T+2,\ldots$ are determined by $\max\{0, B_s\hat{p}_{x,T} - B_s\bar{p}_{x,T}\}$, $s = 1,2,\ldots$. Accordingly, to hedge a proportion h^E, the plan needs to pay a hedge price of

$$HP^E = \frac{h^E\left(1+\delta^E\right)E\left[\sum_{s=1}^{\infty} v^s \max\left\{B_s\hat{p}_{x,T} - B_s\bar{p}_{x,T}, 0\right\}\right]}{(1+\rho)^T}$$

where δ^E is the hedge cost per unit of longevity risk ceded. With the hedge ratio h^E, the plan's liability becomes

$$PBO_t^E = \begin{cases} \dfrac{Ba\left(x(T)\right) - Bh^E \sum_{s=1}^{\infty} v^s \max\left\{0, {}_s\hat{p}_{x,T} - {}_s\bar{p}_{x,T}\right\}}{(1+\rho)^T} & t = 1,2,\ldots,T \\ Ba\left(y(t)\right) - Bh^E \sum_{s-t-T+1}^{\infty} v^{s-(t-T)} \max\left\{0, {}_s\hat{p}_{x,T} - {}_s\bar{p}_{x,T}\right\} & t = T+1, T+2,\ldots \end{cases}$$

With the hedge price HP^E, the fund available for investment at time 0 is reduced to $M^E = M - HP^E$. Again, in our example, we assume $M = 5$ and the pension plan implements the optimal asset allocation and normal contribution strategies shown in Table 8.5. With different combinations of g and the pension asset parameters, we find the same pattern as Table 8.7 with the ground-up hedging strategy (results available on request from the authors). That is, with a positive hedge ratio h^E, $CVaR_{95\%}(TUL)$ and $E(TPC)$ are lower than those without hedge. However, the magnitude of risk reduction achieved by the excess-risk hedging strategy is much lower than that of the ground-up hedging strategy. For example, when $g = -0.20$, the pension asset parameters in Table 8.1 and $h^G = 0.1$, $CVaR_{95\%}(TUL) = 46.91$ with the ground-up hedging strategy. However, at the same levels of g and the pension asset parameters, the excess-risk strategy only reduces $CVaR_{95\%}(TUL)$ to 56.44 even with a full hedge of longevity risk above the expected survival rates (i.e., $h^E = 1$). This is explained by the fact that the excess-risk strategy only transfers the high-end longevity risk but not the pension asset risk, while the ground-up strategy reduces both pension asset and liability risks. In many cases, the capital market risk on pension assets seems to impose a more significant effect on the pension plan than the longevity risk.

Conclusion

Concern regarding capital market risk often eclipses that due to longevity risk in pension management. When it comes to retirement issues, however, these two risks are integrally linked. The number of sustainable years for a retirement portfolio is determined, in part, by market crashes, changes in market volatility, and changes in life expectancy. There are instruments to handle capital market volatility, which include futures and forward contracts to hedge interest rate, currency, and price risks; there are also derivatives to hedge credit risks, weather risks, and more. There are insurance instruments to handle the volatility of life; these instruments include life insurance and life annuities. These insurance instruments have not, however, been designed to deal with the systematic component of the life risks. If life expectancy unexpectedly increases (e.g. a cure for cardiovascular disease or cancer is found), then life insurance becomes more profitable for the insurer but life annuities become less profitable, or may even threaten insurer solvency and adversely impact retirement plans of individuals and pension funds.

To address these issues, we created scenarios to assess risk for both the individual and the institution. In the case of the individual, scenario analysis showed that if the individual invested in a lifecycle fund such as that offered by TIAA-CREF and the financial markets were driven by historical parameters, then a $1 million investment at retirement combined with a withdrawal rate of $75,000 per year would yield approximately 20 sustainable years. This is one year more than the life expectancy of a 65-year-old male in 2013. Most financial planners would consider this as an inadequate retirement horizon, and many would advocate planning for a much longer horizon.[14] The same analysis shows that one could only say that the fund would last for ten years with a 99 percent probability. Similarly, if market parameters were doubled so that crashes occurred more often and the market was more volatile (i.e. BaseX2 case), one could expect the fund to last less than ten years and the fund would last for four years with 99 percent probability. This leaves the investor with considerable uncertainty. Yet the TIAA-CREF-type lifecycle fund held 40 percent in equity, 40 percent in bonds, and 20 percent in T-bills. The analysis also showed that the investor could select an alternative portfolio to increase the number of sustainable years. If the investor held all in the bond fund, he could expect the portfolio to continue paying the same $75,000 per year for almost 35 years. Additionally, if the investor's returns were in the worst 1 percent of the portfolio payoffs then he could still expect almost 18 sustainable retirement years, but only if the portfolio was changed to a 30 percent investment in bonds and a 70 percent investment in T-bills. In the BaseX2 case (i.e. a more volatile market), the same investor could expect the portfolio fund to last almost 24 years if he plunged in the T-bill fund. In this BaseX2 case, if the investor's returns were in the worst 1 percent of the portfolio payoffs then he could expect 11 sustainable retirement years, but only if the portfolio was altered to a 10 percent investment in bonds and a 90 percent investment in T-bills. These numbers do not account for the possible changes in life expectancy that will doubtless make even the best numbers here seem even less sufficient. The DC plans leave the investor with considerable longevity risk, and without the foresight of increasing the size of the investment fund they can only reduce the annual withdrawal or change the portfolio to attempt to keep the retirement fund sustainable for more years. These results emphasize the need for financial instruments that provide a more effective means of transferring some of the longevity risk to those better able to bear it.

Pension providers bear the longevity risk for DB plans. The pension provider has a fiduciary responsibility to act in the interest of the plan members and therefore our scenario objective was to minimize pension underfunding subject to constraints on the expected underfunding, short selling, and the size of the tail of the underfunding distribution. When longevity risk was increased, the solution to the constrained minimization problem showed an 8.3 percent increase in the expected total pension cost. When increased capital market risk was also added to longevity risk, the solution to the constrained minimization problem showed a 24.9 percent increase in the expected total pension cost.

To mitigate risk, two longevity risk-hedging schemes were considered. The first was similar to a partial buyout of the pension plan and the analysis showed that this hedge could lower the pension failure risk. When longevity risk was increased, the reduction in pension risk between the hedged and unhedged scenarios became more pronounced; when capital market risk was also increased, the reduction in pension failure risk between the hedged and unhedged scenarios was even more pronounced. The second hedge was a longevity option. Here there was no exchange of assets; rather, there was only an exchange of liabilities in the tail. As was the case with the partial buyout strategy, the longevity option strategy also demonstrated a reduction in pension failure risk that increased with the size of the hedge.

In sum, improvements can result from managing longevity risk in the context of both defined contribution and defined benefit schemes. Today's DC risk management schemes are currently far too limited (e.g. life annuities and reverse mortgages, among others), and additional financial instruments can help fill the gap. The DB risk management possibilities are limited also, but they have received more attention in academia and in capital markets. Other hedging schemes must also be addressed.

Notes

1. See BBC News (2010).
2. For more discussion of buyouts and buy-ins, see Blake et al. (2013).
3. Embedded value is the present value of future profits plus adjusted net asset value.
4. For example, Vita II–Swiss Re 2005 ($362 million), Vita III–Swiss Re 2007 ($705 million), Vita IV–Swiss Re 2009/10 ($175 million), Vita V–Swiss Re 2012 ($275 million), Tartan–Scottish Re 2006 ($155 million), and OSIRIS–AXA 2006 ($442 million).
5. For more on this, see Feinstein (1993), Blake et al. (2006), Wang et al. (2007), and Coughlan (2014).
6. TIAA-CREF stands for a Teachers Insurance and Annuity Association–College Retirement Equities Fund. A lifecycle fund refers to a fund designed to provide long-term appreciation and capital preservation based on the age and retirement date of the investors in the fund.
7. Data were retrieved from TIAA-CREF (2013).
8. In our simulations based on the parameters estimated from 1989–2010 data, the expected risk premium of S&P 500 over three-month T-bill is around −0.03 each year in the Base case and −0.20 in the BaseX2 case. The negative risk premium of S&P 500 is consistent with the observation that the return on equities has been 7.6 percentage points a year lower than that on government bonds in the U.S. since the end of 1999 (*The Economist* 2012).
9. If there is a Poisson event or equivalent crash in the equity market then the expected loss in the S&P index is approximately 26 percent, while if there is a crash in the bond market then the expected loss in the bond index is approximately 14 percent.
10. The mortality data for 1901–1999 are taken from the Human Life Table Database (MPIDR 2013), and for 2000–2007 from the Human Mortality Database (HMD 2013); these were provided by the University of California at Berkeley and the Max Planck Institute for Demographic Research.
11. The analysis is static and so the portfolio is assumed to remain the same through retirement.
12. The portfolio (0, 0.05, 0.95) also maximizes the sustainable years in the tail of the portfolio distribution.
13. The equality constraint is used rather than an inequality constraint so that the variance is not pushed to zero using T-bills (that would also inflate the total pension cost). The equality constraint is also important because it generates base cases which we later use for comparison with two different longevity risk hedges; there we use the same portfolio of assets generated in the Base case and add a hedging instrument. For this comparison to work, we use the equality constraint for *CVaR* and no constraint on the total pension cost.
14. See Krueger (2011). Also, former Society of Actuaries President Anna Rappaport is quoted in Powell (2012) as saying 'The planning horizon should be long, and if mortality data is used to pick it, it should not be life expectancy, but rather the age that there is a 90 percent or 95 percent chance of survival.'

References

BBC News (2010). 'Annuities and a Question of Age,' *MONEY TALK by Billy Burrows* [website] (updated 18 May 2010). <http://www.bbc.co.uk/news/10122944>.

Baranoff, E., P. L. Brockett, and Y. Kahane (2009). *Risk Management for Enterprises and Individuals, v. 1.0* [electronic publication]. Irvington, NY: Flat World Knowledge. <http://catalog.flatworldknowledge.com/catalog/editions/baranoff-risk-management-for-enterprises-and-individuals-1-0>.

Blake, D., and W. Burrows (2001). 'Survivor Bonds: Helping to Hedge Mortality Risk,' *Journal of Risk and Insurance*, 68: 339–348.

Blake, D., A. J. G. Cairns, and K. Dowd (2006). 'Living with Mortality: Longevity Bonds and other Mortality-linked Securities (with Discussion),' *British Actuarial Journal*, 12(1): 198–214.

Blake, D., A. J. G. Cairns, G. Coughlan, K. Dowd, and R. MacMinn (2013). 'The New Life Markets,' *Journal of Risk and Insurance*, 80(3): 501–558.

Burne, K. (2011). 'Swiss Re Longevity-Risk Deal Opens Door to More,' *Wall Street Journal*. January 7.

Chai, J., W. Horneff, R. Maurer, and O. S. Mitchell (2011). 'Optimal Portfolio Choice over the Life Cycle with Flexible Work, Endogenous Retirement, and Lifetime Payouts,' *Review of Finance*, 15(4): 875–907.

Coughlan, G. (2014). 'Longevity Risk Management, Corporate Finance, and Sustainable Pensions,' in P. B. Hammond, R. Maurer, and O. S. Mitchell, eds., *Recreating Sustainable Retirement: Resilience, Solvency, and Tail Risk*. Oxford, U.K.: Oxford University Press, pp. 89–112.

Cowley, A., and J. D. Cummins (2005). 'Securitization of Life Insurance Assets and Liabilities,' *Journal of Risk and Insurance*, 72(2): 193–226.

Cox, S. H., J. R. Fairchild, and H. W. Pedersen (2000). 'Economic Aspects of Securitization of Risk,' *Astin Bulletin*, 30(1): 157–193.

Cox, S. H., Y. Lin, R. Tian, and J. Yu (2013). 'Managing Capital Market and Longevity Risks in a Defined Benefit Pension Plan,' *Journal of Risk and Insurance*, 80(3): 585–620.

Davidoff, T., J. R. Brown, and P. A. Diamond (2005). 'Annuities and Individual Welfare,' *American Economic Review*, 95(5): 1573–1590.

Dushi, I., L. Friedberg, and A. Webb (2010). 'The Impact of Aggregate Mortality Risk on Defined Benefit Pension Plans,' *Journal of Pension Economics and Finance*, 9(4): 481–503.

The Economist (2012). 'Shares and Shibboleths: How Much Should People Get Paid for Investing in the Stock Market?' 17 March.

Feinstein, J. S. (1993). 'The Relationship between Socioeconomic Status and Health: A Review of the Literature,' *The Milbank Quarterly*, 71(2): 279–322.

Horneff, W. J., R. H. Maurer, O. S. Mitchell, and M. Z. Stamos (2009). 'Asset Allocation and Location over the Life Cycle with Investment-linked Survival-contingent Payouts,' *Journal of Banking and Finance*, 33(9): 1688–1699.

The Human Mortality Database (HMD) (2013). *The Human Mortality Database*. Berkeley, CA: University of California at Berkeley, and Rostock, Germany: Max Planck Institute for Demographic Research.

Kohn, M. (1999). 'Risk Instruments in the Medieval and Early Modern Economy,' Dartmouth College Working Paper no. 99–07. Hanover, NH: Dartmouth College.

Krueger, C. (2011). 'Mortality Assumptions: Are Planners Getting It Right?' *Journal of Financial Planning*, December: 36–37.

Lee, R. D., and L. R. Carter (1992). 'Modeling and Forecasting U.S. Mortality,' *Journal of the American Statistical Association*, 87(419): 659–671.

Lin, Y., and S. H. Cox (2008). 'Securitization of Catastrophe Mortality Risks,' *Insurance: Mathematics and Economics*, 42(2): 628–637.

Loeys, J., N. Panigirtzoglou, and R. M. Ribeiro (2007). 'Longevity: A Market in the Making,' LifeMetrics Research Paper. London, U.K.: J.P. Morgan.

MacMinn, R., P. Brockett, and D. Blake (2006). 'Longevity Risk and Capital Markets,' *Journal of Risk and Insurance*, 73(4): 551–557.

MacMinn, R., and F. Weber (2010). 'The Annuity Puzzle.' Working Paper. Normal, IL: Illinois State University.

Maurer, R., O. S. Mitchell, and R. Rogalla (2009). 'Managing Contribution and Capital Market Risk in a Funded Public Defined Benefit Plan: Impact of CVaR Cost Constraints,' *Insurance: Mathematics and Economics*, 45(1): 25–34.

Max Planck Institute for Demographic Research (MPIDR) (2013). *The Human Life-Table Database* [website]. Rostock, Germany: MPIDR. <http://www.lifetable.de/>.

Milevsky, M. A. (2006). *The Calculus of Retirement Income: Financial Models for Pension Annuities and Life Insurance*. New York: Cambridge University Press.

Oeppen, J., and J. W. Vaupel (2002). 'Broken Limits to Life Expectancy,' *Science*, 296 (5570): 1029–1031.

Oppers, S. E., K. Chikada, F. Eich, P. Imam, J. Kiff, M. Kisser, M. Soto, and T. Sun. (2012). 'The Financial Impact of Longevity Risk,' *Global Financial Stability Report: The Quest for Lasting Stability*. Washington, DC: International Monetary Fund, pp. 123–154.

Panteli, C. (2010). 'Swiss Re Completes First Longevity Trend Bond,' *Professional Pensions*, 23 December.

Powell, R. (2012). 'Planning for Retirement? Plan to Live to 100,' *MarketWatch* [website]. April 12. <http://www.marketwatch.com/story/planning-for-retirement-plan-to-live-to-100-2012-04-12>.

Sinclair, S. H., and K. A. Smetters (2004). 'Health Shocks and the Demand for Annuities,' Congressional Budget Office (CBO) Technical Paper 2004-9. Washington, DC: CBO.

TIAA-CREF (2013). *TIAA-CREF Lifecycle Funds: Save for Retirement in One Easy Step* [website]. <https://www.tiaa-cref.org/public/products-services/mutual-funds/lifecycle>.

Turner, A. (2006). 'Pensions, Risks and Capital Markets,' *Journal of Risk and Insurance*, 73(4): 559–574.

Wang, L., E. Valdez, and J. Piggott (2007). 'Securitization of Longevity Risk in Reverse Mortgages,' *North American Actuarial Journal*, 12(4): 345–371.

Yaari, M. E. (1965). 'Uncertain Lifetime, Life Insurance, and the Theory of the Consumer,' *Review of Economic Studies*, 32(2): 137–150.

Part III
Regulatory and Political Risk

Chapter 9

Evolving Roles for Pension Regulations: Toward Better Risk Control?

E. Philip Davis

Pension regulation has been transformed in recent years, with the central theme being an increasing focus on protection of beneficiaries against various forms of risk. These changes render less relevant much of what was written in the past (e.g. Davis 1995*a*). Underlying forces include the ongoing shift from defined benefit (DB) to defined contribution (DC) pensions, the shift to risk-based supervision for DB and DC plans, changes in accounting standards and transparency (contributing to market discipline), and the turbulence in financial markets in recent years. These forces have engendered a greater awareness of the risks to retirement income security that are inherent in the use of funding to provide for pensions, and given rise to attempts by regulation to seek to reduce these risks to the extent that is feasible and cost-effective.

This chapter offers an overview of the evolution of pension regulation, with a particular focus on regulatory attempts to control risk and using evidence from selected countries under each topic. As regards outcomes, in our view there has been an improvement in retirement income security as a consequence of the focus of regulation on risk. That said, a number of the regulatory developments have stimulated a shift of DB pension portfolios toward lower risk and hence lower return assets, which may yet cause difficulties for future pension income. These shifts also leave open a number of outstanding questions that are related to risk, notably whether education of consumers is sufficient to apprise them of the risk tradeoffs in their pension planning, the neglected role of longevity risk in retirement income provision, and whether regulation can be made more countercyclical to avoid macroprudential risks affecting both pension funds and the wider economy.

In what follows, we first consider the question of why pension plans are regulated, highlighting the role of risk, and then we move to general portfolio regulations, the traditional means of regulating risk. Next we examine the evolving regulation of DB plans focused on risk, including the role of market discipline and accounting standards. We go on to analyze the changing regulation of DC plans, touching on issues again linked directly or indirectly to risk, including costs, annuitization, and outcomes. A final section considers some weaknesses of current pension regulation in respect of risk, and we conclude by considering whether pension funds need a global agreement focusing on risks akin to those addressed by Basel III for banking.

Why Regulate Pension Funds?

Abstracting from issues of redistribution, a case for public intervention in the operation of markets arises when there is a market failure, in other words, when a set of market prices fails to reach a Pareto-optimal outcome. Thus from an economic standpoint, when competitive markets achieve efficient outcomes, there is no case for regulation.

Three key types of market failure arise in finance, namely those relating to information asymmetry, externality, and monopoly. These apply in differing degrees depending on the type of financial institution; in particular, there are quite distinctive problems associated with banks as opposed to pension funds (Davis 2012). But a finance-based approach is not the only way to view pension fund regulation. It can also be argued that enhancing equity, adequacy, and security of pension arrangements can be seen as objectives of pension fund regulation independent of financial aspects, focusing on member rights and the financial security of plans (Laboul and Yermo 2006). Tax privileges to pension funds are emblematic of this alternative approach.

We begin, however, with a discussion of arguments based on pension funds' status as financial institutions (Davis 1995b; McCarthy and Neuberger 2009). Regarding information asymmetry, when it is difficult or costly for the purchaser of a financial service to obtain sufficient information on the quality of the service in question, he may be vulnerable to exploitation. This could entail fraudulent, negligent, incompetent, or unfair treatment, as well as failure of the relevant institution per se.

Such phenomena are of particular importance for retail users of financial services such as those provided by pension funds, because clients seek investment of a sizeable proportion of their wealth, contracts are one-off, and they involve a commitment over time. Moreover, such consumers are unlikely to find it economic to make a full assessment of the risks to which pension funds are exposed—including, for DB funds, the sponsor's solvency and the level of funding backing pension claims in case of sponsor bankruptcy. Participants may not even be aware of costs, returns, volatility, and the range of outcomes for prospective pensions. Hence the need for 'consumer protection'-style regulation for pension funds—and consumer education. We consider this form of risk focus to be the most important element in pension regulation and that on which most recent innovations have largely focused, for example in portfolio regulations for all funds, risk-based regulations and solvency rules for DB funds, and regulation of costs, risks, and outcomes for DC funds as well.

Such asymmetries are evidently less important for wholesale users of financial markets (such as pension funds themselves in their dealings with investment banks), as these typically have better information, hold considerable countervailing power, and carry out repeated transactions with each other. A partial protection against exploitation, even for retail consumers, is likely to arise from the desire of financial institutions such as life insurers offering personal pensions to maintain their reputation, or equally for nonfinancial companies to retain a good reputation in the labor market—a capital asset that would depreciate if customers or employees were to be exploited. Nevertheless, accounting standards can be seen as a protection for wholesale creditors and investors when dealing with funds and their sponsors.

Externalities arise when the actions of certain agents have non-priced consequences on others. The most obvious type of potential externality in financial markets relates to the liquidity risk underlying contagious bank runs, when failure of one bank leads to a heightened risk of failure by others, whether due to direct financial linkages (e.g. interbank claims) or shifts in perceptions on the part of depositors as to the creditworthiness of certain banks in the light of failure of others. 'Runs' may also occur for other types of institutions, such as investment banks. But given the matching of long-run liabilities and long-run assets in pension funds, such externalities are less likely here. There are other possible externalities from failure of pension funds—notably to the state, whether as direct guarantor or as provider of pensions to those lacking them (Impavido and Tower 2009)—and similar investments by pension funds may give rise to macroprudential risks to financial markets as well as to funds themselves. This explains the provision of, for example, guarantee schemes for DB funds and countercyclical regulations. Positive externalities may also lead governments to encourage pension funds, such as a desire to economize on the costs of social security or foster the development of capital markets.

Market failure may also arise when there is some degree of market power. This may be of particular relevance for pension funds, notably when membership is compulsory; here attention to the interests of members is of particular importance, whether there is asymmetric information or not. As argued by Altman (1992), employers in an unregulated environment offering a pension fund effectively on a monopoly basis may structure plans to take care of their own interests and concerns, so for example they can institute onerous vesting rules and better terms for management than for workers. They may also want freedom to fund (or not) as they wish, and maintain pension assets for their own use, regardless of the risk of bankruptcy. They may not take care of the retirement needs of some groups in society, such as frequent job changers, young workers, or women with broken careers due to childbearing. Union pressure may ameliorate some of these problems for employees, but not for the most peripheral groups. This form of regulation, while as important as the others, has undergone less change in recent years than the focus on risk.

Some would argue that pension funds should be regulated independently of these standard justifications, for example to ensure that tax benefits are not misused and that the goals of equity, adequacy, and security of retirement income are achieved—in effect correcting the market failures in annuities markets that necessitate pension funds and social security (Laboul and Yermo 2006). This can be seen as an alternative way of justifying a focus on risk in pension regulation, in that in its absence, equity, adequacy, and security are less likely to be achieved. Annuitization regulations could also be justified in this way. Regulation may also be based on the desire for economic efficiency—for example removing barriers to labor mobility—and indeed financial efficiency, so firms' costs in running pension funds are minimized and pensions are affordable for members.

Moreover, Altman (1992) suggests that the term 'private pension' is itself a misnomer, as the distinction between private and public programs is increasingly blurred. Terms and conditions are often prescribed by the government; they are publicly supported by tax subsidies; there is compulsory provision in several countries; and in some countries, private funds take over part of the earnings-related social security provision function.

Regulations are, of course, not costless, and it is emphasized below that excessive regulatory burdens may discourage provision of private pensions when it is voluntary. It can also reduce the competitiveness of companies when provision is compulsory (Laboul and Yermo 2006). There is a trade-off of cost and benefit security, which regulators must consider and handle. Some would argue that the focus on risk in regulation has been excessive for DB funds and stimulated their replacement by DC, for example.

To guide our overview of developments in pension regulation and their relation to risk, we offer a schematic table which indicates the different types of regulation, the risks they address, their principal level of application, and the main countries cited. Table 9.1 provides an overview and guide to what follows.

Changing Investment Regulations for Collective Pension Funds

Investment regulations are the traditional means whereby pension regulators have sought to control risks arising from funding of pensions, be they corporate or public DC or DB plans (Davis 2002). In a country adopting quantitative asset restrictions (QAR), the government enforces specific regulations, typically limiting holding of particular classes of assets deemed 'risky'. The logic of QAR or 'prudent investment' rules is that prudence is equal to safety, where security of assets is measured instrument-by-instrument according to a fixed standard. Focus is placed on the investment itself.

Typically QAR involves limits on holdings of assets with relatively volatile nominal returns, low liquidity, or high credit risk, such as equities, venture capital/

TABLE 9.1 Types of regulation and related risks

Regulation	Main risk addressed	Principal application	Main countries cited
Portfolio regulations	Risky asset portfolio	Fund-by-fund	U.K. and U.S. (PPR); E.U., Japan (transition); Germany (QAR)
Defined benefit funds:			
Risk-based regulation	Shortfall risk, especially due to asset/liability mismatch	Fund-by-fund	Netherlands, Germany, U.K., U.S.
Tighter solvency rules	Shortfall risk	Fund-by-fund	Netherlands, U.K., U.S.
Guarantees	Bankruptcy of sponsor	System-wide	U.K., U.S.
Accounting standards	Risk to investors and creditors	System-wide	U.K., Netherlands, International accounting standards
Defined contribution funds:			
Costs	Risk of inadequate returns and hence pension	System-wide	U.K., Poland, Argentina, Sweden, Chile, US, Australia
Outcomes and risks	Risk of volatility close to retirement	Individuals and funds	Australia, Denmark, Mexico, Sweden, Chile
Annuitization	Risk of outliving pension assets	Individual by individual	U.S., U.K., Australia, Chile, Switzerland
Transparency and education	Risk of inadequate saving and inappropriate investment	Individual by individual	Denmark, Mexico, Australia, Poland, Chile
Current weaknesses:			
(Mortality tables and mortality risk-sharing)	Longevity risk to both DB and DC funds	System-wide	US, Switzerland, Netherlands
(Counter cyclical funding and investment)	Risks of wider market volatility	System-wide	Canada, U.S., Netherlands, Japan, Switzerland

Source: Author's depiction.

unquoted shares, and real estate, as well as foreign assets, even if their mean returns are relatively high. By contrast, under the prudent person rule (PPR), an OECD definition is that 'a fiduciary must discharge his or her duties with the care, skill, prudence and diligence that a prudent person acting in a like capacity would use in the conduct of an enterprise of like character and aims' (Galer 2002: 45). Hence, there must be an investment strategy whereby pension assets are invested prudently, just as someone would do in the conduct of his own affairs.

The PPR has generally been seen as an economically superior approach, since it permits funds to attain the frontier of efficient portfolios as well as optimize the risk–return trade-off given the maturity of the fund and the risks to which it is exposed (Davis and Hu 2009). PPR allows a free market to operate throughout the investment process, while ensuring, along with solvency regulations (for DB funds) and appropriate decisions regarding contributions in the light of market conditions, that there is both adequacy of assets and an appropriate level of risk. By focusing unduly on the risk and liquidity of individual assets, QAR fails to take into account the fact that, at the portfolio level, both default risk and price volatility can be reduced by diversification. Liquidity risk depends on the overall liquidity position of the investor and not on the liquidity of individual instruments. QAR may prevent taking into account the duration of the liabilities, which can differ sharply between sponsors and funds, as well as over time.

Indeed, in PPR there is usually an implicit or explicit presumption that diversification of investments is a key indicator of prudence, in line with finance theory. Prudent person rules also tend to include limits on self-investment, but this is not the case for 401(k) plans in the U.S., despite the losses at Enron and WorldCom (Galer 2002).

Traditionally there has been a division between countries adopting PPR and QAR that corresponds broadly to that of the Anglo-Saxon countries versus Europe and Japan as well as emerging markets. Nevertheless, the past several years have seen a broad shift from QAR to PPR. The logic of the argument for PPR has been followed, for example, in the Institutions for Occupations Retirement Provision (IORP) Directive in Europe and recent shifts to PPR in countries such as Japan. Nevertheless, this shift is not universal: for example, Germany retains limits such as 35 percent equity for its 'Pensionskassen' and limits on asset classes that can be invested in, and in this it is followed by many emerging market economies (OECD 2013).

The shift to PPR has also involved a change in the roles of regulators, away from evaluating and checking portfolios and toward assessing the validity of a plan's approach to investment. For example, under PPR, regulators must test the behavior of the asset manager, the institutional investor, and the process of decision-making. Regulators must evaluate whether a 'due diligence' investigation has been undertaken in formulating the plan's strategic asset allocation. A pension institution would also be expected to have a coherent and explicit statement of investment principles. PPR thus necessitates a wider degree of transparency for the institutions, including, in particular, identification of lines of responsibility for decisions and of detailed practices of asset management to be discussed in more detail below.

The means of applying PPR varies. For example, trustees in the U.K. are not required to have investment knowledge, but they must obtain proper advice on the topic. Accordingly, regulation has, in effect, been supplemented by the role of the investment consultant. Meanwhile, in the U.S., the pension fund manager's decisions have to be justified by reference to those of investment professionals (prudent expert rule), maximizing risk-adjusted returns on a well-diversified portfolio. These have both tended to involve high equity holdings (OECD 2012). Although Continental European countries have also switched to the prudent person rule, they have held more conservative portfolios. This relates partly to tighter solvency regulations for DB and risk-based regulation for both DB and DC, to be elaborated below.

The Evolving Regulation of DB Plans

Besides the portfolio regulations noted above, the traditional regulation of DB funds has related to the funding of benefits and ownership of surpluses. By definition, a DC plan is always fully funded as assets equal liabilities, whereas with DB plans there is a distinction between the pension plan obligations or contractual rights to the participants and the fund assets to providing collateral for the promised benefits. This in turn gives rise to shortfall risk, which implies a danger that pension promises are not fulfilled.

Key aspects underlying the evolution of DB regulation in different countries relate to differences in how the pension fund is conceptualized, divisions of responsibility, and risk-sharing between employers and employees (Laboul and Yermo 2006). In the Anglo-Saxon region, the basis of safety is the solvency of the sponsor who bears the underwriting risk, backed by an insurance fund. Accordingly, the funds are organized as trusts securing the assets, but the plan is kept close to the company, with considerable flexibility in regulation and amortization of shortfalls. In Continental Europe, by contrast, pension funds have significant operational autonomy and offer guarantees with sponsors providing a form of reinsurance (or even more limited responsibility). Insurance funds are absent and funding rules more strict. Here the pension fund is legally independent, and economically it is akin to a life insurance company and regulated accordingly.

DB plans have suffered successive financial market shocks in the past dozen years, with the dotcom crisis and the subprime crisis affecting their equity holdings severely, the extent of which depended on their prior holdings of such assets. The resultant shortfall risk implied dangers to retirement income security. These crises challenged the traditional flexible approach of Anglo-Saxon regulators, as well as challenging the less flexible approach in Continental Europe (Laboul and

Yermo 2006). As noted by Franzen (2010), the 'perfect pension storm' that has been experienced led the risk management revolution to extend to the pension industry, superimposed on traditional forms of regulation, whereas it had previously been confined to other sectors, notably banks (see also Lundbergh et al. 2014). This has in turn been reinforced by regulation requiring risk management, also justified by the development of guarantees and shaped by the changing accounting standards for pensions and the shift to PPR as noted above.

The Shift to Risk-based Regulation and the Link to Solvency Regulation

Kocken (2006) defines risk management for a financial institution as a process starting at a strategic level. It begins with analyzing risk factors for a pension fund and its stakeholders, which is followed by a decision regarding the acceptable level of risk, and ends at the operational level in measuring and controlling risk. Banks have been in a process of shifting from returns-driven management to risk management for some decades, with a particular milestone being the Basel Capital Adequacy Accord of 1988 and its extension in 1996 to cover use of approved models for market risk to calculate capital (Basel Committee on Banking Supervision 2006). The underlying shift of focus from return to risk was in turn a consequence of the wave of global financial crises that began in 1973 after a long period of quiescence since 1945 (Davis 1995a), and notably the Latin American debt crisis that began in 1982. There is a clear parallel between these seismic events affecting banks and triggering changes in the focus of regulation and the more recent market crises impacting on DB pension fund solvency.

Yet this transition in banking regulation did not initially affect pension funds and their regulators in Europe, although DB plans are clearly subject to underwriting or actuarial risk—risks that they might not fulfill contractual obligations to customers. These, in turn, are linked to longevity risk and inflation risk; they also bear market risk on their assets and the risk of asset/liability mismatch. But, as noted above, pension funds are not subject to liquidity risk, arguably the main concern of banks and their regulators in risk management. Traditionally pension fund risk managers have focused instead on choosing appropriate assets to derive a strategic asset allocation and manage the market risk, largely ignoring liabilities. But increasingly, larger funds have begun to use asset liability management (ALM), eventually deriving the optimal strategic asset allocation in a liability-consistent way, assessing the impact of decisions not only of investment but also of contributions and indexation of benefits. In this sense, risk-based regulation has grown up from best practice in individual pension plans.

Franzen (2010) argues that pension funds in the major industrial countries manage risk today according to differing concepts of the underlying pension promise as defined previously. This explains why Continental pension funds such as the Dutch were in the lead in risk-based regulation. Also, Anglo-Saxon country regulators have been traditionally more lenient with respect to risk-taking than Continentals (Laboul and Yermo 2006).

Risk-based regulation of pension funds was first prompted by the dotcom bust of 2001–3, which led to widespread underfunding of DB pensions (Davis and de Haan 2012). The subprime crisis was a further spur. It can be argued that the introduction of risk-based regulation for DB funds enables pension funds to make proper use of complex markets and instruments, and to allocate scarce supervisory resources efficiently (Brunner et al. 2008). It has also been driven by the integration of financial supervision in the Netherlands, as well as in DC countries Denmark and Australia. Thus, the Dutch and Australians seek to apply a similar form of financial regulation to pension funds as to banks and insurance companies, adapted nonetheless to the economics of pension funds (Brunner et al. 2008).

Risk-based management requires sound risk management within the institution—including a risk management strategy, board involvement, fulfillment of risk management functions, and internal controls. Evaluation of corporate governance rules for risk management architecture becomes an important role of the regulator, although large and small funds are not expected to be equally sophisticated. In practice, regulators typically do not require a specific form of risk management architecture; there are links between the form of risk-based regulation and the varying structural form of pension funds and pension promises discussed above. Thus, for example, asset liability management (ALM) is mandatory in the Netherlands and Germany, whereas in the U.K. it is only encouraged, and in the U.S. regulators are neutral. Accordingly, the role of regulators in the former countries must include evaluation of models and strategies based on ALM, not essential in the Anglo-Saxon countries. In fact, mandatory use of ALM can be criticized, in the sense that it is subject to model risk and the breakdown of underlying assumptions. And if all pension funds were to adopt a similar model, they could be subject to herding, volatility, and liquidity crises in capital markets, worsening aggregate risk.

More fundamentally, it can be argued that when pension fund models include Value-at-Risk (VaR), they could be in danger of imposing an inappropriately short time horizon on pension funds and excessive concern about market risk (Shi and Werker 2012). Indeed, Campbell and Viceira (2002) note that when equities are subject to mean reversion, and taking human capital into account, equities can be secure assets for long-term investors such as pension funds. But this argument may break down when taking into account a plan's integration with the sponsor, which is assumed to provide a backup for shortfalls. Mergers and bankruptcies are examples in which the state of the sponsor limits the horizon of investment of the pension fund. And new accounting standards also impact the time horizon of investment, as will be discussed further on in the chapter.

Stress testing is another key aspect of risk-based regulation. For example, since 2005, the most important tool of the regulator in Germany is a stress test (within the ALM) to ensure that funds retain 100 percent funding under various capital market scenarios (Franzen 2010). Sale of assets may be required to meet the test, so this is one explanation why funds there are typically well below their 35 percent limit on equities. Since 2007, Dutch funds have had to run scenario-based solvency tests showing that they have only a 2.5 percent probability of falling below 100 percent funding (excluding conditional indexation) within a year (Franzen 2010). There are methods based on simplified and standard methods prescribed by the regulator, but also internal models are permitted, as in most recent global accords on banking regulation, Basel II and III. But stress tests are only as useful as the likelihood of the scenarios they depict coming about, and if they are imposed mechanistically they can lead to complacency about exposure to risk.

Risk scoring is a further aspect of risk-based supervision. Pension regulators in the Netherlands use a common model for assessing pension funds for banks and insurance companies (Financial Institutions Risk Analysis Method, or FIRM). This is a four-stage approach to assessing risk, requiring a detailed profile of the fund, identifying relevant management units, assessing gross risks and giving scores, and then seeking insight into the quality of risk controls in each category for a view of overall risk. This, in turn, drives the frequency of on-site inspections. As discussed below, risk scoring is also a feature of risk-based supervision of DC funds in countries such as Denmark, Australia, and Mexico.

In the wake of the dotcom crisis, pension authorities also began to impose higher funding ratios. Franzen (2010) argues that solvency ratios are not an ultimate goal of pension funds, but rather an instrument of risk management imposed by the regulatory authorities. The U.K. 2004 Pensions Act and the 2006 U.S. Pension Protection Act, for example, tightened funding rules in those countries, with the U.S. shortening periods of smoothing of asset values and liability discount rates from five to two years.

Meanwhile the Dutch introduced a full model-based approach to solvency regulation similar to that used for insurance and banking, with longevity, market, currency, and interest rate risks all covered and asset–liability mismatches penalized, though a 15-year period is allowed to amortize shortfalls (Franzen 2010). Whereas the minimum solvency buffer is 5 percent, in practice consideration of the risks and the stress tests require pension funds to be 30 percent overfunded. As noted by Brunner et al. (2008), the new Dutch system is seen as costly and could discourage provision of DB pensions; more onerous supervision may also have played a role in the shift to career-average-based DB and conditional indexation.

These conceptual differences highlighted above are reflected in the differences in the ways in which regulators approach funding. The U.K. approach to funding is principles-based and relies on regulation of governance. It is scheme-specific with no general rules for funding recovery periods. Meanwhile, the Dutch approach is a rule- and risk-based approach focused on fair value, in line with banking concepts. The U.S. offers a hybrid combining governance principles with quantitative rules on funding—amortizing shortfalls in seven years, discounting liabilities with corporate bond yields and limiting smoothing to two years. (Public plans are allowed 30 years to amortize shortfalls; Impavido and Tower 2009.)

The Development of Guarantees

The passage of the Employee Retirement Income Security Act (ERISA) in 1974 led to the introduction of the Pension Benefit Guaranty Corporation (PBGC) for private sector DB funds in the United States. This enterprise has become a model for the extension of such guarantees in other countries seeking to protect beneficiaries against risk of sponsor insolvency. In particular, the U.K. introduced the Pension Protection Fund (PPF) in its 2004 Pension Act to pay compensation to members of eligible DB pension schemes in the event of employer insolvency, where there are insufficient assets in the fund to cover Pension Protection Fund levels of compensation. Existing schemes are charged an annual levy, which is a mixture of scheme-based and risk-based levies (Liu and Tonks 2008).

The scheme-based levy is based on the plan's pension liabilities and makes up 20 percent of the total pension protection levy. The risk-based levy is based on the plan's underfunding risk and the insolvency risk of the sponsoring firm. The PPF Board, a government entity, considers the level of underfunding and the likelihood of sponsoring employer insolvency (based on external rating agencies). It may also consider the plan's asset allocation and any other risk factors.

Although guarantees seek to protect beneficiaries against risk, they pose risks in themselves to the guarantors, particularly if incentives are not appropriate. McCarthy and Neuberger (2005) suggest that there is a large chance that the U.K. PPF will default on its liabilities if it sticks with its proposed levy structure. Also it faces severe moral hazard and agency problems, not least because the financing burdens are placed mainly on riskier funds. More generally, the development of pension insurance involves additional agencies regulating DB funds with the risk of overlap and contradiction. It also puts greater pressure on regulators to impose stricter funding rules and asset/liability management to avoid calls on insurance funds that may themselves discourage DB pension provision.

The Role of Accounting Standards

Whereas pension funds are economically subject to longevity risk and wage or inflation risk, under the influence of accounting standards they must take increasing account of interest rate risk (Franzen 2010). Accounting standards are seen as an aspect of regulation since they are a form of market discipline, but they may also impinge on the investment horizon of pension funds. They integrate the sponsor and the fund into one accounting unit valued at market prices, thus leaving the sponsor's balance sheet vulnerable to short-term market risk arising from pension fund considerations. The sponsor may hence require the fund, independent of regulation, to invest on a shorter time horizon than would otherwise be the case. Accounting pressures and mark-to-market may also limit investment in illiquid assets such as private placements and private equity, which may increase shortfall risk since these assets are potentially high-yielding.

In practice, there is often an inconsistency between the accounting and actuarial approaches to pension fund valuation. Actuarial approaches tend to look at a fund on an ongoing basis, focusing on accrued and not projected liabilities. Traditional accounting approaches recognize the pension contributions as costs on the sponsor's financial statement, but they do not expose the sponsor to market risk from the pension fund, not least given smoothing and long periods between valuations. The mark-to-market approach to assets and liabilities currently growing in popularity means that the focus is increasingly on the current financial situation of the pension fund, allowing for projected values (Franzen 2010). As noted above, in the U.K. there is also a third form of valuation required by the PPF, related to the cost of buying out liabilities with an insurance company. This has created a dilemma for sponsors, since regulators often focus on the actuarial values while, due to capital market pressures, firms need to take the accounting values into account. The importance of interest rates in calculating accounting liabilities means interest rate risk, which is not an economic risk for ongoing pension funds, becomes dominant.

Indeed, the combination of risk-based regulation with market value accounting has led to a focus on liability-driven investment whose goal is to manage interest rate risk such as immunization and dedication (Franzen 2010). These practices are much costlier than traditional strategies that would have been adopted in risk/return optimization or even ALM. Given their high cost, they are also inducing firms in the U.K. to opt out of provision of DB pensions. But on the positive side, liability-driven approaches adopted by the U.K. Boots plc pension fund also appear to have enabled the plans to ride out the subprime crisis without a shortfall (Skypala 2011). The alternative approach of greater diversification using financial innovations such as collateralized debt obligations (CDOs) proved more than counterproductive, due not only to defaults but also to mark-to-market losses as illiquidity set in and false perceptions of credit quality were corrected.

Accounting pressures on pension funds have arguably contributed to a further trend involving market-based calculations of liabilities for regulatory purposes. In the light of the development of guarantee funds, the fragility of sponsors, and recent financial turmoil, some argue that regulators should be more concerned with measures of termination or wind-up liabilities, as opposed to those for an ongoing fund. Recently, the Dutch shifted to a market-value basis for liabilities and not a fixed rate, while in 2004–5 the U.S. shifted from a 30-year Treasury bond yield to a corporate bond yield where the timing of future benefits will determine the yield (Laboul and Yermo 2006). Smoothing of the latter helps reduce the impact of short-run market turbulence.

Evolving Regulation of DC Plans

DC funds have not been immune to the asset market volatility caused by the global financial crisis, with losses of as much as 25 percent of portfolios (OECD 2009). This has naturally put a focus on investment risks, highlighting the ongoing importance of costs and annuitization which can also put retirement income security in jeopardy, as well as that of DC holders' level of financial knowledge.

The Regulation of Costs

Many charges are applied to DC funds, including flat rate fees (e.g. a monthly policy fee unrelated to the fund size), deductions from the fund (e.g. the annual management charge is usually expressed as a percentage of the fund value), initial charges (e.g. set-up costs such as the bid–offer spread: the difference between the prices at which investments are bought and sold), and exit charges (e.g. the transfer fee if a member transfers to a different scheme; U.K. Parliament 2012).

There is a growing awareness that DC plans can be very costly for beneficiaries, considerably reducing the pensions accumulated relative to the returns on the underlying portfolios. For this reason there is a risk that accumulations will fall short of what is desired for a comfortable retirement. This is particularly true if these are individually managed plans, suggesting a need for regulatory intervention to limit costs. In a low-inflation environment the impact of costs is even more noticeable.

One option is direct regulation of costs. Under the U.K. Stakeholder scheme, costs are limited to 1 percent of assets per annum, and the new 'NEST' plan aims to deliver to all employees and the self-employed the opportunity to save for a pension at the annual management charge of 0.3 percent per year or less 'today enjoyed only by employees of large firms, by public sector employees or by high income individuals' (U.K. Parliament 2012: 28).

In mandatory funded schemes, direct regulation of fees is common, with maximum fees imposed in countries such as Argentina, Bolivia, and Colombia as well as in Central and Eastern Europe (Tapia and Yermo 2008). In Poland, progressively lower limits are being imposed on fees to put pressure on providers to economize. There may also be restrictions on types of fees, as, for example, in Argentina, where pension funds may only charge fees on contributions.

Another way to limit costs is to create a market structure that generates competition via a central agency or clearing house for pensions, as in Sweden (Tapia and Yermo 2008). This separates costs of fund collection and management from those of asset management, limits marketing costs, and ensures a government monopsony to put pressure on asset managers' fees. The central clearinghouse negotiates fees with providers, and a proportion of fees must be rebated to participants so they share in economies of scale in asset management. Similar low costs are ensured in Bolivia by limiting the market to two competitors selected by an international bidding process for the lowest fees, and restricting competition between them (Tapia and Yermo 2008). Nevertheless, low costs in Bolivia may also relate to low costs of asset management for government bonds. Competition per se, without such structures, has tended to increase costs owing to the expenditure necessary to encourage members to switch suppliers. Chile is an example of this, with there being no direct regulation limiting fees and the hope that competition would limit them, when in fact fees there have remained high despite the maturity of the system (Tapia and Yermo 2008).

Another regulatory response to the problem of high costs has been to enforce greater transparency, as in the U.S., where 401(k) plans are now required by the SEC to disclose charges. Similarly, in Australia, the Cooper Review led to tough disclosure rules. In the U.K., there have been industry initiatives such as the National Association of Pension Funds (NAPF) code on disclosure. However, given the lack of understanding by beneficiaries, as discussed later in the chapter, such initiatives may not lower charges.

The Regulation of Risks and Outcomes

Besides costs, the outcome of DC plans and consequent risk to beneficiaries depends on the efficiency of the investment process. Accordingly, the nature of portfolio regulations plays a significant role for such schemes. As noted above, there is a trend to move from quantitative restrictions to prudent person rules that apply both to DC and DB schemes. Nevertheless, countries with pure mandatory DC schemes tend to have QAR (Antolín et al. 2009).

Besides limiting holdings of volatile assets, QAR may apply a minimum investment return, as in mandatory funds in Switzerland, which the government has been forced to reduce owing to market conditions. Or there may be an extension of the forms of risk-based regulation discussed above for DB schemes, as in the case of stress tests in Denmark and a daily value-at-risk ceiling as in Mexico based on the volatility of individual member accounts (based, in turn, on asset prices over 500 days; see Brunner et al. 2008). The Danish system is a hybrid of DB and DC with return guarantees and hence risk-sharing, but is classified here as DC. The stress test based on asset composition provides a 'traffic light' indication of solvency, which drives regulatory intervention (Brunner et al. 2008).

In Australia, pension funds are subject to risk scoring as for other financial institutions, in line with the Netherlands. Although funds are DC, the system takes into account institutions' exposure to financial risks and ability to manage them (including investment strategies and asset allocation), by looking not only at portfolio allocations but also how risk management compares to industry best practice. Risk scoring then leads to a degree of supervisory oversight and intervention (Brunner et al. 2008). Denmark and Australia, like the Netherlands, require a risk management plan or risk management guidelines during licensing, and the aim through risk scoring is to induce funds to take on best practice in risk management. Australia introduced licensing of trustees at the same time as risk-based supervision and has seen a number of trustees leave the industry; in other words, there has been industry consolidation.

For DC funds in these countries, risk-based regulation has at times been a *quid pro quo* for easing of investment restrictions (Brunner et al. 2008), and this has entailed a more diversified portfolio in Mexico. On the other hand, the Mexican VaR ceiling is criticized in Antolín et al. (2009), as it is centered on a zero mean return while a pension fund needs to consider non-zero means in the returns distribution. Such tools may force pension funds, which are not subject to liquidity risk, to invest in lower risk assets and thereby harm the outcome at retirement, as well as inducing them to sell equities when markets are falling. They may also be vulnerable to modeling error. Brunner et al. (2008) note that it is only manageable to require such a detailed specification of risk management (including precise details of board structure and risk models to use) for all funds when they are small in number, as in Mexico. Meanwhile, the Danish risk-based supervision system is seen as generating shifts from hybrid to pure DC across the funds, partly driven by workers seeking higher returns that come without guarantees.

Whereas risk-based supervision is readily applied to DB funds, as in the Netherlands, it is less clear whether it is appropriate for DC funds, which lack a concept of 'solvency.' Instead, some suggest that income replacement targets should be implemented, and scenarios based on contributions and returns (Brunner et al. 2008).

For individual contracts, there may be investment rules that apply in addition to—or instead of—QAR or PPR. The provision of a default option is becoming more common across DC schemes, when individuals may not have the information to invest freely with confidence. Particularly in mandatory schemes, this may entail a form of lifestyle or target date fund which may protect individuals from losses in volatile assets as they draw close to retirement. The age of the participant does affect the nature of the portfolio limits in Chile and Mexico, for example. But it does not in E.U. countries with similar schemes. For instance in Estonia, Hungary, and the Slovak Republic, there is a single default option with zero or few equities. Arguably, this may not be appropriate for younger workers who can afford to take more risk. A similar problem arises in a more acute form in Colombia, Israel, and Poland, which allow no fund choice at all.

By contrast, Australia and Sweden allow providers to establish their own choice menus and individuals to elect therein freely, which may lead to excessive equity exposure for older workers. Some types of voluntary DC fund also involve lifestyle default options as in stakeholder funds in the U.K., although default options are less common in voluntary schemes. Impavido and Tower (2009) suggest that default options in the U.S. could reduce the impact of shocks such as the subprime crisis on pension wealth, and hence on household expenditures.

Antolín et al. (2009) show that mean-variance efficient portfolios with low or high equity exposure may not be efficient for pension provision given the trade-off between expected replacement ratio and risk. And a dynamic risk budgeting strategy may be superior to zero equities for the years approaching retirement, although calculating this would be challenging for individuals. They also emphasize that there is no 'single recipe' for DC plans, so factors such as desired participation rates, cultural attitudes to financial risks, and the nature of the pension promise will affect appropriate regulation of outcomes.

Regulation of Annuitization

Annuities can protect individuals from longevity risk, though these are traditionally very little used when voluntary. In the U.S. and Australia, this links to tax disincentives. In Australia, there are no restrictions on payout options from the second pillar, which reduces annuitization demand (Rocha et al. 2010). This is unusual for countries with mandatory funded schemes which typically are tightening regulations on lump sums, as in Chile in 2004 and 2008, where a growing proportion of average wages must be provided in the form of a real annuity for the minimum pension plus a variable annuity or a phased withdrawal.

Other forms of regulation of annuities include those related to prudential regulation of insurance companies, conduct of business regulation of insurance companies, and other aspects of the regulation of annuities within the overall pension system (Davis 2004). These topics are largely beyond the scope of this chapter; suffice to note that risk-based regulation and strict solvency rules are more appropriate for the provision of annuities, which are guaranteed products, than they are for DC and (to a lesser extent) DB pension plans discussed earlier in the chapter.

As regards further regulation of annuities per se, Swiss regulations fix the pricing of annuities—which causes difficulties when bond yields fall (including cross subsidies between individuals). Then the conversion factors have had to be repeatedly lowered, although they are generally higher than could be obtained on the open market, thus encouraging annuitization via the occupational pension fund (Rocha et al. 2010). In Sweden, under the centralized funded system, only two options are offered and annuitization is obligatory. One is a with-profits annuity with minimum guaranteed benefits, which in 2007 had its guarantee cut from 2.75 percent to zero with the hope of raising returns and bonuses. In fact most retirees select the unit-linked alternative from the asset managers where risks and returns are higher (Rocha et al. 2010).

Marketing of annuities is not widely regulated beyond conduct of business rules, except in Chile, which has a licensing regulation for pension advisors as well as caps on broker commissions and an electronic quotation system. This quotation system is aimed to reduce brokers' influence on costs and hence returns by providing consumers with direct access to a full range of commission quotes.

Annuity regulations are changing also in countries with voluntary schemes. In the U.S., withdrawal from DC funds is becoming more restrictive, while in the U.K. it is becoming less so, with former levels of compulsion in annuitization no longer applying, partly under pressure from low bond yields. Turner and Hughes (2008) note that historically lax regulation of DC fund payouts may have accelerated the shift from DB to DC in the U.S., while in contrast, the requirement of annuitization in Canada may have decelerated the shift by ensuring a 'level playing field'. This does not explain the shift in the U.K., where such a level playing field also prevails—the mandatory inflation indexation requirement for DB pensions in payment may be more decisive (Ashcraft 2008; McCarthy and Neuberger 2009).

Transparency and Financial Education

As highlighted earlier in the chapter, pension benefits from DC plans are inherently uncertain and affected by returns on investment, discount rates, inflation, wages, and employment, as well as life expectancies. Participants must make decisions at a time when the outcomes in these factors are unknown.

For risk-based systems of regulation as in Denmark and Mexico, market discipline is established by ensuring individuals and sponsors are well informed, since there is scope to change providers. In Australia and Mexico, auditors also assess the quality of risk management and must report problems to the supervisor. Nevertheless, supervisory ratings are not typically disclosed to the market. Whereas this is understandable for banks, given the risk of a 'run,' this is not a consideration for pension funds and disclosure would seem to be appropriate. In Chile, efforts are made to help members further by communicating those choices and their implications on a regular basis, as well as giving projections showing likely future pensions by way of pension statements and pension risk simulators. These complement the electronic quotation system for annuities highlighted above.

Pension statements usually include a member's current balance asset allocation, and they can also provide projections about future benefits (although projected pension benefits are never certain). Meanwhile, questions regarding the returns on investments, whether the person will lose his job, or how long the person will live are among the factors that generate uncertainty. Pension risk simulators, used in Chile since 2005, can be used to help employees understand related uncertainty about projected future pension benefits.

To convey this uncertainty, members need projections they can readily comprehend. There are two main approaches to providing projected future pension benefits: deterministic or stochastic projections. The latter offer a range with associated probabilities. A particular advantage of stochastic modeling is that it allows for the uncertainty regarding projections of future benefits from DC pension plans to be quantified. The drawback is that results may be complex and difficult to understand.

Despite such advances, surveys cited in Tapia and Yermo (2008) show that knowledge of fees is poor in countries such as Poland and Chile. In Poland, there is limited understanding of types of fees paid and 40 percent did not know there is a transfer fee between accounts. In Chile 96 percent of people did not know pension companies receive management fees as a proportion of monthly payments. Since fees are a major determinant of returns and consequent pensions, transparency is again not sufficient.

This discussion highlights the need for education about pensions to complement these forms of transparency, without which beneficiaries will be unaware of risks to retirement income until it is too late. This remains absent, or at least mainly on paper rather than in practice in most countries. It is of course of particular relevance where there is a major element of choice in pension saving and hence in retirement income, such as in countries without mandatory funded schemes or substantial pay-as-you-go pensions.

The Evolution of Pension Portfolios

Fair valuation principles used for accounting purposes have been a key factor behind the decline in equity allocations in pension fund portfolios in the United Kingdom, according to Severinson and Yermo (2012). Risk-based funding regulations have also contributed to the declining equity allocation among pension funds and pension insurance companies in countries such as Denmark and the Netherlands. In complementary work, Shi and Werker (2012) show that the imposition of an annual expected shortfall constraint, or a VaR constraint on a long-term investor, can lead to an economic cost of 2.5–3.8 percent of initial wealth over a 15-year horizon.

These points should not be exaggerated, however, as there has also been a shift to private equity, hedge funds, real estate, and, most recently, unlisted infrastructure equity held in pension funds. Accordingly, risk in pension portfolios has not necessarily fallen. Although bond allocations have increased, particularly in Sweden and the United Kingdom, derisking is more evident in the growing use of interest risk-hedging instruments (such as swaps and options) than in the net change in investment risk in the main asset portfolio. There are also perceptions of changes in long-term asset returns which underlie shifts in portfolios (see also Moore and Pedersen 2014).

Emerging Concerns

Longevity Risk

Longevity is a key determinant of liabilities of DB plans as well as the retirement income provided by DC plans (Cairns 2014). U.S. DB plans from 1995 to 2007 appear to have retained use of outdated mortality tables (from 1983), and few plans used the latest available data (IMF 2012). Pension liabilities may be underestimated by at least 12 percent as a consequence, implying a major risk of inadequate funding. In Switzerland, despite the mandatory funded system, pension funds can also choose their own mortality tables and discount rates for estimating liabilities (Rocha et al. 2010). In the Netherlands, a change in the mortality table in 2010 led to an increase in measured liabilities of 7 percent. Because of the way in which liabilities are calculated, longevity risk is particularly sizeable in a low interest rate environment. Using the methodology proposed by Impavido (2011), at a 6 percent interest rate, a three-year rise in longevity raises liabilities by 8 percent, but at 2 percent interest liabilities rise 14 percent.

One response has been to increase risk-sharing. Dutch pension regulators have arrived at an accord that stabilizes contributions, ensures up-to-date mortality calculations, and requires the risk of longevity and market performance to be reflected in retirement ages and benefits (IMF 2012). Such a shift is likely to make DB funds in that country more sustainable. Market-based transfers of longevity risk could also occur via buy-ins, buyouts (both with insurers), and longevity bonds. Meanwhile it is essential that countries ensure mortality tables are updated, as was apparently not the case in some U.S. pension funds.

Procyclicality of Funding and Investment Rules

Risk-based regulation and fair value accounting could incentivize procyclical investment behavior such as the fire-sale of assets in market downturns (Severinson and Yermo 2012). Besides generating unnecessary losses for pension funds per se, this could lead to price distortions in less liquid markets, as witnessed during the 2008–9 crisis in some maturity segments of derivatives markets used by pension funds and life insurers to hedge interest rate risks. This effect is compounded by a supply problem in long-term government bonds, as pension and insurance liabilities are often substantially larger than the stock of long-term government debt. Besides fire sales, inappropriately designed regulations could force companies to contribute heavily after a crash while not incentivizing build-up of contributions in an upturn (Impavido and Tower 2009). These can have a macroeconomic impact on company investment, to add to other macroeconomic effects via pension funds, such as those on personal wealth, and via calling of government guarantees. Moreover, Antolín and Stewart (2009) and Yermo and Severinson (2010) show that after the crisis there were measures of regulatory forbearance such as longer periods to recover shortfalls (in Canada, Netherlands, U.K., U.S.), moratoria on contributions (in Japan) and lower minimum returns (in Switzerland). Besides allowing funds to remain viable, they prevented damaging fire sales of assets that could have further destabilized markets.

Yet regulations remain damagingly procyclical (Yermo and Severinson 2010), meaning that it will be important to reduce the reliance on current market values when determining contributions. In particular, it has been suggested that smoothed discount ratios could be used for liabilities, as is already the case in the U.S. and Japan. Or, as in Canada, regulators could use average rather than current solvency ratios in calculating minimum funding requirements. There could be greater encouragement of surpluses in good times via more flexible tax ceilings, while also limiting contribution holidays and sponsor access to surpluses. And the calculation of minimum funding could pay more attention to security mechanisms such as insurance schemes that are in place. These suggestions, of course, are in contrast to the development of risk-based and market value-based regulation highlighted above.

Conclusion

In the wake of the market crises over the last decade, along with a growing awareness of the shortcomings of pension plan finances, there has been widespread innovation in the regulatory field. Increasingly, and appropriately, regulation has grown more focused on risk to beneficiaries both within the portfolio and arising from other aspects of pension systems such as costs and lack of consumer education. In this context, we highlight countries such as the Netherlands (for DB) and Sweden and Australia (for DC) as having regulatory innovations worthy of attention, although some shortcomings remain, as discussed above. We have argued that further progress in managing and controlling risk remains vital, for example in the fields of longevity risk, procyclical behavior of funds, and financial education. These remain threats to retirement income security that regulators need to bear in mind in future reforms.

It has also been shown that a number of regulatory developments have been counterproductive, inducing pension funds to be increasingly short-term in their investments and focusing on interest rate risk, which is not economically relevant for pension funds. In this light it is worth asking whether pension funds need a Basel III in the wake of the crisis—a new global regulation like that currently being introduced for banks (Basel Committee 2012). As noted, the successive Basel agreements have put an increasing focus on the need for sufficient capital to protect against solvency risk, but also measurement of risk and, in the case of Basel III, including consideration of macroprudential as well as individual institution risk.

Some would contend that global agreements are not needed, since pension funds do not compete across borders and pension policy remains national. Moreover, failure of a pension fund does not usually generate significant externalities either within countries or across borders. That said, some global similarity in the regulation of company funds would be beneficial to multinationals, which are forced at present to set up individual and idiosyncratic funds in each of their operating countries. As noted, Basel III tightens solvency regulations for banks, and similar tightening might help pension funds, although it could at some point also become counterproductive by enforcing holding of low-return assets and/or inducing procyclical investment and portfolios. Liquidity regulations for banks are being introduced for the first time at a global level with Basel III. These do not apply to pension funds, given that their liabilities are long-term—although for mature funds and especially those that are winding down, liquidity is more important. Furthermore, one area of particular interest which does feed through from Basel III is the idea of offsetting procyclicality. As noted, the easing of pension regulations on an ad hoc basis has followed the subprime crisis. The next challenge will be to develop and implement risk-based regulation sufficient to ensure there are not undue and counterproductive countercyclical shifts in pension asset portfolios, forcing sponsors to sell shares at the very point when they are likely to be most profitable. This may in turn be generated by inappropriate forms of risk-based supervision. Furthermore, as in Basel III, macroprudential regulation of pension funds may need to be developed, given the often-neglected macroeconomic consequences of their collective behavior.

References

Altman, N. (1992). 'Government Regulation; Enhancing the Equity, Adequacy and Security of Pension Benefits,' in E. Duskin, ed., *Private Pensions and Public Policy*. Paris, France: Organisation for Economic Co-operation and Development, pp. 77–95.

Antolín, P., S. Blome, D. Karim, S. Payet, G. Scheuenstuhl, and J. Yermo (2009). 'Investment Regulations and Defined Contribution Pensions,' OECD Working Paper on Insurance and Private Pensions No. 37. Paris, France: Organisation for Economic Co-operation and Development.

Antolín, P., and F. Stewart (2009). 'Private Pensions and Policy Responses to the Financial and Economic Crisis,' OECD Working Paper on Insurance and Private Pensions No. 36. Paris, France: Organisation for Economic Co-operation and Development.

Ashcraft, J. (2008). 'U.K. Pension Regulation Compared,' NAPF Research Report. London, U.K.: National Association of Pension Funds.

Basel Committee on Banking Supervision (2006). *Basel II: International Convergence of Capital Measurement and Capital Standards: A Revised Framework—Comprehensive Version*. Basel, Switzerland: Bank for International Settlements.

Basel Committee (2012). *Report to G20 Leaders on Basel III Implementation*. Basel, Switzerland: Bank for International Settlements.

Brunner, G., R. Hinz, and R. Rocha (2008). 'Risk-Based Supervision of Pension Funds,' World Bank Policy Research Working Paper No. 4491. Washington, DC: The World Bank.

Cairns, A. (2014). 'Modeling and Management of Longevity Risk,' in P. B. Hammond, R. Maurer, and O. S. Mitchell, eds., *Recreating Sustainable Retirement: Resilience, Solvency, and Tail Risk*. Oxford, U.K.: Oxford University Press, pp. 71–88.

Campbell, J. Y., and L. M. Viceira (2002). *Strategic Asset Allocation: Portfolio Choice for Long-Term Investors*. Oxford, U.K.: Oxford University Press.

Davis, E. P. (1995a). *Debt, Financial Fragility and Systemic Risk.* Oxford: Oxford University Press.

Davis, E. P. (1995b). *Pension Funds.* Oxford: Oxford University Press.

Davis, E. P. (2002). 'Prudent Person Rules or Quantitative Restrictions? The Regulation of Long-Term Institutional Investors' Portfolios,' *Journal of Pension Economics and Finance*, 1: 157–191.

Davis, E. P. (2004). 'Issues in the Regulation of Annuities Markets,' in E. Fornero and E. Luciano, eds., *Developing an Annuities Market in Europe.* Cheltenham, U.K.: Edward Elgar, pp. 49–92.

Davis, E. P. (2012). *Crisis and Kingdom.* Eugene, Oregon: Wipf and Stock.

Davis, E. P., and L. De Haan (2012). 'Pension Fund Finance and Sponsoring Companies,' *Journal of Pension Economics and Finance*, 11: 439–463.

Davis, E. P. and Y. Hu (2009). 'Should Pension Investing be Regulated?' *Rotman International Journal of Pension Management*, 2(1): 34–42.

Franzen, D. (2010). 'Managing Investment Risk in Defined Benefit Pension Funds,' OECD Working Papers on Insurance and Private Pensions No. 37. Paris, France: Organisation for Economic Co-operation and Development.

Galer, R. (2002). 'Prudent Pension Rule Standard for the Investment of Pension Fund Assets,' *Financial Market Trends* No. 83. Paris, France: Organisation for Economic Co-operation and Development.

International Monetary Fund (IMF) (2012). 'The Financial Impact of Longevity Risk,' Chapter 4, *Global Financial Stability Review April 2012.* Washington, DC: IMF.

Impavido, G. (2011). 'Stress Tests for Defined Benefit Pension Plans—a Primer,' IMF Working Paper WP/11/29. Washington, DC: International Monetary Fund.

Impavido, G., and I. Tower (2009). 'How the Financial Crisis Affects Pensions and Insurance and Why the Impacts Matter,' IMF Working Paper WP/09/151. Washington, DC: International Monetary Fund.

Kocken, T. P. (2006). *Curious Contracts: Pension Fund Redesign for the Future.* Den Bosch: Tutein Nolthenius.

Laboul, A., and J. Yermo (2006). 'Regulatory Principles and Institutions,' in G. L. Clark, A. H. Munnell, and J. M. Orszag, eds., *The Oxford Handbook of Pensions and Retirement Income.* Oxford: Oxford University Press, pp. 501–520.

Liu, W., and I. Tonks (2008). 'Alternative Risk-Based Levies in the Pension Protection Fund for Multi-Employee Schemes,' University of Exeter Xfi Centre for Finance and Investment Paper 08/01. Exeter, U.K.: Xfi Centre for Finance and Investment.

Lundbergh, S., R. Cardano, R. Laros, and L. Rebel (2014). 'Developments in European Pension Regulation: Risks and Challenges,' in P. B. Hammond, R. Maurer, and O. S. Mitchell, eds., *Recreating Sustainable Retirement: Resilience, Solvency, and Tail Risk.* Oxford, U.K.: Oxford University Press, pp. 186–214.

McCarthy, D., and A. Neuberger (2005). 'The Pension Protection Fund,' *Fiscal Studies*, 26(2): 139–167.

McCarthy, D., and A. Neuberger (2009). 'The Economic Basis for the Regulation of Pensions,' U.K. Department for Work and Pensions Research Report No 603. London, U.K.: DWP.

Moore, J., and N. K. Pederson (2014). 'Implications for Long-term Investors of the Shifting Distribution of Capital Market Returns,' in P. B. Hammond, R. Maurer, and O.

S. Mitchell, eds., *Recreating Sustainable Retirement: Resilience, Solvency, and Tail Risk*. Oxford, U.K.: Oxford University Press, pp. 30–59.

Organisation for Economic Co-operation and Development (OECD) (2009). *Private Pension Outlook*. Paris, France: OECD.

Organisation for Economic Co-operation and Development (OECD) (2012). 'Pension Markets in Focus,' No. 9, September 2012. Paris, France: OECD.

Organisation for Economic Co-operation and Development (OECD) (2013). *Survey of Investment Regulation for Pension Funds*. Paris, France: OECD.

Rocha, R., D. Vittas, and H. P. Rudolph (2010). 'The Payout Phase of Pension Systems; a Comparison of Five Countries,' World Bank Policy Research Paper No 5288. Washington, DC: The World Bank.

Severinson, C., and J. Yermo (2012). 'The Effect of Solvency Regulation and Accounting Standards on Long-term Investment,' OECD Working Papers on Finance, Insurance and Private Pensions No. 30. Paris, France: Organisation for Economic Co-operation and Development.

Shi, Z., and B. J. M. Werker (2012). 'Short Horizon Regulation for Long-Term Investors,' *Journal of Banking and Finance*, 36: 3227–3238.

Skypala, P. (2011). 'Boots' Bonds Architect on the Merits of Switching,' *Financial Times*, November 6.

Tapia, W., and J. Yermo (2008). 'Fees in Individual Account Pension Systems,' OECD Working Papers on Insurance and Private Pensions No. 27. Paris, France: Organisation for Economic Co-operation and Development.

Turner, J. A., and G. Hughes (2008). 'Large Declines in Defined Benefit Plans are Not Inevitable: The Case of Canada, Ireland, the U.K. and the U.S.,' Pensions Institute Discussion Paper PI-0821. London, U.K.: Cass Business School.

U. K. Parliament (2012). *Pension Scheme Charges*. Standard Note: SN 6209 by Djuna Thurley, House of Commons Library. London, U.K.

Yermo, J., and C. Severinson (2010). 'The Impact of the Financial Crisis on Defined Benefit Plans and the Need for Counter Cyclical Funding Regulations,' OECD Working Papers on Finance, Insurance and Private Pensions No 3. Paris, France: Organisation for Economic Co-operation and Development.

Chapter 10

Developments in European Pension Regulation: Risks and Challenges

Stefan Lundbergh, Ruben Laros, and Laura Rebel

This chapter focuses on developments in the regulatory frameworks for pensions in Europe, and their potential consequences for pension systems in the European Union (E.U.) and possibly other countries as well. Our aim is to outline how these changes in regulatory frameworks may develop, given the underlying demographical and societal trends. Because the rules are still under development, we focus on the key principles involved, rather than specific details.

In what follows, we first discuss retirement systems in the E.U. and how employment-based pensions are organized. Then we outline how the regulatory environment is changing. Next we explore the impact of the global financial crisis on the regulatory framework by highlighting specific experiences of the member states who were early adopters of the stricter regulatory framework. A final section concludes.

Retirement Systems in the European Union

Retirement systems in Europe are often described as having a three pillar structure, where Pillar I refers to the public pension, Pillar II refers to workplace (occupational) retirement plans, and Pillar III consists of private savings through fiscal incentives.

In the E.U. region, the public pension is the foundation of retirement provision, though it is organized in many different ways across member states. Generally, public pensions are redistributive, providing a minimum pension intended to minimize old-age poverty. Most of these are unfunded and paid for out of government budgets. As a consequence, projected low economic growth rates combined with retirements in the baby boomer cohort are placing the systems under pressure. In response to these pressures, many member states have proposed (or passed) laws raising retirement ages to 67.[1] Some countries responded with different types of reforms while others did little to counter these demographic changes. In any event, Pillar I is the bedrock on which the workplace-based retirement plans, Pillar II, rest.

Workplace-based retirement plans are intended to complement public pensions by adding another layer of stable income after retirement. In other words, in the E.U., occupational pensions have traditionally been seen as a tool for income smoothing over the lifecycle. During their productive years, workers save part of their wage to provide for an income in retirement. These pension savings are invested in financial markets, with the goal to maintain retirees' purchasing power as long as they live (primarily aiming to provide compensation for infla-tion). This could also be achieved by offering guaranteed real deferred annuity, as it could provide lifelong inflation-linked benefits, but this product is currently unavailable in the E.U. marketplace. Instead, traditional defined benefit (DB) pension schemes seek to fill the gap with something close to real deferred annui-ties. In these plans, financial market risk, inflation risk, and longevity risk have traditionally been borne by the plan sponsor. But recent developments in longev-ity and financial market volatility have rendered the DB model unattractive for many sponsors. As a consequence, the European market has witnessed both a rapid decline in DB plans and the rise of various forms of defined contribution (DC) plans over time.

Pillar III of the retirement system in Europe consists of individual saving through tax incentives which typically defer income taxes until after retirement. Though the initial objective was to encourage people to build up additional retire-ment assets, over time many countries have lowered such tax deferrals.

Generally speaking in the E.U., governments provide the first pillar, whereas Pillars II and III are managed by pension funds, insurance companies, banks, and investment houses. In some cases, there is some overlap between the institu-tions offering both second and third-pillar pensions. For example, in Sweden, insurance companies and banks offer the same kind of products in both pil-lars, while in the Netherlands the second pillar is dominated by pension funds while the third pillar is dominated by insurance companies and banks. With the demise of traditional DB plans, one might expect providers of second and third-pillar retirement accounts to become less differentiated. The regulatory frameworks are also aligned along these lines. That is, DB pension plans oper-ate under Pillar II and are covered by the regulation regarding Institutions for Occupational Retirement Provision (IORP), while insurance companies oper-ating under both Pillars II and III are covered by Solvency regulation. The European Commission is currently developing what are known as IORP II and Solvency II rules, yet it is clear that the regulatory frameworks are converging. An important factor in the proposed regulation is the further extension of a risk-capital-based framework.

These changes are taking place within the frameworks promulgated by the Basel Committee on Bank Supervision covering banking regulation, which moved banks away from a capital-based regulatory framework and toward a risk-capital-based framework.[2] In a risk-capital-based framework market, consist-ent (i.e. arbitrage-free) valuation of the balance sheet is instrumental. It requires that the financial institution has large enough capital buffers (i.e. risk capital) that the probability of becoming insolvent in the future is sufficiently low should adverse movements in the financial markets occur. The minimum required size of the risk capital is a function of the risks on the balance sheet. The pensions and insurance industries are the last of the financial institutions to have moved toward a similar European framework. The proposed regulatory frameworks on occupational retirement provision in the E.U. are mainly driven by harmonization, transparency, and customer protection.

It should be noted that the current problems in the European pension market such as low funding ratios and unsustainability of some types of pension systems are not attributable to the regulations; rather, the risk-capital-based approach only highlights the underlying problems of demographic changes. Yet the global financial crisis and ongoing problems with the euro provide a unique opportunity to assess how retirement systems in the member states have fared, especially in the case of member states that can be seen as early adopters of the new regulation. Going forward, it is reasonable to assume that there will be a further consolidation of the products, vehicles, and providers in both the second and third pillars, and that the regulatory frameworks will continue to converge (albeit over many years).

To date, the retirement provision industry has responded by moving toward pension solutions that do not embody guarantees. As a result, financial market and longevity risk are devolving to individual workers and retirees. We argue in what follows that both regulators and consumers will in turn demand increased transparency and fairness within group risk pools. If the providers of collective risk pools cannot meet these demands it is likely that low-cost individual DC saving schemes will emerge as the dominant form of workplace retirement provision.

Employer-sponsored Pensions in the European Union

Retirement systems do differ across the member states, which can be explained by differences in historical and cultural backgrounds. Nevertheless, all the E.U. nations face long-term aging, driving the need for reforms. While DB plans were the predominant form of workplace-based pensions in the past, they are being replaced by various forms of DC plans.

Across the E.U., companies traditionally elected one of three formats for DB plans: book reserve schemes, pension funds, or insured plans. In a book reserve scheme, the sponsor keeps future pension payments on its balance sheet as deferred salary. This is an unfunded solution deemed quite cost efficient, since there is no charge for asset management or taxes levied on capital gains. Yet this model requires some sort of insurance in the event of a corporate bankruptcy, as the employee might risk losing all pension rights. While book reserve schemes are less common than they were in the past, examples remain in Germany and Sweden. In a pension fund, the employer and the employees both pay contributions to a fund that is legally separated from the plan sponsor. This is called a funded solution, but one where the sponsor holds the tail risk in the form of a covenant (to be discussed in more detail further on in the chapter). In the case of sponsor bankruptcy, a fully funded pension represents a secure solution since pension capital is maintained at arm's length. A deeply underfunded pension would actually closely resemble a book reserve scheme, and it requires some sort of bankruptcy protection for the members. In the case of an insured plan, an employer will pay pension contributions to a third party that takes over the responsibility to provide retirement income security to the workers. The third party is typically an insurance company, whose shareholders provide the risk capital backing the guarantees. This third solution has attracted strict regulation to protect the interests of the clients in case of insurer bankruptcy.

In the past, many E.U. workers relied on DB schemes for most of the funded retirement component, and only high earners had an individual top-up in the form of an individual DC. Offering DC schemes was an attractive option for both sponsoring companies and financial service providers, and it appeared attractive to the employees during the equity bull market in the 1980s and 90s. While traditional DB schemes based on final wage and inflation indexation worked very well for many years, they were best suited for different times. The DB pension formula was simple to understand as it depended only on years in service and final salary. In Europe, most DB pensions also provided lifelong inflation-linked benefits.

Of late, several economic and social trends have made the traditional DB design even less sustainable. These include increasing longevity, low fertility, worker mobility, and shorter service at an employer. For instance, in the E.U. average life expectancy at birth was close to the retirement age after World War II, but has risen to around 77.7 years and is likely to rise further.[3] The average life expectancy at 65 for both sexes averages 17.3 years in the E.U. and is projected to rise by another 3.4 years up to 2045 (OECD 2012). Moreover, in the E.U. the average woman gives birth to her first child later in life and has fewer children. With average fertility rates now around 1.5, virtually all E.U. member states will experience a declining population without immigration (OECD 2012). To these changes must be added the fact that today's workers are more mobile than in the past. Rather than remaining in a single occupation or industry, many will change employers multiple times, and some will have periods of self-employment and international mobility. Accordingly, a corporate-backed pension plan at a single employer is often not the preferred vehicle for retirement provision in the current labor market.

As we cannot select a single pension model representative of what is going on across all member states, we instead focus our study on three—Sweden, the Netherlands, and the United Kingdom—in detail. All three at one time had a pension system characterized by traditional DB pension schemes, and all three have changed their pension systems, albeit in different directions. Additionally, each country was an early adopter of a stricter regulatory framework for its workplace retirement system, applying to both pension funds and insurance companies. We discuss each in turn.

Sweden

While many Nordic countries have implemented retirement system reforms, Sweden is of particular interest since its first pillar is income-dependent and the second pillar is mainly serviced by insurance companies. From an international perspective, Sweden is quite unusual and is frequently studied by other member states that are considering reforms. In the 1990s, it became clear that the Swedish pension system was not sustainable and that there was a looming retirement crisis with the Baby Boomers retiring. All political parties joined to reach an agreement without making retirement provision an election issue. The main reform was to change all the pension products in the different pillars to DC schemes, since neither the government nor employers offer guarantees anymore.[4]

The first-pillar retirement provision was changed in the late 1990s into a so-called Notional DC pension system, separate from the government budget but governed by Parliament and managed by a governmental agency. The system is partly funded, with a balance sheet where the notional pension rights of individuals represent the liabilities and future pension contributions and buffer funds represent the asset side. The buffer funds act, as the name suggests, as a means of dealing with the demographic bulge due to the Baby Boomers. What makes the system sustainable is the presence of an automatic 'break' that, when needed, will return the balance sheet to parity by reducing liabilities—including pensions in payment. As part of the pension reform, an individual DC component was also introduced to the first pillar, called the premium pension. Initially individuals had to choose from among 800+ funds, a development critiqued by Sunstein and Thaler (2008) as an example of complex choice architecture. In 2011, almost all (98.5 percent) of youth entering the labor market ended up investing in the 'default' choice (Swedish Government 2013). A typical employee pays 23 percent in pension premiums on top of salary: 16.0 percentage points go into the Notional DC system, 2.5 percentage points into the premium pension, and the remaining 4.5 percentage points into occupational retirement provision. There is a cap on the salary level that is covered by the public pension system and the premiums paid above that cap are transferred to the state budget and are to be considered as an additional tax. For employees earning more than that cap, additional pension premiums go into the occupational retirement provision through a collective agreement to compensate for this implicit tax. In 2011, 19 percent of men and 7 percent of women had incomes above the cap (Swedish Pensions Agency 2012). The tax incentives for the third pillar are relatively limited.

The Swedish government continues to review the system, with a committee currently examining the pension age. The Swedish Pensions Agency (2012) has calculated what pension age would be required to maintain current pension incomes, which may indicate what these reforms might look like. The social partners (employer organization and unions) are relatively strong in Sweden, and there are national collective agreements regulating occupational retirement provision. Historically, self-annuitizing mutual insurance companies have dominated occupational retirement provision offering a guaranteed product called 'traditional life' which, in spirit, is quite similar to traditional DB plans. Corporate pension funds are rather uncommon. What is interesting to note is that the social partners manage the procurement process where the individual employee selects his/her provider via an election platform. The employees choose mainly between traditional life products and individual DC platforms, both offered through a limited set of providers. The default choice is typically a traditional life product provided by a self-annuitizing mutual insurance company controlled by the social partners.

The Netherlands

Many cite the Dutch retirement system as a strong one due to its fully funded quasi-mandatory Pillar II pension funds. The Netherlands is also interesting since the traditional DB models have been evolving into hybrid schemes over time, sometimes described as 'collective DC' schemes. This process began, as in many other countries, in the wake of the tech bubble crisis. The terms and conditions of the DB pension deal changed by moving from final wage and full inflation indexation to career average and conditional indexation. This change illustrates the consensus culture wherein the social partners, on behalf of their members, can agree on changes at the negotiation table.

In the Netherlands, Pillar I is a pay-as-you-go program financed from the annual budget; benefits are based on the number of years retirees have lived in the country. Singles receive 70 percent of the minimum wage ($1,337 per month) and couples together receive 100 percent of the minimum wage; this makes the benefits among the lowest first-pillar benefits in the E.U. (along with the U.K.) (OECD 2011). The government has already boosted the retirement age, slated to reach age 67 in 2023, and it will be linked to longevity increases from 2024 onward (SVB 2013). The first pillar is financed through taxes. For income up to $43,500 (2013 figures) the employee pays 17.9 percent of pay into the first pillar.[5] Over the full income (minus a deduction for the first pillar) an employee pays a percentage of his income into the second pillar. On average, 17.4 percent of pay goes to the second pillar, although the largest three pension funds all levied a premium above 25 percent in 2013 (DNB 2012b). The maximum tax levy for third-pillar retirement provisions is relatively small. Overall, the average Dutch employee pays approximately 20 percent of his/her income into all three pillars and it is a widely accepted notion among Dutch people that they work one day a week for their pension.

The fact that Pillar I benefits are low makes the Pillar II benefits more important. There are three types of pension fund in the Netherlands: industry-wide funds (which have 88 percent of the participants and 73 percent of the assets managed), corporate pension funds, and pension funds for a certain occupation (although the latter are rare and relatively small). A clear trend in the Netherlands is that corporations are terminating their own pension funds; since 2000, the number of corporate pension funds has fallen by 63 percent (DNB 2013). They either join an industry-wide plan or opt for an insured solution. Recently a third alternative was introduced, namely the PPI, a Dutch IORP vehicle, which is a way to offer DC pensions without guarantees.

The average Dutch worker receives approximately 40 percent of the total pension income from the first pillar, 50 percent from the second pillar, and 10 percent from the third pillar. The social partners (employer organization and unions) still have a strong position in the Netherlands and they negotiate national collective agreements which include second-pillar pensions. Participation is not mandated by law but rather imposed by social partners in collective agreements. The details of the second-pillar provision can be negotiated for an entire industry, where every employer in an industry will be obliged to join the industry-wide pension scheme and their employees obliged to save for their pension through their employer. There is also a growing group of self-employed, often in low-income jobs, outside the collective system; they must rely on buying individual products in the third pillar. There is also discussion underway as to whether guarantees should be provided in Pillar II plans, and what the maximum tax-favored contribution should be. In the end, Pillar II is also expected to migrate toward a DC model.

United Kingdom

The United Kingdom has transformed its pension system in a different direction from that of the two countries just discussed. Because the U.K. focuses more on enabling individuals to make choices, individual DC schemes have become the dominant pension provision. Part of the difference is that individual fairness is seen to be more important than collective benefits. From a legal perspective, the U.K. has a contract-based legal system (common law), making it difficult to change pension contracts retroactively, even if they prove to be unbalanced.

The U.K. Pillar I is financed from the state budget, and it consists of two parts. The Basic State Pension is a flat-rate amount and provides a pension of $121 per week on average (PPI 2010).[6] The second part, called the State Second Pension, is means-tested. For an average person, it ranges from $27 to $50 per week (PPI 2010).[7] The government introduced an extensive rehaul of the first pillar which will go into effect in 2017. A flat-rate system will replace the means-testing and the overall pension income in the first pillar will be $219 per week ($11,800 per year) plus inflation rises between now and 2017.[8] Additionally, the U.K. will raise the retirement age from 65 to 67 over a 13-year period (U.K. Government 2013).

In the past, most British workers participated in company DB plans providing a decent retirement income. Currently few private sector workers have open and accruing DB plans, while public sector employees are in DB schemes. Most public employees are in unfunded book reserve schemes, with the exception of those working for the local governments, but those plans are in relatively poor financial condition. Recently the government introduced an auto-enrolment reform, which forces all firms to offer workplace pensions where individual employees may still opt out. Contribution rates for the auto-enrolment pensions are relatively low compared to the Netherlands: the minimum is 8 percent of salary (3 percent is contributed by the employer, 4 percent by the employee, and 1 percent through tax relief; DWP 2012). At retirement, workers use all or part of their pension savings to buy an annuity. The government has also set up NEST, a low-cost pension scheme that must accept all employers that want to become clients. In doing so, the government hopes that almost everyone will build up Pillar II pensions in the future. But even with these reforms, contribution levels remain low, which will translate into meager retirement incomes for the low earners. In addition, pension costs and fees are rather high, which can erode future retirement income (Pitt-Watson 2012). Nearly all Pillar II pension plans open to new private sector employees in the U.K. are DC (see Table 10.1).

TABLE 10.1 Overview of first and second pillar for Sweden, the Netherlands, and the United Kingdom

	Sweden	The Netherlands	The United Kingdom
First pillar	Large Notional DC Income-dependent, but with a minimum pension level. A small part of the income-dependent public pension is individual DC.	Small Pay-as-you-go Flat minimum level	Small Pay-as-you-go One part is flat minimum level Second part is means-tested, but will become flat level.
Second pillar	Small Social partners model with collective agreements. Election centrals operated by social partners, where the employee selects pension product and provider. Default choices are typically low-cost mutual insurance companies. Market liberal implementation	Large Social partners model with collective agreements. Quasi-mandatory Industry-wide pension fund operated by social partners. Paternalistic implementation offering limited individual employee choices.	Small Employer must offer occupation retirement, but employee can opt out. Employee has choices within the solution of the pension provider. Market liberal implementation

Source: Authors' compilations.

To summarize, in many E.U. nations, as demonstrated here, traditional DB plans are no longer existing occupational retirement solutions and they are rapidly being replaced by various DC arrangements, especially for new employees. The demise of the traditional DB is attributable to the fact that their design was unsustainable given demographic and societal trends, and because the sponsors did not manage the tail risks well. One should not blame the passing of DB plans on new regulation.

Longer-term Trends in the E.U. Regulatory Environment

Europe has a long history of conflict, and the creation of a single market through the European Coal and Steel Community, the European Economic Community, and later the European Union, was meant to pave the way for economic synergy and political stability. One important aspect of the move toward a single market has been to seek consistent legislation across the different member states. For financial markets, a number of European-wide frameworks have been developed. Of course these reforms do not take place overnight, and changing European regulation is a highly political process with many vested interests. As with most regulatory processes, it also tends to be reactive and moves forward in response to crises or scandals.

Pension regulation currently under development in the E.U. is the result of an evolutionary process driven by harmonization efforts among member states. It aims to create a single market for European retirement provision. One complication is that the vehicles providing pension products are subject to different sets of regulations. For insurance companies the Solvency directive exists, while pension funds are subject to the IORP directive. Additionally, there is a gap between regulatory solvency measures and economic solvency measures in both the regulatory regimes.

The proposed regulatory frameworks (Solvency II for insurance companies and IORP II for pension funds) use the market valuation of the balance sheet to close the regulatory gap. This will incentivize insurers and pension funds to manage their balance sheet risk in a more economically meaningful way. The new regulation will also provide supervisors with an early warning system as well as a set of meaningful tools to bring about changes when needed.

As said, insurance companies are currently subject to the European prudential framework called Solvency; changes and improvements to this framework will result in the implementation of Solvency II. Similarly, pension funds in Europe are subject to the IORP directive, and several changes to the IORP directive will mean the future rollout of IORP II. The banking sector is ahead when it comes to European regulation. Their regulation is called Basel and Basel II is already implemented. When comparing Basel II to IORP II and Solvency II, similarities arise. All three regulatory frameworks operate on a three-pillar model. The first pillar concerns quantitative capital requirements in order to minimize the risk of insolvency of the financial institution. The second pillar sets standards for risk management and governance within a financial institution. It also allows national supervisors to challenge the institutions on the conducted risk management. The third pillar imposes standards for transparency toward supervisors and the public. In Basel I, IORP I, and Solvency I, the focus was mostly on the quantitative rules. The term 'three-pillar model' is not to be confused with the three pillars that are used for the distinction between public pensions, occupational pensions, and individual pensions. To minimize confusion below, we reserve the term 'pillar' for the distinction between public, occupational, and private retirement provision.

Solvency: European Insurance Regulation

European solvency rules for insurance companies have been in place since 1973, when the European insurance legislation took form. Over the years, the rules evolved while the basis remained the same: insurance companies were obliged to hold a minimum amount of regulatory capital to insure against unforeseen events. A revision of the rules in the 1990s resulted in the implementation of the Solvency I directive in 2002. Since then, the regulation has again been reviewed and a new expected Solvency II directive is intended to be implemented in 2014. It is very unlikely, however, that this timetable will hold, so implementation is likely to start in 2015 or 2016 (Nyman 2012).

After a series of unexpected bankruptcies in the insurance industry in Europe, European policymakers realized that the prudential rules of Solvency I do not capture all the risks on the balance sheets of insurance companies. Due to the importance of insurance companies to the financial stability of a country, some member states reacted as early adopters by introducing national legislation that was stricter than just Solvency I, while at the same time the European Parliament pondered the question of how Solvency I should be improved.

IORP: European Pension Fund Regulation

Before the IORP I directive was introduced, a single market for European pensions did not exist. Due to differences in fiscal regimes and social and labor jurisdictions, a pan-European fund was (almost) impossible to set up. This was a practical challenge for many multinationals in Europe. A larger problem was that the lack of a single market caused fractured pension accumulation, which was an obstacle to labor force mobility between member states. In addition, due to the reduction of first-pillar pension benefits throughout Europe, second-pillar pension provision grew in terms of relative importance of the total retirement provision. On June 3, 2003, the European Parliament and the European Council introduced the IORP

I directive (E.U. 2003). The IORP I directive provides a prudential framework for pension funds in which it creates a minimum level of prudential supervision for all member states. As it serves as a minimum level of supervision, all member states adopted IORP in their national regulation and some implemented more restrictive prudential rules.

Some member states recognized the potential to become a haven for pan-European pension funds and were quick to erect new pension vehicles that can facilitate pension schemes from different member states. Most notably, Belgium and Luxembourg created vehicles that could be used by, for example, multinationals to pool pension schemes from different member states. Some member states already had vehicles in place that adhered to the IORP directive, such as the Netherlands and Ireland, but not all vehicles were suitably equipped to service foreign schemes. Belgium actively promoted their IORP vehicle, called the OFP, with the argument that they would apply the minimum level of prudential supervision as the unique selling point. In 2005, Belgium even released a leaflet called 'Belgium, prime location for pan-European pension funds' in which the Prime Minister of that time, Yves Leterme, promoted Belgium as an attractive domicile (Federal Public Service Finance 2008). In June 2012, EIOPA reported 84 cases of IORPs facilitating foreign schemes. Half of these cases are held between Ireland and the United Kingdom (EIOPA 2012).

Similarities and Differences between IORP II and Solvency II

IORP II and Solvency II build on the foundations of their predecessors, and as such, they share similar goals. Solvency I and IORP I provided insurance companies and pension funds with a European passport permitting them to service pension plans from other member states. In addition, regulators seek to take another step in creating a single European market and to strengthen the financial institutions providing second and third-pillar pensions. The general approach of the frameworks is similar; both use an economic risk-based solvency model applied to all member states to avoid regulatory arbitrage between the member states.

An important source of discussion, however, is the underlying vehicle supplying the pension. In the early design stages of IORP II, it appeared as if its risk-based capital approach would be the same as the one in Solvency II. Nevertheless, the pension fund industry resisted this change as it would increase required risk capital. Their main argument was that pension funds and insurance companies have different risk-absorbing potential. The sponsor covenant backing many pension funds implies that the sponsor company will pay a higher premium or lump sum payment if the pension fund falls into financial distress, which could give them more leeway with regard to required risk capital. This may be true in some cases, but many sponsors lack the financial strength to fill the gap, in which case the value of the covenant is relatively small. But in some cases, such as the

Netherlands, accrued benefits can be reduced when a pension fund's funding ratio is low, whereas this is not the case for insurance companies.

Responding to pension fund critiques, the European regulator came up with an extended approach for pension funds termed the Holistic Balance Sheet approach. This represents an integral approach to a pension fund's balance sheet, valuing various recovery methods including the reduction of pension rights and indexation, as well as the backing of a protection fund. But this idea too has come under criticism due to the complexity of valuing some of the instruments in a market-based valuation framework. As yet, European Commission has postponed the implementation of the first pillar of the IORP directive, which focuses on capital requirements, arguing that the solvency rules should be 'an improvement, rather than a punishment' (IPE 2013).

The discussion around Solvency II and IORP II has raised attention to proper risk management, providing a general yet simple framework for financial institutions to use. These institutions can also develop their own more thorough risk management systems, which then must be approved by the regulator. The proposed regulation has also provided impetus to speed up consolidation in the pension market. The increased capital requirements make it advantageous to have different activities under one roof, due to diversification effects in the calculation of the capital requirements. Also, the regulation is likely to raise administration costs and governance costs, making it less attractive to run a small pension fund or insurance company.

Other Drivers of European Reforms

The observed convergence between previously quite differentiated industries such as banking, insurance, and pensions has also helped drive the need for regulatory reforms in the E.U. Current regulation allows pension providers to undertake regulatory arbitrage by managing their regulatory risk instead of the actual economic risk. In times of financial crisis with sharply falling interest rates, regulatory frameworks based on fixed actuarial rates allow the pension provider to maintain a risky investment strategy, whereas applying a market-consistent (risk-neutral) valuation of liabilities could show that the pension provider is technically underfunded or even bankrupt. It is anticipated that future regulation will better measure and regulate these institutions' economic risks to improve customer/member protection and the financial stability of the pension providers. Moreover, it is hoped that increased transparency will provide regulators with an early warning system as well as a framework in which meaningful tools for preventive interventions can be deployed.

This is of particular importance since governments have a moral obligation to handle the consequences if regulation and enforcement are inadequate. Roberts (2012) describes the Equitable Life debacle in the United Kingdom, which represents an example where the U.K. government eventually shouldered some responsibility for those who lost their pension rights. Reducing the regulatory gaps will lower the chances of unexpected and large bankruptcies, but it will also induce management to manage the economic risk and not issue off-balance sheet guarantees.

Collective Risk Pool Regulation

The idea of collective pooling of risk has long been the foundation of group pension provision, based on the notion that individuals can pool their individual longevity risk with a large group of other similar individuals. Insurance companies or pension plans can then offer lifetime annuities by carefully managing those risks that are not significantly diminished by pooling; remaining open-ended risks must be absorbed by the plan sponsor in DB pensions, the collective in mutual insurance companies, or shareholders in stock insurance companies. The goal of regulation in these cases is to provide some degree of certainty that the institutions can honor their promises on an ongoing basis. By contrast, persons holding individual pension accounts bear both longevity and capital market risk on their personal balance sheets; the capital in their accounts is ring-fenced, so most of the new regulatory reforms do not impact individual DC pension systems. This explains the rapid growth of individual pension solutions offered by banks, insurance companies, and pension schemes.

Both the Solvency II and IORP II proposed regulations prescribe that risk management and governance of the financial institutions they speak to must be proportional to the scale, nature, and complexity of the operations. Moreover, they set out requirements for these groups' level of expertise, internal audit, and outsourcing. But they do not prescribe the quality of the financial product from the consumer's perspective. When a 'hard' promise is provided, enough risk-based capital is required to absorb shocks; when a product has a 'softer' promise (an ambition or aspiration), the vehicle is responsible only for implementation risks, while the rest of the risks remain with the client/member. An important side effect of the regulatory reform debate is that it has offered a methodology for determining fairness between different cohorts (or individual members) inside collective risk pools. By applying risk-neutral pricing and valuation mechanisms, members can still benefit from collective risk-sharing and gain clarity over their individual claims in a mark-to-market framework (Kocken 2012).

In many E.U. mandatory occupational retirement provision schemes, intergenerational risk-sharing typically translates into applying intertemporal smoothing of asset returns, so as to dampen the impact of financial market volatility on pension income. The length of the smoothing period determines the degree of intergenerational risk-sharing taking place. A challenge is that risks with a trend, such as systemic longevity risk, can give rise to one-way intergenerational transfers. While intergenerational risk-sharing can be welfare-enhancing in some circumstances, this is a different case which is probably not welfare-improving.[9] And intergenerational risk-sharing may not be appealing for occupational pensions, especially when participation in a specific collective risk pool is not mandatory. For example, proposed changes to the Dutch pension system are clearly moving away from intergenerational risk-sharing by applying a relatively short smoothing window (a maximum of ten years; Rijksoverheid 2012). This was proposed to provide some fairness between generations and stability in pension income for those who have already retired.[10]

Due to the fact that pensions are moving increasingly to DC plans, and the products offered by pension funds, banks, and insurers are becoming more similar over time, it may be less necessary to continue regulating pensions and insurance companies differently in the future. Nevertheless, sensible regulation must consider features distinctive to pension products, such as whether guarantees are offered, collective risk pools or individual accounts, trust-based or contract-based governance, payouts in retirement, and mutual or stock ownership of pension vehicles. The conventional European DB scheme was provided by a mutual vehicle and was a self-annuitizing collective risk pool with a guarantee provided by the plan sponsor. There are still mutual insurance companies in Sweden which offer very similar products, with the difference that the guarantee is provided by the collective instead of the employer. By contrast, individual DC products typically lack guarantees and need to be converted to an annuity at retirement.

Solvency II and IORP II regulatory proposals do not seek to alter the governance structures of collective risk pools. But with pensions moving away from 'hard guarantees,' their governance structures become even more important. Individual products are often associated with contract-based governance: that is, the employer selects a provider of the DC scheme (traditionally an insurance company) on behalf of its employees, and employees participate in the plan by entering into a contract directly with the provider. A danger of contract-based governance is that there might be no entity acting in a role similar to that of a trustee. In other words, trust-based governance has a fiduciary duty to help participants save the best way possible, but contract-based governance need not—and sometimes cannot—help participants due to possible legal consequences.

Regulations Regarding Pension Accounting and Solvency Requirements

In the past, the European pension and insurance industries were heavily regulated and required to invest mostly in national government bonds. Post-deregulation, the industry was able to invest more freely and on the asset side, and valuations changed from book to market value. The introduction of market valuation of assets in the past resolved some adverse behavioral effects that book valuation methodology had had on sound investment principles. In order to protect the solvency, pension funds and insurance companies tended to keep their underperforming investments when the market price was below acquisition cost to avoid realizing losses, and sold their successful investments to enhance solvency. Sometimes 'air' built up on the asset side of the balance sheet, so the introduction of market valuation of assets was quite painful for certain pension funds and insurance companies. Nowadays, pension and insurance liabilities may still be reported at book value. Not surprisingly, discussions about moving to market valuation of the liability side are again raising concerns.

We have not discussed changes in international accounting standards yet, though they are pertinent to E.U. regulatory reforms. The international accounting standards expressed in IAS19/FRS17 stipulate that a corporation must report its pension liabilities in its balance sheet, as per the 2005 revision of international accounting standards (IFRS). One consequence was that traditional DB schemes began to close to new members when their unfunded liabilities had to be reported on the sponsor's balance sheets.

A Look at Solvency and IORP

The current regulatory frameworks, Solvency I and IORP I, could be described as capital-based accounting frameworks. The original E.U. directive on Solvency was ratified in 1973, and the E.U. directive for Institutions for Occupational Retirement Provision came in 2003 (E.U. 2003). The longer history of Solvency shows in the details of the regulation. For example, IORP I set no limits on a pension fund's asset classes, as long as the 'prudent person principle' is upheld (meaning that investments made on a client's behalf should be made in a prudent manner). This involves no quantitative restrictions other than prohibiting holding more than 5 percent in its underlying sponsor (and 10 percent in shares belonging to the same group as the sponsor). By contrast, Solvency I further restricts insurers' permissible asset classes (E.U. 2002), to stimulate diversification. For example, insurers cannot invest more than 10 percent of their gross technical provisions in one piece of real estate, 10 percent of the shares in non-regulated markets, 3 percent in cash, or 5 percent of the shares in one undertaking. IORP I, more than Solvency I, serves as a minimum basis on top of which member states can implement their national prudential framework.

Neither Solvency I nor IORP I prescribed risk management procedures. Rather, the prudential rules were based on the expected long-term mean of the distribution and did not include the (very relevant) short-term tail risk. This is expressed by the freedom that member states have in determining discount rates used for liabilities. As said, the proposed Solvency II and IORP II frameworks are moving toward a mark-to-market valuation of the balance sheet and a risk-based supervisory framework.

Several conceptual challenges arise when thinking of moving to market valuation for liabilities. Using book values for liabilities means that only asset volatility influences solvency; therefore opting for a stable return on the asset side is the rational thing to do. Yet it is conceptually problematic to evaluate cash flows using different methods depending on whether they are on the asset or liability side of the balance sheet. The market valuation approach for liabilities makes it impossible to have both a stable solvency ratio and stable asset returns, since the liability side is sensitive to changes in interest rates. This has a large impact on how pension funds and insurance companies must manage the asset side of the balance sheet.

In our view, using book value for liabilities can make it difficult to prudently manage economic solvency risk, since the official solvency measure does not represent actual economic risk. As a consequence, the current regulatory solvency measure, in combination with the equity bull market until 2000, obscured the impact of falling interest rates. Conversely, when market rates dropped below the discount rate, problems became much more apparent.

An Illustrative Example

The effects of the impact of changes in interest rates, equity prices, and longevity for a pension balance sheet using different valuation methods are illustrated in Table 10.2 for a stylized Dutch corporate DB pension fund having a mature collective risk pool. At the beginning of 2007, its initial asset mix was set at half equities (MSCI World) and half fixed income with a duration of six years (equal to the duration of Barclays Capital Aggregate Bond Index for Europe). The duration of the liability side was 15 years. We assume that, prior to 2007, the fund used an actuarial discount rate of 4 percent leading to a (nominal) regulatory solvency ratio of 135 percent, approximately the average in the Netherlands at the time.

At the beginning of 2007, usage of the actuarial discount rate was discontinued and the regulator forced the fund to adopt a market valuation approach. The timing of the implementation was favorable, since then the valuation gap between regulatory solvency and economic solvency was positive. The market funding ratio was slightly higher than the previous regulatory funding ratio since swap rates exceeded the fixed actuarial discount rate of 4 percent. This stylized DB pension fund had two significant market exposures: equity risk and a duration mismatch. The stylized pension fund was also exposed to changes in longevity. Sensitivity of

TABLE 10.2 Sensitivity analysis for a stylized DB pension scheme at January 1, 2007

	Solvency based on market valuation of liabilities (%)	Solvency based on book valuation of liabilities (%)
Starting point	139	135
1% point decline in interest rates	124	139
10% falling equity prices	132	128
1-year increase in longevity	136	132

Source: Authors' compilations.

the solvency to shocks in yields, equity prices, and longevity increases is illustrated under market and book valuation of liabilities.

As we can see, the regulation in place creates perverse incentives that conflict with sound risk management principles. To reduce the regulatory solvency risk, the DB pension fund could reduce the duration of its fixed income assets, but, as a consequence, economic solvency risk will actually increase. With a fixed actuarial discount rate, the balance sheet volatility only depends on the volatility of the asset portfolio, and senior management is therefore evaluated on its ability to create high and stable returns on the assets. Falling interest rates since the 1970s and booming equity markets until 2000 made the 'asset-only balance sheet' appear strong, but this was an illusion. And the existing regulatory framework also made it a challenge for the organization to manage both the economic solvency risk and the business/reputational risks at the same time. This conflict of interest is similar to that leading to the collapse of many financial institutions in the global financial crisis: a regulatory framework which allowed for off-balance sheet risk-taking and stock investors demanding higher ROEs produced a downward spiral where sound management of the real economic risk in the financial institution was actively punished and generated excessive leverage. This conflict of interest was accentuated by Chuck Prince, the Citigroup CEO, in 2007 when he famously told *Financial Times* (2007): '. . . as long as the music is playing, you've got to get up and dance.'

The sensitivity results in Table 10.2 illustrate that book valuation of liabilities encourages asset portfolio strategies that had an expected negative impact on the economic balance sheet. In essence, the traditional DB pension fund borrowed money from its members at the long end of the yield curve by issuing long-dated promises. It then invested the contributions at the short end of the curve. A popular hedge fund investment strategy is the so-called 'carry trade,' where an investor borrows at the short end of the curve to invest at the long end of the curve. During normal cases, when the yield curve is upward-sloping, this can be a profitable strategy in expectation. By contrast, pension funds and insurers had systematic exposure to the exact opposite situation, a 'negative carry trade.' This trade is only profitable when the yield curve shifts upwards enough that the decline in net valuation is larger than the yield pick-up, but this strategy loses money when the yield curve is stable or falling.

This example shows that the current DB pension fund crisis is an unfortunate consequence of long-term trends that were disguised by problematic regulation in combination with poor risk management. These insights are not new, and the E.U. commission worked for years on new regulatory frameworks to better align the regulatory and economic risks. In our view, the new regulatory frameworks are probably best described as risk-based accounting frameworks aimed at reducing the gap between the regulatory measure and the real economic risk.

Some E.U. member states have introduced stricter national regulations, in anticipation of the proposed E.U. regulation. To illustrate what the early adopters have done, we turn again to Sweden, the United Kingdom, and the Netherlands.

Sweden

In 2006, Sweden introduced market valuation for liabilities using the Swedish yield curve as the market rate (previously various other methods were used). The Swedish FSA (*Finansinspektionen*) introduced the so-called traffic light system, where a company's solvency risk is categorized as green, amber, or red. When a company is moving from yellow to red, the Swedish FSA has a set of pre-determined actions that will take place, with the final action being the closure of an insurer or pension fund. Since there are few pension funds in Sweden, similar rules applied to both. Moreover, the Swedish financial minister has suggested that there will soon be one framework for both pensions and insurers. Yet many insurers and pensions have not changed their risk management practices to date, instead continuing with the business model and investment strategy from the old regulatory regime.

Netherlands

Market valuation of liabilities was introduced in the Netherlands in 2007, using a yield curve based on interbank swap rates provided by the regulator, the Dutch Central Bank (DNB). Before that, an actuarial discount rate of 4 percent was used. While pensions and insurers face similar regulatory frameworks, there are some details with large consequence. The chance of underfunding of a pension fund can only be 2.5 percent, while an insurer can only have a 0.5 percent chance of underfunding. The Dutch Central Bank introduced the FTK (Financial Assessment Framework) for pension funds, which is similar to the Swedish traffic light system. FTK set two thresholds for nominal solvency of (approximately) 105 percent and 125 percent requiring regulatory actions (Pensioenfederatie 2012). Pension funds may remain below 105 percent for a maximum of three years but they must submit a recovery plan to the supervisor, including raising contributions and, ultimately, reduction of pension payments. Those who do not comply may be closed. Some pension funds did change their business models and applied sound risk management principles, though many have not.

The United Kingdom

The Pension Act of 2004 initiated a move toward market valuation of liabilities for the DB schemes, along with a minimum funding requirement and the installation of a Pension Regulator and Pension Protection Fund. Trustees of a DB scheme are responsible for a prudent valuation of the liabilities, for which they have to seek professional advice. A specific interest rate is not prescribed, unlike in Sweden and the Netherlands. In practice, most DB pension schemes use a discount rate of gilts (U.K. inflation-linked bonds) plus x percentage points, where x typically ranges between 0.5 percent and 1.5 percent. When setting the discount rate, several factors are taken into account, such as plan demographics, current asset values, and the sponsor's strength. In case of underfunding, a recovery plan is required by the pension regulator where remedial actions must be outlined. The insurance industry was quite early in moving toward market valuation of liabilities in anticipation of a stricter regulation.

Ongoing Debate

Member states continue to debate the correct market discount rate for pension liabilities. There is no market for the liabilities in corporate retirement plans, and some recommend that the selected yield curve should be without credit risk and based on liquid instruments to avoid valuation distortions. The pension and insurance industry frequently propose that a smoothed yield curve, for example using the average yields over the previous five-year period, would be better to use, since that would eliminate short-term fluctuations in the yield. Walschots and van Capelleveen (2009) argue that, from an economic perspective, using smoothed returns causes refinance returns to be incorrectly evaluated. Especially for long smoothing periods, the true economic return only becomes apparent after a long time, when it might be too late to take corrective actions.

The proposed risk-based accounting framework is disruptive for the traditional pension funds and insurance contracts providing guarantees, so it is not surprising that governments are being lobbied to try to weaken the impacts of these proposed regulatory changes. Opponents to market-based valuation argue that it is too sensitive to short-term volatility, and that book value better represents the true value of the liabilities. But, given recent market experiences, in our view a market valuation approach for both assets and liabilities better represents the quality of the balance sheet. Pensions or insurers paying out on the hope that markets will recover during downturns might end up in bankruptcy, if the adverse scenario is persistent enough and economic risks are not managed in prudent way.

Regulations Regarding Fair Treatment of Customers/Members

While traditional DB plans historically sought to pay a stable income in retirement, most DC plans do not put an emphasis on the pay-out phase. As the transition toward non-guaranteed retirement payouts continues, with the risks pushed to individuals, regulation becomes even more important to protect individuals' interests. The E.U. regulation seeks to ensure fair treatment for consumers, with greater transparency as well. The IORP and Solvency regulations prescribe minimum information that must be provided to participants; this includes an annual report, the target level of retirement benefits, the level of benefits in case of cessation of employment, the participants' capital market risk exposure, and arrangements relating to the transfer of pension rights to another institution for second-pillar pension provision (E.U. 2003: Article 11).

Yet this required information serves only as a minimum, and some member states have additional requirements. For example, second-pillar Netherlands members receive an annual statement called the Uniform Pension Overview (UPO) that is, as the name implies, uniform. This makes sure that all participants receive the same level of information, although many pension funds have a broader communication platform than just the UPO. Continuing the stronger focus on protecting the consumer, Sweden and the Netherlands have banned commission-driven independent financial advisors. The United Kingdom has introduced a Retail Distribution Review (RDR) and Treat Customers Fairly (TCF) policies which focus on restoring trust in the financial system.

The Global Financial Crisis: A Stress Test of the E.U. Regulatory and Supervisory Reforms

Next we ask how European pensions and insurers fared during the global financial crisis, since this period served as a stress test of the regulatory framework, as well as of the political willingness of the E.U. member states to stick to the principles when their local financial industry is struggling. Since the crisis started in 2007, equity markets in the E.U. have been very volatile, and interest rates have fallen to historically low levels. It is unclear how long these low interest rates will persist, since structural economic problems will take time to address.

To illustrate how the financial crisis affected these industries of interest, it is useful to recall the hypothetical Dutch scheme from Table 10.2. We focus on the six-year period January 1, 2007–January 1, 2013, which includes the global financial crisis as well as the euro crisis, and we expose this pension fund to these developments as well as longevity improvements. First we assume that the fund made the strategic decision to stick to its investment strategy, keeping its asset mix constant by annual rebalancing to the 50/50 asset mix, and not hedging the duration risk. During this period, the 30-year euro swap rate dropped from just above 4 percent to approximately 3 percent, and the MSCI World had a negative return in euros of 12.9 percent. Average life expectancy also rose by 0.8 years during this period.[11]

Table 10.3 indicates how the individual effects affected solvency (for clarity we have not attributed the cross effects and thus the impact of the individual effects does not add up to the total impact). The optical illusion due to book valuation can readily be seen. If the regulatory framework continued to use the actuarial discount rate (i.e. that used for the book value of liabilities), the global financial crisis and the euro crisis would have had little impact on the pension fund's solvency. Actually, with a fixed actuarial discount rate, the falling interest rates seemed to compensate for the decline in equity markets. Hence the pension fund seemed to be in strong financial shape during this difficult period.

TABLE 10.3 Impact on solvency due to markets and longevity developments between January 1, 2007, and January 1, 2013

	Solvency based on market valuation of liabilities (%)	Solvency based on book valuation of liabilities (%)
Solvency at January 1, 2007	139	139
Solvency at January 1, 2013	103	135
Change in Solvency (percentage point)	−36	+0
due to interest rates	111 (−28)	146 (+11)
due to equity	130 (−9)	126 (−9)
due to longevity	137 (−2)	133 (−2)

Source: Authors' compilations.

But the fund's problems become very clear after applying market valuations to the liabilities: using the solvency criterion of 103 percent, the pension fund is almost insolvent. The investment strategy of a static asset mix was exposed to both falling interest rates and falling equity markets; these combined with increased longevity eroded solvency by 36 percentage points over a six-year period. Under the proposed market valuation framework, management's investment strategy wiped out most of the fund's risk capital. This very simple example illustrates how following a regulatory framework based on an actuarial discount rate can provide a false sense of security. In fact, the Netherlands was an early adopter of market-based liability valuation and some funds managed their solvency risk successfully.

Corporate Sponsor Risk

Not only did the crisis hurt DB plan solvency; it also hurt the sponsor's profitability as well. And if the current economic scenario continues for another five to ten years, some closed DB plans may not be able to maintain their guarantees. Kocken and Potters (2009) showed that the financial status is quite path dependent for aging pension funds following a traditional static 50/50 asset mix. Should real asset returns be poor during the plan's early years, and the pension payment be large, the fund's economic solvency might eventually be depleted. Conversely, if real returns early on are strong, solvency is likely to persist.

Transition Problems

When moving from the old to the new regulatory regime, there may also be transition problems. For instance, DB schemes that did not carefully manage their economic solvency risk could drag their sponsors down with them, if the proposed regulation were introduced and enforced at current low interest rate levels. E.U. policymakers must then decide whether to require the stricter regulatory framework to better protect retirees' accrued rights, versus risking losing jobs today. Policy regarding the insurance industry faces a similar conundrum, since a stricter regulatory framework may better protect customers, while at the same time threatening the survival of the local insurance industry.

Again, it is of interest to analyze how the early adopters of a stricter local regulatory framework fared during the crisis. In many cases, local regulators were strict in enforcing their local regulatory frameworks, since most pensions and insurers had decent balance sheets entering the crisis period. The collapse in risky asset values did hurt initially but markets rebounded, and so there was limited impact on the economic balance sheet. Falling interest rates, on the other hand, had a huge impact on the economic balance sheet of pensions that implicitly (or explicitly) speculated, following the negative carry strategy on their economic balance sheet.

Sweden

As a result of the crisis, many mutual and stock insurers stopped selling their traditional life products. Most of this occurred on a voluntary basis, though some were forced to close by the Swedish regulator due to insufficient solvency.

The Netherlands

In early 2013, the Netherlands experienced the bankruptcy of an insurer, SNS Reeal, after which the company was nationalized. Dutch pension funds with a solvency level below 105 are being forced to reduce their liabilities by cutting real pension rights for both active and retired members. Benefits cuts have been announced at approximately 70 pension funds, to be implemented in 2014; this will affect more than two million active participants, 1.1 million retirees, and 2.5 million deferred members. In 2011, the Dutch regulator also found that the metal workers' pension trustees (PME) had taken excessive investment risks, and forced a change in trustees and investment policy.

The United Kingdom

In the U.K., the Pension Regulator effectively put several sponsor companies into bankruptcy and the Pension Protection Fund took over their DB liabilities. There are no prescribed discount rates in this case, so the pension regulator has substantial freedom to act. Nevertheless, the Pension Regulator has permitted lengthening of proposed recovery periods and more optimistic assumptions on expected returns, in some cases.

Easing of the Rules

The regulators in some of the early adopter member states decided to ease the rules due to the low interest rates in mid-2012. They announced that the low interest levels were exceptional and took measures such as introducing a temporary floor on the yield curve in Sweden or temporarily introducing the Ultimate Forward Rate (UFR) in the Netherlands. In June 2012, when the interest rate level hit an all-time low, some Swedish insurers that did not manage their economic solvency risk were on the brink of either becoming insolvent or having to sell their remaining risky assets at a large scale. In Sweden, insurers were then given the choice to apply either a temporary interest rate floor or actual market rates. Those who opted for the temporary floor faced some restrictions on dividend payouts to shareholders (Finansinpektion 2012). Recently, the Swedish FSA announced that it will move toward an UFR methodology as described in Solvency II (Finansinspektion 2013).

More on the Ultimate Forward Rate

The UFR is a weighting scheme blending market rates and an assumed steady-state long-term interest rate (like an actuarial discount rate). Market rates are used for the part of the swap curve that is liquid, set at 20 years. Beyond that last point of liquidity (in the literature this point is referred to as the LLP, 'Last Liquid Point'), the forward (UFR) interest rate is a weighted average of the last liquid forward rate (year 19 into year 20) and the UFR of 4.2 percent so that the forward rate converges to 4.2 percent in ten years (the Smith–Wilson 20-30 UFR methodology; EIOPA 2010).

It is worth mentioning that the Dutch regulator adopted a slightly different UFR methodology for pension funds where the last liquid market forward rate is not used; instead, a weighted average of the market forward rates and the UFR of 4.2 percent is used during the convergence period. Furthermore the convergence period is ten years instead of ten years, so that the forward rate equals 4.2 percent at the 60-year point (DNB 2012a). Table 10.4 shows that solvency based on the two UFR methodologies is higher than the solvency based on market rates, since the UFR rate of 4.2 percent currently exceeds market rates. Yet the discrepancy between the economic solvency and the regulatory solvency concepts is much less striking than when a fixed discount rate of 4 percent is used (see Table 10.3). The number 4.2 percent is a bit arbitrary since it is based on 'expert opinions' for the

TABLE 10.4 Impact on solvency due to UFR methodology, January 1, 2013

	Solvency based on market valuation of liabilities (%)	Solvency based on Smith-Wilson 20-30 UFR methodology (%)	Solvency based on Dutch UFR methodology for pension funds (%)
Solvency at January 1, 2013	103	108	106

Source: Authors' compilations.

long-term real rate (2.2 percent) and inflation (2 percent); it is unclear how easy it will be to change the UFR rate in the future.

From a policy perspective, the introduction of the UFR methodology is of particular interest since it represents a step back toward applying a book valuation methodology for the long end of the yield curve. This re-introduces a gap between the regulatory solvency risk and the economic solvency risk, the gap that the regulatory reforms sought to close in the first place. The regulatory gap introduced by the UFR methodology causes a dilemma for managers of a pension fund or insurance company. Should they be street-smart and manage the regulatory solvency risk, hoping for the best, or should they be prudent and manage the actual economic solvency risk? In our view, managers are likely to once again begin managing the regulatory solvency risk. Applying different interest rates (i.e. valuations) for the same cash flows depending on whether they show up on the asset or liability side of the balance sheet is technically challenging, since adopting UFR does not mean that economic risk disappears.

In our view, an insurance company or pension fund will do best by fully hedging the economic risk; in addition to this neutral position, management can have an active view on the expected development of interest rates. In other words, having an active view on interest rates is a management decision and can be evaluated as such, rather than disguised as an asset liability management decision (or implicitly supported by a regulatory framework).

Precedent-setting Concerns

As noted above, some effort was devoted to save weaker local insurers and pension funds in the wake of the financial crisis. This is understandable, since the early adopters implemented stricter local solvency regulations compared to the current E.U. directive. And it would have been difficult for politicians to explain why they closed down one of their own insurers or pension funds due to insolvency, while others with similar (or worse) financial situations could have continued to operate just because they were regulated by a different E.U. member state which applied the minimum requirements under the current regulatory framework. Yet saving one local company creates a precedent, giving pensions and insurers mixed signals that could stimulate moral hazard; additionally, large local players may seek to game the regulatory framework.

European pension and insurer regulation is being driven by the European Commission and EIOPA, the European supervisor for pension funds and insurance companies. While these entities seek to create a single market by bringing in stricter regulation, there is much lobbying underway in Brussels seeking to weaken the capital requirements under the proposed regulatory frameworks. Indeed, introducing the UFR methodology into Solvency II and IORP II may be one of the lobby's most important achievements.

Conclusion

Retirees seek stable retirement incomes, and traditional DB pension schemes met this goal by offering real deferred annuities to their members. Yet the traditional DB design proved to be unsustainable due to demographic and financial market developments. Nevertheless, DB plans serve as a guide for what a good pension system should provide to participants, namely lifelong and stable inflation-linked cash flows throughout retirement. This objective translates into a risk-free investment for the consumer or a portfolio that matches retirement spending needs. From this viewpoint, risk refers to not being able to achieve this stable income. Naturally this perspective on risk differs from the wealth management portfolio, where risk is typically measured as asset volatility in relation to cash.

The E.U. regulatory changes reviewed here are intended to create a single market for retirement provision across the region. If successful, the reforms will remove an obstacle to labor mobility in the E.U. and create a single European market for pension provision. The proposed regulatory frameworks are based on market valuation of liabilities, and they aim to close the gap between regulatory and economic solvency measures. This will increase transparency and create incentives for insurers and pension funds to manage the balance sheet risks in an economically meaningful way. It also provides the regulator with an early warning system and tools for intervention. Moreover, as the barriers between traditional DB and DC plans are becoming less relevant, regulation is keeping up: for instance, pension plans will be identified as individual or collective DC plans, with or without guarantees, and as trust- or contract-based. For this reason, the natural barriers are melting between regulation covering pensions (IORP), insurers (Solvency), and banks (Basel). In the longer run, the different regulatory frameworks (Solvency, IORP, and Basel) will also converge, but since it is a political process, it is difficult to say much about the timetable or path to that end.

Although the E.U. faces many unique challenges, some lessons can be drawn. Moving to a risk-based regulatory framework where both assets and liabilities are valued according to mark-to-market principles increases transparency. Putting a fair price on guarantees acknowledges the market value of cash flows, rather than concealing problems with book values based on wishful thinking. Policymakers outside the E.U. contemplating new regulations based on economic solvency measures will want to carefully consider the timing of the implementation and the transition rules. Ideally, it would be useful to implement new frameworks in robust economic periods when interest rates are closer to long-term averages. Regarding enforcement, a valuable lesson can be learned from the early adopters of the new E.U. regulatory framework. Regulatory enforcement must be credible and the prompt corrective actions have to be strong. If the industry does not consider regulators to be credible, business will continue as usual and business models will not be adapted to the new regulatory framework. The global financial crisis showed that it was too difficult for early adopters to enforce their local regulatory framework, so they relaxed regulations to avoid having insurers become insolvent. This response has set precedents, and the industry is most likely to try to game the regulators in the future by playing the 'too big to fail' card.

The E.U. regulatory developments also offer useful insights for those seeking to improve the pension product. Collective self-annuitizing schemes can be useful, but these must be transparent and internal fairness issues resolved. If not, contract-based individual solutions will dominate pension provision, which could be a loss from the consumer perspective. A leading design principle is that risks which cannot be hedged in the market or naturally reduced by risk pooling in the collective should be passed back to the individual. The proposed E.U. regulation illustrates that there is a way to implement an internal risk-based accounting framework that will increase the transparency and fairness across cohorts. Another lesson learned for product design is that by applying the principles of market-consistent valuation and pricing mechanisms, one can construct a collective product that is fair to members/customers and offers promise with respect to looming risk-based regulatory frameworks.

Notes

1. Pensions are high on the policy agenda because most member states are confronting enormous challenges in the Pillar I systems as Baby Boomers enter retirement. Often public pensions are pay-as-you-go systems paid directly from government budgets. While this mode worked reasonably well given a growing workforce, it has come under challenge given population aging, forcing many countries to implement reforms boosting the retirement age to 67. In the Netherlands, the proposed transition period is eight years; in the United Kingdom it is 13 years, and in Germany the process will take 17 years. One exception to this trend is France, where some have proposed lowering the minimum retirement age from 62 to 60; nevertheless, the age to receive a full public pension in France went up from 65 to 68. In addition to the increasing first-pillar pension payments, many governments also have unfunded DB occupation pensions for civil servants on their economic balance sheets.
2. Basel III standards were agreed on in 2010–11 but implementation in the banking arena has been delayed until 2019 (*Financial Times* 2012).
3. See the Human Mortality Database (2013): <http://www.mortality.org/>.
4. Trampusch et al. (2010) provides a comprehensive overview of the pension reforms in the Swedish system.
5. €33,363. Exchange rate EUR:US$ 1.3043 (July 1, 2013)
6. 79.31 GBP. Exchange rate GBP:US$ 1.5232 (July 1, 2013)
7. 18 to 33 GBP. Exchange rate GBP:US$ 1.5232 (July 1, 2013)
8. 144 GBP. Exchange rate GBP:US$ 1.5232 (July 1, 2013)
9. See Diamond (1977), Gordon and Varian (1988), and Ball and Mankiw (2007), among others.
10. There might be still some unfair distribution among the generations inside the pension fund; see Lever et al. (2012).

11. According to the CBS (2013) life expectancy after retirement (age 65) increased by 1.11 years for men and 0.49 years for women between 2007 and 2013. On average, life expectancy after retirement increased by 0.8 years for this period.

References

Ball, L. and N. G. Mankiw (2007). 'Intergenerational Risk Sharing in the Spirit of Arrow, Debreu, and Rawls, with Applications to Social Security Design,' *Journal of Political Economy*, 115(4): 523–547.

Centraal Bureau Statistiek (CBS) (2013). *StatLine Database* [website]. Den Haag/Herleen, The Netherlands: CBS. <http://www.cbs.nl/en-GB/menu/cijfers/statline/zelf-tabellen-maken/default.htm>.

De Nederlandsche Bank (DNB) (2012*a*). *DNB Anticipeert op Solvency II Voor Verzekeraars* [website]. Amsterdam, The Netherlands: DNB. <http://www.dnb.nl/nieuws/nieuwsoverzicht-en-archief/persberichten-2012/dnb275027.jsp>.

De Nederlandsche Bank (DNB) (2012*b*). *Uitkomsten Enquête DNB Naar Pensioenpremies en Toeslagverlening in 2012* [website]. Amsterdam, The Netherlands: DNB. <http://www.dnb.nl/nieuws/nieuwsoverzicht-en-archief/dnbulletin-2012/dnb276524.jsp>.

De Nederlandsche Bank (DNB) (2013). *Statistieken Pensioenregelingen Tabel 8.12* [website]. Amsterdam, The Netherlands: DNB. Accessed in March 2013. <http://www.statistics.dnb.nl/financieele-instellingen/pensioenfondsen/pensioenregelingen/index.jsp>.

Department of Work and Pensions (DWP) (2012). *Automatic Enrolment and Pensions Language Guide* [website]. London, U.K.: DWP. <http://www.dwp.gov.uk/docs/auto-enrol-language-guide.pdf>.

Diamond, P. (1977). 'A Framework for Social Security Analysis,' *Journal of Public Economics*, 8(3): 275–298.

European Insurance and Occupational Pensions Authority (EIOPA) (2010). *QIS 5 Risk-Free Interest Rate Extrapolation Method* [electronic publication]. Frankfurt am Main, Germany: EIOPA. <http://eiopa.europa.eu/fileadmin/tx_dam/files/consultations/QIS/QIS5/ceiops-paper-extrapolation-risk-free-rates_en-20100802.pdf>.

European Insurance and Occupational Pensions Authority (EIOPA) (2012). *2012 Report on Market Developments* [electronic publication]. Frankfurt am Main, Germany: EIOPA. July 25, <https://eiopa.europa.eu/fileadmin/tx_dam/files/publications/reports/2012-07-25_EIOPA-OPC-12-046_Report_on_market_developments_2012__1_.pdf>.

European Union (E.U.) (2002). *Directive 2002/83/EC of the European Parliament and the Council of 5 November 2002 Concerning Life Assurance* [website]. Brussels, Belgium: E.U. <http://eur-lex.europa.eu/LexUriServ/LexUriServ.do?uri=CELEX:32002L0083:EN:HTML>.

European Union (E.U.) (2003). *Directive 2003/41/EC of the European Parliament and the Council of 3 June 2003 on the Activities and Supervision of Institutions for Occupational Retirement Provision* [website]. Brussels, Belgium: E.U. <http://eur-lex.europa.eu/LexUriServ/LexUriServ.do?uri=CELEX:32003L0041:EN:HTML>.

Federal Public Service Finance (2008). *Belgium, Prime Location for Pan-European Pension Funds* [electronic publication]. Brussels, Belgium: Administration of the Treasury. <http://minfin.fgov.be/portail2/belinvest/downloads/en/publications/bro_pension.pdf>.

Financial Times (2007). 'Citigroup Chief Stays Bullish on Buy-outs,' 9 July. <http://www.ft.com/intl/cms/s/0/80e2987a-2e50-11dc-821c-0000779fd2ac.html#axzz2Z7gaIGWo>.

Financial Times (2012). 'And Now for Some Real Basel 3 Inspired Deleveraging,' *FT Alphaville* [website], 24 October. <http://ftalphaville.ft.com/2012/10/24/1225821/and-now-for-some-basel-3-inspired-deleveraging/>.

Finansinspektion (2013). 'Pressmeddelande: FI Planerar Införa Solvens 2-Anpassad Diskonteringsränta för Försäkringsföretagen,' press release. Stockholm, Sweden: February 18.

Gordon, R. H. and H. R. Varian (1988). 'Intergenerational Risk Sharing,' *Journal of Public Economics*, 37(2): 185–202.

The Human Mortality Database (2013). *The Human Mortality Database* [website]. Berkeley, CA: University of California, Berkeley, and Rostock, Germany: Max Planck Institute for Demographic Research. <http://www.mortality.org>.

Investments & Pensions Europe (IPE) (2013). 'Brussels Postpones Introduction of Pillar One for Revised IORP,' 23 May 2013. <http://www.ipe.com/guest/brussels-postpones-introduction-of-pillar-one-for-revised-iorp_52577.php#.UiCi3z-zIyY>.

Kocken, T. (2012). 'Pension Liability and Intergenerational Fairness: Two Case Studies,' *Rotman International Journal of Pension Management*, 5(1): 16–25.

Kocken, T. and J. Potters (2009). 'Sinking Giants,' *Life and Pensions* [electronic publication]. London, U.K.: Cardano, May. <http://www.cardano.com/cms/upload/100501_Sinking_Giants.pdf>.

Lever, M., R. Mehlkopf, and C. Van Ewijk (2012). 'Generatie-Effecten Pensioenakkoord,' *CPB Notitie*, 30 May. Den Haag, The Netherlands: Centraal Planbureau.

Nyman, F. (2012). 'Solvency II Unlikely to be Implemented Until 2016,' *Insurance Insight* [website], 18 October. <http://www.insuranceinsight.com/insurancxe-insight/news/2218289/solvency-ii-unlikely-to-be-implemented-until-201>.

Organisation for Economic Co-operation and Development (OECD) (2011). *Pensions at a Glance*. Paris, France: OECD.

Organisation for Economic Co-operation and Development (OECD) (2012). 'OECD Pension Indicators,' *Social Policies and Data* [website]. Paris, France: OECD. <http://www.oecd.org/els/soc/oecdpensionsindicators.htm>.

Pensioenfederatie (2012). *Roadshow Hoofdlijnennotitie Pensioenakkoord/FTK* [electronic publication]. Den Haag, The Netherlands: Pensioenfederatie. <http://www.pensioenfederatie.nl/Document/Presentaties/Presentatie%20Roadshow%20Hoofdlijnen%20def.pdf>.

Pension Policy Institute (PPI) (2010). 'State Pensions: Basic State and State Second Pension (March 2010)' [website]. <https://www.pensionspolicyinstitute.org.uk/default.asp?p=73> and <https://www.pensionspolicyinstitute.org.uk/default.asp?p=76>.

Pitt-Watson, D. (2012). 'Seeing through the British Pension System,' *RSA Projects*. London, U.K.: Royal Society for the Encouragement of Arts, Manufactures and Commerce.

Rijksoverheid (2012). 'Uitwerking van het Nieuwe Financieel Toetsingskader (ftk),' 30 May. Den Haag, The Netherlands: Rijksoverheid.

Roberts R. (2012). 'Did Anyone Learn Anything from the Equitable Life? Lessons and Learning from Financial Crises,' Institute of Contemporary British History report. London, U.K.: King's College.

Sociale Verzekeringsbank (SVB) (2013). 'AOW-Leeftijd Verhoogd,' [website], 8 January. Den Haag, The Netherlands: SVB. <http://www.svb.nl/int/nl/aow/actueel/nieuws overzicht/130108_aow_leeftijd_verhoogd.jsp>.

Statens Offentliga Utredningar (Swedish Pensions Agency) (2012). *Orange Report: Annual Report of the Swedish Pension System.* Stockholm, Sweden: Swedish Pensions Agency.

Sunstein, C. R. and R. H. Thaler (2008). 'Privatizing Social Security: Smorgasbord Style,' in *Nudge: Improving Decisions about Health, Wealth, and Happiness.* New Haven, CT: Yale University Press, pp. 147–161.

Swedish Government (2013). 'Vägval för Premiepensionen 2013,' DS 2013:35. Stockholm, Sweden: Swedish Government.

Trampusch, C., P. Eichenberger, M. de Roo, R. Bartlett Rissi, I. Bieri, L. Schmid, and S. Steinlin (2010). 'Pension in Sweden,' *REBECA (Research on Social Benefits in Collective Agreements) Database, Part 2, 'Social Benefits in Collective Agreements.'* SNF-Project No. 100012-119898. Bern, Switzerland: University of Bern Institute of Political Science.

U.K. Government (2013). 'Changes to the State Pension,' *GOV.UK* [website]. <https://www.gov.uk/changes-state-pension>.

Walschots, B. and H. Van Capelleveen (2009). 'Uitzonderlijke periode voor het FTK?', *VBA Journaal* [electronic publication]. Amsterdam, The Netherlands: Dutch Association of Investment Professionals (VBA). <http://www.cardano.com/cms/upload/091001_VBA,_Uitzonderlijke_periode_voor_FTK.pdf>.

Chapter 11

Extreme Risks and the Retirement Anomaly

Tim Hodgson

Retirement for the masses represents the briefest of anomalies over the broad sweep of human history. While the rich have always enjoyed their leisure, most of our ancestors worked until they were physically or mentally incapable of carrying on. The idea of self-sufficient time over many years in old age—what today we call retirement—is a very modern invention. To explore whether the concept of retirement is sustainable in the future, this chapter asks whether modern retirement systems are likely to be resilient to extreme risks—low-probability, but very high-impact shocks. To do so, we evaluate how certain we are in thinking the probability of such shocks is low and how to think about probabilistic modeling in this context.

In what follows, we begin by considering a 'straw man' worldview of stability, linear relationships, predictability, and equilibrium. Next we introduce an alternative perspective, one of complex adaptive systems with jumps, non-linearities, and punctuated equilibria; this perspective offers less predictability and higher likelihoods of extreme events. In this second case, it is less possible to diversify risk across time; hence one must weight more heavily the consequences of outcomes. Accordingly, it becomes essential to evaluate extreme risks so as to identify potential threats to retirement as we know it. In particular, we focus on political, environmental, social, and technological risks, as these receive far less attention than the much more evident financial and economic risks. We conclude that extreme risks matter and deserve far more attention than given thus far. Partly as a consequence but also due to economic risks, retirement for the masses is also at risk.

Alternative Worldviews

Early developers of financial economics relied on economic theory, which itself drew on the mathematics and statistics of physics (Lo and Mueller 2010). Its initial inspiration was Newtonian physics with its cause-and-effect approach and linear relationships. In many economic models, therefore, the economy is assumed to be in, or moving toward, long-term equilibrium with stable parameters through time. Dynamics are permitted, with short-term cycles typically generated by external shocks to the system. Moreover, economics frequently uses the phrase *ceteris paribus*, or 'all else being equal,' but this cannot hold in a dynamic system. This mindset has made it difficult to focus on rare 'tail events' and only recently have analysts devoted much attention to developing a theory of systemic risk.

By contrast, complexity science, or the study of complex adaptive systems,[1] has as its focus how system-level conduct emerges from interactions between components (cf. Bostrom 2013). In particular, this approach explores how complex collective behavior can emerge if individual actors operate with simple rules and lacking central control. Moreover, signaling and information processing become key: a form of network arises when the actors produce and use information from internal and external sources. And finally, complex systems adapt and change their behavior over time, implying an absence of stable equilibrium.

Viewing financial markets as complex adaptive systems rather than as linear systems tending toward equilibrium has important implications (see Table 11.1). First, understanding each component's behavior may not provide insight into the system as a whole. Thus, even if all investors were fully rational optimizers, this still may not imply rational, well-ordered, efficient markets. Second, one must grapple with the 'interconnectedness of all things.'[2] For example, the collapse of Lehman Brothers in September 2008 shows that counterparty risk is subject to non-linear contagion. Third, sudden and violent regime change is possible. Rather than returning to equilibrium after a nasty shock, it may be that turbulence endures for some time. Fourth, and most material to the consideration of extreme risks, is that the tails of the 'complexity distribution' are considerably fatter than those of the normal distribution. Complex adaptive systems tend to have scale-free distributions (power laws), so extreme events will be much more likely. Fifth, modeling becomes much more complex. That is, shocks can be modeled with fatter tails and higher probabilities, but complexity science has not yet developed sufficiently to provide readily usable quantitative models for finance and economics.

The Irreversibility of Time

The conventional approach to thinking about risk considers all possible outcomes and weights them in accordance with their probability. In effect, the exercise freezes time, taking multiple copies of the world and running them forward as 'parallel universes.' For instance, consider the following fair gamble: we will roll a fair die and stipulate that if I roll any number from one to five, I must pay you 50 percent of your current wealth including the present value of your future earnings.[3] Imagine how much better your life would be if you were one-and-a-half times richer in the time it took to roll a die. The downside, paltry in comparison, is that if you roll a six you must pay me your entire wealth. The expected value of the bet is a 25 percent expected return.

While this seems attractive from an odds perspective, many would not take the bet, perhaps because people might think about it as follows. Instead of rolling

TABLE 11.1 Characteristics of complex adaptive systems

Characteristic[a]	Financial market[b]
Underlying simplicity	An individual buys, or sells, a security.
Many components	Many investor types, many intermediaries, exchanges, payment systems.
Many individual actors	Each major market has thousands of institutional investors, and multiple thousands of individual investors. The investors span markets resulting in interconnectedness of apparently separate systems.
Coupled/interacting	Transactions cause a security's price to change, which triggers subsequent transactions and further price changes. In addition, news flow can cause coupling when unrelated parties trade on the same story.
Multiple spatial and temporal scales	Stock price charts over different lengths of time cannot be distinguished, meaning that stock price movement is scale-free with respect to time. It is therefore better proxied by a power law distribution than a normal distribution. This is consistent with stock price movements being self-similar (fractals) (Mandelbrot and Hudson 2004).
Unintended consequences	The repeal of the Glass–Steagall Act, which separated retail and commercial banking, was justified on the grounds of increased financial sophistication and new risk management technology. However, in retrospect it allowed deposit-taking banks to leverage their balance sheets, thereby contributing to the severity of the global financial crisis.
Emergent phenomena	Bubbles and busts are unintended, and are not controlled by any single actor or group. Consequently they can be considered as a behavior of financial markets that emerges from multiple individual interactions.
Historically contingent/ path-dependent	Bond market returns over the past 30 years were heavily dependent on yields falling from around 14% to around 2%. If we agree that yields will not fall another 12% over the next 30 years (to −10%) then it follows that bond returns cannot be as good in the next 30-year period. Future bond returns are historically contingent on what happened in the prior period. If returns were i.i.d. (independent and identically distributed), the returns over the next 30 years could be the same as in the previous 30. In equities, the concept of path dependency can be illustrated by Soros's concept of 'reflexivity' where 'the mispricing of financial instruments can affect the fundamentals that market prices are supposed to reflect' (Soros 2009).
Multiple phases (regimes)	Academics have identified different market regimes in monthly returns data (Kritzman and Li 2010) and over spans of a decade or more (Brock 2003). The difference in these timescales is interesting and refers back to the multiple time scales characteristic above.
Non-linear	Most, if not all, bubbles and busts would qualify as non-linear market events. However, there is an interesting example in the quantitative equity crisis of August 2007. David Viniar, then CFO of Goldman Sachs, explained that 'we were seeing things that were 25-standard deviation moves, several days in a row' (Larsen 2007). This quote inspired academic papers exploring the implications. In short, a 25-sigma event would be so incredibly rare that most other things would be more likely. My argument is that the confluence of quantitative equity trades caused prices to move in a non-linear way.
Robust/resilient	The global financial crisis notwithstanding, it is remarkable given the volume and size of daily transactions, as well as the ongoing attempts by unethical players to pervert markets for their own ends, that more doesn't go wrong more often.

(*Continued*)

Table 11.1 (Continued)

Characteristic[a]	Financial market[b]
Adaptive/evolving	If we compare financial markets today with any previous point in time we will see remarkable changes, and yet seldom have these changes appeared material at the time. The underlying simplicity remains— the buying and selling of securities—but now the trades are in decimals, occur in fractions of a second, and may not happen on an exchange. In addition the number and variety of securities available to transact has ballooned, particularly derivatives.
Non-equilibrium	There is no proof that can be offered to demonstrate conclusively that financial markets do not have an underlying equilibrium. Ultimately it comes down to an individual's belief about how the market operates. However, the clear exhibition of the other characteristics suggests, to the author at least, that financial markets do not exist in equilibrium. Instead they exhibit 'punctuated equilibria' where they appear to be in equilibrium while in fact cumulative change is occurring 'beneath the surface' which at a certain point leads to a non-linear jump. Hyman Minsky's financial instability hypothesis is an example of a punctuated equilibrium model.
Complicated vs complex	An aeroplane is complicated as it requires many different parts and systems to come together in a precise way in order to be able to fly safely. However it is not complex. Once those parts and systems have been assembled according to the design the plane will fly predictably. In contrast a complex system is non-repeatable and unique, in that slightly different interactions will lead the system down a different path. While not possible to rewind time and prove by experimentation, financial markets by dint of their reflexive nature appear more likely to be complex than complicated.

[a] This column lists the characteristics of complex adaptive systems as given in a presentation by Geoffrey West, Distinguished Professor and Past President, Santa Fe Institute to the Foundational Questions Institute (West 2011).
[b] This column indicates how financial markets exhibit the characteristics of complex adaptive systems.
Source: West (2011) and the author.

the die once in each of six parallel universes, we stay in our familiar universe and roll the same die six times in succession: the time average takes each of the six possible independent outcomes and makes them occur one after the other. When we compound returns over the six periods and take the sixth-root to calculate the per-period expected (time average) return, the time average is negative (−100 percent). In other words, the ensemble average *is* misleading; the 25 percent expected return unhelpfully disguises the meaningful (16.7 percent) likelihood that you lose everything. And when you have lost everything, you cannot go back and try again.

A more subtle point is that the expected return calculation effectively underweights the impact of extreme risk. To illustrate this, consider a world in which one invests a portfolio of financial assets with either a good or bad outcome. In the good case, one earns a return of 5 percent and this occurs most of the time; in the bad case, which only occurs once in the distribution, it causes severe or total loss. Table 11.2 shows that for a number of runs of the thought experiment, the ensemble average return exceeds the time average return. The column pairs represent worlds with different probabilities for the single extreme outcome, starting with one-in-1,000 and moving right to one-in-100. The rows show cases where the severity of portfolio loss rises from 99 percent in the first row to 100 percent in the bottom row. For all 20 combinations of probability and severity, the ensemble average return is always higher than the time average return, and in some cases significantly higher. Once the probability of the extreme event rises to one-in-100 or higher, then 99 good outcomes of 5 percent are wiped out by a single extreme event. Finally, note the difference in the time average return between extreme losses of 99.999 percent and 100 percent: as in the die-throwing experiment, once you have lost all your wealth, the game is over and your return is −100 percent, whether that occurs in the first or the last period. Losing 99.999 percent of your portfolio would clearly be painful, but the little that is left can then start to grow again. This highlights the difference between an existential risk and a risk where 'life' continues to the next period, albeit in very poor shape.

Of course one might object that a 99 percent or higher portfolio loss is too extreme to contemplate realistically. Yet some of the extreme risks discussed below might cause financial portfolios to become worthless, and history has offered several examples of entire stock market losses. In the pension case, if the retirement fund were a defined benefit arrangement and the plan sponsor has ceased to exist, then a large portfolio loss could mean that the fund's mission failed: assets will run out before the liabilities are paid and, absent an insurance arrangement, some beneficiaries will receive nothing. So for them, at least, this would equate to a total portfolio loss. If the retirement fund were a defined contribution arrangement, a large portfolio loss would not qualify as existential since there is no contractual benefit to be broken. Instead, the adjustment is borne by individual participants, perhaps by accepting a lower retirement standard of living than anticipated. Even here, however, not all members are equal. A 50 percent loss for a 29-year-old is fundamentally different to a 50 percent loss for a 59-year-old; the older participant could perceive the loss as bordering on the existential. The practical takeaway is that avoiding or reducing the probability of 100 percent (existential) losses is incredibly valuable.

Using a different lens to regard the world can increase our perception of the qualitative chances of an extreme event occurring,[4] and embracing the reality of irreversible time meaningfully increases the significance of extreme risks. Next we consider what events might be considered extreme, in the context of their impact on retirement systems.

TABLE 11.2 Expected returns (percent) from a distribution comprising good outcomes with a 5 percent return and a single extreme outcome

Loss given extreme event (%)	Probability of extreme event occurring:							
	1 in 1,000		1 in 500		1 in 250		1 in 100	
	Ensemble average	Time average	Ensemble average	Time average	Ensemble average	Time average	Ensemble average	Time average
−99.000	4.90	4.51	4.79	4.03	4.58	3.06	3.96	0.23
−99.900	4.90	4.27	4.79	3.55	4.58	2.12	3.95	−2.06
−99.990	4.90	4.03	4.79	3.07	4.58	1.18	3.95	−4.29
−99.999	4.90	3.79	4.79	2.60	4.58	0.25	3.95	−6.46
−100.000	4.90	−100	4.79	−00	4.58	−100	3.95	−100

Notes: The ensemble average is calculated using the formula: $E(r) = \sum_{i=1}^{N} \frac{r(t)}{N}$. The time average is calculated using the formula:
$T(r) = \prod_{i=1}^{N} [1 + r(i)]^{1/N} - 1$.

Source: Author's calculations.

Identifying Extreme Risks

A large variety of risks could be included on a list of extreme events. Here we propose a framework or set of filters that can help identify which risks are of most import, and which can be safely ignored. Here we consider only first-order impacts and discuss them in isolation. We do, however, make an attempt to move toward second-order considerations in the form of an 'association matrix,' a qualitative assessment of whether there is likely to be a causal link between the individual risks. Moreover, context-specific risk assessment considers whether a chain of events could occur; whether the conditional probability of a subsequent event is substantially higher than the unconditional probability; and whether the combined events have a different scale of impact.[5]

Since our focus is on sustainability of the retirement system, we focus mainly on risks that can erode assets or increase liabilities; we also omit discussion of legal, process, and operational risks. Having acknowledged these limitations, our overall framework consists of six categories: finance, economics, politics, environment, society, and technology. We also touch only lightly on financial and economic categories, since these are widely commented on in other chapters in this volume (and Towers Watson 2010, 2011). Financial extreme risks would be sovereign default, banking crises, and insurance crises. Economic extreme risks would include depression, hyperinflation, currency crises, and the end of fiat money.

The six categories in our framework are not independent. In fact, some of the most interesting insights can be found at points of confluence; see Table 11.3 (and the Appendix). To be clear, some of these risks may seem quite extreme (and perhaps amusingly or ridiculously so). But our goal is to allow for 'black swan' or highly unusual events. Within a category, the risks are listed in alphabetical order and do not represent any form of ranking. The risks listed are also intentionally extreme: in effect, we ask 'is it plausible?' or, perhaps more accurately, 'does our current state of knowledge suggest it is completely implausible?' Next we evaluate, assuming this event occurred, what the consequences might be.

Political

This category of extreme risks derives from policy decisions. In two cases, the link is direct: global trade collapse follows policy decisions to favor protectionism over openness and globalization, and a World War III would flow from active decisions to declare war. For anarchy and political extremism, the link is less direct, yet poor prior policy decisions are likely to be necessary, if not sufficient, conditions for these risks to foment. Terrorism is included in the political category due to its ideological foundation, and because the target chosen for the act of terrorism is likely to have political ramifications.[6]

TABLE 11.3 Extreme risks by category

Political

P1 Anarchy	An extreme form of social disorder in a major economy, resulting in a loss of power by government and possible imposition of martial law.
P2 Global trade collapse	Extreme rise in protectionism causing global trade and investment to collapse, requiring a rise in self-sufficiency.
P3 Political extremism	The rise to power in a major economy of a brutal and oppressive government, typically causing a large number of civilian deaths and becoming a major threat to global peace (e.g. totalitarianism, whether fascism or Stalinism).
P4 Terrorism	A major (ideologically driven) terrorist attack, targeted at a region of global economic and/or political importance.
P5 World War III	A military war involving many of the world's most powerful and populous countries causing multiple millions of deaths (could involve a nuclear holocaust).

Environmental

E1 Alien invasion	Invasion of non-peace-seeking extra-terrestrial beings that either remove the planet's resources or enslave or exterminate humanity.
E2 Biodiversity collapse	The destruction of the world's ecosystem and therefore the loss to humans of ecosystem services: provision (food and clean water), regulation (climate and disease), support (nutrient cycles and crop pollination), and culture (spiritual and recreational benefits).
E3 Cosmic threats	Existential risks arising beyond earth, such as a major meteorite impact, being pulled out of orbit (or the solar system) by a passing asteroid, or a giant solar flare (which would be compounded if it were during a reversal of the earth's magnetic field).
E4 Global temperature change	Habitable areas on the Earth are significantly reduced due to excessive heat or cold, associated with significant sea level rises or 'ice age' respectively.
E5 Natural catastrophe	Earthquakes, tsunamis, hurricanes, flooding (including atmospheric river storms), and volcanic eruptions. The extreme risk would either be a confluence of connected extreme natural catastrophes or the eruption of a supervolcano (ejecta >1,000 km³ threatening species extinction).

Social

S1 Extreme longevity
An unanticipated, significant increase in life expectancy for much, or the majority, of humans. Possibly the result of a major breakthrough in medical or human genome science.

S2 Food/water/energy crisis
Major shortfall in the supply of food, water, or energy causing political strife and widespread death and severe damage to the quality of life for many survivors.

S3 Health progress backfire
A reversal in the trend of improved health. Possibly caused by societal trends such as mental health problems or obesity, the unintended consequences of current healthcare practices (e.g. antibiotic resistance), or a slowing in the rate of medical advancement below the rate of pathogen evolution. Economic output falls and liabilities increase.

S4 Organized crime
A significant increase in the scale of illegal operation in a major economy or region to the extent that legitimate economic activity becomes non-viable.

S5 Pandemic
An epidemic of highly infectious and fatal disease that spreads through human, animal, or plant populations worldwide.

Technological

T1 Biotech catastrophe
An instance of error or terror causing widespread deaths. The risk arises from the easy synthesis of DNA, as well as other biological manipulations being increasingly available to small groups of technically competent and even individual users.

T2 Cyber warfare
Politically motivated computer hacking to conduct sabotage and espionage on a national or global-power scale.

T3 Infrastructure failure
An interruption of a major infrastructure network for a relatively long period due to human behaviors, natural disasters, or even cosmic threats.

T4 Nuclear contamination
A major nuclear accident or attack that leads to lethal effects to individuals and large radioactivity release to the environment.

T5 Technological singularity
An extreme risk resulting from technological advancement proceeding beyond the point of human understanding. The creation of a computer more powerful than the human brain, which can then design and build an even more advanced machine creating an environment where human survival is at risk.

Note: The risks are listed alphabetically within the categories.
Source: Author's analysis.

Environmental

These risks represent threats to human safety and well-being arising from a disruption to the planet's environment. Two of these, alien invasion and cosmic threats, can be considered exogenous. While some might think that an alien invasion is too extreme to consider seriously, and its probability and consequences are unknowable, good risk management requires taking action in advance to protect against possible future consequences. Accordingly, the exercise is to scan the horizon with an open mind; one can always apply additional filters later, to protect finite risk management resources. For now, all we can say is that too little is known to rule out the possibility of an alien invasion.

Two other environmental risks, biodiversity collapse and global temperature change, could be the result of human activity, and thus they represent serious challenges given the absence of effective global governance. Other possible sources of both risks are shown in Table 11.4.

The final risk in this category is natural catastrophe. As earthquakes, for example, occur every day, the extreme version of this risk is either a confluence of extreme natural catastrophes (e.g., a magnitude 10 earthquake combined with a 25-meter tsunami, helped along by a Category Five windstorm) or the eruption of a supervolcano.

Social

Social extreme risks are threats that could adversely affect the smooth functioning of society. As noted above, the table categories are not independent and social risks link to policy decisions, the environment, and, in some cases, to technology. This is clearest in the case of a food/water/energy crisis which would have political, environmental, and technological drivers, as well as offsets.

Three of the risks are health-related. Pandemics are a favorite of commentators on extreme risks, as there are good data (at least in relative terms). Here we postulate that a new disease agent hits the 'disease sweet spot' of both high infectivity and high mortality (in practice these have often been trade-offs). Health progress backfire refers to a reversal in the trend of improved health while, working in the other direction, extreme longevity becomes a risk when viewed through the lens of a retirement provider. The final risk identified in this category is organized crime, to the extent that legitimate economic activity ceases to be viable in a major country or region.

Technological

Our last category of extreme risks concerns technology. Here one might contemplate a failure in current technology (nuclear contamination or infrastructure failure); possible consequences of emerging technology (cyber warfare and biotech

TABLE 11.4 Extreme risk scoring

	Likelihood 1—one in 10 years 2—one in 20 years 3—one in 100 years 4—one in 100+ years	Uncertainty A degree of High (H), Medium (M), Low (L)	Impact—intensity 1—Endurable 2—Crushing 3—Existential	Impact—scope 1—Local 2—Global 3—Trans-generational 4—Pan-generational
Political				
P1 Anarchy	3	M	2	1
P2 Global trade collapse	1	M	1	2
P3 Political extremism	3	H	2	1
P4 Terrorism	2	M	1	1
P5 World War III	3	M	2	2
Environmental				
E1 Alien invasion	4	H	3	4
E2 Biodiversity collapse	3	M	2	3
E3 Cosmic threats	4	M	3	4
E4 Global temperature change	2	L	2	3
E5 Natural catastrophe	4	M	2	3
Social				
S1 Extreme longevity	3	L	1	2
S2 Food/water/energy crisis	1	L	2	1
S3 Health progress backfire	2	M	1	3
S4 Organized crime	2	M	1	1
S5 Pandemic	2	H	2	2
Technological				
T1 Biotech catastrophe	3	H	2	2
T2 Cyber warfare	2	H	1	2
T3 Infrastructure failure	2	M		1
T4 Nuclear contamination	2	M	2	1
T5 Technological singularity	3	H	3	4

Source: Author's analysis.

catastrophe); or a technological singularity—the point in time when humans have designed super-intelligence into machines. What happens beyond that point is unknowable and therefore the subject of speculation.

Assessing Extreme Risks

Next we seek to determine which of these risks might be more or less material in the context of a retirement system. The traditional risk assessment approach would be to learn from historical data; a qualitative overlay can be added, if for example, a structural change is believed to have occurred. But when thinking about extreme risks, by definition there may be no or very small historical evidence.

For this reason, we take a deliberately qualitative (deductive) approach to the assessment process. In the first phase, a team of Towers Watson researchers reviewed the research literature and historical data on past extreme events. Team members then independently generated scores. In phase two, the independent scores were compared and debated, with a single consolidated scoring approach generated. For stage three, the consolidated scores were reviewed by a senior committee and further refinements suggested. Hence what we propose has been subjected to a rigorous oversight process, making our conclusions robust, albeit qualitative.

We score each of the extreme risks in Table 11.4, and results are illustrated graphically in Figure 11.1. Each risk has four scores: for likelihood, uncertainty, intensity of impact, and scope of impact. For the grading of the intensity and scope of impact we draw on and adapt the qualitative risk categories of Bostrom (2013). These scores relate to the most extremely negative manifestation of the risk. For instance, the consequences of earth being visited by aliens span a massive range from the beneficial to the extinction of the human species. As we are concerned here with extreme negative risks, it is the latter potential outcome we score. Also, rather than assign each risk a probability (the quantitative route), we assign it one of four categories representing a likelihood of occurrence of 1-in-10 years, 1-in-20 years, 1-in-100 years, and less than 1-in-100 years. (For the technically minded, this is akin to a high-alpha power law for the distribution and implies we believe these events should be considered far more likely than if a normal distribution were used.)

We split the potential impact of each risk into two separate dimensions, namely the intensity and the scope (or geographical/temporal spread). The intensity is assigned to one of three states labeled 'endurable,' 'crushing,' and 'existential.'[7] The scope of the impact attempts to convey both spatial and temporal information by use of four categories: local, global, trans-generational, and pan-generational. The first two imply a temporary impact, while the latter two imply a lasting impact. We use 'trans-generational' to describe an impact affecting more than one generation, but that would then fade or reverse. 'Pan-generational' refers to an impact that would affect all subsequent or all previously potential generations (such as extinction of the human species). Of course there is a danger that these two dimensions are not independent; for instance, a food/water/energy crisis could be described as either locally crushing or globally endurable. For the majority of other cases, we believe the two dimensions are sufficiently independent to provide useful additional information.

The final score assigned to each risk is uncertainty, assessed as low, medium, or high. In the graphical representation (Figure 11.1), this is shown as a semi-transparent border around the shape, with higher uncertainty shown by a larger 'fuzzy' border (or 'location'). As indicated by the shapes, the uncertainty is

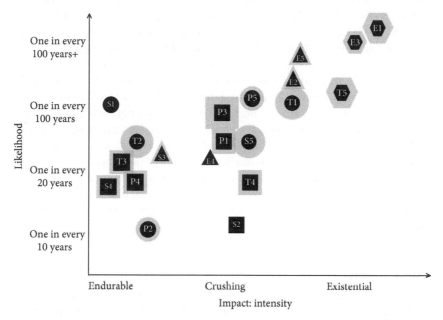

Figure 11.1. Extreme risk scoring.

Notes: the scope of the impact is shown in different shapes (Local—Square; Global—Circle; Trans-generational—Triangle; Pan-generational—Hexagon). The size of the shape is indicative of the level of uncertainty with regards to the likelihood/impact of each risk:

P1 Anarchy	E1 Alien invasion	S1 Extreme longevity	T1 Biotech catastrophe
P2 Global trade collapse	E2 Biodiversity collapse	S2 Food/water/ energy crisis	T2 Cyber warfare
P3 Political extremism	E3 Cosmic threats	S3 Health progress backfire	T3 Infrastructure failure
P4 Terrorism	E4 Global temperature change	S4 Organized crime	T4 Nuclear contamination
P5 World War III	E5 Natural catastrophe	S5 Pandemic	T5 Technological singularity

Source: Author's analysis.

in two dimensions: uncertainty regarding the likelihood, and uncertainty regarding the impact.[8] Figure 11.1 is perhaps more useful for assessing the overall findings. One might have hoped that the most likely risks were endurable and the existential risks less likely, and the Figure does show this general shape. One might have also anticipated that local impact was more frequent than global, global more frequent than trans-generational, and pan-generation the least frequent; this too is the case in our view.

Of course in the retirement context, we are most interested in impacts on assets and liabilities. If we split Figure 11.1 into three regions, the first comprises the six points in the top right corner, which are the existential and crushing-bordering-on-existential risks. Should these events happen, we will not be particularly worried about the assets or the liabilities, as assets are likely to be worthless and the value of the liabilities may well have fallen to zero too. The second group comprises the seven points to the left with crushing intensity of impact. For these events, the effect on assets will be global and materially negative. There will also be a reduction in the value of liabilities, but as liabilities tend to be more local than assets, the effect would be much more case-specific. That is, if your nation is at war, you lose lives and your liabilities go down. If your neighbors are neutral, their liabilities do not change. On balance, therefore, we would expect asset losses to be larger than any reduction in liabilities, and so funding levels would deteriorate.

The third group is the left-most seven points (endurable intensity). These are less homogenous, but in general we would expect a more muted impact on assets and liabilities. The clear outlier in this group is extreme longevity, which would explicitly increase the liabilities.

Association

As noted above, these risks are not entirely independent, so we have also developed an 'association' matrix (see Table 11.5). This is not a correlation matrix: correlations require data to calculate and even then they say nothing about causality. Instead, here we use the term association to communicate that this is a qualitative assessment of whether there is likely to be any causality between the events. If evaluating whether a particular event, X, might cause another, select X in the first column and read across the row. A blank cell means that, in our opinion, X does not cause Y to any material extent. 'L' for low means that we believe X could cause Y, or is a contributory factor. 'H' for high means we believe the causality is material, so X is likely to, or will, cause Y. For example, reading across the first row of entries shows that we believe anarchy (P1) *could* cause, or contribute to, global trade collapse (P2), World War III (P5), a food/water/energy crisis (S2), biotech catastrophe (T1), infrastructure failure (T3), and nuclear contamination (T4). Anarchy *is likely to* cause political extremism (P3) and a sharp rise in organized crime (S4).

The table can also be read down the columns. Here column entries mean event Y could or is likely to 'be caused by' events corresponding to the cell entries. As

TABLE 11.5 Extreme risk association matrix

	P1 Anarchy	P2 Global trade collapse	P3 Political extremism	P4 Terrorism	P5 World War III	E1 Alien invasion	E2 Biodiversity collapse	E3 Cosmic threats	E4 Global temperature change	E5 Natural catastrophe	S1 Extreme longevity	S2 Food/water/energy crisis	S3 Health progress backfire	S4 Organized crime	S5 Pandemic	T1 Biotech catastrophe	T2 Cyber warfare	T3 Infrastructure failure	T4 Nuclear contamination	T5 Technological singularity
P1 Anarchy		LL	HH		LL							LL		hH		IL		LL	IL	
P2 Global trade collapse	HH		LL		LL							HH		hH			IL	LL	IL	
P3 Political extremism	L	HL		LL	HH							LL		h			IL		IL	
P4 Terrorism			LL				LL									IL	hH	hH	hH	
P5 World War III	LL	LL	HH				LL					LL			IL	IL		hH	IL	
E1 Alien invasion					LL															
E2 Biodiversity collapse	HH		LL		LL				HH			HH	HH	IL				IL		
E3 Cosmic threats	HH	HH					HH		HH			HH						hH		
E4 Global temperature change	LL		LL				HH			LL		HH	IL	IL	IL			IL		
E5 Natural catastrophe	HH	HH					HH		HH			HH						hH		
S1 Extreme longevity												LL								
S2 Food/water/energy crisis	HH				LL									IL						
S3 Health progress backfire															IL					
S4 Organized crime	LL	LL																		
S5 Pandemic																				
T1 Biotech catastrophe	HH				LL							LL	IL		IL			hH		
T2 Cyber warfare					LL														IL	
T3 Infrastructure failure												IL								
T4 Nuclear contamination												IL						IL		
T5 Technological singularity	LL	LL	LL																	
	PP1	PP2	PP3	PP4	PP5	EE1	EE2	EE3	EE4	EE5	SS1	SS2	SS3	SS4	SS5	TT1	TT2	TT3	TT4	TT5

Notes: This table is a qualitative assessment of the likelihood the events in the left column could lead to events in the right columns (reading across the rows). A blank cell means that X does not cause Y to any material extent. L (low) means that we believe X could cause Y, or is a contributory factor. H (high) means we believe the causality is material, so X is likely to, or will, cause Y. The table can also be read down the columns in a 'this risk is "caused by. . ." ' sense. For example, E1, alien invasion, is not caused by" any of the other risks considered here.

Source: Author's analysis.

an example, global temperature change (E4) is likely to be caused by biodiversity collapse (E2), cosmic threats (E3), and natural catastrophe (E5). We emphasize that this is an association matrix between only the risks we are considering, and therefore it is silent on whether other contributory factors outside our current consideration also matter.

Many comments could be made about the associations, but here we focus on the key ones for our purpose. The environmental risks (rows E1 to E5) are powerfully causal, so, contingent on one of them occurring, other extreme risks could be triggered. By contrast, the social extreme risks (rows S1 to S5) have low causal power: they are unlikely to trigger further extreme events. Yet the social risks could have multiple triggers, as indicated by the number of entries in columns S2 to S5. This is especially the case for food/water/energy crisis (S2), attributable to our assessment that the demand for water and food may soon start to exceed supply. With little current buffer, it would take little to tip the balance the wrong way. We also note that there are some truly independent risks in the table. Columns E1, E3, S1, and T5 imply that an alien invasion, cosmic threats, extreme longevity, and technological singularity are unlikely to be triggered by any of the other extreme events considered here.

Next we create a ranking of the importance of the risks; this introduces no new information, but rather combines the scores for each risk into a single number that can then be ranked. The approach is straightforward: the more likely a risk, the higher the ranking it receives. Likewise, the more certain a risk, the greater its intensity of impact; the larger the scope of the risk impact, the higher its ranking. The scoring necessarily involves some element of rough justice, in that it requires trading off between, say, likelihood and intensity. But instead of focusing overly much on precise ranking, it is more useful to arrive at an overall judgment as to whether the ranking is satisfactory, inquiring whether the risks at the top and at the bottom seem reasonable. Results appear in Table 11.6.

At the top of the list is a food/water/energy crisis (S2), driven by our assessment that this is one of the most likely risks; hence there is *relatively* little uncertainty attached to either its likelihood or the consequences. The consequences themselves, while locally crushing, are not globally severe (in relative terms), so these do not imply a top ranking. In contrast, the second ranked risk, global temperature change (E4), has much more severe consequences (trans-generationally crushing), but it is assessed to have a lower likelihood of occurring.

It is interesting to note that the three extreme risks assessed as having the worst consequences (existential and pan-generational) all rank in the bottom 10 overall, with alien invasion (E1) ranked at 19. This is because their poor consequences are diluted by our assessment of low likelihood and relatively high uncertainty. At the very bottom is political extremism (P3), where the locally crushing consequences are not particularly severe, the likelihood is relatively low, but there is a high degree of uncertainty over how assets and liabilities would be affected.

TABLE 11.6 Extreme risk ranking

1.	S2 Food/water/energy crisis
2.	E4 Global temperature change
3.	P2 Global trade collapse
4.	S3 Health progress backfire
5.	T4 Nuclear contamination
6.	S1 Extreme longevity
7.	P4 Terrorism
8.	T3 Infrastructure failure
9.	E2 Biodiversity collapse
10.	S5 Pandemic
11.	P5 World War III
12.	T5 Technological singularity
13.	E3 Cosmic threats
14	T2 Cyber warfare
15.	P1 Anarchy
16.	S4 Organized crime
17.	E5 Natural catastrophe
18.	T1 Biotech catastrophe
19.	E1 Alien invasion
20.	P3 Political extremism

Source: Author's analysis.

As noted above, different scoring systems and weights could produce somewhat different rankings, but the power of our approach is that it combines and trades off the four risk scores in a consistent manner. Overall, the value of this approach is to challenge preconceptions and highlight which risks to prioritize when it comes to management actions.

Implications for Retirement and Retirement Systems

Above we showed that adequate saving is necessary but not sufficient for a comfortable retirement period. And extreme risks pose a threat to the quality of retirement in terms of security and/or wellbeing, whether political, environmental, sociological, or technological. Similarly, extreme risks pose a risk to retirement systems. To protect against these, we require more robust investment portfolios and balance sheets. Accordingly, we consider how to incorporate the framework developed above in the process of managing a retirement fund's balance sheet.

One option would be to slightly reduce expected returns, or push up volatilities and/or correlations, so as to incorporate the impact of infrequent extreme events (Towers Watson 2011). Another approach is to model dynamic switching: here one must make explicit two sets of assumptions ('normal' and 'extreme'), or one could design a second, extreme risk, portfolio directly (Moore and Pedersen 2014). A third option is to construct a hedging overlay, though hedging comes with its own set of problems, including high carrying cost and often the use of derivatives. Not all extreme risks can be hedged, and hedges are imprecise. In fact, once one moves beyond financial and economic extreme risks to confront the extreme risks described above, hedging becomes very difficult indeed. Whether the counterparties would be willing to and capable of paying out if the extreme event happened is also unclear.

Retirement systems have three broad hedging strategies. The first is to hold cash; this is likely the 'oldest, easiest, and most underrated source of tail risk protection' (Montier 2011) and is closest to a generic hedge for all of the risks considered in this chapter. Over long historical periods, in many countries, cash has held its real value through both episodes of deflation and inflation, but there is no guarantee that this will be the case in the future. Cash is likely to be effective in partially hedging risk up to and including crushing intensity, but it is likely to become worthless once we cross over to existential intensity (all other assets are also likely to become worthless, but the funding ratio could be quite good if all the liabilities have been extinguished). Also there could be non-linear breakpoints between crushing intensity and existential intensity. Another consideration regarding holding cash is which currency (or currencies) to favor. Since retirement system liabilities tend to be domestic, there is a natural draw to domestic currency cash. Yet this represents a relatively concentrated risk position and so a degree of diversification may be preferable.

A second hedging strategy for retirement systems is to use derivatives, though cost and usefulness are often in opposition. The cost of derivatives protection can often be reduced by specifying more precise conditions for the payout, but the more precise the conditions, the greater the chance that these will not be met exactly, so the protection will not pay. Derivatives in the form of swaps are an obvious way to hedge the risk of extreme longevity, but capacity is likely to be severely constrained relative to potential demand (cf Coughlan 2014). Beyond longevity hedging, derivatives could possibly be used to help with one or two of the risks, such as global trade collapse, or commodities futures could be used to hedge a food/water/energy crisis. In the main, however, derivatives are probably better suited to hedging financial and economic risks.

A third retirement system hedging strategy is to hold assets that are negatively correlated with their liabilities. Typical hedging assets include the highest quality sovereign nominal and inflation-linked bonds, as well as precious metals. More creativity is probably required to handle some of the risks. For example, with respect to a World War III, one strategy would be to hold assets in neutral countries; of course, this would require foresight and willingness to hold a portfolio very different from that of peers. In fact, all of the political risks require some sort of portfolio-exclusion approach, avoiding assets in jurisdictions likely to be affected. In any event, no single asset is likely to protect against all possible bad outcomes. Moreover, there is no guarantee that the expected performance of the hedge asset will actually transpire in the event.

To make retirement funds more resilient in the face of extreme risks, we suggest they undertake a prioritization exercise. At the top of the list is to focus on the events that might permanently impair the investor's mission, to identify which extreme risks matter and which can be ignored. For the former, insurance is indicated since the investor cannot afford to self-insure. For the latter, an investor should do the 'simple' things, including diversifying the portfolio across as many return drivers as possible; today many institutional portfolios are heavily concentrated in equity or growth risk. Additionally it is useful to diversify within asset classes; today most pension funds are heavily exposed to domestic sovereign bonds for liability-matching purposes. Extreme risk thinking would suggest reducing the quality of the match to reduce the risk concentration. Holding cash strategically also provides optionality. And finally, over time, greater complexity can be added assuming it passes a considered cost/benefit analysis. This is likely to involve adding long-dated derivative contracts in a contrarian manner—that is, when they are inexpensive rather than popular.

Extreme Risks and the Retirement Anomaly

At the outset we posed the question of whether retirement in the modern sense is sustainable or a passing anomaly. Our review of extreme risks casts doubt on society's ability to defer sufficient current consumption to fund future consumption. A simple model of a retirement system where individuals work for 45 years, set aside 10 percent of earnings, and earn a real return of 3.5 percent each year, implies that they could live for 21 years without working (Towers Watson 2012). But all the assumptions embedded in this model require the household to build up a pension or assets worth just over 10 times annual earnings by the retirement date. If the population were distributed evenly by age, this would mean the economy would need to accumulate steady-state pension wealth equal to 4.7 times total earnings, or around 235 percent of GDP.

Unfortunately, this target is far from met. The 13 largest pension markets in the world have pension assets amounting to less than 80 percent of GDP (Towers Watson 2013), implying much too few resources available to support retirement. So we have either chronically undersaved for retirement and need to do better, or other assets outside the pension system may be the answer. If the diagnosis is chronic undersaving, it will be necessary to greatly boost saving without reducing the rate of return on investment. Unfortunately this could result in Keynes's paradox of thrift: even if it is rational for an individual to save more, if everyone saves more, the real rate of return is likely to be driven down. The same thought holds true for non-pension saving, and so it may not be possible for society to defer consumption in sufficient size to give people the retirement they currently expect.

It appears, then, that society will struggle to support a retired population in the style to which it aspires. The past half-century has witnessed a historical 'retirement sweet spot,' where rising expectations were affordable due to well-documented economic and social factors post-World War II, including favorable demographics and the run-up in debt levels. For the future, the outlook is less sanguine.

Conclusion

This chapter has suggested that the world is a complex adaptive system. A consequence of this perspective is that the probabilities of extreme events are higher than anticipated by those accustomed to viewing the world linearly and predictably. We also noted that understanding that time is irreversible for decision-makers implies that we must give greater weight to the consequences of outcomes and less weight to their likelihood. In turn, we must acknowledge that political, environmental, social, and technological risks can play havoc with the quality of life for retirees, and cause sustainability issues for retirement systems everywhere.

The range of potential consequences of these risks is very wide. Locally endurable risks would be uncomfortable for retirement funds caught in the wrong locale, or with the wrong exposures, and would likely be enough to cause the weaker funds to become incapable of completing their mission. At the other end of the spectrum, existential and pan-generational risks represent a systemic and terminal outcome for retirement funds, and perhaps the human species. We also proposed a ranking system as a useful way to prioritize efforts to consider and manage potential risk exposures. Since political, environmental, social, and technological risks are difficult to hedge, a relatively high cash weighting appears versatile and effective. Perhaps rather than changing investment strategy, we must save more and build a larger risk buffer, a course of action currently forced onto banks.

Among the issues we lacked space to discuss include two worth mentioning. First, embedded in our likelihood scores is the fact that the world lacks effective global governance, 'G0.'[9] Many of the political, social, and technological risks, and two of the environmental risks, identified are clearly exacerbated by an absence of effective global governance. Conversely, such governance could materially reduce the likelihood of these multiple risks. Second, we noted the possibility that technology could 'run amok.' Naturally, technology has been of substantial benefit to humankind, but many unintended consequences arise from complex adaptive systems.

In sum, extreme risks matter and they deserve more attention than has been given thus far. As a consequence, retirement for the masses is at serious risk, at least in terms of current expectations regarding length, quality of life, and degree of financial freedom. Alternatively, retirement as currently configured probably was never affordable, but this fact was obscured by demographic and debt trends over the past half-century.

Acknowledgements

The author acknowledges his colleague, Liang Yin, for support in this research, though any errors and omissions are those of the author alone.

Appendix: A Taxonomy of Extreme Risks

The extreme risks developed in the text are described in greater detail here.

Political Risk

P1 Anarchy. The Arab Spring that started in December 2010 has removed existing rulers in Tunisia, Egypt, Libya, and Yemen to date. It was prompted by dissatisfaction with the rule of governments and likely by wide gaps in income levels. Welfare cuts and unemployment during the global financial crisis fuelled protests and anxiety across Europe. According to Europe China Research and Advice Network, social unrest in China has been increasing at an alarming rate—8,700 'mass incidents' were recorded in 1993; by 2005 it had grown tenfold to 87,000 and estimates for 2010 range between 180,000 and 230,000, highlighting an increasing threat to the stability of the world's second largest economy (Göbel and Ong 2012). In a world of growing income inequality and hyper-connected communication, the risk is an extreme form of social disorder in a major state, resulting in a loss of power by government and causing its economy to collapse.

P2 Global trade collapse. Protectionism is the policy of restricting trade with the aim of 'protecting' businesses and workers in the domestic economy from the full force of external competition. There have been a number of studies that suggest an increase in barriers to trade since the global financial crisis (Lowrey 2012). The concern is that short-term political expediency can override long-term economic logic, with the extreme risk being a populist backlash against cross-border mobility of labor, goods, and capital, causing global trade and investment to collapse. The consequences will include more uncertainty in financial markets, greater fragmentation of capital markets, and eventually a reversal in globalization.

P3 Political extremism. During the twentieth century, many nations suffered under extraordinarily brutal governments seeking to retain total authority over the society and control all aspects of public and private life (totalitarianism). The Soviet Union and Nazi Germany are the two most studied totalitarian regimes. The risk of political extremism is defined by the rise to power in a major economy of an oppressive government (including but not limited to totalitarianism). Political extremism typically causes a large number of civilian deaths (by modern calculations, the Soviets killed approximately 20 million civilians, the Nazis 25 million) and could become a major threat to global peace (Nazi Germany directly caused World War II). Bryan Caplan from George Mason University speculates that the chance of a world totalitarian government emerging during the next 1,000 years and lasting for 1,000 years or more is 5 percent (Caplan 2006).

P4 Terrorism. 9/11 caused almost 3,000 deaths and the Dow Jones Industrial Average index fell by more than 14 percent within the first week of market reopening. New York City's GDP was estimated to have lost $27.3 billion for 2001–2012 (Wikipedia 2013*a*). Its impact extended beyond geopolitics into society and culture in general. The extreme risk here is a major ideologically driven terrorist attack of a similar, or larger, scale to 9/11, targeted at a region of global economic and/or political importance and inflicting large-scale human and financial damage.

P5 World War III. This extreme risk is a military war involving many of the world's most powerful and populous countries, causing multiple millions of deaths. One consequence of war is the destruction of capital—both physical and human. War tends to kill those in prime ages (predominantly males), which leaves a reduced younger workforce base and in turn reduces economic output and consumption. World War II caused deaths of between 65 and 75 million, and the total number of deaths in wars and conflicts for the entire twentieth century was between 136.5 and 148.5 million (Leitenberg 2006). The availability of weapons of mass destruction means the next world war could destroy an order of magnitude more capital than the previous ones. As Albert Einstein put it, 'I know not with what weapons World War III will be fought, but World War IV will be fought with sticks and stones' (Calaprice et al. 2005). The invention of nuclear and biological weapons raises the possibility that the future war could put much of the human race at risk.

Environmental Risk

E1 Alien invasion. An alien invasion is a very common theme in science fiction stories and films, despite the fact that evidence of extra-terrestrial life has never been documented. NASA's Kepler mission to identify earth-size planets around stars was launched in March 2009 and has already discovered thousands of candidates (2,740 planet candidates and 105 confirmed planets as of February 11, 2013; NASA 2013), including one the size of Earth. The range of outcomes of an alien life contact can be vast and entirely unpredictable, but if the contact is indeed hostile it is more likely that the human race will be unable to defend itself due to the potentially overwhelming technological gap. The extreme risk is therefore an invasion of non-peace-seeking extra-terrestrials that look to either remove the planet's resources or enslave or exterminate human life.

E2 Biodiversity collapse. It is estimated that less than 1 percent of the species that have existed on earth are extant and there have been five known mass extinctions since life began on earth that led to large and sudden drops in biodiversity (Wikipedia 2013*b*). Human activity has accelerated the species loss and these losses could reach a point beyond which it becomes irreversible. It is believed earth is not far away from its sixth mass extinction. Although about 80 percent of humans' food supply comes from just 20 types of plant, humans use at least 40,000 species. Earth's surviving biodiversity provides resources for increasing the range of food and other products suitable for human use, although the present extinction rate shrinks that potential. The subsequent destruction of the world's ecosystem could cause the loss to humans of ecosystem services, such as provision (food and clean water), regulation (climate and disease), support (nutrient cycles and crop pollination), and culture (spiritual and recreational benefits).

E3 Cosmic threats. There are risks arising beyond earth, such as a major meteorite impact, being pulled out of orbit (or the solar system) by a passing asteroid, or a giant solar flare (the effects of which would be compounded if it were during a reversal of the Earth's magnetic field). The impact of these events could range from severely inconvenient to existential. A big enough solar eruption could trigger a magnetic storm and damage electricity distribution lines or disable critical communication and navigation systems, while a 10-kilometer-wide meteorite (like the one that hit Earth around 65 million years ago causing, as widely believed, the extinction of dinosaurs) could release the equivalent to 100 million megatons of energy. It is estimated that such a meteorite could trigger magnitude 10 earthquakes and a 300-meter-high tsunami spreading to all of the earth's coastal regions, costing millions if not billions of human lives. Noxious gases and dust would then accumulate in the atmosphere, cutting out sunlight and potentially terminating all lives that survived the direct impact—a mass extinction event.

E4 Global temperature change. There is little doubt in science that rising greenhouse gas emissions produced by human activities are leading to rising global temperature. Natural feedbacks (e.g. the ice-albedo feedback means that melting ice reveals darker land and water surfaces below, which absorb more solar heat, causing more melting and warming) in the system have the potential of amplifying global warming. They are expected to be followed by serious consequences including more frequent extreme weather and rising sea levels (of several meters) making much of the current coastal communities uninhabitable. The extreme risk is that the earth's atmosphere passes a point of return and tips into a less habitable state. On the other hand, while this thesis has gained less support in the science community, earth's surface and atmosphere could experience excessive cold, slipping into an ice age. This could be caused by a drop in the sun's emission of energy (for a temporary but prolonged period), or by another extreme event such as a meteorite strike or supervolcano eruption. In either situation, habitable areas will be significantly reduced, causing large-scale migration and reducing the quality of life for most of humankind.

E5 Natural catastrophe. These are the disasters resulting from natural processes of the earth including earthquakes, tsunamis, hurricanes, flooding (including atmospheric river storms), and volcanic eruptions. The extreme risk would either be a confluence of connected extreme natural catastrophes (e.g. a magnitude 10 earthquake causing a giant tsunami and triggering volcanic eruptions) or the eruption of a supervolcano. The latter would cause global effects on climate (from the ash fallout and aerosol clouds; 'volcanic winter'), agriculture (collapse as a result of the loss of one or more growing seasons), health (famine and spread of infectious disease), and transportation (air travel halted for years). It is believed that a supervolcanic event at Lake Toba around 71,000 years ago led directly to a cooling event that lasted over 1,000 years (Zielinski et al. 1996).

Social Risk

S1 Extreme longevity. A major breakthrough in medical or human genome science—it is hoped that cures for common banes such as heart disease, cancer, and stroke may be in the offing—could result in an unanticipated, significant increase in life expectancy for many, or the majority, of humans. A direct impact of people living longer on a retirement plan is increased liabilities. In addition, even though life expectancy has increased steadily in recent history, these gains do not necessarily lead to better health in later life. The risk therefore also includes an emergence of a society of a growing number of the elderly who suffer chronic but nonfatal diseases—people live longer but their 'productive' years stay more or less the same. The economy will be struggling to support the health care of a mass of the elderly who are in need of long-term health care.

S2 Food/water/energy crisis. It was estimated in 2010 that 600 million people in 21 countries were facing either cropland or freshwater scarcity, and that number is projected to increase to 1.4 billion people in 36 countries by 2025. Over one billion people live in areas where human use of available water supplies exceeds sustainable limits and by 2025 this figure is projected to rise to 1.8 billion, with up to two-thirds of the world's population living in water-stressed conditions (NIC and EUISS 2010). On the energy side, the supply of fossil fuels has a known limited time span, while no viable alternatives are currently available with comparable energy returns on energy invested (EROEI). There is a risk that the necessary technological breakthrough will not arrive in time to prevent a global economic collapse due to an energy crisis. Consequently, given the current fine balance between supply and demand and the projections of demand growing faster than supply for food, water, and energy, we see this as a particular area of vulnerability. The extreme risk refers to the occurrence of a major shortfall in the supply of, or access to, food/water/energy for a large proportion of the world's population, causing severe societal issues such as widespread death and damage to the quality of life of many survivors.

S3 Health progress backfire. Modern medicine has been consistently meeting existing and new diseases with new treatments, giving rise to improved human health. There is no guarantee that the rate of medical advancement can always outpace the rate of pathogen evolution and a catastrophic event could emerge should biological mutation eventually outpace human innovation. This could result from the unintended consequences of current healthcare practices such as antibiotic resistance. The World Economic Forum warns (WEF 2013) that we are decades behind in comparison with the historical rate at which we have discovered and developed new antibiotics and none of the drugs currently in the development pipeline would be effective against certain killer bacteria. Social trends such as widespread mental health problems and obesity are additive to the problem. Stephen Petranek, then editor-in-chief of *Discover* magazine, pointed out in a TED talk that despite improved physical health, the human race is mentally falling apart—one in five people in the west is believed to be clinically depressed (2002). The extreme risk from a societal point of view is a massive increase in morbidity for a large proportion of the population. Not only does this directly reduce quality of life; it would also reduce economic output. From a retirement viewpoint the extreme risk is that the increase in morbidity is not accompanied by a reduction in longevity. In other words, economic output falls and liabilities increase.

S4 Organized crime. Organized crime is a common reality for most if not all countries. The U.K. Home Office (2013) suggests that organized crime costs the U.K. between £20 and £40 billion each year, and its impact is felt by the state, businesses, communities, families, and individuals. The extreme risk is a significant increase in the scale of illegal operation in a major economy to the extent that legitimate economic activity becomes non-viable. Extreme-form organized crime could bring severe disruption to normal activities in affected areas, typically associated with high homicide rates, wide use of illegal drugs and the collapse of legal business activity potentially followed by social unrest.

S5 Pandemic. Recent pandemics (e.g. SARS, avian flu, and swine flu), despite being successfully contained (for now?), demonstrate how easily deadly viruses can mutate and history is full of significant pandemics with an extremely high number of causalities. For example, it is believed that the Plague of Justinian in CE 541–2 killed 50 percent of the world's population; the Black Death in the thirteenth century caused the death of one-third of the population of Europe; and 'Spanish flu' during 1918–19 killed 20–50 million people (Kilbourne 2006). (We need to distinguish between those pandemics occurring before the advent of modern medicine and those after. For example, the Black Death is believed to have been a bacterial infection which would, today, be treated with antibiotics. However, please note the threat of antibiotic resistance referred to in S3.) Pandemics can be attended by high morbidity within a very short period of time (e.g. influenza), increasing the difficulty of developing effective vaccines in time. Modern traveling patterns make it almost impossible to contain a contagious disease within a specific region. While we have relatively more knowledge about human disease pandemics than other events, the extreme risk here is a pandemic of a new highly infectious and fatal disease that spreads through human, animal, or plant populations worldwide.

Technological Risk

T1 Biotech catastrophe. DNA sequencing and synthesizing machines are available to anyone with enough money to afford a used car. Nasty nucleotide sequences such as the Ebola virus and the 1918 influenza virus are accessible online and genetic engineering of viruses is much less complex and far less expensive than sequencing human DNA. This makes it a lot easier to apply this technology to destructive uses than constructive ones. Adding to the problem is the fact that the biotech industry is highly unregulated. Regulating and controlling current and new developments would require strong global governance, which the world currently lacks. British cosmologist and astronomer Martin Rees speculates that by the year 2020, an instance of bio-error or bio-terror could have killed a million people (Rees 2003), which is the extreme risk considered here.

T2 Cyber warfare. This refers to politically sponsored computer hacking to conduct sabotage and espionage on a national or global-power scale. It is reported that a series of cyber-attacks on businesses and institutions in the United States have prompted fears of a looming 'cyber cold war' and former United States Defense Secretary Leon Panetta predicted a cyber-version of Pearl Harbor might soon take the United States by surprise. Cyber war could cause severe damage to physical infrastructure—bridges, tunnels, air traffic control, and energy pipelines. Social security, financial, and medical systems connected to the Internet could all become the target of cyber-attacks. A cyber-attack on the defense system might precede a military attack in all future wars.

T3 Infrastructure failure. This extreme risk refers to an interruption (prolonged but not permanent) of a major infrastructure network due to either human activity (e.g. cyber-attack), natural disasters (e.g. earthquake or flooding), or even cosmic threats (e.g. giant solar flare). An extended shutdown of a critical network or electricity grid would bring increasing disruption to economies within the geographical area of impact. People's basic needs would be threatened in such circumstances, raising the possibility of social unrest and law-breaking behaviors for survival.

T4 Nuclear contamination. The risk is a major nuclear accident or attack that leads to lethal effects on individuals and large radioactivity release to the environment. It is reported that worldwide there were 99 accidents at nuclear power plants between 1952 and 2009 (defined as incidents that either resulted in the loss of human life or more than US$50,000 of property damage), totaling US$20.5 billion in property damages (Sovacool 2010). One of the worst nuclear contamination events to date is the Chernobyl disaster which occurred in 1986 in Ukraine, killing 30 people directly, causing thousands of indirect deaths due to radiation-induced cancer, and damaging approximately $7 billion of property (Wikipedia 2013c). Nuclear contamination could also be a direct consequence of a nuclear terrorist attack or a full-blown nuclear war among states.

T5 Technological singularity. This refers to an extreme risk resulting from technological advancement proceeding beyond the point of human understanding. It is possible that the creation of a computer more powerful than the human brain, which can then design and build an even more advanced machine, would create an environment where human survival is at risk. Bill Joy, then Chief Scientist at Sun Microsystems, has argued that '21st century technologies—robotics, genetic engineering, and nanotech—are threatening to make humans an endangered species' because 'they share a dangerous amplifying factor: they can self-replicate' (Joy 2000). Another possibility is a so-called nanotechnology 'grey goo' scenario, in which nano-robots self-replicate in an uncontrolled manner and eventually consume everything on the Earth (Wikipedia 2013d). The University of Cambridge has recently established a research center named 'The Centre for the Study of Existential Risk,' devoted to studying possible catastrophic threats posed by present or future technology.

Notes

1. See for instance the Santa Fe Institute, <http://www.santafe.edu/about/history/> (Santa Fe Institute 2013).
2. A phrase borrowed from Dirk Gently, a fictional 'holistic' detective who believed all things were connected in some way (Adams 1987, 1991).
3. This is a thought experiment so we will gloss over my ability to pay; assume my credit is pristine.
4. With extreme risks all probabilities are qualitative, however derived. By definition we are dealing with very small sample sizes of previous occurrences so even using extreme value theory to fit a tail distribution requires the application of significant qualitative judgment.
5. Clustering of risks is the basis of scenario analysis which should be done; this is outside the scope of the present chapter.
6. We acknowledge that terrorism is a weekly, if not daily, occurrence somewhere around the world; the extreme risk here would be a terrorist act comparable to, or worse than, 9/11.
7. We do not define these states, as the labels are self-explanatory. But one might think about oneself in the three states as follows: an endurable risk could represent a broken leg; a crushing risk might imply the loss of a limb or paralysis; and an existential risk might refer to the loss of self-awareness or loss of life.

8. An extra layer of sophistication could have been added by extending the shapes in either the vertical or horizontal direction, implying greater certainty in one dimension and less in the other. But there is no reason to stop there; one could also move the border off-center to show that the uncertainty is asymmetric. In view of the high intrinsic uncertainty involved when considering extreme risks, this extra sophistication would likely provide the impression of spurious accuracy and give a false impression of the level of signal relative to the noise.
9. This is a term and concept coined by Ian Bremmer of Eurasia Group.

References

Adams, D. (1987). *Dirk Gently's Holistic Detective Agency*. London, U.K.: William Heinemann Ltd.

Adams, D. (1991). *The Long Dark Tea-Time of the Soul*. New York, NY: Pocket Books.

Bostrom, N. (2013). 'Existential Risk Prevention as Global Priority,' *Global Policy*, 4(1): 15–31.

Brock, H. W. (2003). 'Advent of a New "Investment Regime",' *SED Profile*, 68: I1–I25.

Calaprice, A., F. Dyson, and A. Einstein (2005). *The New Quotable Einstein*. Princeton: Princeton University Press, p. 173.

Caplan, B. (2006). 'The Totalitarian Threat,' in N. Bostrom and M.M. Cirkovic, eds. *Global Catastrophic Risks*. Oxford, U.K.: Oxford University Press, pp. 504–519.

Coughlan, G. (2014). 'Longevity Risk Management, Corporate Finance and Sustainable Pensions,' in P. B. Hammond, R. Maurer, and O. S. Mitchell, eds., *Recreating Sustainable Retirement: Resilience, Solvency, and Tail Risk*. Oxford, U.K.: Oxford University Press, pp. 89–112.

Göbel, C., and L. H. Ong (2012). *Social Unrest in China*. London, U.K.: Europe–China Research and Advice Network.

Joy, B. (2000). 'Why the Future Doesn't Need Us,' *Wired*, April: 8.04.

Kilbourne, E. D. (2006). 'Plagues and Pandemics: Past, Present, and Future,' in N. Bostrom and M. M. Cirkovic, eds., *Global Catastrophic Risks*. Oxford, U.K.: Oxford University Press: 287–307.

Kritzman, M., and Y. Li (2010). 'Skulls, Financial Turbulence, and Risk Management,' *Financial Analysts Journal*, 66(5): 30–41.

Larsen, P.T. (2007). 'Goldman Pays the Price of Being Big,' *Financial Times*, August 13.

Leitenberg, M. (2006). 'Deaths in Wars and Conflicts in the 20th Century,' Cornell University Peace Studies Program Occasional Paper, No. 29, 3rd ed. Ithaca, NY: Cornell University.

Lo, A., and M. Mueller (2010). 'WARNING! Physics Envy May Be Hazardous To Your Wealth,' *Journal of Investment Management*, 8: 13–63.

Lowrey, A. (2012). 'An Increase in Barriers to Trade is Reported,' *The New York Times*, June 22.

Mandelbrot, M., and R. L. Hudson (2004). *The Misbehavior of Markets: A Fractal View of Financial Turbulence*. New York, NY: Basic Books.

Montier, J. (2011). 'A Value Investor's Perspective on Tail Risk Protection: An Ode to the Joy of Cash,' GMO white paper.

Moore, J., and N. K. Pederson (2014). 'Implications for Long-term Investors of the Shifting Distribution of Capital Market Returns,' in P. B. Hammond, R. Maurer, and O. S. Mitchell, eds., *Recreating Sustainable Retirement: Resilience, Solvency, and Tail Risk*. Oxford, U.K.: Oxford University Press, pp. 30–59.

National Aeronautics and Space Administration (NASA) (2013). *Kepler: A Search for Habitable Planets* [website]. <http://kepler.nasa.gov/>.

Petranek, S. (2002). *10 Ways the World Could End* [Video file]. <http://www.ted.com/talks/stephen_petranek_counts_down_to_armageddon.html>.

Rees, M. (2003). *Our Final Century: The 50/50 Threat to Humanity's Survival: Will the Human Race Survive the Twenty-first Century?* London, U.K.: William Heinemann Ltd.

Santa Fe Institute. *History of the Santa Fe Institute* [website]. Santa Fe: Santa Fe Institute. <http://www.santafe.edu/about/history/>.

Soros, G. (2009). 'One Way to Stop Bear Raids,' *The Wall Street Journal*, March 24.

Sovacool, B. K. (2010). 'A Critical Evaluation of Nuclear Power and Renewable Electricity in Asia,' *Journal of Contemporary Asia*, 40(3): 369–400.

Towers Watson (2010). *Extreme Risks*, TW-NA-2009-14398. London, U.K.: Towers Watson.

Towers Watson (2011). *Extreme Risks—The 2011 Update*, TW-2011-INV-00130. London, U.K.: Towers Watson.

Towers Watson (2012). *The Impossibility of Pensions*, TW-EU-2012-25855. London, U.K.: Towers Watson.

Towers Watson (2013). *Global Pension Asset Study 2013*. London, U.K.: Towers Watson.

United Kingdom Home Office (2013). *Reducing Knife, Gun and Gang Crime* [electronic publication]. London, U.K.: Home Office. <https://www.gov.uk/government/policies/reducing-knife-gun-and-gang-crime>.

United States National Intelligence Council (NIC) and European Union Institution for Security Studies (EUISS) (2010). *Global Governance 2025: at a Critical Juncture*. NIC 2010-08.

West, G. (2011). 'Emergence of "Universal" Time in Living Systems from Cells to Cities,' [lecture]. Santa Fe, AZ: Santa Fe Institute.

Wikipedia (2013*a*). 'September 11 Attacks' [website]. Accessed April 2013. <en.wikipedia.org/wiki/September_11_attacks>.

Wikipedia (2013*b*). 'Biodiversity' [website]. Accessed April 2013. <http://en.wikipedia.org/wiki/Biodiversity>.

Wikipedia (2013*c*). 'Nuclear and Radiation Accidents' [website]. Accessed April 2013. <http://en.wikipedia.org/wiki/Nuclear_and_radiation_accidents>.

Wikipedia (2013*d*). 'Grey Goo' [website]. Accessed April 2013. <http://en.wikipedia.org/wiki/Grey_goo>.

World Economic Forum (WEF) (2013). *Global Risks 2013—An Initiative of the Risk Response Network*. Geneva, Switzerland: WEF.

Zielinski, G. A., P. A. Mayewski, L. D. Meeker, S. Whitlow, M. Twickler, and K. Taylor (1996). 'Potential Atmospheric Impact of the Toba Mega-Eruption ~71,000 years ago,' *Geophysical Research Letters*, American Geophysical Union, 23(8): 837–840.

Part IV
Implications for Plan Sponsors

Chapter 12

Risk Budgeting and Longevity Insurance: Strategies for Sustainable Defined Benefit Pension Funds

Amy Kessler

The extreme losses incurred in defined benefit (DB) pension plans during the financial crisis have called into question the conventional approach to managing pension risk. In the aftermath of the financial crisis, many plans have closed and stopped accruing benefits for new or existing members. Closing a plan, however, only stems the growth in the pension risk—it does nothing to manage the risk the plan already has. Today, in the wake of unprecedented losses and with a new understanding of longevity risk, open and closed DB plans in the United Kingdom, the Netherlands, the United States, Canada, Switzerland, and other countries continue to search for a new paradigm that manages investment risk, longevity risk, and intergenerational risk.

Investment risk is the risk that asset performance falls short of expected returns. Twice in the past dozen years, plans that maintained a high allocation to risky assets have incurred losses severe enough to overwhelm many plan sponsors. Longevity risk is the risk that plan participants and eligible dependents live longer than expected. While longer life is a welcome development, it is also a significant financial obligation for pension plan sponsors, particularly where the retirement age has remained the same for decades. Intergenerational risk is the risk that current employees contributing to a pension plan will support current retirees at the expense of securing their own future retirement benefits. In most open plans, the number of retired participants is rising much more quickly than the number of working age people contributing to the plan. This raises questions about sustainability and fairness, particularly where pension deficits are acute, the credit quality of the plan sponsor is weak, and life expectancy is underestimated. Current employees contributing to such plans are exposed to the risk that the plan sponsor may not be able to fulfill its future obligations to them.

In today's low interest rate and low-growth environment, these risks are particularly daunting and the failure to manage them is behind the growing funding gap for the many DB pensions. The key question is how to develop the strategies and solutions that will help pension funds regain and maintain a path toward a stable and sustainable future.

A 'DB Pension Sustainability Model' will combine techniques that already exist to achieve more predictable outcomes and manage risk within the plan sponsor's financial wherewithal to absorb losses. The goal is to create a new paradigm for DB risk that draws from the best available practices in risk budgeting, asset management, and insurance. One possible approach is described in this chapter and it includes three components.

First, sustainable risk budgeting involves measuring the key sources of risk that a pension plan has in order to quantify potential losses, identify areas where risks compound each other, and establish a targeted level of potential risk of loss from which the plan and its sponsor could recover over the medium term.

Second is a sustainable asset management approach. With its risk budget in place, a pension plan can chart a course for a lower risk future, shedding the risks that are unrewarded (such as interest rate risk) and creating the opportunity to take risk that is rewarded (such as credit and exposure to equities and alternatives), all within a sustainable risk budget. Also, custom liability-driven investing (LDI), alternative fixed income investments, and absolute return strategies are among the key changes pension funds can make. As asset management choices evolve, a key paradigm shift takes place, bringing the liabilities squarely into the equation to choose assets designed to support the liabilities. The overall goal is a lower risk, lower volatility portfolio that creates a stable base for risk management and a good expected return relative to its risk of loss in funded status.

Finally, longevity insurance can be used to cover a DB plan's most significant demographic risk and achieve three key objectives: (a) to create a known and knowable future obligation and ease the challenge of managing assets against unknown future liabilities; (b) to protect the solvency of the pension fund (and its sponsor) and secure the promises made to plan participants in the event of unexpected longevity; and (c) to addresses the impact of intergenerational risk on current employees in the event of increasing obligations to retirees.

These strategies go hand in hand with the ability to increase the normal retirement age as healthy life expectancy extends, and this approach can put pension funds on a path to a more sustainable future. To succeed, the DB Pension Sustainability Model must enhance retirement security for plan participants, include a robust safety net for disabled workers to retire early, and be flexible enough to adapt to the risk tolerance and financial wherewithal of plan sponsors of varied size, credit quality, and sophistication.

In what follows, we describe an approach to the DB Pension Sustainability Model. We look forward to a vibrant discussion of these ideas as the pension industry focuses on helping individuals and institutions prepare for a longer retirement.

The Nature of Pension Risk

A DB pension is a promise to pay monthly retirement benefits to participants for as long as they live, no matter what happens to the assets. Plan sponsors who have

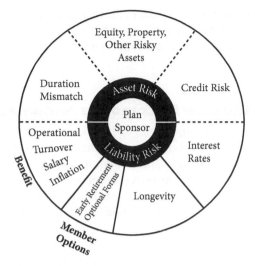

Figure 12.1. DB plan sponsors are surrounded by risk.

Note: Categories of asset and liability risks for sponsors of DB plans.

Source: Author's illustration.

made these promises are surrounded by risk. The risk dial in Figure 12.1 shows the key sources of asset and liability risk that are part of the pension promise.

Liability Risk

The liability risks shown on the bottom half of the risk dial in Figure 12.1 include anything that might increase the amount of the benefit the pension fund owes to its members. Longevity risk is the key source of liability risk and is common to all DB plans. Many plans base retirement benefits on final or average salary, creating exposure to salary inflation until plan participants reach retirement age. In addition, some pension plans offer cost of living adjustments to retired participants and for them, inflation risk after retirement compounds the longevity risk exposure. Finally, interest rate risk is included in the liability risks because most pension liabilities are valued by discounting at a high-grade bond yield curve (the 'liability discount rate'). This approach is consistent with the fact that pension liabilities are often the most senior debt of the plan sponsor.

The liability discount rate a pension fund uses to value its future obligations is the largest driver of the effective rate at which the liabilities grow from one year to the next (the 'liability growth rate'). Other factors driving the liability growth rate include unexpected improvements in longevity and cost of living adjustments offered to plan participants, if any. Failure to earn the liability growth rate on actual invested assets results in an increasing funding gap for the pension plan, with the liabilities growing faster than the assets. This challenge can be particularly acute for pension funds that offer cost of living adjustments to plan participants.

Asset Risk—The View for Corporate Pension Funds

Asset risks are shown on the upper half of the risk dial in Figure 12.1. As long-term investors, the conventional wisdom has been that pension funds should take asset risk, and so investing in equities, private equity, real estate, hedge funds, commodities and other risky asset classes has become the norm. Many pension funds invest 50 percent to 75 percent of their assets in these risky asset classes by choosing asset managers in each desired 'style box,' rebalancing periodically to a pre-set asset allocation and measuring performance strictly against benchmarks that are not linked to the liability growth rate. The result of applying this strategy is that the value of the risky assets fluctuates in ways that bear no relation to the liabilities. In effect, with risky assets that have no duration and liabilities that have very long duration, the plan is 'short duration' and thus, duration mismatch is also shown on the risk dial as a key challenge for pension funds.

In the generally falling interest rate environment that has prevailed from June 2007 to the present, remaining in a 'short duration' position has meant taking a bet that rates would not fall any farther. Unfortunately, with US\$ ten-year Treasury bonds falling in yields above 350 basis points over the same time period (U.S. Treasury 2013),[1] betting on steady or rising rates has been a losing proposition for pension funds, particularly given their present level of underfunding. For pension funds that remain in a short duration position and continue to bet on rising rates, it is useful to note that after the Great Depression, rates remained low (with the ten-year Treasury below 3 percent) for 19 years (Shiller 2013).[2] In light of the severity of the recent financial crisis, as well as the credit contraction and deleveraging that ensued, low interest rates and low growth may persist for a prolonged period.

The key concern in maintaining a high allocation to risky assets and a short duration position is the risk of losing money that is not recovered over a manageable time horizon. Corporate pension funds generally think about this volatility in terms of the plan's funded status, which is calculated as the market value of assets divided by liabilities discounted at the liability discount rate. When viewed from the perspective of the pension plan's funded status, it is the extreme volatility of the conventional approach that is causing corporate pension funds the world over to rethink their risk and consider lowering their risk profile to the point where the potential losses are more affordable and more likely to be recovered over the medium term.

The evidence of volatility abounds and is directly linked to two facts. First, the average U.S. pension plan maintains a high allocation to risky assets of 50 percent to 75 percent. Second, the average U.S. pension plan is underfunded and finished

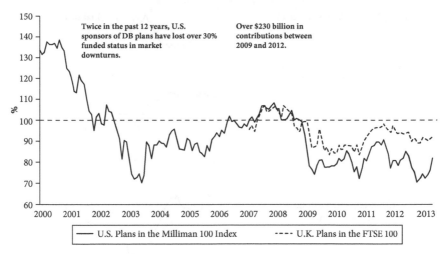

Figure 12.2. Funded status volatility.

Note: Funded status data depicts the ratio of assets divided by liabilities of U.S. DB plans in the Milliman 100 (Milliman 2013) and U.K. DB plans in the FTSE 100 (Aon Hewitt 2013). Cumulative assets and liabilities are shown aggregated on an accounting basis.

Source: Milliman (2013) (Milliman 100 data); Aon Hewitt (2013) (FTSE 100 data).

2012 with assets equal to just 76.4 percent of its liabilities (Milliman 2013). The unfunded liability is leverage and, as in any leveraged investing strategy, gains and losses will be magnified when measured relative to the full amount of the liability.

Figure 12.2 depicts the funded status of U.S. pension plans in the Milliman 100 since the beginning of 2000, and U.K. pension plans in the FTSE 100 since the beginning of 2007. With regard to U.S. pension funds, these data show that from 2000 through 2012, there have twice been losses of over 30 percent in funded status terms. First there was the 'dot-com bust,' and then, from 2002 through 2007, U.S. sponsors of DB pension funds in the Milliman 100 contributed over $245 billion. With help from favorable markets, these U.S. plans returned to good health in 2007, just in time for the financial crisis of 2008, when they lost 30 percent in the downturn. The plans denoted made over $230 billion in contributions between 2009 and 2012, and they will likely face significant contributions for many more years in order to approach full funding.

One of the most dramatic things about Figure 12.2 is the fact that, despite contributing so much cash from the end of the financial crisis through the middle of 2013, U.S. plan sponsors did not move to a sustained higher funded status. This is precisely because risk-taking remained the norm for the average U.S. plan throughout this period. Most U.S. plans in 2013 combine leveraged, high allocations to risky assets and a short duration position.

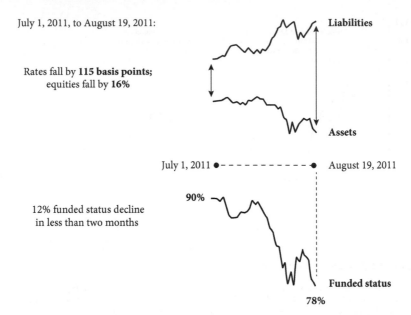

July 1, 2011, to August 19, 2011:

Rates fall by **115 basis points;**
equities fall by **16%**

Liabilities

Assets

July 1, 2011 ● ─ ─ ─ ─ ─ ─ ─ ─ ─ ─ ● August 19, 2011

12% funded status decline
in less than two months

90%

Funded status

78%

Figure 12.3. Scenario—real life!

Note: For the period between July 1, 2011, and August 19, 2011, depicts the changes in assets, liabilities and funded status of U.S. DB pension funds in the S&P 500.

Source: Aon Hewitt (2013).

Consider the period from July 1, 2011, to August 19, 2011 (depicted in Figure 12.3), when interest rates in the U.S. fell by 115 basis points and equities plummeted 16 percent (U.S. Treasury 2013; Bloomberg 2013).[3] Given the asset and liability mismatch of the average U.S. pension plan in the S&P 500 at that time, their asset and liability values were independently volatile. Liabilities rose dramatically due to the decline in interest rates. In the meantime, assets plummeted because most of the assets were at risk in equities and other risk asset classes.

U.S. corporate pension funds have encountered this challenge before. In fact, any time bad news in the economy has caused interest rates and equities to fall simultaneously, the average U.S. pension plan has experienced dramatic losses in funded status. The 34 business days from July 1, 2011, to August 19, 2011, were no exception: with liabilities rising and assets falling, the average U.S. pension plan fell from 90 percent funded to only 78 percent funded (Aon Hewitt 2013).[4] With so much exposure to risk, the rebound one would have hoped for after such a dramatic six-week period was slow to materialize. U.S. plan sponsors ended 2011 only 4 percent higher, with a funded status of 82 percent, and at the end of 2012, there was still no more sustained movement toward higher ground: the average U.S. plan was only 76 percent funded (Milliman 2013).[5]

Asset Risk for Public Pension Funds

While corporate pension funds in the United States, the United Kingdom, and Canada are focused on funded status, public plans are much more focused on long-term realized returns. Figure 12.4 shows the volatility of this approach over the most recent 20 years, assuming investment in the Russell 2000 Equity Index (Russell Investments 2013) and the Barclays U.S. Aggregate Bond Index (Barclays 2013).

The key goal for most public plans is meeting long-term return expectations, and the data show that a public pension plan investing in this manner will likely achieve its long-term targeted returns (often between 7.5 percent and 8.0 percent) on the assets it has invested. However, U.S. public pension funds rarely have assets invested that are commensurate with their liabilities; for most underfunded plans, the current approach is unsustainable.

A hypothetical U.S. public pension plan might have an expected return on assets of 7.75 percent. Its effective liability growth rate is also at least 7.75 percent of the liabilities, because the future liabilities are discounted at the expected return on assets. This means that a failure to earn at least 7.75 percent on the full amount of the liability will result in a growing funding gap for the pension plan. It is worth noting that the actual liability growth rate may exceed 7.75 percent, once unexpected increases in longevity and benefit cost of living

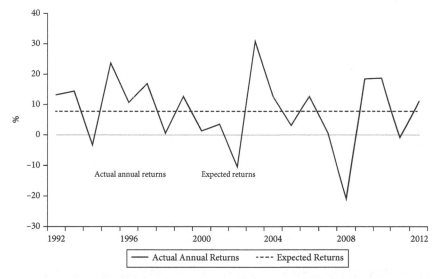

Figure 12.4. Volatility of returns—65 percent equities/35 percent bonds and cash.

Notes: The returns depicted are weighted actual returns, assuming 65 percent from the Russell 2000 Equity Index and 35 percent from the Barclays U.S. Aggregate Bond Index. Weighted returns are shown from December 1990 to December 2012.

Sources: Author's calculations from Barclays (2013); and Russell Investments (2013).

adjustments are included. Figure 12.4 indicates that using a ten-year return on assets of 7.75 percent will lead many to believe that the plan is achieving its target. However, the public pension plan may be only 60–65 percent funded, so it only has 60–65 percent of the assets it needs earning returns. Historical data show that plans can reasonably expect to earn 7.75 percent on the invested assets. But plans can reasonably expect to earn zero percent on the unfunded liability, which can best be thought of as the 'allocation to air' in the portfolio. In fact, the unfunded liability represents leverage in the investment strategy. As in any levered investment strategy, gains and losses will be magnified when measured in relation to the liability.

A natural question thus arises: how difficult will it be for this hypothetical public pension fund to overcome the unfunded liability, meet current benefit payments, and maintain or improve funded status? Figure 12.5 shows how daunting this challenge is. With 62.8 percent of the liabilities invested and earning 7.75 percent, and the remainder unfunded and earning zero percent: (a) the plan likely needs to earn 10.9 percent or 11 percent to remain at its present funded status and avoid an increasing funding gap; and (b) without cash contributions to improve the funded status, the plan likely needs to earn 12.7 percent or more on a sustained basis to

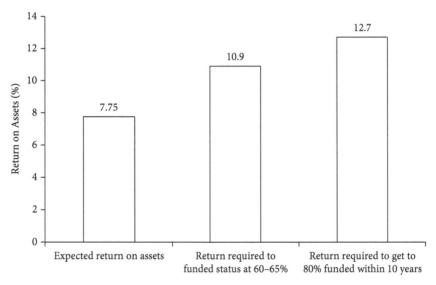

Figure 12.5. The impact of leverage and the disconnect between assets and liabilities.

Note: The return required to maintain or improve the funded status is calculated by Prudential assuming a typical open public plan in the U.S. with cost of living adjustments in its benefits, a starting funded status of approximately 63 percent, and benefit payments that increase by 5 percent per year.

Source: Author's calculations.

reach 80 percent funding within ten years. This analysis assumes no unexpected increase in longevity and no periods of higher than expected inflation.

This analysis demonstrates the depth of the public pension crisis in the United States and in many other countries where the leverage in the pension fund requires an unrealistically high realized rate of return in order to avoid an increasing funding gap. It is for this reason that most public pension funds need to consider one further aspect of a DB Pension Sustainability Model—a Sustainable Contribution Strategy that will bring potential earnings on actual invested assets into line with the year-on-year growth in the liabilities.

Longevity Risk Is Material and Often Left Out of the Risk Equation

A recent Global Financial Stability Report by the International Monetary Fund (IMF 2012) explains that actuarial science has historically underestimated life expectancy by a period of three years. To be fair, the poor record around the accuracy of longevity projections has been driven by the incredible power of human ingenuity to develop medical treatments that extend human life and it is clear that increasing longevity is a very positive outcome for many. However, for sponsors of DB pension funds, increasing longevity also creates a significant financial obligation that governments, institutions, and corporations will struggle to afford.

The IMF report also points out that 'appropriate longevity assumptions should use the most recent longevity data and allow for future increases in longevity' (2012: 6). The same report suggests that 'the use of outdated mortality tables has been a common practice' among U.S. pension plans and that many in the IMF sample analysis exhibited a 'lag of almost a quarter century in their mortality assumptions' (2012: 13). A similar challenge exists in many countries, where measurement of current liabilities has not kept pace with known and observable improvements in longevity that have already occurred. The U.K. and the Netherlands are global role models in mandating the use of up-to-date tables, while progress remains slow in North America.

As the IMF has pointed out, updating pension mortality assumptions for purposes of estimating today's liabilities is fundamental in creating the transparency that key stakeholders need in order to evaluate the impact of longevity risk on the credit quality of governmental, institutional, and corporate plan sponsors. Merely updating mortality assumptions is not enough, because there is still uncertainty around today's best estimate projections of future pension liabilities. Pension funds must begin to consider how longevity risk interacts with all of their other risks and, in many cases, compounds them!

Figure 12.6 depicts the pure longevity risk in a pension fund with 36 percent retiree liabilities and 64 percent deferred and active liabilities, though no future

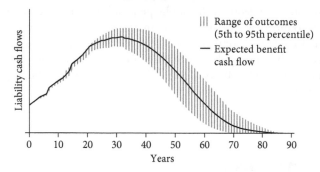

**Potential variability in future benefit cash flows
due to longevity risk**

||| Range of outcomes
(5th to 95th percentile)

— Expected benefit
cash flow

For every year that life
expectancy extends, the
liability will likely increase
by 5% or more.

A 95th percentile outcome
might increase the liability
by 8–10% from current
annuitant mortality tables.

Figure 12.6. Materiality of longevity risk assuming fixed inflation.

Notes: Shows the projected benefits and longevity risk for a pension fund with 36 percent retiree liabilities and 64 percent deferred and active liabilities, though no future accrual is assumed for active members. The average age of retired members is 69 and the average age of deferred and active members is 46. Benefits include cost of living adjustments, which are assumed at a fixed escalation rate of 3 percent. Longevity improvements are simulated in a fully stochastic analysis.

Source: Author's calculations.

accrual is assumed for active members. The average age of retired members is 69 and the average age of deferred and active members is 46. Benefits include cost of living adjustments, which are assumed at a fixed escalation rate of 3 percent in the graph. The solid line is the best estimate projection of the liability assuming the fixed cost of living adjustments and the grey bars indicate the risk around the best estimate determined on a stochastic basis where longevity is the only risk factor simulated in the stochastic analysis. For every year that life expectancy extends, the liability will likely increase by 5 percent or more. A more severe stress would increase the liability by 8 percent to 10 percent from current annuitant mortality tables but this analysis only stresses longevity.

Since this pension plan offers cost of living adjustments to plan participants, the risk of longevity and inflation combined is much larger. In the event that plan participants live longer than expected and inflation is higher than expected, the liability could increase by 20 percent because the longevity risk is compounded by inflation risk (see Figure 12.7).[6] The increase in risk is relevant for any U.S. public pension plan and any plan (public, institutional, or corporate) in the U.K., Canada, or elsewhere that offers a cost of living adjustment.

The fact that liability-side risks compound each other leads to an important conclusion about risk modeling and risk management. It suggests that hedging and risk transfer decisions must be made in the context of a fully stochastic analysis of all risks. Hedging and risk transfer decisions made without a combined stochastic model that brings liability risks into the picture will consistently undervalue the benefits of risk management strategies.

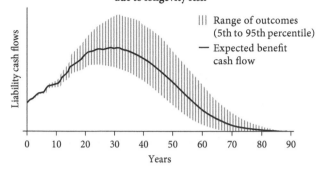

**Potential variability in future benefit cash flows
due to longevity risk**

||| Range of outcomes
(5th to 95th percentile)

— Expected benefit
cash flow

A 95th percentile outcome
might increase the liability
by 20% if both longevity
and inflation are stressed.

Figure 12.7. Compounding of longevity risk and inflation risk.

Note: Shows the same pension liability as depicted in Figure 12.6 with both longevity improvements and future inflation simulated in a fully stochastic analysis.

Source: Author's calculations.

Bringing Longevity Risk into the Picture

To demonstrate the importance of the compound nature of longevity risk, interest rate risk, and inflation risk, it is useful to consider a different example provided by Guy Coughlan of Pacific Global Advisors. In this example, there are 1,000 retired pension plan participants, all aged 65 and all receiving the same level of benefit today. There are also 1,000 active pension plan participants, all aged 45 and all expecting to receive the same benefit at their retirement in 20 years. The base mortality tables assume the U.S. male population, taken from the LifeMetrics Index. Inflation is expected to be 2.5 percent. In the fixed liability results, only salary inflation is assumed through the retirement date of the active pension plan participants with no benefit escalation after retirement. In the inflation-linked liability results, both salary inflation to the retirement date and escalation after the retirement date are assumed. The benefit payments are shown in Figure 12.8 for the fixed liability and the inflation-linked liability cases.

Thus the pension fund is not well funded and is holding assets of $600, equal to only 60 percent of the liabilities, assumed to be $1,000. Despite its underfunded position, the plan has already begun to make its way down a de-risking path and holds its assets invested in 45 percent fixed income, 33 percent equities, 19 percent alternatives and 3 percent cash. Figure 12.9 provides a risk overview for this plan. It shows the funded status-at-risk or value-at-risk ('VaR') in the pension fund, reflecting the financial risk in the asset portfolio, as well as the market and longevity risks impacting the liabilities. For pension funds, funded status-at-risk is analogous to the VaR measures used by other types of financial institutions.

Panel A. Fixed liability.

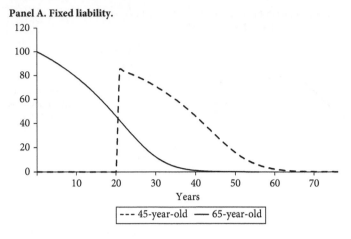

Panel B. Inflation-linked liability.

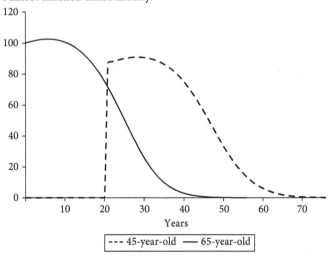

Figure 12.8. Illustration of fixed liability and inflation-linked liability cash flows (normalized pension payment).

Notes: Panel A: Fixed liability; Panel B: Inflation-linked liability. Depicts normalized pension payments for 1,000 retired and active plan participants aged 65 and 45, respectively, for fixed liabilities and inflation-linked liabilities.

Source: Analysis from Pacific Global Advisors.

Funded status-at-risk measures the level of financial risk to the funded status of the pension fund, taking assets and liabilities into account. Figure 12.9 shows the amount of the potential loss in funded status at a 95th percentile stochastic stress over a period of one year. The stress depicted below can be considered a reasonable worst-case scenario for a one-year period.

The individual asset and liability risks shown here depict the 95th percentile outcome of a stress in each risk in isolation. For example, asset risks (shown in the left-most column on each graph) include the risks to equities, interest rates, and alternatives and they reflect a 95th percentile risk of loss in each asset class stressed independently. The asset risks are the same in the two cases because each assumes a portfolio of $600 invested identically. In normal market conditions, these losses would not be expected to occur simultaneously—rather, some of these losses will be diversified away, as described further on in the chapter.

The liability risks are shown in the second column of each graph in Figure 12.9. The liability risks differ in the fixed liability and inflation-linked liability cases. Relatively speaking, the inflation-linked liability has greater longevity exposure. This is intuitive, in light of the graphs shown in Figures 12.6 and 12.7, which demonstrate that the risk of longer life and high inflation compound each other. In other words, with inflation-linked benefits, a pension fund promises to make monthly benefit payments to its members that will keep pace with cost of living

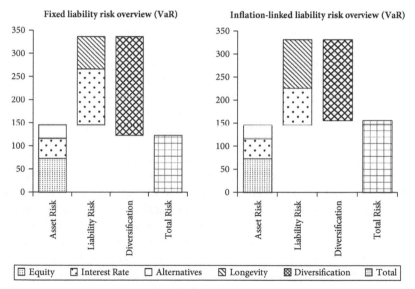

Figure 12.9. Risk overview for fixed liability and inflation-linked liability cases (VaR). Analysis of a reasonable worst-case loss scenario for a one-year period for the hypothetical pension plan depicted in Figure 12.8.

Panel A. Fixed liability deterministic stress.
Panel B. Inflation-linked liability deterministic stress.

Source: Analysis from Pacific Global Advisors.

adjustments. Should inflation be higher than expected, each additional year of life carries with it approximately twice the impact on the liability, because the benefit will be payable in future value terms. For years, we have described this exposure as 'longevity risk on steroids.'

It is also of interest to note that the inflation-linked liability has less interest rate risk than the fixed liability. This is due to the fact that liabilities rise in low interest rate conditions, which are also commonly linked to low inflation environments. If inflation is low, the inflation-linked liability would benefit from lower-than-expected cost of living adjustments. This finding (in which inflation-linked liabilities are less interest rate-sensitive than nominal liabilities) is consistent with the fact that inflation-linked government bonds are less volatile in price terms than comparable nominal bonds.

The third bar in each graph in Figure 12.9 shows the diversification benefit that naturally arises because the risks detailed in the first two columns are not all expected to arise at their 95th percentile levels at the same time. Risks in the pension fund, whether on the asset or the liability side, are not perfectly correlated and they generally are not expected to occur together and *in extremis*. Consequently, the risks should diversify each other.

One of the best examples of a natural diversification benefit is longevity risk and equity risk, which are often thought to be unrelated risks—they may both occur *in extremis* by chance but the conventional wisdom is that there is no reason to expect them to both occur simultaneously *in extremis* and thus, the diversification benefit of holding the combination of risks is significant.

Another key source of diversification benefit is the relationship between interest rate risks on the asset and liability side. A 95th percentile outcome for interest rate risk on the asset side would generally occur when rates rise and fixed income assets fall in value. In contrast, a 95th percentile outcome for interest rate risk on the liability side would generally occur when rates fall, pulling down the discount rates used to value the liability and causing the present value of the liability to rise. These two circumstances are negatively correlated and offer a fairly direct hedge to the extent that the pension plan holds fixed income assets that are key rate duration-matched to the liability and are of similar credit quality to the liability measurement benchmark. The diversification benefit of the individual risks is substantial and can be thought of as reducing the pension fund's funded status-at-risk by taking into consideration the fact that some of the risks are not correlated (such as longevity and equity risk), while others are negatively correlated (interest rate risk on liabilities vs. interest rate risk on assets).

The Total Risk column in Figure 12.9 is shown on the right of each graph. As a result of the diversification benefit, the Total Risk column is materially lower than the sum of the Asset Risk and Liability Risk columns, which depict the 95th percentile risk of funded status loss on each risk measured in isolation. For clarity, the Total Risk column shows the 95th percentile risk of funded status loss on the total combination of asset and liability risks, after taking the diversification benefit into account. As expected, the total risk results show that the inflation-linked liability has more total risk and less diversification benefit than the fixed liability case. This is the natural conclusion because the actual liability growth rate of the inflation-linked liability (with cost of living adjustments) is more likely to outpace the earning power of the assets than in the fixed liability case, and this risk of growth in the liability outpacing the growth in the assets is unlikely to be diversified away by the assets this pension plan is holding.

A Simpler View of Crossover Risk

Many find the three-dimensional nature of stochastic VaR analysis challenging to interpret because the conclusions depend on the correlation matrix embedded in the statistical risk analysis, which drives the degree of diversification benefit among the risks. To address these concerns and provide a two-dimensional anchor for the risk analysis, it is also useful to look at deterministic stress alongside the stochastic analysis.

Coughlan's approach to the deterministic stress is to construct a stress that is reassuringly similar to a duration calculation.[7] For the fixed liability and the inflation-linked liability, Figure 12.10 shows the impact on the liability of a 1 percent decline in interest rates and a 1 percent per year increase in the future projected trend for mortality improvements (also referred to as 'q-duration'). Results are shown separately for the older retiree population (the 65-year-olds) compared to the younger deferred members (the 45-year-olds) who have yet to retire. We conclude that longevity risk, interest rate risk, and inflation risk compound each other. In each case, the combined stress is greater than the sum of its parts (the interest rate stress and the mortality stress), because an interest rate shock will have a bigger impact on the liability if the liability increases due to an expectation of longer life. The difference between the value of the combined shock and the sum of the two individual shocks (interest rates and mortality) is referred to as the 'crossover rate and mortality risk,' and is broken out separately in Figure 12.10.

Both the combined stress and the crossover rate and mortality risk are bigger in the inflation-linked liability case than in the fixed liability case because inflation compounds both the mortality and interest rate risks. Also, both the combined stress and the crossover rate and mortality risk are bigger for the deferred liabilities (the 45-year-olds) than the retiree liabilities (the 65-year-olds) because of their longer duration. The analysis proves that deferred liabilities are the most risky obligations for the pension fund.

Implications of Crossover Risk for Risk Analysis and Risk Management

Given the key conclusion that interest rate risk, longevity risk, and inflation risk compound one another in the pension liability, it is clear that the current standard

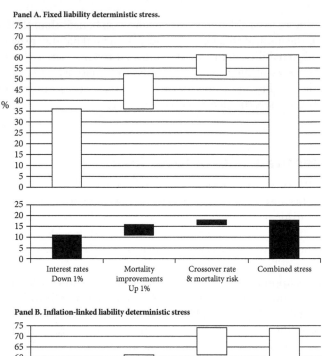

Panel A. Fixed liability deterministic stress.

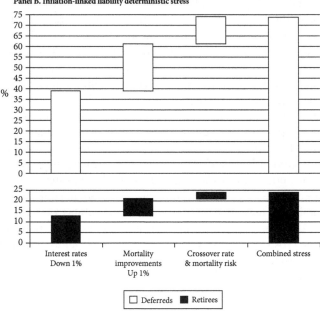

Panel B. Inflation-linked liability deterministic stress

Deferreds ☐ Retirees ■

Figure 12.10. Deterministic stress on liabilities (impact of a 1 percent decline in rates and a 1 percent increase in mortality improvements). Panel A: Fixed liability deterministic stress. Panel B: Inflation-linked liability deterministic stress.

Note: Depicts the impact on the liability of a 1 percent decline in interest rates and a 1 percent per year increase in the future projected trend for mortality improvements.

Source: Analysis from Pacific Global Advisors.

practice of leaving longevity risk out of pension risk analysis will lead to an under-estimation of total risk. This is particularly acute for inflation-linked liabilities and deferred liabilities, where their longer duration makes them significantly more sensitive to adverse outcomes. Pension funds and industry practitioners that make risk budgeting, risk management, and risk transfer decisions without taking these crossover risks into consideration will underestimate potential losses as well as the potential benefits from risk management and risk transfer strategies.

To this point, we have focused on pension asset and liability risk and on quantifying and understanding these risks in a manner that is more comprehensive than current general market practice. From this point forward, we focus on what these conclusions about risk actually suggest for risk management in the context of a DB Pension Sustainability Model.

The Role of Risk

For most pension funds, the conventional strategy has relied upon asset risk-taking activities to minimize overall contributions to the pension plan. Toward that end, investment activities are often focused on endowment principles of retaining liquidity premiums, earning risk premiums, and maximizing diversification benefit. In carrying out this strategy, most pension funds have hoped to earn enough return to outrun increasing life expectancy and offer generous pension benefits with modest contributions. As shown in Figures 12.2 through 12.4 of this chapter, the key issues associated with this strategy include: (a) the lack of focus on the liability and its risks; (b) the volatility; and (c) the risk of loss that cannot be overcome in the medium term.

The challenge for the pension industry today is to modify the conventional endowment strategy to moderate the role of risk. Figures 12.2 through 12.5 provide the historical data that demonstrate the need for a change in general pension risk management practices. In the new paradigm, the role of risk must be more carefully harnessed than has been the case in the past. Potential losses must be budgeted so their impact on required pension contributions in the medium term is affordable for the plan sponsor. Within the overall risk budget, pension plans should still retain liquidity premiums, earn risk premiums, maximize diversification benefit, and seek to minimize overall contributions.

The key change is that all of these activities would be limited and controlled within the risk budget and, within that risk budget, risk-taking would still have an important role to play in pension risk management.

Managing Total Risk and Risk Budgeting

In managing the total risk exposure of a pension fund, we have said that it is important to ensure that the potential losses are budgeted so that their impact on required pension contributions in the medium term is affordable for the plan sponsor. We expect very few to disagree with this goal because losses that are not affordable can impair the sponsor's credit quality or render the sponsor insolvent, leaving the plan without adequate resources to pay benefits to plan participants. To bring our broadly stated objective forward into risk practice, it is important to be specific and define each element.

Potential losses refer to funded status-at-risk or total risk as shown in the right-most bar in each of the graphs in Figure 12.9. This is the potential loss in funded status in a reasonable worst-case (95th percentile) scenario that takes into consideration asset risks, liability risks, and diversification benefits. We are focused on funded status-at-risk because this is the amount the plan sponsor would need to contribute in cash to overcome these potential losses.

Budgeting the impact on required pension contributions refers to managing the pension fund's asset and liability risks to try to keep potential losses below a specific funded status-at-risk or total risk level. Again, the plan sponsor may have to make contributions of cash to overcome these potential losses, and it is the potential cash contributions that need to be budgeted and affordable in order to ensure sustainability.

Medium term refers to the plan sponsor's reasonable time horizon for recovery from a market disruption. In some circumstances, the reasonable time horizon will be driven by regulation in the home country or province of the plan sponsor. For example, U.K. corporate pension funds are generally required to make cash contributions to recover from pension deficits within three to five years. U.S. corporate pension funds will increasingly focus on a seven-year horizon in light of the guidelines in the Pension Protection Act (PPA). Plan sponsors in Ontario also have a prescribed period over which they must recover. These regulatory recovery periods can help plan sponsors define the 'medium term' because cash contributions may be required over this period to restore the pension fund to good health. In instances where there is no regulatory requirement for recovery, as is the case for U.S. public sector pension funds, it will be more challenging, though no less important, to establish a disciplined construct for budgeting potential losses.

Affordable for the plan sponsor will have a different meaning for every sponsor. In tailoring the definition of 'affordability' to each unique obligor, we recognize that public pension plans will need to control the impact of potential losses to ensure the loss is affordable in terms of the sponsor's debt burden or future tax burden. In contrast, corporate plan sponsors will need to control the impact of potential losses to ensure the loss is affordable in terms of their debt burden, considered alongside such other factors as shareholders' equity and free cash flow. Today, the vast majority of pension plan sponsors fail to manage the funded status-at-risk so that it is affordable in the context of debt burden, future tax burden, shareholders' equity or free cash flow, but this is the key step in risk budgeting. It is worth considering each of these key metrics in turn.

Debt burden. Today, credit analysts are increasingly aware of the nature of unfunded pension liabilities, which are the debt of the plan sponsor and which may come ahead of any other debt or equity. Losses in the pension fund increase the sponsor's debt and, as such, growing pension deficits are increasingly a factor in rating downgrades and credit analyst commentary. A corporate, institutional, or municipal plan sponsor must determine whether losses in an amount equal to the funded status-at-risk would have a detrimental impact on its debt burden if the potential losses were realized. Given the nature of unfunded pension liabilities, key stakeholders consider: (a) whether potential losses would cause a debt rating downgrade or result in negative credit analyst reviews if realized; (b) whether any debt covenants would be violated; and (c) whether market access or other credit objectives (such as target debt ratios) of the sponsor would be threatened.

Impact on tax burden. This metric is relevant only to public plan sponsors whose pension plan contributions are funded by tax revenues or user fees. Losses in the pension fund may increase the sponsor's required contributions and create pressure on tax revenues or, where tax revenues cannot be raised, the pension contributions may displace needed public services. A public plan sponsor must consider whether losses in an amount equal to the funded status-at-risk would have a detrimental impact on its tax burden if the potential losses were realized and the requisite contributions were made to restore the pension fund to good health. Key stakeholders consider: (a) whether the potential losses and resulting contributions would cause tax rates to rise substantially; (b) whether there are legal, constitutional, or practical limits on the potential tax increases that might be violated; (c) whether tax revenues would need to be diverted from public services to make the contributions; (d) the probability that the municipal entity would be downgraded; (e) whether market access or other credit objectives of the sponsor would be threatened; and (f) whether residents and businesses would choose to locate in other municipalities to avoid the increasing burden of pension risk.

Impact on shareholders' equity. For corporate plan sponsors, losses in the pension fund that increase the company's debt burden also reduce its shareholders' equity because the increase in net effective debt does not create any investment in the enterprise nor any earning power for the firm. Current accounting rules appropriately capture this reality in the balance sheet mark-to-market approach that prevails today for corporate pension assets and liabilities in the U.S., U.K., and Canada, among other countries. Given the importance of shareholders' equity to investors, many companies are now considering whether the funded status-at-risk would have a detrimental impact on shareholders' equity if the potential losses were realized. It is particularly important to do this analysis for the plan sponsor alongside all of the other companies in the plan sponsor's industry peer group to determine the extent to which the plan sponsor would underperform its peers in a down market. Cyclical companies must also be very focused on these calculations because cyclical companies are likely to see declining equity values in the same market conditions that are challenging for the pension fund.

Impact on free cash flow. To the extent that pension losses trigger a requirement to contribute cash to the pension fund, a corporation's free cash flow can be severely impacted by pension risk. Moreover, free cash flow is at the foundation of shareholder value creation, which has led to the reasonable conclusion that 'cash is king.' Toward that end, we see companies with limited free cash flow taking the lead in pension de-risking to minimize potential cash calls on the company and ensure more consistent financial results within their industry peer groups. There was a raging debate in the United States before the recent financial crisis as to whether it was in the best interest of plan participants to moderate or budget the risk taken in the pension plan to ensure that potential losses would be affordable from the perspective of the plan sponsor. However, by the end of 2012, the Pension Benefit Guaranty Corporation in the United States was responsible for benefits to members of over 25,000 U.S. pension funds whose sponsors had previously filed for bankruptcy (PBGC 2013). As a result of these insolvencies, the benefits payable to many of the plan participants were capped below their original levels and the plan participants experienced the double challenge of a simultaneous decline in their retirement security and their job security. If potential pension losses are unaffordable for the plan sponsor, plan participants may face this difficult situation.

Allocating the Risk Budget: Choosing Your Risks

Once a plan sponsor defines its risk budget, the focus often turns to trimming overall risk to bring funded status-at-risk down to the targeted level. In this exercise, pension plans most often begin with a risk assessment such as the one shown in Figure 12.9 of this chapter. The risk assessment helps to quantify the risks the pension fund is running in order to begin an analysis of which risks to keep, which risks to manage, and which risks to shed.

From the point of the initial risk assessment, there are three key considerations in determining a risk reduction strategy. First, the risk assessment clearly identifies the largest sources of risk, where the greatest impact of risk management can be achieved but charting a successful course to a lower risk future is never as simple as attacking the largest risks and trimming them back. Second, it is critically important to consider which risks the plan believes are rewarded risks and which are unrewarded in order to prioritize rewarded risk-taking within the risk budget. Finally, the balance of risks is the key to an optimal outcome so that the plan makes the most of the diversification benefit available in its portfolio of risks.

In the risk reduction journey, we have seen several leading plans establish the following core principles. First, before risk reduction, interest rate risk, inflation risk, and longevity risk create a substantial amount of risk for the plan, but: (a) these risks compound each other; (b) each carries with it a lower expectation of returns than equity risk and investments in alternatives; and (c) within the overall risk budget, prioritizing rewarded over unrewarded risks is fundamental. Second, in reducing the overall level of risk, interest rate risk, inflation risk, and longevity risk should be trimmed ahead of equity risk and investments in alternatives. Third, to make the most of the diversification benefit among the risks, no risk should be completely eliminated. Fourth, the liabilities matter, so younger plans with a lot of deferred and active participants will take more risk than mature plans that are primarily composed of retirees.

The following section describes two real pension plans—one corporate and one public—that have applied these principles to successfully reduce their pension risk.

Case Study: A Closed Corporate Plan in a Cyclical Industry

Several closed corporate plans in the United Kingdom have dramatically reduced risk by applying the principles described above. They typically began with the realization that longevity risk, interest rate risk, and inflation risk are 'unrewarded' risks that need to be balanced and managed carefully within a risk budget.

One such plan (depicted in Figure 12.11) was extremely good at fixed income asset management; it brought its portfolio allocation up to 70 percent to 75 percent fixed income, including illiquid fixed income (such as private placement loans, commercial mortgages, inflation-linked ground leases, and high-quality credit card and auto loan ABS). The fixed income portfolio was built over many years and in many interest rate environments and allowed the plan to address its interest rate risk very effectively. Inflation risk was hedged or managed through investments. The remaining 25 percent to 30 percent of the portfolio was in equities, absolute return, and other alternatives, meaning that the plan could benefit from the diversification of risk among its various asset classes.

By the time the pension plan was invested in 70 to 75 percent fixed income, its downside risk was very well managed, but its upside earnings potential was greatly diminished too. The plan no longer had enough potential in its portfolio to earn its way out of an unexpected increase in life expectancy. The solution chosen by this plan was to run its asset portfolio alongside a longevity insurance transaction providing both asset and liability risk management. This strategy works for any large, sophisticated plan sponsor, though cyclical companies have the biggest incentive to reduce risk because the biggest pension losses arrive in downturns when equities and interest rates are falling simultaneously. These are the same moments when the business would need to conserve cash to manage through the business cycle. For this cyclical company, having a properly risk-managed pension plan (with a funded status-at-risk below its risk budget) meant that it could solidify its industry leadership, create more consistent financial results, and manage from a position of strength in down markets. Eliminating this fundamental risk to the company also enhanced the retirement security and the job security of the plan participants.

Case Study: An Open Public Plan

The risk budgeting and risk management strategy described above is not only for corporate plans. Public pension plans can pursue these strategies as well even though many public plans are still open and actively accruing benefit for plan participants. In these circumstances, the plan is likely to insure its longevity risk and target a higher asset risk level than a closed, mature plan, as shown on the right side of Figure 12.11. One public plan that pursued this strategy combines longevity insurance with a diversified asset portfolio that is one-third bonds and cash, one-third equities, and one-third absolute return. Its strategy is based upon risk budgeting and the strong belief that longevity risk is unrewarded, particularly when combined with (and compounded by) interest rate risk and inflation risk. The plan's CIO saw the exposure to longevity risk as a bond that routinely lost 2 percent or more each year. To put a floor on those losses, the plan decided to hedge away the longevity risk on the retirees and turn the liability into a known and knowable future obligation. The risk budget previously taken up by longevity exposure could then be re-allocated to rewarded risk-taking in the asset portfolio.

This is a revolutionary concept, made possible by longevity insurance. Pension funds can now choose to hedge longevity risk as an unrewarded risk and redeploy that risk allocation to rewarded risk-taking in the asset portfolio.

Many have asked what plan participants might gain from this risk management approach. The answer is likely retirement security. In an open plan for a public entity that is still accruing benefits for current employees, there is a fundamental

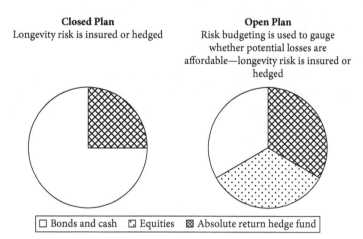

Closed Plan   Open Plan
Longevity risk is insured or hedged   Risk budgeting is used to gauge
                                            whether potential losses are
                                            affordable—longevity risk is insured or
                                            hedged

☐ Bonds and cash   ☐ Equities   ▨ Absolute return hedge fund

Figure 12.11. Sustainability model.

Note: Summarizes a sustainable asset and liability strategy for a closed plan and an open plan, respectively.

Source: Author's illustration.

question of whether the plan is adequately reserved for the longevity risk of current retirees and, if it is not, what impact that will have on current employees contributing to the plan. Managing asset risk and hedging the longevity risk of the retirees in the plan can address the intergenerational risk current employees face in circumstances where pension deficits are acute, the credit quality of the plan sponsor is weak, and life expectancy is underestimated. This is the essence of the DB Pension Sustainability Model as it brings into practice techniques for managing investment risk, longevity risk, and intergenerational risk in today's open pension plans.

Lessons Learned from Monoline Pension Insurers

There are many differences between most pension funds and the world's best-run pension insurers, but first we will focus on the similarities. Both are monolines that have written pension annuities and therefore grapple with asset risk and longevity risk. The similarities generally end there, because monoline pension insurers manage their blocks of business under insurance principles, while the pension funds, with the same annuity liabilities, remain focused on the endowment principles of retaining liquidity premiums, earning risk premiums, and maximizing diversification benefit to minimize overall contributions. The key differences are presented in Table 12.1.

The key to bringing the DB Pension Sustainability Model into practice is not to bring pension funds to manage risk fully under the insurance principles applied to the monoline pension insurers. Rather (in order to address the risks shown in Figures 12.2 through 12.5 of this chapter), the focus is on finding the happy medium between the two models for pension funds that seek to sustain themselves for the long run. The goal is to be able to keep the pension promises they have made and provide retirement security for plan participants even in the face of shifting demographics and increasing longevity. The halfway point between the insurance model and the conventional pension model is a moderate approach with plans: (a) managing just below fully funded status without any reserves or capital behind the risk; (b) maintaining a low volatility asset strategy that is heavy in fixed income and absolute return with a modest allocation to risky assets to

TABLE 12.1 Comparison of pension funds and monoline pension insurers

	Pension Funds	Monoline Pension Insurers
Funded level	Generally underfunded	Fully funded plus reserves & capital
Asset strategy	High allocation to risky assets	Asset and liability matching
Longevity risk strategy	Generally unhedged	Generally reinsured
Risk budgeting	Generally not applicable	Potential losses < capital and reserves

Source: Author's tabulation.

benefit from diversification of asset classes; and (c) hedging the longevity risk of their retirees to ensure sustainability even in the face of longer life.

This moderate approach is designed to benefit from much of the stability of the insurance model, without the extra capital and reserves it requires. At the same time, the moderate approach continues to take advantage of some of the diversification benefit among asset classes that is the hallmark of the conventional pension approach. By combining the two models, it is possible to help pension funds develop an approach to moderate risk and bring potential losses into an affordable range.

Conclusion

People are living longer lives but the normal retirement age in most countries has been the same for decades. As a result, there is a demographic shift observable within many pension plans: the number of retired persons to be supported by the plan is rising much faster than the number of working age people contributing to the plan. This intergenerational risk creates an acute need for open pension plans to move retirement age later with increases in healthy life expectancy.

While this demographic shift continues unabated, a low-growth/low interest rate environment is creating a substantial funding gap for plan sponsors. Maintaining a high risk profile to bridge the gap may result in investment losses as unaffordable as they have proven to be in the first decades of the twenty-first century.

Today's path for pensions is unsustainable. This chapter develops a way to budget and moderate risk, provide for increasing longevity, manage the intergenerational risk in the pension plan, and create greater certainty that participant benefits can be met. The retirement security of many pension plan participants depends upon it.

Acknowledgements

The author thanks Guy Coughlan for providing the analysis for Figures 12.8 through 12.10 and for being a willing collaborator to so many in our industry. She also appreciates excellent comments from Gary Knapp, Peter Patrician, Jo Alvarez, and Daniel Bertram. Finally, she thanks the many pension funds with whom she works for sharing their concerns about risk and their aspirations for a better future.

Notes

1. This reflects the history of the ten-year U.S. Treasury, taken from the Daily Treasury Yield Curve, which was at its highest level in nearly six years on June 12, 2007, at 5.26 percent and has generally fallen for the five ensuing years, to 1.43 percent on July 25, 2012.

2. The ten-year Treasury rate data collected by Shiller (2013) show rates below 3 percent for 19 years from 1934 to 1953.
3. Interest rate data are for ten-year U.S. Treasuries, taken from the Daily Treasury Yield Curve (U.S. Treasury 2013), which was at 3.22 percent on July 1, 2011, and 2.07 percent on August 19, 2011. Equity data reflect the S&P 500 Index, which closed at 1339.67 on July 1, 2011, and 1123.53 on August 19, 2011 (Bloomberg 2013).
4. Cumulative assets (in US$billions) and liabilities of all pension schemes in the S&P 500 index on the accounting basis.
5. This assumes a pension fund with 36 percent retiree liabilities and 64 percent deferred and active liabilities, though no future accrual is assumed for active members. The average age of retired members is 69 and the average age of deferred and active members is 46. Benefits include cost of living adjustments, which are simulated in a fully stochastic analysis. Longevity improvements are also simulated in a fully stochastic analysis.
6. This assumes a pension fund with 36 percent retiree liabilities and 64 percent deferred and active liabilities, though no future accrual is assumed for active members. The average age of retired members is 69 and the average age of deferred and active members is 46. Benefits include cost of living adjustments, which are simulated in a fully stochastic analysis. Longevity improvements are also simulated in a fully stochastic analysis.
7. See also Coughlan (2014).

References

Aon Hewitt (2013). *Aon Hewitt Global Pension Risk Tracker* [website]. <https://rfmtools. hewitt.com/PensionRiskTracker>.

Barclays (2013). *Barclays Indices* [website]. London, U.K.: Barclays. <https://indices.bar cap.com/index.dxml>.

Bloomberg (2013). *S&P 500 Index* [website]. New York, NY: Bloomberg, Inc. <http:// www.bloomberg.com/quote/SPX:IND>.

Coughlan, G. (2014). 'Longevity Risk Management, Corporate Finance, and Sustainable Pensions,' in P. B. Hammond, R. Maurer, and O. S. Mitchell, eds., *Recreating Sustainable Retirement: Resilience, Solvency, and Tail Risk.* Oxford, U.K.: Oxford University Press, pp. 89–112.

International Monetary Fund (IMF) (2012). 'The Financial Impact of Longevity Risk,' in *Global Financial Stability Report 2012.* Washington, DC: IMF, pp. 123–153.

Milliman (2013). *Milliman 100 Pension Funding Index* [website]. New York, NY: Milliman. <www.milliman.com/expertise/employee-benefits/products-tools/ pension-funding-index/>.

Pension Benefit Guaranty Corporation (PBGC) (2013). *Pension Benefit Guaranty Corporation Fact Sheet* [website]. Washington, DC: PBGC, April. <http://pbgc.gov/res/factsheets/ page/pbgc-facts.html>.

Russell Investments (2013). *Russell 2000 Index* [website]. Seattle, WA: Russell Investments. <http://www.russell.com/indexes/>.

Shiller, R. (2013). '10-Year Treasury Rate,' *Online Data Robert Shiller* [website]. New Haven, CT: Yale University. <http://www.econ.yale.edu/~shiller/data.htm>.

U.S. Department of the Treasury (U.S. Treasury) (2013). 'Daily Treasury Yield Curve,' *Resource Center* [website]. Washington, DC: U.S. Treasury. <http://www.treasury.gov/resource-center/data-chart-center/interest-rates/Pages/TextView.aspx?data=yield All>.

Chapter 13

The Funding Debate: Optimizing Pension Risk within a Corporate Risk Budget

Geoff Bauer, Gordon Fletcher, Julien Halfon, and Stacy Scapino

To assess the merits of using company cash to fund pension obligations instead of other corporate strategies, we believe a corporate finance approach is needed. Corporate finance theory generally suggests that companies should pursue projects offering returns above a certain hurdle rate for a given risk level. These approaches are more useful for decision-making in a multi-country environment than assessing each pension plan individually. By considering the pension funding policy alongside other potential corporate actions within the same net present value (NPV), internal rate of return (IRR), or similar analytical framework, a company can further optimize the use of available cash resources and balance alternative strategies against each other.

In developing a model for determining whether to provide additional voluntary funding to pension plans, we begin with a 'holistic' view of a company's financial statements, which we use to consider the pension plans and the employer covenant alongside other balance sheet, income statement, and cash flow statement elements. This step establishes the nature and extent of the linkages between a company and its pension plan(s). Next we develop a risk optimization process and framework for selecting the optimal combination of pension funding, investment, and risk management strategies together with desired corporate activities. In particular, we discuss how to compare the relative merits of additional pension contributions against other potential uses of available company resources and how to assess the impact on the covenant. We then extend the debate beyond the strategic aspects by outlining high-level governance and practical implementation issues. Last, we provide some examples of how certain companies have applied these concepts in practice.

The Scale of the Global DB Pension Problem

At the end of 1999, large multinational company exposures to sizeable pension deficits and the perceived level of corporate risk related to the pension liability were considered to be quite limited and rarely mentioned as potential concerns. At that time, DB pension plan investment strategies typically had large equity holdings and interest rates were higher than in the current environment, leading to lower liability valuations and, in some cases, decisions to take contribution holidays.

Conditions have changed in the wake of two significant global equity market corrections and a trend toward loose monetary policy across the largest developed countries. As Figure 13.1 shows, the total value of pension assets for 498 of the largest European and American multinationals have increased by 1.2 percent *per annum* over the past five years while their total liabilities increased by 2.5 percent *per annum* over this same period. As seen in Figure 13.2, these 498 multinational companies together made pension contributions of roughly €419 billion in total during this five-year period, at an average rate of €84 billion per year. While such efforts to eliminate pension deficits are notable, they have had little impact and one could even say that the past five years of pension contributions have been completely lost.

This global pension funding position has developed against a backdrop of corporate deleveraging and considerable declines in market capitalization. Figure 13.3 shows that for our sample of 498 multinational companies, total net debt declined from a peak of €12.1 trillion in 2007 to €10.8 trillion in 2011, while total market capitalization declined from €8.6 trillion to €8.2 trillion over this same period. Similarly, Figure 13.4 shows that their combined total net income declined from a peak of €837 billion in 2007 to €812 billion in 2011, while total free cash flow increased from €375 billion in 2007 to €832 billion in 2011 (although this is lower than the €1.2 trillion observed in 2009).[1]

Therefore, corporations have continued to make contributions to their DB pension plans despite the ongoing difficulties posed by the financial environment. Yet the continued existence of large pension deficits suggests they could probably have been more effective in the use of their cash. This analysis suggests two key points. First, pension plan investment and risk management strategies adopted by these companies were not suitably adapted to the changing nature of the market environment. Second, the considerable proportion of free cash flow used for pension contribution purposes may have been better invested elsewhere—potentially to boost core productive activities or enhance shareholder value.

A Holistic View of Pension Risk

To arrive at a framework and methodology for assessing whether a company should fund its DB pension liabilities or use its resources to pursue other corporate activities, one must understand the company's options, as it chooses between paying additional, non-statutory contributions to a given pension plan or investing more into the business.

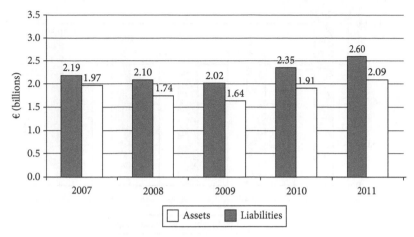

Figure 13.1. Overall funding position on IAS 19 basis for 498 of the largest European and American multinationals.

Source: Authors' compilation from annual financial statements.

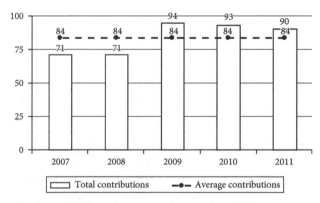

Figure 13.2. Total combined employer contributions for 498 of the largest European and American multinationals.

Source: Authors' compilation of annual financial statements.

What Do DB Pension Plans Actually Mean for a Corporate Sponsor?

A company's financial statements summarize its ability to generate returns for shareholders and provide a detailed understanding of the firm's overall viability. A well-run company should always attempt to find the optimal balance between

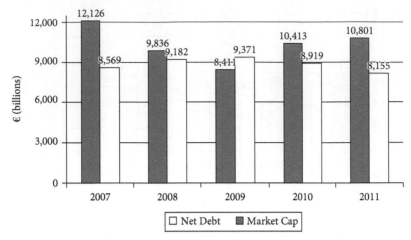

Figure 13.3. Total combined net debt and market cap for 498 of the largest European and American multinationals.

Source: Authors' compilation of annual financial statements.

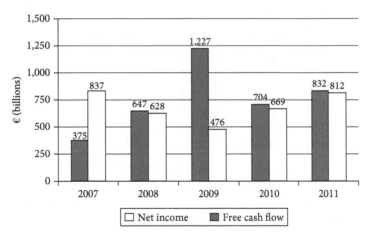

Figure 13.4. Total combined net income and free cash flow for 498 of the largest European and American multinationals.

Source: Authors' compilation of annual financial statements.

its balance sheet, income/expenses, and cash flow objectives, to maximize the value of shareholder equity.

Companies with material pension exposures cannot define their key corporate objectives (e.g. valuation, earnings volatility, capital requirements, capital expenditures, etc.) without considering their pension exposures and associated pension risks. Trying to achieve key corporate objectives without considering the potential impact of pension risks creates imbalances that will affect the company's ability to achieve its goals and the pension plan's ability to meet long-term obligations. Within this context, one must consider what exactly a DB plan represents for a corporate sponsor.

Corporate sponsors have three levers to manage DB pension risks so that their impact is predictable and manageable: the funding strategy, the investment strategy, and the risk management strategy. In turn these three levers determine how much money is paid into the plan, the trade-off between risk and expected return, and the specific actions that can be taken to reduce either the size or volatility of a DB pension deficit. The ideal balance between these levers depends on the sponsor's financial health. For example, a very strong company may be able to accept higher levels of investment risk or higher contribution levels than a weaker company.

Corporate Risks

Any investment or strategic decision brings potential rewards but also exposes a corporation to a set of risks. As shown in Figure 13.5, these risks can be broken down into three: core business risks, other general risks, and financial risks. Together these risks provide the references against which the success of and return on any corporate strategy can be measured. For our purposes, we shall define corporate risks as any threat to a corporation's objectives measured in financial terms, including all of the individual risks shown in Figure 13.5.

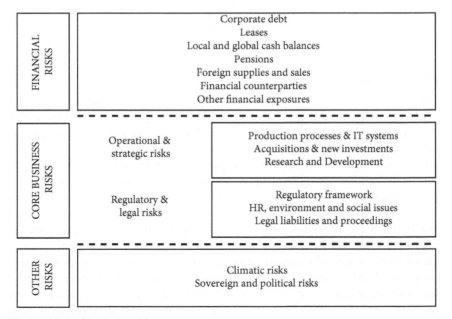

Figure 13.5. Corporate risks.

Source: Authors' compilation.

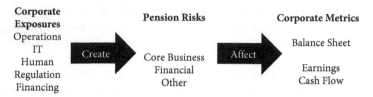

Figure 13.6. Impact of corporate risks on key corporate metrics.

Source: Authors' compilation.

Figure 13.7. Impact of pension risks on key pension metrics.

Source: Authors' compilation.

A company's operations and internal functions, along with the wider economic and regulatory environment, impact its corporate risks. As shown in Figure 13.6, exposure to these corporate risks can in turn result in an unwanted adverse impact on the company's financial statements and overall market standing.

Pension Risks

Pension liabilities and asset valuations affect pension risk; the latter arise as a result of changes in the market value of assets held to meet pension liabilities, the underlying nature of the pension benefits provided to plan members, the demographic profile of the membership group to which benefits are provided, and the financial and demographic assumptions used to place a value on the liabilities. At a consolidated corporate group level, aggregate pension risks are reflected in the company's financial statements. Under the revised IAS 19 accounting standard, the full value of the pension deficit (or surplus) will be reflected on the consolidated balance sheet, while the consolidated income statement will reflect the total operating cost (i.e. service costs) and finance cost (i.e. the net-interest cost without allowance for subjective expected return on assets assumptions) from a company's DB pension plans. Furthermore, the value of all actuarial gains and losses incurred during the year will be fully recognized through the consolidated statement of other comprehensive income, with the total value of pension contributions reflected in the consolidated cash flow statement. Just as corporate risks affect corporate metrics, pension risks influence key pension metrics, as illustrated in Figure 13.7.

The Interaction Between Corporate Risks and Pension Risks

Pension risk drivers can be the same as the corporation's risk drivers. For example, a large financial institution will most likely have considerable interest rate exposure through its outstanding debt. In some cases, pension risk drivers can act as diversifiers or even offset some corporate risks when viewed within an enterprise risk management framework. For example, a utility company whose revenues are linked to inflation may be less worried about the level of inflation risk exposure in its pension plans. As a result, it is possible that decisions taken to manage pension risk may result in an increase in overall risk when the pension scheme and company are viewed together.

The asset-liability risks associated with a company's DB pension plans can have a significant impact on the company's financial risks; however, non-financial pension risks can also have an important impact on a company's core business and other risks. Figure 13.8 shows how pension risks can be viewed within a corporate-wide risk budget.

A company's pension deficit directly affects its balance sheet. The pension plan's risk levels and key risk drivers determine pension deficit volatility. Consequently,

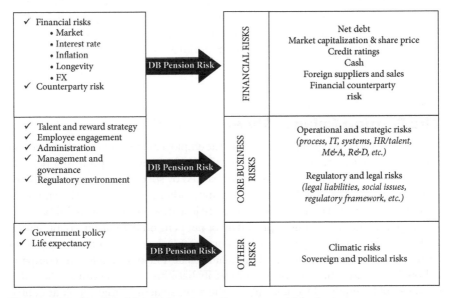

Figure 13.8. Pension risks within an overall corporate risk budget.

Source: Authors' compilation.

pension risk can cause increased volatility of total balance sheet liabilities, thereby affecting all corporate finance metrics that include the company's total liabilities, such as net debt, enterprise value, or the company's credit rating. Similarly, pension expense can dilute the company's consolidated net earnings. Any earnings volatility arising from exposure to pension risks at a local level can, therefore, have a knock-on effect for the company's dividend policy and other corporate finance metrics, including earnings measures such as net debt to EBITDA (earnings before interest, taxes, depreciation, and amortization) ratios. Finally, the pension contributions a company is required to make can ultimately drain overall free cash flow, thereby reducing its ability to develop its business and undertake profitable ventures.

Pension benefits can be met either from the pension plan's existing assets (and the expected future return earned on these assets) or by making additional contributions (i.e. the funding plan). A company considering additional contributions is essentially faced with a choice between contributing money to increase pension plan assets in the hope that these contributions and the associated additional investment returns will help minimize the probability that the company will have to meet pension obligations using additional financial resources,[2] and using the available funds to invest in 'corporate activities' (i.e. invest in research and development, productive capacity, a debt or equity buyback program, or other similar activities). In the latter case, the pension plan is left either unfunded or underfunded for a period of time. The assumption is that the company's financial position will be strengthened as a result of its other corporate activities and the stronger company should be better placed to meet its future pension obligations. The company is trying to 'grow out of the pension problem': a pension deficit of €50 million may be seen as a material problem for a company whose total value is €100 million but might be considered immaterial for a company whose total value is €1 billion.

The Pension Balance Sheet

When considering a DB plan in isolation, the employer covenant reflects the notion that the company bears ultimate responsibility for providing promised pension benefits; therefore, pension liabilities not backed by specific assets ear-marked for this purpose must be met from the company's other resources (i.e. the employer covenant). Unfunded pension obligations are just another financial liability.

Corporate liabilities consist primarily of net pension obligations, debt, leases, and other financial obligations, while corporate assets are mostly composed of cash and other long-term real and financial assets. The question for the company is how best to structure its assets to meet its liabilities and maximize the value of shareholder equity. Decisions about the asset structure might look at contributions and cash flow (described further on in the chapter), but will also include decisions about investment and risk management strategies, which affect the balance sheet if they result in reduced volatility of the pension deficit.[3] The company must find an acceptable balance between pension deficits and overall company debt capacity.

Deciding to leave the pension plan either unfunded or underfunded for a period of time might also be viewed as a form of inexpensive borrowing for companies, especially for those companies with high borrowing costs. This flexibility may be an attractive factor from a corporate finance perspective. On the other hand, companies may feel uncomfortable borrowing from employees. Importantly, this issue may be mitigated where there is some form of pension insolvency insurance, such as the Pensions-Sicherungs-Verien (PSV) in Germany, the Pension Protection Fund (PPF) in the United Kingdom, and the Pension Benefit Guaranty Corporation (PBGC) in the United States.

The Pension Income Statement and the Statement of Other Comprehensive Income

Under the revised IAS 19 accounting standard, the annual cost of running a DB pension plan is the sum of total service costs (including current and past service costs plus any curtailment and settlement gains and losses recognized on the income statement), the net-interest cost recognized on the income statement, and 're-measurements,' including actuarial gains and losses, recognized in 'other comprehensive income.' By making additional contributions to a DB pension plan, the sponsoring firm could achieve a lower net-interest cost (*ceteris paribus*) and effect a transfer of some pension liabilities and risks,[4] thus reducing the pension plan size and expense levels, or achieve a better degree of asset-liability matching,[5] leading to less volatility in annual 're-measurements' through the statement of other comprehensive income and on the balance sheet.

These potential benefits contrast with possible increases in operating or investment income should the company choose to invest in other corporate activities. In this case, the expected increase in earnings in the long term may overwhelm pension expense volatility in the short term. If an acceptable balance between pension deficit and deficit volatility on one hand and earnings dilution and volatility on the other is not reached, there could be a material impact on the valuation of the company and/or the strength of the covenant.

The Pension Cash Flow Statement

Using an example of a single underfunded DB pension plan, and assuming that the sponsor is not required to fund the deficit in advance, we can look at the choice between making no immediate contributions to the plan, making a large contribution up front, and making regular but relatively smaller contributions over time. A graphical illustration of each of these choices is provided in Figures 13.9, 13.10, and 13.11.

If the company does not make immediate contributions, the pension plan's benefit payments will be met from the plan assets in prior years. When these assets are expended, the rest of the liability cash flows must be covered by the employer. In this case, the company will be left free to invest in corporate activities in the early years until the point in the future when it will need to cover the ongoing benefit payments from its own operating cash flow. If the company were to consider monetizing the existing pension covenant by making additional contributions to the pension plan, it could do so by front-end loading the required contribution. Under this option, the hope is that that this contribution, along with the additional returns earned on the investment, would be sufficient to meet ongoing benefit payments with no further sponsor involvement. Alternatively, the company could make regular contributions over time, which might balance the need (or priority) to invest in corporate activities with the potential objective of reducing the requirement for additional sponsor investment in the future. The selected approach constrains to some extent the company's non-pension investment program and can affect the long-term strength of the pension covenant. Structuring additional contributions should reflect a balance between the level and timing of contributions needed to meet the legal and regulatory funding requirements of the pension plans, which differ greatly across countries, and pursue other planned

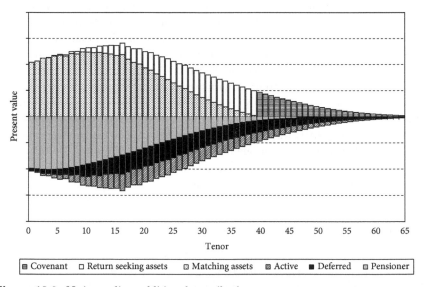

Figure 13.9. No immediate additional contributions.

Source: Authors' compilation.

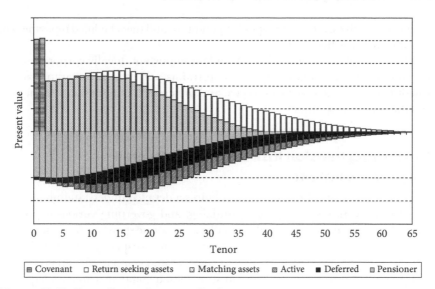

Figure 13.10. Immediate upfront contribution.

Source: Authors' compilation.

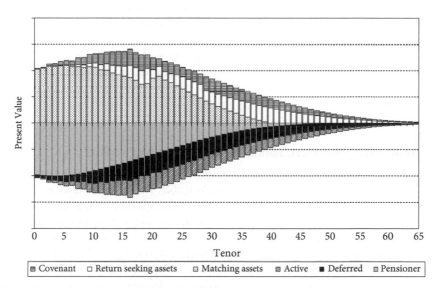

Figure 13.11. Regular additional contributions over time.

Source: Authors' compilation.

business initiatives, including capital expenditure and the scheduled repayment of existing company borrowings.

The shape of the contribution schedule is important. Ideally corporate sponsors should take account of liquidity constraints and attempt to customize the schedule to meet the objectives, needs, and preferences of both the pension plan and the corporate sponsor.

Optimizing Pension Risk within the Overall Corporate Context

Achieving corporate objectives often requires a detailed understanding of and a sound framework for managing, optimizing, and governing various exposures and risks, including pensions. Additionally, a corporate sponsor's financial health is instrumental in ensuring its pension plans' long-term capacity to meet their obligations. Without some objective way to consider and compare the different risks and potential returns from changes in strategies, a company cannot adequately assess how much pension risk it can afford to take, where risks can be taken to ensure they are satisfactorily rewarded, which risks need to be hedged or transferred, and which risks need to be governed.

To this end, we focus on the processes that can help optimize and govern pension risks. This can be achieved in three phases. First, a risk optimization process is required, where changes in funding, investment, and risk management strategies are analyzed in terms of their impacts on corporate metrics and objectives. This is then supplemented by a cost/benefit analysis to determine the relative merits of each alternative pension strategy and how changes to the pension risk/return profile affect the sponsor covenant. Last, another cost/benefit analysis will be carried out to compare the best pension strategy to other corporate options available.

Optimizing the Pension Risk and Return Profile

Ideally the plan sponsor will form a view on the level of pension risk that might be regarded as acceptable, tolerable, or desirable. At a corporate level, aggregate pension risk must be commensurate with the sponsor's capacity to absorb potential costs/losses. For example, for a company sponsoring multiple pension plans, reducing pension risks in one or more plans may allow additional risk to be taken in other core business activities within the overall risk budget. But for the sponsor to appreciate the scale of its pension risk, it must specify an overall pension risk limit that reflects risk levels in its pension plan(s) and the impact that these risks have on wider corporate metrics. The steps set out below can be used to achieve this.

Identify Corporate Objectives and Key Corporate Metrics

Key corporate metrics and ratios determine the extent to which corporate objectives have been met. These metrics must include traditional valuation metrics, such as the stability of earnings, the level of net debt, earnings targets, etc., and sector and company-specific ones (e.g. the Basel 2 capital requirements for banking institutions, cash flow levels for utilities, etc.).

With a Detailed Understanding of the Overall Corporate Objectives, Develop 'Proxy Corporate-Pension Metrics'

Simple 'proxy corporate-pension metrics' can combine corporate metrics and pension metrics such as the following ratios: net pension deficit as percentage of market cap and/or net debt, pension expense as percentage of net earnings, pension-driven net earnings volatility, and contributions as percentage of pension-adjusted free cash flow.

Companies may also consider more complex ratios as proxies, using pension-adjusted figures such as funds from operations (FFO)/pension-adjusted net debt, pension-adjusted net debt/EBITDA, and pension-adjusted net debt/capital. The appropriate metrics vary from sector to sector. Individual company circumstances can lead to different levels of importance attached to each metric. These 'proxy corporate-pension metrics' should illustrate the materiality of a company's pension exposures, while their volatility provides an indication of pension risk levels and their potential impact on the company.

Set an Explicit Limit on the Level of Pension Risk Regarded as Acceptable, Tolerable, or Desirable

For companies valued on the basis of Net Debt to EBITDA or enterprise value to EBITDA ratios, a simple risk limit could be specified as a maximum value for the ratio of either [pension-adjusted net debt + one-year 95 percent Value-at-Risk][6] to pension-adjusted EBITDA or [Pension-adjusted enterprise value less one-year 95 percent Value-at-Risk] to pension-adjusted EBITDA.

For others, the dilution of earnings from DB pensions and the corresponding volatility can give a good indication of pension cost in terms of overall company valuation. For such companies, one might consider ratios such as the volatility of net earnings to the volatility of net earnings excluding the pension expense or, alternatively, net earnings (current pension expense + impact of one-year 95 percent Value-at-Risk on expected pension expense) to net earnings (current pension expense).

The appropriate definition of a risk limit is complex and must reflect the company's specific circumstances and objectives. The risk budget is likely to be multi-faceted with several risk limits, including the maximum increase in deficit over a given period of time, the maximum value of additional contribution over a given period of time, or the maximum increase in pension expense over a given period of time.

Develop Alternative Pension Funding, Investment, and Risk Management Strategies Focused on Meeting Desired Return Objectives While Remaining Within the Set Risk Limits

To ensure pension risk is within the acceptable levels set out in the previous step, a range of strategies must be considered, including changes to planned pension funding or the period over which funding will occur, changes to investment strategy (i.e. asset allocation, diversification within asset classes, and hedge ratios), and other risk management options (e.g. initiatives to reshape the size or profile of the liabilities, risk transfer options, and alternative finance solutions).

Bringing pension risk to an acceptable limit may require contributing money and using contributions to affect the investment strategy or risk management changes. These additional contributions may affect other corporate activities, so the combined overall pension and corporate strategy should be fully analyzed. The sponsor must decide whether making additional pension contributions as part of a revised contribution policy or funding strategy is preferable to using the available cash elsewhere in the sponsor's business.

Assess the Appropriateness of a Given Investment and Risk Management Strategy for the Pension Plan Based on the Pre-Defined 'Proxy Corporate-Pension Metrics,' Acceptable Risk Limits, and Other Evaluation Criteria Such as NPV, IRR, etc.

One must maintain consistency when comparing pension funding and corporate investment decisions. One way to maintain consistency is to complement the 'proxy corporate-pension metrics' and acceptable risk limits defined earlier with risk-adjusted hurdle rates, IRR, or NPV, so pension strategies can be compared to other alternatives.

Any single available pension or corporate strategy cannot be considered in isolation; as noted above, it is the overall pension and corporate strategy that must be analyzed. For example, consider a company with a material pension deficit faced with a simplified decision between contributing money into its pension plans to remove the deficit and buy out the liabilities with an insurance company, or continuing with its existing contribution policy, using available cash resources to develop, say, a new production plant over the next ten years. In this example, the appropriate comparison is between (a) the risk-adjusted NPV or IRR for the company's ongoing business initiatives, including the initial cash contribution to settle the pension liabilities, but without any future balance sheet or earnings volatility or any potential cash calls from DB pension plans; and (b) the risk-adjusted NPV or IRR for the company's ongoing business initiatives and the new production plant, but taking into account the impact on this risk-adjusted NPV or IRR of the remaining pension risks (and hence the potential need for additional future pension contributions).

If this example company pursued the second option, and a new medical breakthrough resulted in a substantial increase in life expectancy, the financial analysis of the company's business initiatives and new production plant could remain unchanged. The increased cost of having to pay pension benefits for significantly longer periods of time may make it difficult for the company to effectively complete its planned development of the new production plant. Allowance for such factors may reduce the NPV of this option.

Two pension investment and risk management strategies can have similar risk/return profiles, yet different overall impacts and combined NPV or IRR results. A feedback loop can help separate strategies that increase the strength and value of the covenant (e.g. generate positive NPV) from those that decrease it.

Select the Most Effective Pension Strategy from those Deemed Appropriate by Ensuring that Risk Is Taken in the Most Efficient Manner and that the Combined Pension and Corporate Strategies and Activities Maximize the Chosen Evaluation Criteria

The main differentiating factor between different strategies remains the overall impact on the covenant. This impact is best captured using evaluation criteria like NPV or IRR.

Risk should be taken in areas that are expected to be rewarded and any potential diversification benefits between different risk sources should be maximized. In deciding which strategy is most efficient, one must consider both the company's views and factors specific to the company and its operating environment. An illustration of how this framework might work in practice is shown in Figure 13.12.

Governance and Implementation Considerations

In the extended framework set out above, a company must ensure that the process for comparing alternative strategies is rigorous and reliable. Consequently, sponsors would do well to consider the implications of these decisions from a governance and implementation perspective.

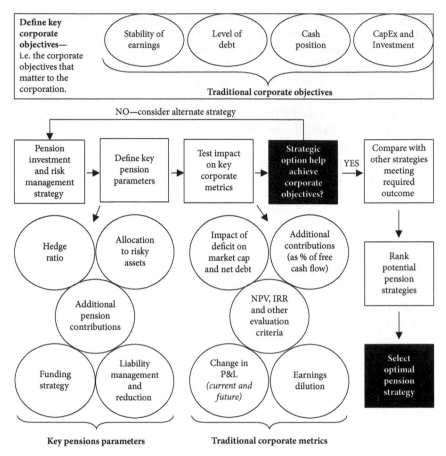

Figure 13.12. Optimizing the DB pension risk and return profile.

Source: Authors' compilation.

Governance Implications of the Funding Debate Framework

The framework and approach advocated has several distinct advantages for managing pension risk. Nevertheless, these methods introduce complexity because a company may need to implement various corporate and pension strategies simultaneously. This increased complexity requires robust governance and monitoring. In particular, a company must be aware of implementation requirements for a given pension or corporate action, the need for coordination between different services, geographies or lines of business, potential disparities between different stakeholders, advisors, and providers (which would require the sponsor to clearly define responsibilities and assign them to named individuals, define policies and processes, articulate risk tolerances, implement a forward-looking monitoring process, and manage internal and external communications), and the potential need for the company to take corrective action in the face of unfavorable outcomes and its capacity to actually develop and take such actions.

Understanding Cash Sources

Another dimension that must be considered is whether potential pension contributions are sourced from excess cash within the business or raised on the market. This decision could affect the level of relative leveraging in the company's balance sheet and the company's long-term borrowing capacity. In certain industries, companies may have a regulatory arbitrage opportunity. Although the cost of capital is assumed to be the same, changes in the company's debt-to-equity ratio as a result of raising the funds externally should be considered. Tax considerations and the existence of potential tax shields should also be taken into account when determining the most appropriate source of additional cash.

Implementation Constraints

One reason for testing and ranking many alternative strategies is that structural and organizational limitations can affect their implementation. For example, the sponsor may not be capable of making additional contributions as its financial standing is weak, or due to liquidity issues. This affordability constraint may limit the universe and nature of the pension strategies and activities that can be implemented. Alternatively, legal and regulatory requirements might determine the way in which pensions are financed. For example, in the Netherlands or the United Kingdom, companies are required by regulation to make pension contributions if their pension plan solvency falls below some pre-defined short-term or long-term level.

Furthermore, the company may run into opposition from trustees or other third parties. For example, in the Netherlands and United Kingdom, DB plans are typically set up as trust arrangements with a set of fiduciaries that have ultimate responsibility for investment strategy and compliance with local funding requirements. If the merits of the company's pension decisions cannot be communicated clearly to such third parties, it is entirely possible that their opposition could complicate matters significantly and, in the worst case, could render the entire approach impossible.

If the most favored strategy is not implementable, the company may well need to consider whether the second or third ranked strategies (shown in the previous figure) would be sensible and desirable, and whether this approach could offer an attractive strategy that can actually be carried out in practice.

Practical Application of the Proposed Framework

Our suggested framework provides companies with an innovative way to assess the relative merits of using available cash for pension funding. Moreover, we are aware of a number of cases where companies have successfully applied some of its individual components. This is because companies are increasingly evaluating pension funding decisions with reference to the potential impact these decisions could have on their key performance indicators and business plans, rather than just considering changes in typical 'pension-only' metrics like Value-at-Risk. One such example comes from a large European telecom firm with significant pension liabilities. This company was faced with calls from their largest plan's trustee to adopt a very prudent long-term funding target; by considering the specific components of their core business that could offset pension risks to some extent and how the pension deficit (and risk) was expected to develop over time relative to the expected progression of the employer covenant, the company was able to demonstrate that it would need to increase the current level of risk in the pension plan by 50 percent in order to have a reasonable chance of meeting the trustee's prudent funding target. The company was then able to clearly illustrate the potential detrimental impact that this risk increase could have on its debt and equity holders, and how the increased risk might impact the perceived strength of the covenant in the shorter term and, hence, the security of member benefits. In this way, the company was able to negotiate a pension contribution policy that did not adversely impact its development plans and ensured that pension risk levels relative to the employer covenant were reasonable in future years.

A second example comes from a European bank that has developed an approach to pension risk monitoring as set out above. The bank identified the financial metrics most important to its shareholders and then restated these metrics to explicitly include the size and potential volatility of global DB liabilities. As a result, the bank gained better control over global risk exposures, with the ability to quantify and qualify risk sources and evaluate the impact of pension risk on its capital requirements. This provided the bank with an 'early warning system' to identify when risk limits were close to being breached and provided senior management with a better understanding of the potential impact that pension risk management actions could have on their key financial metrics. The bank has now also developed a governance framework with clearly defined responsibilities for identifying potential risk management and investment opportunities.

Furthermore, companies and external stakeholders (e.g. equity and credit rating analysts) appear to have increasingly greater appreciation for the potential positive impact that reducing or removing pension risks can have on expected future company performance, even if this involves substantial initial contributions that might have been used elsewhere in the business. For example, in mid-2012, a large U.S. manufacturing company announced an offer of lump sum payments to a significant percentage of salaried retirees in the U.S., with other retirees offered a continued monthly pension, insured by a large U.S. insurance company. The company contributed approximately $4 billion to help fund a group annuity contract purchase and improve the funded status of the pension plan for active employees. The company took a one-off charge to earnings of approximately $3 billion, as well as an ongoing annual reduction in earnings of approximately $200 million. Despite the substantial additional contribution requirements and the reduction in overall company earnings, reactions from investors and credit rating agencies were positive to neutral. The successful completion alleviated many concerns that the market would view accounting charges unfavorably.

Conclusion

For many companies, DB pension liabilities are material and can have a significant impact on their ability to achieve the firm's business objectives. Consequently, companies increasingly need an integrated governance and pension risk management framework that will allow them to evaluate the relative merits of using cash to fund pension obligations versus using it for other corporate objectives. There is no simple solution to the pension problem; we have argued here that the answer lies in adopting a corporate finance approach. While we have yet to see a company fully adopt the framework set out here, there are clear examples that many corporations are moving in this direction. We believe this momentum will continue and that companies adopting a corporate finance approach will be far better placed to manage DB pension risk in the future.

Appendix: Defining the 'Sponsor's Covenant'

As with other company debtors, the company owes money to pension plan(s) that it sponsors. For a pension plan, the value of the sponsor's financial support is crucial if it wants to meet the pension obligations of its members. The 'sponsor's covenant' in relation to a pension plan is defined as 'the combination of (a) the ability and (b) the willingness of the sponsor to pay (or the ability of the trustees to require the sponsor to pay) sufficient advance contributions to ensure that the scheme's benefits can be paid as they fall due' (IFoA 2005).

If a company is looking for a solution that leaves it free to pursue its corporate agenda while ensuring DB pension risk is well managed, it might look to maximize the value of the sponsor's covenant and reach a balanced position where corporate finance and pension risk management decisions are optimized.

Notes

1. Free cash flow is taken to be cash flow from operating activities less total capital expenditure.
2. In this example, 'money' is intended to capture not only direct cash contributions but also the transfer of a wide range of contingent or conditional assets.
3. With the changes in IAS 19 disclosure requirements, deficit volatility will feed into the balance sheet through recognition in Other Comprehensive Income.
4. In this example, risk transfer is intended to cover liability management exercises, such as enhanced transfer values or pension increase exchange, as well as either a partial or complete buy-in or buyout.
5. To the extent that additional contributions are used to reduce risky assets and increase hedging.
6. Value-at-Risk is the potential increase in pension deficit that would be expected to occur over a given time horizon with a defined probability and is typically measured in monetary terms.

Reference

Institute and Faculty of Actuaries (IFoA) (2005). *Sponsor Covenant Working Party Final Report: Allowing for the Sponsor Covenant in Actuarial Advice*. London, U.K.: IFoA.

The Pension Research Council

The Pension Research Council of the Wharton School at the University of Pennsylvania is committed to generating debate on key policy issues affecting pensions and other employee benefits. The Council sponsors interdisciplinary research on private and social retirement security and related benefit plans in the United States and around the world. It seeks to broaden understanding of these complex arrangements through basic research into their economic, social, legal, actuarial, and financial foundations. Members of the Advisory Board of the Council, appointed by the Dean of the Wharton School, are leaders in the employee benefits field, and they recognize the essential role of social security and other public sector income maintenance programs while sharing a desire to strengthen private sector approaches to economic security. For more information, see <http://www.pensionresearchcouncil.org>.

The Boettner Center for Pensions and Retirement Security

Founded at the Wharton School to support scholarly research, teaching, and outreach on global aging, retirement, and public and private pensions, the Center is named after Joseph E. Boettner. Funding to the University of Pennsylvania was provided through the generosity of the Boettner family, whose intent was to spur financial wellbeing at older ages through work on how aging influences financial security and life satisfaction. The Center disseminates research and evaluation on challenges and opportunities associated with global aging and retirement, how to strengthen retirement income systems, saving and investment behavior of the young and the old, interactions between physical and mental health, and successful retirement. For more information, see <http://www.pensionresearchcouncil.org/boettner/>.

Executive Director

Olivia S. Mitchell, *International Foundation of Employee Benefit Plans Professor*, Department of Business Economics and Public Policy, The Wharton School, University of Pennsylvania.

Institutional Members

Allianz AM/Project M
International Foundation of Employee Benefit Plans
Ontario Pension Board
Society of Actuaries

Recent Pension Research Council Publications

The Market for Retirement Financial Advice. Olivia S. Mitchell and Kent Smetters, eds. 2013. (ISBN 0-19-968377-2)

Reshaping Retirement Security: Lessons from the Global Financial Crisis. Raimond Maurer, Olivia S. Mitchell, and Mark Warshawsky, eds. 2012. (ISBN 0-19-966069-7)

Financial Literacy. Olivia S. Mitchell and Annamaria Lusardi, eds. 2011. (ISBN 0-19-969681-9)

Securing Lifelong Retirement Income. Olivia S. Mitchell, John Piggott, and Noriyuki Takayama, eds. 2011. (ISBN 0-19-959484-9)

Reorienting Retirement Risk Management. Robert L. Clark and Olivia S. Mitchell, eds. 2010. (ISBN 0-19-959260-9)

Fundamentals of Private Pensions. Dan M. McGill, Kyle N. Brown, John J. Haley, Sylvester Schieber, and Mark J. Warshawsky. 9th ed. 2010. (ISBN 0-19-954451-6)

The Future of Public Employees Retirement Systems. Olivia S. Mitchell and Gary Anderson, eds. 2009. (ISBN 0-19-957334-9)

Recalibrating Retirement Spending and Saving. John Ameriks and Olivia S. Mitchell, eds. 2008. (ISBN 0-19-954910-8)

Lessons from Pension Reform in the Americas. Stephen J. Kay and Tapen Sinha, eds. 2008. (ISBN 0-19-922680-6)

Redefining Retirement: How Will Boomers Fare? Brigitte Madrian, Olivia S. Mitchell, and Beth J. Soldo, eds. 2007. (ISBN 0-19-923077-3)

Restructuring Retirement Risks. David Blitzstein, Olivia S. Mitchell, and Steven P. Utkus, eds. 2006. (ISBN 0-19-920465-9)

Reinventing the Retirement Paradigm. Robert L. Clark and Olivia S. Mitchell, eds. 2005. (ISBN 0-19-928460-1)

Pension Design and Structure: New Lessons from Behavioral Finance. Olivia S. Mitchell and Steven P. Utkus, eds. 2004. (ISBN 0-19-927339-1)

The Pension Challenge: Risk Transfers and Retirement Income Security. Olivia S. Mitchell and Kent Smetters, eds. 2003. (ISBN 0-19-926691-3)

A History of Public Sector Pensions in the United States. Robert L. Clark, Lee A. Craig, and Jack W. Wilson, eds. 2003. (ISBN 0-8122-3714-5)

Benefits for the Workplace of the Future. Olivia S. Mitchell, David Blitzstein, Michael Gordon, and Judith Mazo, eds. 2003. (ISBN 0-8122-3708-0)

Innovations in Retirement Financing. Olivia S. Mitchell, Zvi Bodie, P. Brett Hammond, and Stephen Zeldes, eds. 2002. (ISBN 0-8122-3641-6)

To Retire or Not: Retirement Policy and Practice in Higher Education. Robert L. Clark and P. Brett Hammond, eds. 2001. (ISBN 0-8122-3572-X)

Pensions in the Public Sector. Olivia S. Mitchell and Edwin Hustead, eds. 2001. (ISBN 0-8122-3578-9)

The Role of Annuity Markets in Financing Retirement. Jeffrey Brown, Olivia S. Mitchell, James Poterba, and Mark Warshawsky. 2001. (ISBN 0-262-02509-4)

Forecasting Retirement Needs and Retirement Wealth. Olivia S. Mitchell, P. Brett Hammond, and Anna Rappaport, eds. 2000. (ISBN 0-8122-3529-0)

Prospects for Social Security Reform. Olivia S. Mitchell, Robert J. Myers, and Howard Young, eds. 1999. (ISBN 0-8122-3479-0)

Living with Defined Contribution Pensions: Remaking Responsibility for Retirement. Olivia S. Mitchell and Sylvester J. Schieber, eds. 1998. (ISBN 0-8122-3439-1)

Positioning Pensions for the Twenty-First Century. Michael S. Gordon, Olivia S. Mitchell, and Marc M. Twinney, eds. 1997. (ISBN 0-8122-3391-3)

Securing Employer-Based Pensions: An International Perspective. Zvi Bodie, Olivia S. Mitchell, and John A. Turner, eds. 1996. (ISBN 0-8122-3334-4)

Available from the Pension Research Council website: <http://www.pensionresearchcoun cil.org/>.

Index

Bold entries refer to figures and tables. Notes are indicated by 'n.'